Acting in the Cinema

Acting in the Cinema

James Naremore

University of California Press
Berkeley   Los Angeles   London

University of California Press
Berkeley and Los Angeles

University of California Press, Ltd.
London, England

© 1988 by The Regents of the University of California
First Paperback Printing 1990
Library of Congress Cataloging-in-Publication Data

Naremore, James.
    Acting and performance in the American cinema /
James Naremore.
        p.   cm.
    Bibliography: p.
    Includes index.
    ISBN 0-520-06228-0 (alk. paper)
    ISBN 0-520-07194-8 (ppb.)
    1. Motion picture acting.   2. Motion pictures—
United States.
    I.   Title.
    PN1995.9.A26N37 1988
    791.43′028—dc19   87-30180

Printed in the United States of America

2   3   4   5   6   7   8   9

Illustrations courtesy of Columbia Pictures, MGM/UA,
RKO, Paramount Pictures, Samuel Goldwyn, Universal Pictures, and Warner Communications.

For Darlene J. Sadlier

Contents

Acknowledgments

Portions of the following text, in different form, appeared originally in *Film Quarterly, Mosaic, Quarterly Review of Film Studies,* and *Studies in the Literary Imagination.* I am grateful to those journals for their interest in my work, and I would also like to thank the Indiana University Office of Research and Graduate Development for a fellowship that enabled me to complete the manuscript.

My colleagues in the Film Studies program at Indiana University were especially helpful. Harry M. Geduld shared his enormous fund of knowledge about Chaplin and the silent cinema; and Claudia Gorbman, Barbara Klinger, Aaron Baker, and Kathleen McHugh read certain chapters and offered useful suggestions. I was also assisted by scholars at other institutions, particularly by Charles Affron and Virginia Wright Wexman, two important contributors to the literature on film acting, who were generous advisors. Robert B. Ray and Rebecca Bell-Metereau were around from the beginning, listening to my problems and contributing valuable ideas; and at various points along the way I received support from Rick Altman, Patrick Brantlinger, Mary Burgan, Robert Carringer, Sandra M. Gilbert, Ronald Gottesman, Donald Gray, R. Barton Palmer, Richard Peña, Michael P. Rogin, George E. Toles, Michael Wood, Ulrich Weisstein, and the late Dennis Turner.

The book might never have been written without the encouragement and patient, wise counsel of my editor, Ernest Callenbach; and at the University of California Press, I owe additional thanks to Stephanie Fay, Andrew Joron, and Barbara Ras. Most of all, the book was made possible by the extensive help and daily companionship of Darlene J. Sadlier, to whom it is dedicated.

1

Introduction

This is a book about the art of film acting, but I had better make clear from the outset that it will not teach anyone how to become a successful performer. My approach is theoretical, historical, and critical, and I write from the point of view of a voyeur in the audience. Terry Eagleton has remarked that such writing ought to produce bad actors. Perhaps he is correct, but my own aim is simply to make readers conscious of behavior they usually take for granted.

At a certain level, of course, we easily recognize the flourishes, emotional intensities, and expressive nuances of acting in the movies—indeed we are supposed to recognize them. Even so, the most interesting figures on the screen often look "natural," as if they were merely lending themselves to the manipulations of script, camera, and editing; the work they do is variable and vague, and critics usually discuss them as personalities rather than as craftspeople. This potentially contradictory attitude is significant, suggesting that the very technique of film acting has ideological importance. After all, one purpose of ideology (as defined by most contemporary theory), is to seem the most natural thing in the world, understandable only in terms of common sense. In the book that follows, therefore, I have tried to analyze conventions of filmed performance in some detail, isolating them both at points where they are obvious and at points where they are relatively invisible. By such means I hope to reveal buried, paradoxical assumptions about society and the self.

I hope also to indicate something about the theatrical quality of movies and of ideology in general—an issue that has been neglected in criticism, partly because intellectuals have wanted to legitimize cinema by emphasizing its difference from the stage, and partly because analysis and interpretation of drama have always given priority to matters of plot. In one sense, the traditional strategy is perfectly understandable; as I shall argue later, the actor hardly exists except as an agent of narrative, and movie performers cannot be discussed apart from the many crafts that surround and construct them. Nevertheless, most academic film critics, even when they exhibit a sophisticated knowledge of technology, are excessively novelistic. Clearly films depend on a form of communication whereby meanings are *acted out;* the experience of watching them involves not only a pleasure in storytelling but also a delight in bodies and expressive movement, an enjoyment of familiar performing skills, and an interest in players as "real persons."

Unfortunately, the attempt to describe some of these things in writing is rather like wrestling with Proteus. As many theorists have noted, actors use analog techniques; their movements, gestures, and inflections are presented in gradations of *more* and *less*—subtle degrees of everchanging expression that are easy to comprehend in the context of a given film but difficult to analyze without falling back on unwieldy tables of statistics or fuzzy, adjectival language. I have not been able to avoid this problem entirely, although I prefer adjectives to statistical tables. At best, I try to mix phenomenological description with other methods, showing how performances can be understood in roughly the same way as "narratology" has understood plots. In the process, I have been aided by a series of writers on performance from outside film—especially by Stanislavsky, Brecht, and the "Chicago school" of social anthropology.

Among these writers, Stanislavsky is perhaps the best known and most influential on the culture at large. Nearly all forms of actor training in the United States today are approximately Stanislavskian, whether or not he is recognized as a source, and most film reviewers operate from Stanislavskian assumptions; in fact, Stanislavsky's disciple, V. I. Pudovkin, is responsible for the first important book on the technique of film acting. As a result, I have used Stanislavsky's name in two ways, sometimes quoting him directly, sometimes referring to "Stanislavskian aesthetics" to designate an expressive-realist attitude that determines most of the films we see. The hallmark of such an attitude is the belief that good acting is "true to life" and at the same time expressive of the actor's authentic, "organic" self—hence the typical movie advertisement: "Clint Eastwood *is* Dirty Harry." In more specific terms, however, Stanislavsky is the great exponent of naturalism. All varieties of teaching derived from his work try to inculcate spontaneity, improvisation, and low-key psychological introspection; they devalue anything that looks stagy, and in their extreme form—namely in the work of Lee Strasberg—they lead to quasi-psychoanalytic rehearsal techniques, inviting the actor to delve into the unconscious, searching out "truthful" behavior.

Stanislavsky and his followers are essentially romantics, contested at every point by the radical modernism of Brecht. The antirealistic Brechtian player is more like a comic than a tragedian, concerned less with emotional truth than with critical awareness; instead of expressing an essential self, she or he examines the relation between roles on the stage and roles in society, deliberately calling attention to the artificiality of performance, foregrounding the staginess of spectacle, and addressing the audience in didactic fashion. The movement from Stanislavsky to Brecht therefore involves a shift in emphasis from psychoanalysis to semiotics, from inner contemplation to social praxis. Indeed Brecht's writings have something in common with traditional social science, which uses concepts like "performance" and "role playing" to analyze nontheatrical behavior. This tendency is especially marked in the theoretical work of Erving Goffman, who suggests that all forms of human interaction are in one sense stagy and that notions of "character," "personality," and "self" are merely outgrowths of the various roles we play in life.

Throughout my own study, I have tried to keep the old tensions between Stanislavsky and Brecht alive, criticizing the dominant form without dismissing it. I have also drawn a good deal from Goffman. As a "scientist," he never makes judgments about art; like Brecht, however, he is interested in defamiliarizing actorly behavior, and he makes useful distinctions between theater and the daily presentation of self, ultimately helping us to understand how these two fundamentally important but quite different modes are interrelated.

Having suggested my interests and influences, I need only comment on the organization of the book. The text is divided into three sections, each devoted to a slightly different task. Part 1, "Performance in the Age of Mechanical Reproduction," is mainly theoretical, employing a wide frame of reference. Although I concentrate throughout on the Hollywood narrative cinema, I needed to place my discussion in a larger context, alluding to everyday life, to traditional theater, to television, and to "foreign" directors like Wenders, Godard, and Bresson. By including such materials, I was able to define the central terms of my argument, to offer a general description of the work of film acting, and to comment on the ideological assumptions certain performances can involve. I was also trying to develop what Roland Barthes might have called a structuration, or a set of formal distinctions that can be applied to all types of theatrical performance. As a result, the chapters in part 1 are designed to treat systematically the following concerns:

(1) A framing or cuing process that establishes a boundary between performers and audience, producing an elementary theatrical event. The boundary can be more or less ambiguous, eliciting different sorts of interaction between two social groups.

(2) A set of rhetorical conventions, controlling the ostensiveness of the players, their relative positions within the performing space, and their mode of address to the audience.

(3) A series of expressive techniques governing such matters as posture, gesture, and voice, and regulating the entire body as an index of gender, age, ethnicity, and social class.

(4) A logic of coherence, enabling the players to seem more or less in step with changes in the story, more or less in character, and more or less "true to themselves."

(5) A *mise-en-scène,* shaping the performance to a greater or lesser degree by clothing, makeup, and a variety of inanimate objects with which the actor comes into direct contact.

I might have termed this structure the "five codes" of performance, inventing names for each item in the list: the boundary code, the rhetorical code, the expressive code, the harmonic code, and the anthropomorphic code. I have preferred, however, to repress jargon and not pursue the analogy with Barthes too far; instead I allow my distinctions to emerge in more general ways from a series of four rather discursive chapters, sometimes invoking them again later when they seem appropriate to the analysis of individual actors. At the same time, I try to indicate how the basic formal structure can be mapped onto history, technology, and the politics of spectacle.

Part 2, "Star Performances," deals with particular circumstances, where exceptions to the general rules begin to appear. In this section, composed largely of practical criticism, I examine the techniques of seven important players in specific films. As stars, they are special cases: each is an extraliterary character whose name circulates through publicity, biography, and everyday language; each is also known for an ideolect, a set of performing traits that is systematically highlighted in films and sometimes copied by impressionists. To deal with such matters, and to suggest the influence stars have had over scripts and directors, I have usually placed my discussions in the context of more general accounts of entire careers, relating individual actors and pictures to the themes of fame, celebrity, and myth.

The people I selected to discuss in part 2 have little in common except an expressive vivacity, a certain androgynous quality, and a tendency to make acting or role playing the subject of their performances. They all have legendary status, and I have not concealed my admiration for their work; in fact one of my purposes is to stress the important artistic contributions players usually make to films. I should emphasize, however, that my choices are not meant to suggest a pantheon, or even a list of personal favorites. These chapters will probably indicate something about my obsessions, but I was not writing purely out of my own desire. Had I done so, the book would have been more aestheticized or hedonistic, filled with idiosyncratic commentary on relatively minor figures like Diana Lynn, Gloria Grahame, Claude Rains, and Alan Ladd. My overriding aim is merely to illustrate a variety of acting styles and star personae, ranging from the silents of Griffith and Chaplin to the advent of the Method. I have avoided performers of musical comedy, staying mainly within the confines of realistic drama, and in most cases I have selected films my readers would know fairly well. Seven names seem enough for my purpose, but I am painfully aware of many fine actors I chose to eliminate. (I especially regret the omission of Barbara Stanwyck, to whom I refer several times in part 1, and of Richard Pryor, who seems to me more gifted than Chaplin but whose best work has been done in concert films. Had I included Pryor, I might have been able to discuss indirectly an issue that is in need of further research: the influence of blacks on the American performing idiom, despite the fact that they are usually unrepresented, marginalized, or parodied by Hollywood cinema.)

Part 3, "Film as a Performance Text," is a synthesis of the previous sections, dealing with the work of ensembles in two films. Both films depend on the audience's familiarity with the star system, both involve the theme of performance, and both use a complex variety of casting techniques, rhetorical strategies, and acting styles. By analyzing them in detail, I attempt to show the many ways a narrative motion picture can be discussed under the rubric of "theatricality," and I summarize the argument of the book as a whole.

Running behind these last chapters, and behind the entire book, is an indirect commentary on the social and psychological foundations of identity. Fairly early on, I indicate that one job of mainstream acting is to sustain "the illusion of the unified self," or what Pudovkin called "the organic unity of the acted image." Western culture as a whole, from at least the Renaissance onward, has depended on a roughly similar kind of work; thus we tend to think of ourselves as unified, transcendent subjects of experience who express an innate personality through daily activity, ultimately becoming star players in our personal scenarios. Our "commonsense" view of life might be described, in the words of critic Catherine Belsey, as a blend of empiricism, humanism, and idealism—a philosophy that conceives of reality as a camera-eye narrative, with human consciousness as the seat of truth. (Consider John Locke, the founder of British empiricism, who regarded the mind as a camera obscura, or "dark room," receiving impressions and transforming them into reasonable wholes through the power of the soul.) In fact, however, as a great deal of recent work in linguistics, literary theory, psychoanalysis, and film studies has attempted to show, common sense is illusory; the self is more like an effect of structure—a crowd of signifiers, without any particular origin or essence, held in place by ideology and codes of representation.

Perhaps we can learn something about this phenomenon by looking at the insubstantial images of movie players, who persuade us so convincingly of their individual reality. By analyzing the paradoxes of performance in film, by showing how roles, star personae, and individual "texts" can be broken down into various expressive attributes and ideological functions, we inevitably reflect upon the pervasive theatricality of society itself. Such an approach will necessarily involve a reversal of the priorities usually adopted by film criticism; nevertheless it leads to many of the same themes, and it seems true to the way audiences and the movies in general have always focused on actors.

Part One

Performance in the Age of Mechanical Reproduction

2

Protocols

The Performance Frame

If we take a professional actor, . . . to film him through the "Kino-eye" would be to show the agreement or disagreement between the man and the actor. . . . Not Petrov in front of you, but Ivanov playing the role of Petrov.

—Dziga Vertov

Imagine for a moment that the short film I am about to describe was shot by some Los Angeles–based Dziga Vertov, a man with a movie camera setting out to record an incident on the streets. (The illusion will be dispelled almost immediately.)

The date was early 1914. In Venice, California, next door to Santa Monica, the citizens were staging a soapbox derby, and a director and his cameraman went out to catch some of the action, bringing along a second crew that would take pictures of them at work. They were well prepared to get candid footage, and everything was set up correctly to demonstrate a dialectic between life and the camera. All they had to do was undercrank and overcrank a few shots, and then head back to their studio to photograph the process of editing: the documentary material would be cut together with scenes of the filmmakers at work, producing a conflict between the camera as recording instrument and the camera as instrument of semiosis. But almost from the beginning something went wrong. To be precise, an actor got in the way.

A brief account of the film's opening scenes will illustrate what happened.

It begins with a newsreel-style shot of the main street in Venice, with the camera positioned beside the roadway, looking diagonally across at a crowd of spectators. We see a couple of officials dressed in dark suits and lots of kids in knickers, a few of them scrambling across the street in the far distance. In the center of the image are a couple of soapbox race cars, one of them being pushed by hand across a starting line. But contemporary viewers can hardly register this information. They immediately notice a man at the far left of the screen, standing out a bit from the crowd. He is wearing a derby hat, a tight Edwardian coat, and baggy pants; he stands in a dancer's first position, the toes of his shoes pointed up like wings, and he is holding a curved-handled bamboo walking stick.

As the soapbox racer rolls off to the right, this man turns to watch it go, and we glimpse his face. He is more unkempt and mean-looking than the poetic fellow we know from later appearances, with a rather large nose, bushy brows, and a scruffy mustache. He seems to be drunk—his hair is sticking out beneath the bowler, he is weaving a little, and he is puffing madly at a cigarette. When the car passes, he wanders into the roadway, partly blocking the camera's view of the race. Somebody taps him on the back. He tips the bowler apologetically but turns toward us, walking a half dozen jerky, turned-out paces along the curb until he is in the exact center of the composition,

now completely blocking the view of a second car that has been rolled up to the starting line. He turns and stands for a moment, his back once more to the camera, his hat tilted at a raffish angle, and then suddenly spins around as if he had been yelled at by the cameraman. Looking toward us and frowning, he points a dainty finger offscreen right, responding to a "direction." Hurrying to go, he stays, shifting from foot to foot, clearly aware that he is being photographed. He then makes a quick right face and marches off, knees locked and toes pointed out. For a moment we glimpse a race car passing the starting line, but then, as if pulled by an invisible rubber band, the bowler-hatted figure pops back into the picture, looking into the camera. Curious, he pauses at the edge of the frame, gazing at us, twirling his cane in feigned nonchalance, and then exits.

After a brief shot of the race in progress, we see a title card, "The Grand Stand," followed by a slow pan along a reviewing box, with a line of seated figures and a few rows of people standing behind. Several faces are smiling shyly, glancing sidelong at the camera with the tense pose of people who are trying to ignore it. The panorama is fascinating—boys in tight collars and walking caps, grizzled men and plain women; but suddenly, there, at the bottom corner of the picture, sitting on the curb alongside a grubby child, is the fellow from the previous scene. An unlit cigarette in his mouth, he is looking off to the right, ostentatiously oblivious. When the camera starts to reverse its pan, he turns toward it, craning his head. As the panning movement continues, he casually stands up, blocking the view and sauntering along with the camera until he has moved clear out into the street. Apparently somebody yells at him again, because he looks toward the lens, gesturing to the right and then the left, pretending to be confused about where he should exit, all the while remaining at center stage.

By now the director (Henry Lehrman) has had enough. He walks briefly into the picture, shoves the intruder off, and then ducks behind the camera, which continues to pan. But the drunken tramp pops back, staring indignantly in our direction. The director returns and pushes him out of the picture again. Again he bounces back, easing along, pausing to raise a leg and strike a match on his pants. The camera has now moved a full 180 degrees and is aimed at the opposite side of the road. In the background a couple of dogs are circling at the edge of the crowd, sniffing one another; a few boys are craning their necks to watch the race and a few others are laughing, amused by the antics in front of the camera. As if inspired, the drunk now begins showing off: he lights his cigarette, shakes out the match, flicks it over his shoulder, and does a fancy little dance kick with his heel, bouncing the dead match away before it hits the road.

The film is only about four minutes long, and it consists of nothing more than this single gimmick, repeated over and over. The "drunk" keeps hamming it up for the camera, growing ever more aggressive and determined to ignore the director. When the camera crew tries to photograph the end of the race, he comes running and skipping down the middle of the street, flapping his arms like a bird, tripping over the finish line; when stray kids wander between him and the camera, he shoves them in the face; when the director starts knocking him out of the way, he dances around in little circles at the periphery of the shot and sticks out his tongue. Ultimately he "spoils" every scene in the newsreel.

He is, of course, Charlie Chaplin, and the film is *Kid's Auto Race,* a minor landmark in cinema history because it is the first film in which Chaplin appeared in the costume of the Tramp. When it is viewed in the light of Chaplin's later career, it becomes fascinating in many ways. For example, the pretended battle between Charlie and the director can be read prophetically, as an ironic dramatization of Chaplin's egocentricity, his determination to become a star and control every aspect of his films. (There was in fact a real-life conflict between Chaplin and the director Henry Lehrman, who is described in Chaplin's autobiography as a "vain" fellow, given to leaving the actor's best work on the cutting-room floor. Significantly, Chaplin describes an entirely different film as the one where he first wore the famous costume and conveniently forgets that Lehrman was directing when the Tramp was born [143–46].) As I have already suggested, it can also be read as an alle-

gory about the way the cinema tended to center on actors, relegating Vertov's Kino-eye to a secondary importance behind filmed versions of nineteenth-century theatrics. Where my own subject is concerned, however, *Kid's Auto Race* is especially interesting because it makes a structural use of two modes of performance, establishing a fundamental distinction that is important to the analysis of performance in general.

Like a great many of the early comedies produced by Mack Sennett, this small film involves a comic "turn" played off against life in the streets. Its humor and aesthetic pleasure depend on audiences' eventually recognizing Chaplin as an *actor*, distinguishable from the "real" people behind him. The paradox here is that the people in the background are performing, too—not only the soapbox drivers in the race, which is a performed event, but also the kids who scurry across the street and gawk at the camera, unwittingly providing a true version of Chaplin's mock hamminess. Everybody plays a role, from the stolid men who stand with hands in their pockets, pretending the camera isn't there, to the woman in a Victorian bonnet who sits in the reviewing stand and covers her face with a sheet of paper so as not to be photographed. The difference between Chaplin's performance and that of the others is that his is a clever professional mimesis, staged for the camera, whereas theirs is an everyday response, provoked by the camera or caught unawares. Chaplin's performance is theatrical, and theirs is aleatory.

Kid's Auto Race illustrates how the distinction between theatrical and aleatory events can be thrown into sharp relief and the audience can be invited to take pleasure in the difference between acting and accident. The technique derives not from cinema but from a very old tradition of street-corner mime that still survives today. I have seen a greasepainted and distinctly Chaplinesque clown create a show by standing across from people at a sidewalk café, designating some of his watchers as audience, others as participants. First he mimicked a traffic cop, lining up bystanders on the other side of the street; having cleared a sort of corridor, he began performing on the sidewalk, slipping behind innocent passersby and playing jokes on them. He could even move the playing area, drawing some of his audience into the spectacle by crossing the street and sitting at one of the sidewalk tables—where, for example, he tried to pick up a pretty young woman. By means of his costume and his elaborate gestures, he was able to establish what Erving Goffman calls a conceptual or cognitive "frame," bestowing a special performing significance on all the people or objects that came inside (*Frame Analysis*, 123–55). Ultimately, his show demonstrated that all social life is a kind of performance; after all, he was simply exaggerating the role-playing that was already happening on the street, turning it into theater.

The early semiotic theorists in the Prague Circle emphasized that this theatrical transformation happens in any exchange between a performer and an audience. A more recent writer on the subject, Keir Elam, has described the "first principle" of Prague theory as the observation that anything designated a stage or playing area tends to "suppress the practical function of phenomena in favor of a symbolic or signifying role, allowing them to participate in dramatic representation" (8). In the simpler words of Jiří Veltruský, "All that is on the stage is a sign" (quoted by Elam, 8). Thus, given that cinema makes all the world a potential stage or performing frame, even a dog going about his doggy business (like the canines on a Venice street in *Kid's Auto Race*) can become a player.

Nevertheless, the primary frame that designates spectacle can contain various kinds of performance, and the audience does not usually regard dogs in the same way as humans. We commonly make a distinction between "real people" and actors, but we also assign the purely theatrical performers to different registers of dramatized action. For example, when the characters portrayed by John Forsythe and Linda Evans were married on an episode of the television show "Dynasty," Peter Duchin was the pianist at their wedding reception. Forsythe and Evans walked over and said hello to Duchin, using his real name, and he in turn congratulated them on their wedding, using their fictional names. On an earlier episode of the same show, Henry Kissinger appeared as Henry Kissinger—roughly like Napoleon showing up in a historical novel, except that Kissinger was really there, playing himself, the way John Wayne and William Holden once played themselves on "I Love Lucy." This suggests that people in a film can be regarded in at least three different senses: as actors playing theatrical personages, as public figures playing theatrical versions of themselves, and as documentary evidence. If the term *performance* is defined in its broadest sense, it covers the last category as much as the first: when people are caught unawares by a camera, they become objects to be looked at, and they usually provide evidence of role-playing in everyday life; when they know they are being photographed, they become role-players of another sort.

Technically, at least, *Kid's Auto Race* contains all these basic kinds of performance, with Chaplin playing a character, the director Lehrman playing a director, and the crowd simply fulfilling their role as the anonymous masses in a newsreel. Notice, however, that the Lehrman role does not actually qualify as a different type of performance because he is not enough of a celebrity for us to recognize him. True celebrity characters do not make their way into Hollywood fiction until a couple of years later, in 1916, when Chaplin appeared in a cameo role in one of Bronco Billy Anderson's Essanay pictures; in the same year Anderson reciprocated by doing a walk-on as "himself" in a Chaplin short.[1] The phenomenon had reached full-blown comic self-consciousness by the time of King Vidor's *Show People* (1928), where Mar-

---

1. I am grateful to Harry M. Geduld for calling this fact to my attention, and for showing me *Kid's Auto Race*. In *Chapliniana* (1987), Geduld notes that *Kid's Auto Race* was the title used in the original Keystone logo. Most histories of cinema refer to the film as *Kid Auto Races at Venice*, but this is actually an abbreviation of the first insert title: "Kid Auto Races at Venice, California."

ion Davies plays Peggy Pepper, a callow youth who travels to Hollywood to become a "serious" actor: during her rise to success, Peggy meets a great many luminaries, including W. S. Hart, John Gilbert, Douglas Fairbanks, and Charles Chaplin (who appears in his own clothes rather than those of the Tramp, and who asks Peggy for her autograph). At one point, standing on the back lot of MGM, Peggy nudges her companion and points offscreen. "Isn't that Marion Davies?" a title card asks. Cut to a shot of Davies getting out of a car and walking across the lot. Cut back to "Peggy Pepper," who stares in awe at "herself."

Even the distinction between Chaplin and the bystanders (who could have been carefully trained actors) depends largely on the way *Kid's Auto Race* is received, because in the last analysis the aleatory quality of any film has less to do with how it was made than with what happens in an audience's mind. The point about *Kid's Auto Race* is simply that it allows, indeed encourages, its audience to recognize a difference between Chaplin and the bystanders. The makers of the film assume our familiarity with street-corner life, our knowledge of how people behave when they are photographed, and our awareness of a certain type of early documentary that they have parodied. Chaplin himself does certain things to notify us that he is a man pretending to be a drunken show-off rather than the thing itself. First of all he is a costumed figure, even if his clothing initially makes him blend with the crowd. On closer inspection, it becomes apparent that no one else in Venice, California, on that day was wearing a bowler hat, a frock coat, or an Edwardian collar. Looked at still more closely, his dress speaks to us in a systematic, orderly language that is different from the haphazard dialect of everyday life. In a famous passage of his autobiography he says he chose this outfit because "I wanted everything a contradiction" (144)—thus he is part tramp, part gentleman, with coat too tight and pants too baggy; his scruffy mustache indicates that he is a rascal, but dark makeup brings out the liveliness and sensitivity in his eyes; a bowler hat and cane give him dignity, but oversize shoes make him a clown. At every level his costuming is built on a set of formal contrasts that signify he is an art object, a figure who says, "I am an actor."

The same message is communicated by his position in the frame and his movements. Although the director is supposed to be avoiding Charlie, *Kid's Auto Race* is never allowed to become a decentered modernist film or a casual documentary. Much of its pleasure and comedy derive from Chaplin's ability to imitate and exaggerate a type of everyday performance and from his tendency to occupy a space on the screen that denotes theatrical interest. He is drawn to that area like a metal filing to a magnet, wandering off with great reluctance or being shoved out of view only to come jogging back. (At one point, infatuated with cinema and determined to ignore the director, he stands looking straight into the camera with haughty, chin-up dignity and wiggles his eyebrows.) Although he imitates a man whose entrances and exits are inappropriate, we can sense his comic timing.[2] No matter how often he trips or falls, we know it is an act; despite the apparent foolishness of his character, he moves with theatrical eloquence, never using the transparent gestures of offstage communication. He walks with an eccentric, ballet dancer's waddle, feet splayed to the side and arms jauntily swinging. He turns on his toes, once or twice executing a perfect pirouette. He never simply stands, he *poses*. When he pretends to be a man who is pretending the camera isn't there, he does so with an exaggerated nonchalance or with the intense gaze of an explorer preoccupied with something on the far horizon. Even when the director shoves him down in the street, he somersaults, never losing his hat, cane, or pretended dignity, and snaps upright to resume his position.

All theatrical performance (even the naturalism of actors like Spencer Tracy and Robert Duvall) involves a degree of ostensiveness that marks it off from quotidian behavior. Chaplin, however, was one of the most ostentatious actors in the history of movies, so intent on exhibiting the virtuosity of theatrical movement that he is nearly always more stylized and poetically unnatural than the people he plays alongside. In this sense his work differs from the general run of movies, which do not make sharp contrasts between codes and styles of performance. Even today, when most films are shot on location, there is seldom any attempt to foreground theatricality by setting it off against accidental or found material. And although we recognize a difference between John Forsythe and Henry Kissinger, that is only because we know them from the media; both men have modeled their behavior on the effortless, transparent manner of everyday life. In fact the dramatic film has always fostered a neutral, "invisible" form of acting, so that highly theatrical techniques—Chaplin's pantomime, Dietrich's expressionist posing—are exceptions to the rule.

There is, however, a type of modernism—Brechtian or Pirandellian in its inspiration—that neither foregrounds the actor's gesture nor allows conventional transparency to go unexamined. Instead of making a clear demarcation between theatrical and aleatory codes, this sort of film problematizes the relation between actors, roles, and audiences, sometimes confounding the audience's ability to "frame" or "key" the action on the screen. Godard's *Breathless* (1960) is a case in point. A movie about the connection between roles played on film and roles played on the street, it casts Jean Paul Belmondo and Jean Seberg self-reflexively, photographing them in quasi-documentary style. More than that, it requires them to imitate characters who imitate movie stars and who borrow their dialogue from the *roman policier;*

---

2. Commentators sometimes equate timing with pace, but the two things are different. A waltz, for example, is defined mainly by timing, or the temporal relation between movements; at any pace, it can be recognized as basically the same dance.

thus a great many of Belmondo's gestures become allusions, and his otherwise naturalistic performance evokes Brecht's notion that an actor should always behave as if he were quoting.[3] Sometimes, too, Belmondo's work is deliberately set off against what appears to be aleatory material. Near the end of the film he staggers away from the camera, histrionically clutching a wound in the style of countless Hollywood gangster movies; as he struggles for a ridiculously long way down a street, we can see pedestrians on the sidewalk, going about their business or looking at his performance as if they were bystanders watching a movie. The sequence echoes a technique we have seen earlier when Belmondo and Seberg stroll down the Champs-Elysées, surrounded by people who turn to watch them or who glance at the camera. The effect here is slightly different from that of *Kid's Auto Race* because Godard has clearly introduced extras into the crowd—as when a Seberg lookalike does a double take as she walks past; at other moments, chiefly on the margins of the screen, it becomes impossible to distinguish actual pedestrians from actors, and theater and life seem to intersect.[4]

Godard's deliberate confusion of theatrical and aleatory codes serves to undermine the conventional notion of film performance. Unlike *Breathless,* the typical dramatic film regards acting as an artful imitation of unmediated behavior in the real world. The actor is taken to be an already completely formed person who learns to "think" for the camera. Thus a substantial body of intelligent critical writing has described the performances of the classic stars as if they were little more than fictional extensions of the actor's true personalities,[5] and in America the most celebrated postwar theater actors were actually *schooled* in how to perform themselves. "We believe," wrote Lee Strasberg, "that the actor need not imitate a human being. The actor is himself a human being and can create out of himself" (Cole and Chinoy, 623). Strasberg's reification of the self was so crucial to his thinking that Method training often extended to psychological therapy. An actor, he wrote, "can possess technical ability to do certain things and yet may have difficulty expressing them because of his emotional life. The approach to this actor's problem must therefore deal first with whatever difficulties are inherent in himself that negate his freedom of expression and block the capacities he possesses" (Cole and Chinoy, 623). Not surprisingly, Method-trained actors—many of whom

---

3. Godard's penchant for quotation is more evident in his later work. The following bit of dialogue in *Breathless* is borrowed from Dashiell Hammett's *The Glass Key:* A friend of Belmondo meets him on the street and remarks, "You oughtn't to wear silk socks with tweeds." Belmondo looks at his socks. "No? I like the feel of silk." His pal shrugs. "Then lay off tweeds."

4. A number of contemporary films have relied on a similar effect. See, for example, Henry Jaglom's *Can She Bake a Cherry Pie?* (1983).

5. Here, for example, is David Thomson, writing about Louise Brooks: "[She] was one of the first performers to penetrate to the heart of screen acting. . . . Quite simply, she appreciated that the power of the screen actress lay not in impersonation or performance, in the carefully worked out personal narrative of stage acting . . . [but] in thinking out for herself the self-consuming rapture of Lulu" (*A Biographical Dictionary,* 72).

adapted well to Hollywood—all had an introspective, neurotic style vastly different from Chaplin's open theatricality.

A film like *Breathless,* for all its rough-and-ready appearance, tends to reverse such assumptions. Instead of treating performance as an outgrowth of an essential self, it implies that the self is an outgrowth of performance. "Performance," in turn, is understood in its broadest, most social, sense, as what we do when we interact with the world—a concept embracing not only theater but also public celebrity and everyday life. In its own brief, modest, and quite different way, *Kid's Auto Race* has similar implications: after all, comic theatrical performance has always been designed to expose and make fun of our social roles, and Chaplin was one of its masters.

Still another approach, in some ways like Godard's but in others more complex and contradictory, may be seen in Wim Wenders's *Lightning over Water* (1981). Conceived as a tribute to Nicholas Ray, it began as a thinly fictionalized work based on the real-life relation between two directors; but as Ray's disastrously failing health grew worse, the film was transformed into a self-conscious mix of theatricality, celebrity acting, and aleatory happening—a drama in which the leading player very nearly performs his own death. An extreme instance, it may help to complete and summarize the themes I have been discussing.

To emphasize a symbiosis between life and art, Wenders and his collaborators structured their work as a Pirandellian regression, employing a radical mixture of techniques that pay homage to Ray's last film, an unclassifiable piece entitled *We Can't Go Home Again*. Instead of producing a *cinéma-vérité* documentary or a set of interviews with Ray, they staged "true-life" scenes, occasionally shooting in *noir* style; alternatively, they recorded their own activity, often videotaping themselves with a Betamax. Throughout, the performances are so naturalistic, so much grounded in the actual situation, that we cannot distinguish what was planned from what was accidental—for example, near the beginning of the film we suddenly cut to a videotaped segment showing the preparation for a scene we have been watching: "Do you want this to be like *acting, Wim?"* Ray asks. "No, not at all," Wenders replies. Ray reclines weakly on a bed, coughing and gazing blankly into space, just as he has done in the "theatrical" sequence we have just seen.

By such means *Lightning over Water* indicates the way everyday behavior overlaps with theater; it also points to the social formation of personality, because the very process of working on the picture has created a role for Ray to act out.[6] At the same time it documents his suffering—revealing the signs

6. In other ways, the film seems romantic and Stanislavskian. "An actor," Ray tells Wenders at one point, "has to work from a character whose needs are his [own] greatest needs." Perhaps because of Ray's indebtedness to the Method, the plot of *Lightning over Water* involves a search for a hidden essence of personality, a true self that is supposedly revealed through documentary and psychological analysis of the players. Whenever it depends on these transcendent "needs," it becomes a less radical work.

of his cancer, filming him in an actual hospital bed, allowing miscues or other signs of the aleatory to break into scenes that have been rehearsed. Its chief strategy is to give Ray's performance an unstable, vulnerable, or ambiguous conceptual frame. Initially it creates a theatrical context for people to play "themselves," but as Ray's illness worsens, it allows normally out-of-frame activity to intrude upon illusion, making drama out of the way biology disrupts art.

And yet, even while the film lets an aleatory, biological fact become the center of dramatic interest, it cannot allow Ray's body to become an exclusive focus of the spectacle; it must place his suffering in the context of a story, if only the story of the film itself. This paradox runs through the history of theater: imperial Rome in the days of Livy might have put real sex and death on the stage, but in other cultures an involuntary biological process is seldom performed outright. Examples of pure biological performance on film tend to be marginal, like the deaths of animals in films such films as *Le sang des bêtes* (1948) and *Weekend* (1967), plus such oddities as Fred Ott's sneeze, stag movies, snuff films, instructional cinema, and Warhol's *Sleep;* at the same time, all acting has a biological dimension, and biology often contributes powerfully to theatrical effect—witness De Niro's fatness in *Raging Bull* (1980) or the many cases where film exploits the decay of celebrity players (Montgomery Clift's ravaged face in *Judgment at Nuremberg* [1961], Randolph Scott and Joel McCrea's visible agedness in *Ride the High Country* [1962], and so forth). Hence *Lightning over Water* makes an interesting contrast with Don Siegel's *The Shootist* (1978), starring John Wayne. In both films the leading actor is a celebrity and a mythical figure who is dying of cancer; but *Lightning over Water* is a more direct, urgent, and makeshift work, and it rarely romanticizes its subject. Ironically, it shows Wenders and Ray talking in a hospital while a television set in the background announces that John Wayne has been hospitalized elsewhere.

Godard (paraphrasing Cocteau but echoing André Bazin's argument in "The Ontology of the Photographic Image") once wrote that cinema differs from painting because it "seizes life and the mortal aspect of life." "The person one films," he said, "is growing older and will die. We film, therefore, a moment when death is working" (81). Wenders gives a clear demonstration of this thesis in a lengthy close-up of Ray near the end of his film. The shot has something in common with the close-up of the dying Major Amberson (Charles Bennett) in Welles's *The Magnificent Ambersons* (1942); in both cases the actor himself was dying as he played his role, but in *Lightning over Water* the actor looks back at us and testifies to his condition. He pauses in the midst of his dialogue, breathing heavily, trying to regain composure but unable to fight off illness. Moaning and cursing, he begins to make jokes, threatening to puke all over the camera. "I'm beginning to drool," he says, confessing embarrassment. Finally his situation becomes intolerable and he wants the scene to stop. Offscreen, we hear Wenders's voice telling Ray to order a cut. Ray looks at the cameraman urgently and rather pathetically, anxiety showing in his one good eye, his lips drawn back over his false teeth like parchment over bone. "Cut!" he says, but the camera keeps running. For just a moment Ray looks angry and helpless. "Cut!" he says again, and he is forced to repeat the order before the screen fades to black.

"By exhibiting his proximity to death," Tom Farell has written, "Nick's acting was organic; it was genuine behavior" (87). In one sense this is true, because the actor's body is different from the social construct we call the actor's "self." But in another sense *Lightning over Water,* like most movies, tends to put biology in the service of character. Ray becomes a man who wants to die in private, similar to the wounded soldier Hemingway writes about in *Death in the Afternoon* (later fictionalized by Thomas Mitchell in *Only Angels Have Wings* [1939]). In his close-up, culture interacts with nature, so that a familiar narrative type, a celebrity who is playing himself, and a man who is dying all merge into a single performed event. As a result, the image seems to partake equally of documentary and animated cartoon: we glimpse an empirical fact, a specific individual; but we "read" the individual's face and body in terms of expressive convention, just as we might read a line drawing. For a moment, the performance frame is extended more broadly than even Sennett or Godard attempted, until we can see its virtual limits.

What Is Acting?

The actor can only be said to be reproducing something when he is copying *another* actor.
   —Georg Simmel, *On the Theory of Theatrical Performance*

The preceding section describes Chaplin as an actor who mimes, mimics, or somehow imitates "real persons." In its simplest form, however, acting is nothing more than the transposition of everyday behavior into a theatrical realm. Just as the language of poetry is no different in kind from the language in a newspaper, so the materials and techniques used by players on the stage are no different in kind from those we use in ordinary social intercourse. This may explain why the metaphor of life as theater is so ubiquitous and convincing.[7] After all, in daily activity we constitute ourselves rather like dra-

---

7. Consider the situation in "real life," as described by Robert Ezra Park:

It is probably no mere historical accident that the word person, in its first meaning, is a mask. It is rather a recognition of the fact that everyone is always and everywhere, more or less consciously, playing a role . . . It is in these roles that we know each other; it is in these roles that we know ourselves. . . .

In a sense, and in so far as this mask represents the conception we have formed of ourselves—the role we are striving to live up to—this mask is our truer self, the self we

matic characters, making use of our voices, our bodies, our gestures and costumes, oscillating between deeply ingrained, habitual acts (our "true mask") and acts we more or less consciously adopt to obtain jobs, mates, or power. There is no question of breaking through this condition to arrive at some unstaged, unimitated essence, because our selves are determined by our social relations and because the very nature of communication requires us, like Prufrock, to put on a face to meet the faces that we meet. Hence Lee Strasberg's notion that the stage actor does not need to "imitate a human being" is at one level entirely correct: to become "human" in the first place we put on an act.

As a result, words like "drama," "performance," and "acting" can designate a great variety of behavior, only some of which is theatrical in the purest sense. But given the affinity between theater and the world, how do we know this purity? How do we determine the important and obvious difference between performers in everyday life and performers who are behaving theatrically? The answer is not altogether clear, even though we often make such distinctions, and even though the basis on which we make them is crucial to the study of acting as an art or as a vehicle for ideology.

One solution to the problem has been offered by Erving Goffman, who defines theatrical performance as "an arrangement which transforms an individual into . . . an object that can be looked at in the round and without offense, and looked to for engaging behavior by persons in an audience role" (*Frame Analysis,* 124). The "arrangement" of which Goffman speaks may take a variety of forms, so long as it divides people into two fundamental groups, designating some as performers and others as watchers. Its purpose is to establish an unusually high degree of ostentation, a quality the actor Sam Waterston has called "visibility": "People can see you . . . all the lights

---

would like to be. In the end, our conception of our role becomes second nature and an integral part of our personality. We come into the world as individuals, achieve character, and become persons (quoted by Goffman in *The Presentation of Self,* 19).

On the question of whether acting involves imitation, one of my early childhood memories seems appropriate. (Coincidentally, it belongs to a category of recollection that Freud once termed "screen memory" [III, 303–22].) I can recall asking my parents, at the age of four or five, whether the people in movies were really kissing. The question involved a moral dilemma, and it revealed a paradox: in fact, actors both do and pretend, sometimes at one and the same moment—hence the potentially scandalous nature of their work. In certain contexts, their actions can become *too* real, breaking the hold of illusion. For instance, film reviewer Vincent Canby was disturbed by a scene in *Devil in the Flesh* (1987), in which Maruschka Detmers performs fellatio: "One's first response [is], 'Gee whiz, they're actually doing it!' Then one begins to wonder how it was staged. . . . It's a recorded, documented fact, which destroys the illusion as throughly as hairpieces that don't fit." ("Sex Can Spoil the Scene," *New York Times,* 28 June 1987, 17.)

are turned out, and there is nothing else to look at" (quoted in Kalter, 156).

This showing (or showing off) is the most elementary form of human signification, and it can turn any event into theater. For example, the New York performance artists of the fifties and sixties were able to stage "happenings" by standing on a street corner and waiting for an auto accident or any chance occurrence that their role as audience would transform into a show; their experiments demonstrated that anyone—a juggler, a dancer, or an ordinary passerby—who steps into a space previously designated as theatrical automatically becomes a performer. Furthermore, not much conscious artistic manipulation or special skill is required to provide some kinds of "engaging behavior." When art theatricalizes contingency, as in *Kid's Auto Race,* John Cage's music, or Andy Warhol's movies, it puts a conceptual bracket around a force field of sensations, an ever-present stratum of sound, shade, and movement that both precedes meaning and makes it possible. Julia Kristeva seems to be talking about such a process when she refers to a "geno-text" or an "other scene" made available to communication by "*significance,*" a preverbal activity she equates with the "*anaphoric* function." "Before and after the *voice* and the *script* is the *anaphora:* the gesture which *indicates,* establishes *relations* and eliminates entities" (270). Meaningless in itself, the anaphora is a purely relational activity whose free play allows meaning to circulate, even when meaning is unintended. All forms of human and animal exchange involve anaphoric behavior, and the "arrangement" Erving Goffman calls a theatrical frame could be understood in exactly those terms, as a primary gesture. It might take the form of a stage or a spot on the street; in the absence of these things, it could be a simple flourish of the hand or an indication to "look there." Whatever its shape, it always separates audience from performer, holding other gestures and signs up for show.

The motion picture screen is just such a theatrical anaphora, a physical arrangement that arrays spectacle for persons in an audience role. As in most types of theater, however, the actions and voices in movies are seldom allowed to "mean" by simply displaying themselves. This is especially true when the film involves *acting*—a term I shall use to designate a special type of theatrical performance in which the persons held up for show have become agents in a narrative.

At its most sophisticated, acting in theater or movies is an art devoted to the systematic ostentatious depiction of character, or to what seventeenth-century England described as "personation." Unplotted theatrics can partake of acting, as when rock musicians like Madonna or Prince develop a persona that has narrative implications; but to be called an actor in the sense I am using, a performer does not have to invent anything or master a discipline, so long as he or she is embedded in a story. The following example from the proscenium stage, cited by Michael Kirby, may serve to illustrate the point:

> Some time ago I remember reading about a play in which John Garfield—I am fairly sure it was he, although I no longer know the title of the play—was an extra. During each performance he played cards and gambled with friends on the stage. They really played, and the article emphasized how much money someone had won (or lost). At any rate, since my memory is incomplete, let us imagine a setting representing a bar. In one of the upstage booths, several men play cards throughout the act. Let us say that none of them has lines in the play; they do not react in any way to the characters in the story we are observing. . . . They merely play cards. And yet we also see them as characters, however minor, in the story and we say that they, too, are acting. ("On Acting and Not-Acting," Battcock and Nicas, 101)

This kind of "received" acting is fairly typical of theater, but in the movies it has much greater importance, extending even to the work of the star players, who sometimes perform gestures without knowing how they will be used in the story. For example, it is rumored that during the making of *Casablanca* (1942), director Michael Curtiz positioned Bogart in close-up, telling him to look off to his left and nod. Bogart did so, having no idea what the action was supposed to signify (the film, after all, was being written as it was shot). Later, when Bogart saw the completed picture, he realized his nod had been a turning point for the character he was playing: Rick's signal to the band in the Café Américain to strike up the *Marseillaise*.

A more "scientific" illustration of the same effect is the so-called Kuleshov experiment, in which an actor's inexpressive offscreen glance was intercut with various objects, thus creating the illusion that he was emoting. Kuleshov described the process as if he were a chemist working in a lab: "I alternated the same shot of Mozhukhin with various other shots (a plate of soup, a girl, a child's coffin), and these shots acquired a different meaning. The discovery stunned me" (200). There is, unfortunately, something disingenuous about Kuleshov's account, which has created what Norman Holland calls a "myth" of film history.[8] Even so, the "Kuleshov effect" is a useful term in film criticism, and anyone who has ever worked at a movie-editing table knows that a wide range of meanings or nuances, none of them intended by the script, the playing, or the *découpage,* can be produced through the cutting. Audiences, too, are aware of a potential for trickery, and a certain genre of comedy or parody foregrounds the process: a recent TV commercial uses close-ups from the original "Dragnet," editing them to make Joe Friday and his partner seem to discuss the merits of a brand of potato chips; a video on MTV shows

---

8. Holland has pointed out that Kuleshov and Pudovkin, who worked together to produce the famous sequence, disagreed about exactly what it contained. The original footage has not survived, and there is no evidence that it was shown to an innocent audience ("Psychoanalysis and Film: The Kuleshov Experiment," 1–2). The sequence therefore has dubious status as either history or science, although a formal experiment seems unnecessary when movies have always proved Kuleshov's point.

Ronald Reagan piloting a dive bomber, gleefully attacking a rock and roll band; and Paramount's *Dead Men Don't Wear Plaid* (1982) allows Steve Martin to play scenes with half the stars of Hollywood in the forties.

One reason these jokes are possible is that expression is polysemous, capable of multiple signification; its meaning in a film is usually narrowed and held in place by a controlling narrative, a context that can rule out some meanings and highlight others. As a result, some of the most enjoyable screen performances have been produced by nothing more than *typage*,[9] and it is commonplace to see dogs, babies, and rank amateurs who seem as interesting as trained thespians. In fact, the power of movies to recontextualize detail is so great that a single role frequently involves more than one player: Cary Grant acts the part of Johnny Case in *Holiday* (1938), but he performs only two of the character's many somersaults; Rita Hayworth does a "striptease" in *Gilda* (1946), but the voice that issues from the character's mouth as she sings "Put the Blame on Mame" belongs to Anita Ellis.

By slightly extending Walter Benjamin's well-known argument about painting in the age of photography, we could say that mechanical reproduction deprives performance of authority and "aura," even as it greatly enhances the possibility of stardom. Significantly, another of Kuleshov's "experiments" had involved the creation of a synthetic person out of fragmentary details of different bodies—a technique that undermines the humanist conception of acting, turning every movie editor into a potential Dr. Frankenstein. Nevertheless, Kuleshov was intensely concerned with the training of players, and audiences continue to make distinctions between figures on the screen, claiming that some of them are a bit more actorly than others.

Up to a point we can make such claims by simply quantifying the character traits exhibited by the performer. As a test case, notice a brief sequence early in *North by Northwest* (1958), when Cary Grant/Roger Thornhill goes to the Oak Room bar in the Plaza Hotel for a business meeting: Grant arrives late, introduces himself to three men waiting at a table, and orders a martini; after chatting for a moment, he suddenly remembers that he needs to call his mother, so he signals across the room to a messenger, asking that a telephone be brought to the table. The sequence involves a great many players, and we can rank them on an "actorly" scale, ranging from the extras in the background, who are rather like decor or furnishings for the hotel set, to Grant himself, who brings a fully shaped star image into the film and acts as the

---

9. *Typage*, a term coined by Soviet directors in the twenties, should not be confused with "type casting." *Typage* depends on cultural stereotypes, but, more important, it emphasizes the physical eccentricities of actors (often, by preference, nonprofessionals). Kuleshov argued that "because film needs real material and not a pretense of reality . . . it is not theater actors but 'types' who should act in film—that is, people who, in themselves, as they were born, present some kind of interest for cinematic treatment. . . . A person with an ordinary, normal exterior, however good-looking he may be, is not needed in cinema" (63–4).

central agent in the story. Between these extremes are the messenger boy, who must respond to Grant's signal, and the three businessmen around the table, who are given a few lines of dialogue. One of these men, however, is different from the others. For some reason—perhaps for the sake of verisimilitude, perhaps out of sheer playfulness—he has been allowed to cup a hand over his ear, lean over the table, and frown in bafflement because he cannot follow the conversation. His gestures, unnecessary to the cause-effect chain of the story, make him a slightly more identifiable character than his companions, and in one sense more of an actor.

In a more obvious form, acting in movies involves still another quality—a mastery, skill, or inventiveness that is implied in the normative use of the word performance. In fact all types of art or social behavior are concerned at some level with this sort of parading of expertise. Writing about Balzac, Roland Barthes remarks that "the classic author becomes a performer at the moment he evinces his power of *conducting* meaning" (*S/Z*, 174). One might say the same thing of a modernist like James Joyce, or of Barthes himself, whose verbal skill is foregrounded on every page and whose intellectual *tours de force* made him a celebrity. In literature, we can even speak of a "performative" sentence, as on the opening page of *Moby Dick:*

> Whenever I find myself growing grim about the mouth; whenever it is a damp, drizzly November in my soul; whenever I find myself pausing before coffin warehouses, and bringing up the rear of every funeral I meet; and especially whenever my hypos get such an upper hand of me, that it requires a strong moral principle to prevent me from deliberately stepping into the street, and methodically knocking people's hats off—then, I account it high time to get to sea as soon as I can.

Melville keeps the sentence in play, stringing out parallel constructions like a singer holding his breath, until that final moment when the period brings us to rest beside the sea. To read his words, we need to employ skills of our own, mentally repeating the rhythms, or perhaps interpreting them aloud so that our vocal cords participate in a dance of meaning. Oratory and most kinds of theatrical acting involve similar effects, and for that reason star performances in movies are often structured so as to give the audience a chance to appreciate the player's physical or mental accomplishments. Film problematizes our ability to measure these effects simply because it allows for so much manipulation of the image, throwing the power of "conducting" meaning into the hands of a director; nevertheless, one of the common pleasures of moviegoing derives from our feeling that an actor is doing something remarkable. Garfield playing poker, Bogart nodding his head, a minor player in a crowded scene—all these are clearly different from Chaplin/Hinkle in *The Great Dictator* (1940), bouncing a globe around a room in a long shot, executing a brilliant comic ballet while dressed as Hitler.

In succeeding chapters I spend a good deal of time illustrating or tracing out varieties of ostentatious, actorly expertise; but at the outset it is important to stress that deliberate imitation or theatrical mimesis is not necessary to acting or to the effect of a "good" performance. In one sense it is misleading to call even Chaplin a mimic when the materials of his art—his body, his gestures, his facial expression, and all the techniques he uses to create character—are the same materials we use in everyday life. We are all imitators, and the terms *mime* and *mimicry* come into play only at an extreme end of the scale of theatrical behavior, where the performer uses neither speech nor props or where the voice and body duplicate conventionalized stage gestures, creating recognizable stereotypes. Thus if a man shaves in front of a camera, he is transforming an everyday action into theater; if he shaves in the service of a story (like Nate Hardman in *Bless Their Little Hearts* [1985]), he is acting; if he goes through the same motions without a razor, he is miming, engaging in a "pure" imitation that A. J. Greimas has termed *mimetic gesturality* (35–37). Chaplin is an impressive performer in part because he is able to exploit the entire scale: at one moment in *The Gold Rush* (1925) he boils a shoe, but at the next he mimes eating, poking the laces into his mouth and chewing them as if they were spaghetti. During all this, he mimics a set of stereotypical characters, changing from cook to fussy waiter to gourmet as he moves through various stages of the meal.

The typical realist dramatic film affords few opportunities for such virtuoso imitation, although we occasionally see "copying" in naturalistic contexts: Belmondo mimics Bogart's gestures in *Breathless,* and in *Badlands* (1973) Martin Sheen takes on a remarkable resemblance to James Dean. To understand the skills involved in less visible forms of acting, it is necessary to examine behavior at a much more elementary level, analyzing the "transforming" elements or conventions that distinguish everyday utilitarian expressions from staged or scripted signs. One of the best ways to start such a project is to think of film in relation to the conventions that govern proscenium theater—a task I propose to undertake in the next chapter. Before that, however, I should like to add a few remarks about the motion picture screen, which creates a boundary between audience and performer unlike any other in theatrical history.

The Actor and the Audience

"Are you talkin' to me?"
  —Robert De Niro/Travis Bickle in
  Taxi Driver (1976)

All public institutions—classrooms, churches, houses of government—have a quasi-theatrical structure, an architecture that creates a performing space. The space can take various forms, from lecture halls to roundtable discussions, allowing for more or less ambiguity in the relation between performer and audience. Even in the most formal situations, however, paying customers sometimes get into the act: professors call on students, magicians solicit volunteers, and stand-up comics endure hecklers. Where live theater is concerned, there are different degrees of freedom in the basic relation: at one extreme are the relatively participatory arrangements of circus, music hall, and most types of "epic theater." (The most completely open form is the theater of Jerzy Grotowski, in which a select group engages in communal activity, everyone becoming simultaneously audience and performer.) At the other extreme is the proscenium arch, which situates the audience in numbered rows of seats inside a darkened room, looking toward a rectangular opening on a lighted stage.

The proscenium, or "picture-frame," arrangement became the dominant form of Western theatrical architecture some time in the late seventeenth century, when theaters in England were permanently established indoors. At about that time—soon after the restoration of Charles II but coincident with the growth of a mercantile economy throughout Europe—playhouses underwent several other changes, all of them signaling the birth of modern drama: artificial lighting was introduced; female actors were allowed on the stage; extensive scenery and props were designed; and hidden wings were constructed at either side of the arch to permit movable sets. Such conventions fostered a "representational," illusionist theater, different from the relatively "presentational" style of Shakespeare and the Elizabethans. Eventually, the actor on the proscenium stage became a part of the decor—an object in a realist *mise-en-scène*—so that it was no longer necessary to describe elaborate settings with speeches or to invoke abstract spaces with gestures. Equally important, the actor's physical relation to the audience underwent subtle changes, as if an invisible "fourth wall" had descended between the drama and the auditorium. The public was seldom addressed directly; in fact, as increasingly sophisticated methods of stage lighting were developed, the audience became less visible to the actor, until it was simply out there somewhere, represented by a dark limbo, like the void that Susan Alexander sings to in *Citizen Kane*.

To some degree, the movement from presentational to representational theatrics corresponds to what Orson Welles, in a lecture on "The New Actor," delivered in 1940, described as a transition from "formal" to "informal" drama. The formal drama, Welles explained, belongs to rigidly hierarchical cultures; ritualistic in the true sense of the term, it inculcates no sense of actorly "style" or "personality." Informal drama, by contrast, grows out of a relatively flexible social organization; its actors are celebrated public figures who treat the audience on a somewhat personal basis. In the informal tradition, which for Welles included Shakespeare and all modern theater, "it is impossible to be a great actor unless you deal with your audience" (2). Before the establishment of fully representational, picture-frame techniques, this "dealing" took specific forms: "We know that Chaliapin adored the gallery and loathed the expensive seats. The greatest moment for the Russian peasants was when Chaliapin sneered at the big people and played for the gallery when he did Boris Goudonof" (3). But in more recent times, Welles argued, the situation changed. "Even before the movies, actors stopped considering their audiences. It was the constant effort of people like Stanislavsky in a very serious way and John Drew in a frivolous way to pretend there is a fourth wall. This is death to acting style. It is practically impossible to create a new acting style which excludes the direct address to the audience" (3).

Even in the most pictorial proscenium drama, however, the audience remains present to the actor, sending out vibrations or signs that influence the intensity, pace, and content of a given performance. Live theater is always what Brecht described as "provisional," because it depends on an immediate interaction between two specific groups; and in the more presentational forms, this interaction is a major determinant of the show. Here is Mae West describing the vaudeville act she performed between 1912 and 1916:

> I used to have to work an audience, appeal to them with little private gestures, twists of my head, the way I spoke a word, or winked over a song line. . . . I brought my own sophisticated ideas and style to the vaudeville stage but I had to adjust it to the standard of each theater, and even to each night's audience in the theater. . . . I usually found that one night a week you would get a top society crowd, and another night you'd get mostly working-class people. Other nights there would be family groups—especially on Friday nights when the kids didn't have to go to school the next day. (quoted in Stein, 25)

At the movies, on the other hand, the existential bond between audience and performer is broken. The physical arrangement is permanently closed, and it cannot be opened even if the performer speaks to us directly or if we make catcalls back at the show. Audiences can sometimes become part of the spectacle, especially at cult films like *The Rocky Horror Picture Show* (1975), but the images never change to accommodate them. Likewise, movie performers can invite viewers to respond—as when James Cagney looks out at us in *Yankee Doodle Dandy* (1942), asking that we join him in singing "Over There," or when David Byrne ironically pokes a microphone at the camera during one of his numbers in *Stop Making Sense* (1984). Nevertheless Cagney and Byrne will never know if their invitation is accepted. The unique property of film as spectacle is that the two groups that constitute theatrical events cannot momentarily change social roles. To do so would involve a magical transformation, like the one in *Sherlock, Jr.* (1924), when the dreaming Buster Keaton walks down the aisle of a theater and steps right into the silver screen—or like the roughly similar one in *The Purple Rose of Cairo* (1985), when the figures in a movie begin chatting with Mia Farrow as she sits in the diegetic audience.[10]

Clearly, the impenetrable barrier of the screen favors representational playing styles. (Presentational theatrics are possible in movies, but usually they are played for a fictional audience *inside* the film, a surrogate crowd.) The barrier also promotes a fetishistic dynamic in the spectator; the actor is manifestly *there* in the image, but *not there* in the room, "present" in a more intimate way than even the *Kammerspiel* could provide, but also impervious and inaccessible. Thus every filmed performance partakes of what John Ellis and other theorists have described as the "photo effect"—a teasing sense of presence and absence, preservation and loss (Ellis, 58–61). And because the performance has been printed on emulsion, it evokes feelings of nostalgia as it grows old, heightening fetishistic pleasure. Like the speaker in Philip Larkin's "Lines on a Young Lady's Photograph Album," the viewer sometimes feels a mingling of voyeuristic desire and bittersweet regret:

> My swivel eye hungers from pose to pose—
> ....
>
> In every sense empirically true;
> Or is it just *the past*? Those flowers, that gate
> These misty parts and motors, lacerate
> Simply by being over; you
> Contract my heart by looking out of date.[11]

Recent developments in technology allow us to evade such feelings, inserting ourselves into the act by taking control of the machinery. We can purchase a VCR or an analyzing projector, manipulating the images and repeating them forever; in doing so, however, we usually prolong the sense of

---

10. The terms "diegetic" and "nondiegetic" have become commonplace in contemporary film theory, enabling us to make important formal distinctions. A film's diegesis is composed of everything that belongs to an imaginary world or "story space." Thus if a character turns on a radio and we seem to hear music coming from it, we can describe the music as "diegetic." If we hear music that does not have a source in the story—for example if we see lovers on a barren heath embrace to the accompaniment of a full orchestra—we describe the music as "nondiegetic." Besides music, typical nondiegetic elements in Hollywood movies include credits, superimposed titles such as "Phoenix, Arizona," and certain types of spoken narration.

11. Larkin's male persona is more articulate and self-aware than most viewers. He recognizes that he derives pleasure from photographs because they make no demands; by passively allowing themselves to be watched, they free him of responsibility:

> in the end, surely, we cry
> Not only at exclusion, but because
> It leaves us free to cry. We know *what was*
> Won't call on us to justify
> Our grief, however hard we yowl across
> The gap from eye to page.

private play, elaborating a *fort/da* game that film has always encouraged.[12] Consider, for example, Charles Affron's rapt discussion of what he calls the "power" and "dominion" given to spectators by the apparatus: "Garbo can die for me around the clock. I can stay her in that final moment of her life; I can turn off the sound and watch, turn off the picture and listen, work myriad transformations in speed and brilliance, and then restore the original without losing a particle of its intensity" (5). For all his emphasis on the power of the viewer, however, Affron is talking less about freedom than about the erotics of textual analysis. Garbo has become the perfect fetish object, the ultimate Romantic Image, her performance balanced between an imaginary plenitude and what Yeats described as "the cold snows of dream."

There is, of course, another side to this issue, and I think it is implicit in what Affron says. The same machinery that fetishizes performance also permits it to be deconstructed or replayed in ways that run counter to its original intentions; the apparatus (especially when joined with video technology) allows the audience to become postmodernists, alienating the spectacle, producing a heightened awareness of the artificiality in all acting—even the kind of acting that constitutes our daily life.[13] By freezing the frames of a movie, by running them at different speeds, we can institute what Terry Eagleton has described as a "Derridian 'spacing,' rendering a piece of stage business exterior to itself . . . and thus, it is hoped, dismantling the ideological self-identity of our routine social behavior" (633). Here again Walter Benjamin's arguments about the effect of photography on painting seem to apply equally to the effect of media on acting. The performance, having become a text, is no longer part of a specific architecture; it now comes to people, who can glimpse it at home in bits and pieces. Under these circumstances, it has less to contribute toward the "theology of art."

The closed boundary between audience and performer has had similarly complex effects on society in the aggregate, partly because the actor's work is no longer "provisional" but fixed, geared toward an imaginary individual

12. In *Beyond the Pleasure Principle*, Freud describes a game he once saw an infant playing. The child enjoyed "taking any small objects he could get hold of and throwing them away from him into a corner, under the bed, and so on." As he did this, he always shouted a syllable that Freud interpreted to mean *"fort,"* the German word for "gone." One day Freud observed him playing with a wooden reel attached to a piece of string. Shouting *"fort,"* the boy held the string and tossed the object away; he then pulled it back, celebrating its reappearance "with a joyful *'da'* ['there']." Freud called this the *fort/da* game, and used it to illustrate the "economics" of the libido. According to Freud, the child was compensating for the fact that his mother sometimes went away, "by himself staging the disappearance and return of objects within his reach" (XVIII, 14–16). For a commentary on this process in relation to cinema, see Stephen Heath, "*Anata mo,*" *Screen* (Winter 1976–77): 49–66.

13. Throughout this discussion I have collapsed film and television together, but I should point out they often promote a quite different relation between audience and performer. For an interesting commentary on the issue, and on ways video has been made to conform to more traditional conceptions of the audience, see Lili Berko, "Discursive Imperialism," *USC Spectator* (Spring 1986): 10–11.

who represents the mass. Thus when Mae West brought her vaudeville persona to talking pictures, her old technique of adjusting to the makeup of a
specific audience was useless. Like a writer imagining a reader, she had to
play for an idealized viewer—or for her directors, producers, and fellow
players. One result of this new arrangement was an increasing homogeniza-
tion of the culture, which began to seem like a global village. "Today," West
observed in 1959,

> motion pictures, radio, and television have brought Broadway sophistication
> and big city ideas to even the remotest of green communities. Today there is no
> longer such a thing as a "hick" audience. Almost anything goes, anywhere, if
> it is good and fast and amusing. Risqué material is only offensive if badly done
> without style and charm. (Stein, 280)

But definitions of "style and charm" can vary, depending on the cycles of
liberalism and conservatism in society at large—a fact West herself must have
realized in the mid thirties, when the Production Code made her work in
movies increasingly problematic.

Like West, film actors must respond indirectly to mass opinion; but cinema
also "constructs" its spectators more rigorously than any other form of theater, so that both players and viewers ultimately resemble lonely individuals,
looking into a mirror. This profound change in the dynamic of performance
was a matter of great concern to the intellectuals who wrote about early movies, although they sometimes disagreed about its influence for good or for
evil. Populist Americans like Vachel Lindsay and Hugo Münsterberg were
optimistic; worshippers of the "universal language" of the silent screen, they
believed mass media could democratize society—raising the level of sophistication, spreading sweetness and light, working as a force of education. By
contrast, most Europeans and Anglophiles were pessimistic. In the twenties,
T. S. Eliot was convinced that the rise of the movie house and the subsequent
death of the English music hall would contribute to a deadening *embourgoise-
ment* of English culture:

> With the death of the music-hall, with the encroachment of the cheap and rapid-
> breeding cinema, the lower classes will tend to drop into the same state of
> protoplasm as the bourgeoise. The working man who went to the music-hall
> and saw Marie Lloyd and joined in the chorus was himself performing part of
> the act; he was engaged in that collaboration of the audience with the artist
> which is necessary in all art and most obviously in dramatic art. He will now
> go to the cinema, where his mind is lulled by continuous senseless music and
> continuous action . . . , and will receive, without giving, in that same listless
> apathy with which the middle and upper classes regard any entertainment of the
> nature of art. He will have also lost some of his interest in life. (225)

Eliot's essentially right-wing argument has something in common with the left-wing responses of Adorno and the Frankfurt School, who regarded cinema as opiate for the masses. Among the Germans, Brecht was perhaps the most aware of mixed blessings in the new media. His short essay on radio, written in the thirties, could be used to summarize the concerns that lie behind all discussions of the relation between audience and performer in the age of mechanical reproduction:

> Radio is one-sided when it should be two-. It is purely an apparatus of distribution, for mere sharing out. So here is a positive suggestion: change the apparatus over from distribution to communication. The radio would be the finest possible communication apparatus in public life, a vast network of pipes. That is to say, it would be if it knew how to let the listener speak as well as hear, how to bring him into a relationship instead of isolating him. (52)

Unfortunately, Brecht's proposed solution cannot be applied to movies, and other types of "mass communication" have seldom realized their potential for democratic exchange: examples of "two-way" performances in America today would range from progressive broadcasts such as "The Phil Donahue Show" to various "prayerline" evangelists. Where ordinary film acting is concerned, the point to be remembered is that even though modern society has brought performers close to us, in many ways it has made them seem farther away, more fabulous than ever.

3

Rhetoric and Expressive Technique

Must not anyone who wants to move the crowd be an actor who impersonates himself? Must he not first translate himself into grotesque obviousness and then present his whole person and cause in this coarsened and simplified version?
—Friedrich Nietzsche, *The Gay Science,* 1882

I would almost say that the best screen actor is the man who can do nothing extremely well.
—Alfred Hitchcock, "Direction," 1937

The quotations above indicate how much our conception of acting has changed during the past century. Hitchcock's remark sounds a good deal like Spencer Tracy's famous advice to his fellow players: "Just know your lines and don't bump into the furniture." Charmingly unpretentious as Hitchcock and Tracy may sound, however, they are quite misleading. All performing situations employ a physics of movement and gesture that makes signs readable; in this sense Nietzsche's observation that actors translate their person into a simplified version still holds true. The actual work for people who appear in movies or television seems to involve a compromise between "obviousness" and "doing nothing." Spencer Tracy was a master of such practical considerations, and as a result his behavior in films differs from ordinary social interaction.

At its simplest level, the activity of any performer can be described in terms of a mode of address and a degree of ostensiveness. For example, in most circumstances of everyday communication the interlocutor's gaze is directed toward an individual or a small group in the immediate vicinity; no special energy is required for the "presentation of self," and considerable latitude is allowed for insignificant lapses, irrelevant movement, or glances away from the audience. In theatrical events, the voice and body are subject to a more rigorous control. Thus in oratory, the performance is formalized and "projected"—movements are at once less frequent and more emphatic, and the speaker tries to maintain eye contact by distributing his or her glance around a crowd. By contrast, the typical TV newscast makes its rhetorical strategy nearly invisible, indirectly confirming Derrida's argument about the cultural valuation of "speech" over "writing." The news anchorman is framed in a bust-sized close-up, directing his gaze at the camera; he speaks to a crowd, but he thinks of it as an abstracted, generalized individual with an intimate frontal view. The performance therefore becomes a blend of public speaking and everyday behavior—more formalized, intense, and "sincere" than ordinary conversation but projected less strongly than a talk from a podium. The speaker's balancing act between clear, standardized enunciation (once known as the "telephone voice") and warm, close-up address also requires him to adopt a fairly rigid posture, since any quick movement threatens to disrupt what Goffman has called the "front" for the performance. At this range, even a minute shift of the body could decenter the careful framing, and a glance downward could fill the screen with a bald spot or a meaningless expanse of hair. Hence the player uses a teleprompter, "anchoring" us with a forthright gaze, masking the fact that he is reading. If any part of the machinery were to refuse to collaborate in this rhetoric—if, for example, the camera were to move a few degrees to the left or right, so that Dan Rather seemed to be looking offscreen toward nothing—then we would witness a sudden transformation of naturalized communication into artifice, a revelation that televised speech is simply another form of writing.

On television variety or talk shows of the Carson type, both the degree of ostensiveness and the mode of address can change rapidly, moving from vaudeville comedy to intimate exchanges, from showbiz to semidocumentary. In the chatty episodes, players cultivate a shifting gaze, aimed now at the interviewer or interviewee, now at the studio audience, now at the lens of the camera. Whatever the situation, they behave more theatrically than they would in an everyday encounter. The more skillful and eager performers know how to enter a stage and find a mark, how to shake hands with the host without turning their backs to the camera, and how to sit down without "bumping into the furniture" or searching too much behind them for the seat. They know how to align their bodies with the slightly outturned position of the chairs, and for the most part they take care to focus their attention on the center of theatrical interest, seldom turning to look randomly at the monitor or the crew. During conversations they usually take turns speaking, treating the camera with the good manners of polite society, as if they were drawing it into the circle of talk with brief glances toward the lens. The trick behind their act is to stage a "natural" give-and-take that is tightly framed, directed at several potential audiences, and viewed somewhat obliquely.

Dramatic theater involves still another strategy, marked by two broadly different playing styles. Imagine two ways of staging *Hamlet:* in the first, the actor places his hand to his brow, turns slightly away from the audience, and mutters "To be or not to be" as if speaking to himself. In the second, the actor poses the question with full rhetorical force, remaining in character but look-ing directly at the audience like an orator who is genuinely baffled by the philosophical issue. These two styles—the representational and the presen-tational—can make up a formal dialectic, as they do in Shakespeare, where characters frequently step outside the ongoing action and become commen-tators. A number of dramatic movies (usually adapted from theater pieces) have employed a similar technique: consider Brando in *Teahouse of the Au-gust Moon* (1955), Michael Caine in *Alfie* (1966), Glenda Jackson in *Stevie* (1983), and so on. Likewise, in certain types of vaudeville-inspired comedy the actors use direct address to disrupt illusion: Groucho Marx steps up to the camera and advises us to go out to the lobby for popcorn; Bob Hope turns to the lens and makes wisecracks; George Burns interrupts the action of his TV sitcom to chat with viewers about the plot. In radical or modernist cinema, speeches of the same sort have didactic or perhaps deconstructive implica-tions. Godard's films provide the best-known examples, but notice also *Fran-cisca* (1983), a masterwork by Manoel de Oliveira, which sometimes gives us two versions of an action, first in representational and then in presenta-tional form.

Brecht's quarrel with Stanislavsky had centered largely on a need to restore presentational techniques to the stage (when he and Piscator adopted the term "epic theater," they were borrowing not from a Hollywood press agent but from Goethe, who had used "epic poetry" to designate a technique of narra-tion). For that reason, it is tempting to link presentational rhetoric with activ-ist or "progressive" strategies. We should remember, however, that direct address appears just as often in television commercials or hard-core pornog-raphy as in radical drama. In the next chapter I shall have more to say about Godard's particular use of the technique to foster the *Verfremdungseffekt;* for now, I want only to emphasize that narrative movies depend chiefly on rep-resentation—in other words, the characters seem to be speaking to one an-other even though their performance is aimed at an audience beyond the "fourth wall." Different performing methods or styles of blocking can make acting seem more or less presentational, depending on the emotional tone of the players, their movements in relation to the camera, and the degree to which they mimic well-known forms of behavior; nevertheless, screen actors usually pretend that the audience is not present.

This representational rhetoric extends to every aspect of the filmed spectacle. The screen is a picture-frame arrangement rather like the proscenium arch (until fairly recently motion picture theaters were outfitted with curtains that drew apart as the projection began); hence it is common for Hollywood directors to speak of the 180-degree rule as the "stage line," and in arranging a given shot they necessarily think in many of the same spatial terms as a theatrical *metteur-en-scène*. For the most part, performance in film, as in theater, is a matter of "acting sideways," so that audiences are given a clear view into every encounter. The essential difference from stage convention, as the British actor Peter Barkworth has remarked, is that "in the theatre you need to *widen* your performance so the whole audience can see you, whereas for the cameras you need to narrow it down" (52).

In either case, the need to make events at least obliquely visible puts a good many constraints on behavior. Suppose, for example, that a scene on the proscenium stage involves a single player in a standing pose. He or she may take a variety of stances relative to the audience, ranging from full front to full back; the front view is the strongest and "stagiest" position, whereas the full back view is usually regarded as "weak"—a device used to give the platform an added dimension, to conceal or suggest emotions, or to lend an air of verisimilitude. The stance most common in representational theater is a profile, usually of an "open," three-quarter variety, which gives the audience a clear view of the actor's expression while maintaining the illusion that spectators are not present. When another actor is added to the scene, the two players are said to "share" or "give" positions, depending on whether their faces are equally visible: if they line up parallel to the arch, they are in a shared relation; but if they are set on the diagonal, they cannot exchange glances without one player assuming a "weak" stance.[1] Thus players with important narrative or expositional functions usually receive the strong focus of the arrangement, facing more or less toward the auditorium, and crossing movements or changes of position are executed so as to preserve the audience's view.

The chief mark of realistic, psychological drama from the late nineteenth century onward has been the tendency of the actors to turn away, moving out of the strong or shared positions, facing one another on the diagonal so as to make the stage seem less "rhetorical," more "natural." Hence the Moscow Art Theater's famous production of *The Seagull* in 1898 opened with the actors standing with their backs to the audience, and the American tour of the Abbey Theater in 1911–12 was heralded by critics because the company frequently played to the rear of the stage; at about the same time, Mrs. Fiske created a sensation by speaking with her back turned or by walking into dark corners at highly dramatic moments.

---

1. I have adapted these terms from a recent textbook, *An Introduction to Acting,* by Stanley Kahan (Boston: Allyn and Bacon, 1985).

Roughly contemporary developments in cinema can be understood similarly as the creation of cinematic strategies to conceal the fundamental "staginess" of acting. As Janet Staiger has shown, a full-scale change toward the rhetoric of psychological realism occurred in Hollywood between 1908 and the mid-teens, when the industry shifted to a director-centered mode of production and began to manufacture feature-length dramatic films that took their subject matter, aesthetic values, and talent from the increasingly intimate and naturalistic New York stage (18). By contrast, the "primitive" cinema had been devoted to straightforward action sequences, paying little or no attention to the psychological motives of characters. Except in kissing scenes, portrait shots, or occasional inserts, the camera was positioned at a distance, so that figures on the screen approximated proscenium scale and the spectator seemed to occupy an orchestra seat. Performers in these early films sometimes behaved with easygoing restraint; in general, however, they moved parallel to the camera, stood in three-quarter profile when they addressed one another, and gesticulated vividly to compensate for their relative distance from the audience. (Edwin Porter's *Uncle Tom's Cabin* [1903] is a good example of the technique, as is F. S. Armitage's somewhat more realistic *The Nihilists* [1906].) Sometimes, too, they adopted a rudimentary sign language in place of intertitles; Kristin Thompson has noted that an actor in the earliest films might signal his desire for "just one drink" by pointing to himself, holding up one finger, and then miming the action of drinking. Thompson calls the technique "pantomime" (189), but a better term would be "codified gesture," because the actors were relying on a sort of writing with the hands rather than on the culturally transmitted, broadly expressive gestures of most nineteenth-century theater.[2]

The first step in facilitating the change toward psychological realism was to shorten the distance between actors and camera. Prior to 1909, scenes were usually played up to a line drawn perpendicular to the lens axis at a distance of twelve feet, with the camera set at eye level; soon afterward, a "nine-foot line" came into vogue, so that the standard group shot framed the upper three-quarters of the actors' bodies, with the camera at chest height (Salt, 106). The screen now seemed a Bazinian *mask,* suggesting a world beyond its edges and giving the spectator a sense of being in the theatrical space. The new arrangement (called "the American foreground" by some producers and later dubbed the *plan américain* by the French) facilitated a wider, more subtle range of gesture and allowed greater variety in the staging of entrances and exits. Actors could turn their backs when they moved into the foreground; eventually they walked on and off from behind the camera, something they had done previously only in films shot outdoors. By these means, the move-

---

2. A similar distinction between "pantomime" and "codified gesture" may be found in Betty and Franz Bauml, *A Dictionary of Gestures,* 1.

ments of players could be rigorously subordinated to a narrative economy: as Chaplin remarked, "you don't want an actor to walk an unnecessary distance unless there is a special reason, for walking is not dramatic" (151). Equally important, the actors could now pose in conversational situations, allowing the camera to focus on extended emotional exchanges between two characters at close quarters.

Griffith's later work depended heavily on these medium shots, and on "cut-ins" for tight framings of faces and details. In general, however, when his players conversed, they stood parallel to the camera in shared relationships. Subsequent directors relied more on the shot/reverse shot combination, which allowed actors to remain still, their bodies largely out of sight, while the camera selected whose face was "given." With this technique, a certain amount of visibly rhetorical blocking could be eliminated, and the smallest psychological nuances could be acted in a pattern of action and reaction. Once the system of interlocking eyeline matches and "cinematographic" camera angles was in place, the actor could play a given shot in *any* relation to the camera and still seem to be working in representational form. The camera was no longer simply an audience; it had become a kind of narrator, so that it could momentarily take up the position of a player in the scene, looking another player in the eye.

Realistic *découpage* made the most extreme frontal stances seem natural-istic, and the talkies ultimately provided everything else that was necessary to "transparent," fully representational performances. Directional micro-phones, multitrack sound editing, looping, sound mixes—all these devices were ultimately employed to render intimate, low-key behavior in ways that would have dazzled Stanislavsky. The highly artificial conventions of the sound mix even allowed viewers to spy on "private" behavior in the midst of "public" settings: as one of countless examples that could be chosen, notice the scene early in William Wyler's adaptation of the popular Broadway play *The Heiress* (1949), where a quiet, shyly flirtatious conversation between Montgomery Clift and Olivia de Havilland can be heard in the midst of a party, while an orchestra is supposedly playing for a crowd of dancers nearby.

Prior to the full advent of sound, however, the movies had already achieved something akin to a Stanislavskian ideal, as in the performances of Eleanor Boardman in *The Crowd* (1925) or Louise Brooks in *Diary of a Lost Girl* (1929). The most important technical device in fostering this naturalism was the close-up, which became a perfect vehicle for what Stanislavsky had called "gestureless moments." Here is V. I. Pudovkin, commenting on behav-ior in portrait shots:

> Stanislavski felt that an actor striving towards truth should be able to avoid the element of *portraying* his feelings to the audience, and should be able to trans-mit to it the whole fullness of the content of the acted image in some moment

of half-mystic communion. Of course, he came up against a brick wall in his endeavors to find a solution to this problem in the theater.

It is amazing that the solution to this very problem is not only not impracticable in the cinema, but extreme paucity of gesture, often literal immobility, is absolutely indispensable in it. For example, in the close-up, in which gesture is completely dispensed with, inasmuch as the body of the actor is simply not seen. (334–35)

Nowhere is the romantic idealism underlying Stanislavskian aesthetics more apparent than in this quote, where the close-up is regarded as a mirror of the soul; Brecht, of course, would have argued that actors are always and everywhere "portraying," and that they ought to be forthright about the process. Pudovkin writes as if "truth" could be seen shining transparently through faces, forgetting that the muscular arrangement of the eyes and mouth are themselves a form of gesture, even when the actor is "living the part." And yet Pudovkin is correct when he describes typical film acting as a relatively passive phenomenon—not only because the meaning of expressions can be determined by editing, but because the camera takes on a rhetorical function when it selects details or changes the scale of an image.

The camera's mobility and tight framing of faces, its ability to "give" the focus of the screen to any player at any moment, also means that films tend to favor *reactions*. On stage or in the standard middle-distance shot of a movie, the eye of the spectator automatically follows whoever moves or speaks; but in film it is possible to cut away, focusing on a relatively immobile bystander. As a result, some of the most memorable Hollywood performances have consisted largely of players isolated in close-up, responding nonverbally to offscreen events: William Powell trying to maintain his decorum while Mischa Auer acts like an ape in *My Man Godfrey* (1935); Brandon de Wilde gasping in bug-eyed awe at Alan Ladd's fast draw in *Shane* (1953); James Stewart squirming in helpless anxiety as he watches Grace Kelly being manhandled in *Rear Window* (1954). In each of these cases, one character becomes audience for another; the close-ups usually involve intense, rather exaggerated facial expressions, but in one sense the actors could be regarded as "doing nothing extremely well."

The "gestureless" form of classic cinema nevertheless involves a good many physical problems for the actors. Tight framing requires them to cultivate unusual stillness or restraint; in two-shots, for example, they often stand closer together than they would in actual encounters, sometimes working from ludicrous positions that look perfectly natural to the camera. Occasionally a small mannerism or emotional reaction that would be automatic in real life can utterly destroy a scene, so that players move counter to their normal instincts. Hume Cronyn has recalled how he learned this lesson in a scene from Hitchcock's *Shadow of a Doubt* (1943):

During the meal, I said something upsetting to the character played by Teresa Wright. She turned to me with unexpected violence. I stood up in embarrassment and surprise and automatically took a step backward. However, at the point of the rise, the camera moved in to hold us in a close two-shot, and to accommodate it—that is, to stay in the frame—it became necessary for me to change that instinctive movement so that when I got up from the chair, *I took a step toward the person from whom I was retreating*. . . . I was convinced that the action would look idiotic on the screen, but I was wrong . . . I had to admit that the occasion passed almost unnoticed even by me. (quoted in Kahan, 297–98)

The filming of physical actions can become so complex that the set has to be dotted with gaffer's tape indicating where the simplest movements must start or end. Even such details as the tilt of a head or the position of a hand are matters of great concern, and the combined action of camera and players in the longer takes creates problems of timing and body placement equivalent to those of a formal dance. Later in this book, I comment on one such scene in *Holiday* (1938), where Katharine Hepburn descends a staircase at a crowded wedding reception, urgently searching for Cary Grant. The action is viewed from a considerable distance, yet Hepburn's alternating expressions—friendly smiles and worried glances around the room—are always visible; throughout the shot she remains at the center of the composition, her dark dress contrasting with the white walls, her quick descent set against the upward flow of massed bodies, her face bobbing into full view at strategic moments between the shoulders of extras.

Movie actors therefore learn to control and modulate behavior to fit a variety of situations, suiting their actions to a medium that might view them at any distance, height, or angle and that sometimes changes the vantage point within a single shot. Different directors have exercised authority over these patterns in different ways—some, like Hitchcock, relying heavily on reaction shots, others, like Hawks, cultivating a looser, middle-distance framing and a greater sense of spontaneous interplay. In all films, however, the behavior of players is designed to make significant faces and gestures visible, important dialogue audible. Hence the average two- or three-figure composition will involve a "shared" position, with the actors in three-quarter profile to the camera; larger groupings will be arranged so that figures on the outer fringes of a crowd stand to the sides of the frame, their faces turned slightly toward the lens, leaving an open space for the sight line of a hypothetical viewer. David Bordwell has described the technique as a "classical use of frontality." The result, he notes, "is an odd rubbernecking. . . . Standing groups are arranged in horizontal or diagonal lines or in half-circles; people seldom close ranks as they would in real life" (51). Once again, directors have different ways of managing these ensembles. John Ford's *The Man Who Shot Liberty*

"Frontality" in Touch of Evil.

Valance (1962) is blocked in shallow, one-dimensional fashion, so much like a high-school play that it looks almost Brechtian; by contrast, Orson Welles's *Touch of Evil* (1958) is filled with decentered arrangements, extreme diagonals, and figures who pop in and out of distant corners. And yet the problem for actors in both films is much the same: they must respect the principle of "frontality," playing within the sight line of a camera, never letting their actions disintegrate into truly random, contingent behavior.

The job of making expression visible is further complicated by the fact that people in films do more than just stand, talk, and maneuver themselves into different arrangements. An important principle of realist acting, borrowed from theater, is to devise situations in which the characters *talk about one thing while doing something else.* Lombard and Powell wash dishes as they discuss their future in *My Man Godfrey;* Hepburn and Tracy give one another a massage as they debate courtroom ethics in *Adam's Rib* (1949); Kirk Douglas and Mitzi Gaynor dance the twist as they have a quarrel in *For Love or Money* (1963), and so forth.[3] If the script does not actually call for

3. The technique is enshrined in a modest little scene in *The Bad and the Beautiful* (1953), when movie-producer Kirk Douglas gives aspiring star Lana Turner a lesson in acting. In the movie-within-the-movie, Turner plays a young woman in a tobacco shop, looking over a paper-

some combination of doing and talking, the better actors usually try to invent business, or they sometimes use the simplest action as a rhythmic counterpoint to speech (one of Olivier's favorite tricks was to walk slowly while talking quickly, or vice versa). Some situations create special problems: a small book could be written about eating scenes in movies, showing how actors regulate their biting, chewing, and swallowing, or only toy with the dish to accommodate dialogue. By the same token, scenes involving kissing, fighting, and social dancing always put complicated rhetorical demands on the participants, turning them into virtual marionettes.

And though it is true that movies have helped to foster a restrained, intimate style, it is wrong to assume that "good" film acting always conforms to the low-level ostensiveness of ordinary conversation. As a general rule, Hollywood has required that supporting players, ethnic minorities, and women be more animated or broadly expressive than white male leads. The intensity of behavior also varies somewhat between genres, and a great many nonmusical films involve the actors in "putting on a show"—consider the music hall sequence at the beginning of *39 Steps* (1935), or the "Tonight Show" monologue delivered by Robert De Niro at the end of *King of Comedy* (1983). The most ordinary settings can involve highly theatrical moments, indications of the way "staginess" interpenetrates everyday life: in *Old Acquaintance* (1946), Miriam Hopkins plays a neurotic, self-dramatizing novelist who constantly wrings her hands and holds her brow like a heroine of Victorian melodrama; and near the beginning of *Mean Streets* (1976), Robert De Niro enters a neighborhood bar with all the brassy, outrageous showmanship of a burlesque comic. In fact a single role in a film can involve an extraordinary range of actorly energy—at one moment Charles Foster Kane is whispering "Rosebud," his mouth filling the entire screen, and at the next he is a tiny figure at the end of a hall delivering a campaign speech; in one scene he holds an intimate *tête à tête* with Susan Alexander, and in another he screams from the top of a stairwell, threatening to "get" Boss Jim Gettys. Some films pitch the entire performance at the level of a quiet, personal interaction, as in the conversation between Wally Shawn and Andre Gregory in *My Dinner with Andre* (1980)—a middlebrow philosophical movie that is deeply concerned with the ideology of "being" instead of "acting." Other films play everything at full tilt: both *The Man Who Shot Liberty Valance* and *Touch of Evil*, despite

---

back novel as Gilbert Roland enters to buy a pack of cigarettes. Roland stares at her and she glances up from the book to ask, "See anything interesting?" The director yells "cut," and Douglas takes Turner aside, whispering something we cannot hear. The scene is shot again, and this time she makes her line more provocative by continuing to read as she speaks.

4. For a particularly instructive example of the rhetoric of eating in films, notice the scene in *Desk Set* (1957), when Tracy gives Hepburn an IQ test as they both munch on sandwiches. At appropriate moments, Tracy leaves a shred of food visible on his lips, and Hepburn makes a great show of trying to talk around a stuffed mouth.

their differences, are acted with a volume and intensity suitable to a fair-sized theater. For the purpose of analysis, therefore, it is better to speak of the specific performing circumstances required by a given movie, acknowledging a shifting cinematic rhetoric that allows room for the full spectrum of behavior.

In general, naturalistic styles of performance try to conceal or modify all the rhetorical devices I have been describing. Actors in "ethnic" films like *The Godfather* (1972) or in middle-class domestic dramas like *Heartburn* (1986) tend to slop down food and talk with their mouths full. Likewise, they occasionally turn away from the camera, speak softly and rapidly, repeat words, slur or throw away lines, sometimes ask "Huh?" or let dialogue overlap.[5] To achieve the effect of spontaneity, they preface speeches with meaningless intensifiers or qualifiers—a technique especially apparent on television soap operas, where nearly every remark is preceded with "look," "now," or "well." Naturalistic actors also cultivate a halting, somewhat groping style of speech: instead of saying "I am very distressed," the actor will say "I am dis- . . . very distressed." By the same logic, he or she will start an action, such as drinking from a glass, and then pause to speak before carrying the action through.[6]

Because naturalistic filmmakers are enamored of what William Gillette called "the illusion of the first time," they also encourage a good deal of improvisation, trying to create situations where the actors will be forced to fumble along, or where one player will do something unexpected, forcing the others to react spontaneously. In one sense, of course, there is no such thing as improvisation in movies because everything is recorded and subject to manipulation; nevertheless, certain directors (Hawks, Cassavetes, Altman) have encouraged their casts to develop scenes as the cameras roll, and players sometimes transform mistakes into clever pieces of business; just as they do

5. The technique of overlapping dialogue seems to have been popularized by Alfred Lunt and Lynn Fontaine on the Broadway stage in the twenties. It was quite standard at the beginning of the talkies, but some of the early sound technicians advised actors against it. Mary Astor has commented on those days: "In [*Holiday* (1930)], it was impossible to 'overlap,' which is natural in conversation . . . the sound man was king. If he couldn't hear it, we couldn't shoot it. . . . You couldn't talk and pace up and down. For example, if the action started with you standing beside a table and then included a move to a chair by the fireplace, you could speak into a mike at the table, but you couldn't talk on the way over; you'd have to wait until you sat down—where there was another mike in the fireplace" (quoted in Leyda, 16).

6. One recent example of these naturalistic rhetorical qualities is Woody Allen's *Hannah and Her Sisters* (1986)—a profoundly Stanislavskian movie, despite its comedy and its occasional use of intertitles. (Significantly, Allen's script alludes to Chekhov, the Moscow Art Theater's favorite playwright, and with a friend, one of Hannah's sisters starts up a business called "The Stanislavsky Catering Company.") The film depends on an ensemble of actors who are sharply attuned to the manners of a specific New York social set. In two-shots, one of these players either delivers crucial lines from a "closed" position or steps briefly out of sight; likewise, some of the most intimate conversations are staged in parks or city streets, with the microphone capturing every low-key word while the actors are viewed as tiny figures in the distance.

on the stage.[7] Even when they improvise in this restricted sense, however, actors usually observe the rules of classical rhetoric, aiming everything obliquely toward the camera. When they develop their own lines, they tend to lapse into monologue, playing from relatively static, frontal positions with a second actor nearby who nods or makes short interjections. (See Jane Fonda's rambling talks with her psychiatrist in *Klute* [1971], or Robert De Niro's long, comic explanation of his gambling debts to Harvey Keitel in *Mean Streets*.) Thus naturalism, which began as an attack on rhetoric or "staginess," remains in the end an orderly, formal construction, never radically challenging the conventions of proscenium drama.

Consequently, even when naturalistic movie actors appear to be doing nothing, they are often quite busy. As one last example, consider *Father of the Bride* (1950), in which Spencer Tracy plays the role of a suburban paterfamilias who sometimes has trouble remembering his lines and avoiding awkward contact with the furniture. At his daughter's wedding ceremony, Tracy's character has to speak two words, step backward a couple of paces, and sit on an empty church pew. On the eve of the wedding, he dreams that he cannot speak, that the church floor has turned to rubber, and that the audience is laughing wildly at his helpless condition. Meanwhile Tracy the actor, impersonating this beleaguered fellow, has to perform a variety of complex rhetorical tasks. Occasionally he speaks directly to the camera—as in the opening shots, where he addresses us while slumping back in an armchair and wearily removing his shoes. Elsewhere he plays fully representational scenes that involve talking about one thing while doing something else: he has an argument with Elizabeth Taylor as he eats ice cream, and then patches up the quarrel during a midnight snack, as he munches bread and butter. During the climactic wedding reception, his character is trapped in the kitchen, trying to mix dozens of different drinks for the guests while making small talk. Throughout the scene, Tracy verges on slapstick comedy, fumbling with ice cubes and glasses, spraying a bottle of coke on himself as he tries to open it—all the while timing every joke and registering every pained expression with exactly the proper ostensiveness. We might say that the effectiveness of his performance, and of good naturalistic playing in general, consists in part of an ability to suggest disorder by means of orderliness—thereby letting us see the distance between a character who is awkward and a player who is in full theatrical control.

*   *   *

7. Katharine Hepburn accidentally broke a heel off her shoe during a scene in *Bringing Up Baby* (1938), and transformed the mishap into a comic walk that remains in the film. George C. Scott slips on the floor during a big speech in *Dr. Strangelove* (1963), and simply turns the fall into a somersault, popping up to finish his sentence. A minor instance of this sort of "playing through" is a scene in *Chinatown* (1974), when Jack Nicholson can't get his cigarette lighter to function. Director Roman Polanski chose to preserve that take, not only because it lends a quality of verisimilitude, but because it makes us vaguely aware of the actor behind the performance.

The ancient texts on rhetoric say little about the matters I have been discussing, perhaps because performing situations in classical Greece and Rome were relatively inflexible. Nevertheless writers like Demetrius and Cicero were able to develop what E. H. Gombrich has called "the most careful analysis of any expressive medium ever undertaken," treating language, voice, and gesture as an "organon, an instrument which offers its master a variety of different scales and 'stops'" (74–75). Throughout these texts, early theorists of oratory understand rhetoric less as a technique of adjusting to the theatrical environment than as an artful deployment of "expressions" to move, persuade, and embody traits of character. For that reason among others, acting and poetics in Western culture have frequently been studied in the context of public speaking. The very word *actor* in English was originally meant to suggest the "action" of orators, and in Shakespeare's day the style of players on the stage was influenced by guidebooks to Euphuistic eloquence. This tradition was sustained in nineteenth-century America, where the first attempts at formal training of actors issued from elocution schools, and where the theater was long regarded as a declamatory medium (McArthur, 99–100).

The connection between acting and speechmaking began to disappear at the turn of the century as drama became increasingly visual, representational, and responsive to the tastes of a larger audience. Since then, technology has widened the gap still further. The microphone is capable of bringing us the "grain" of an actor's voice, but in usual practice it tames and naturalizes the vocal instrument, detheatricalizing language in much the same way as close-ups detheatricalize gesture. Pudovkin, for example, argues that movie actors should ignore old-fashioned vocal training: "When the actor works on his voice and his intonation, he is guided not by the dictates of his role, but by the distance separating stage from audience. Actors on the stage whisper loudly, thereby contradicting the very meaning of the act of whispering" (317). The weight and strength of the actor's vocal cords, he suggests, are mere technical supports for ostensiveness, unnecessary in the age of cinema.

Of course, not all actors have obeyed Pudovkin's injunction. Elocutionists like James Earl Jones or Laurence Olivier are valued precisely because of the musical power of their voices; thus Olivier frequently *lofts* his words, creating effects that mechanical control of volume cannot duplicate. (He is also adept at preserving the cadences of Shakespeare's blank verse, even while he adjusts them to the realist, psychological rhythms of "cinematic" speech—a technique especially evident in his quiet reading of "So oft it chances in particular men . . ." in *Hamlet* [1949].) John Gielgud goes further, virtually singing movie dialogue, shifting the volume and timbre of his mellifluous drawl to bring out emotional contrasts, notably in the long soliloquies of *Providence* (1977). Orson Welles is even more unorthodox; one of the virtues of *Macbeth* (1948) is that whenever Welles exploits sound mixes, dubbing, and whispers for the microphone, he continues to let us hear the power of a vocal instrument alongside his interpretation. Still another actor of the same sort is George C. Scott. In *Patton* (1969), portraying what the script calls "a seventeenth-century man," Scott has an opportunity to open the film with a profane burst of platform bombast; from that point onward, whether he is praying to God or delivering an address to English housewives, whether he is cursing soldiers or speaking in diplomatic French, he resembles Barthes's description of a Russian bass singing in church: "Something is there . . . which is directly the cantor's body, brought to your ears in one and the same movement from deep down in the cavities . . . the muscles, the membranes, the cartilages . . . here, thrown in front of us like a packet, is the Father, his phallic stature" (*Image/Music/Text,* 182).

The ancient rhetoricians appreciated such technical effects—as did the hams of the nineteenth-century stage. But if movie actors have sometimes rendered voices in all their stagy glory, they have usually done so with the sense of harking back to an earlier time, when vocal power was an important sign of "phallic" performing skill, and when class distinctions were indicated by careful deployment of "standard" language. By the same token, one effect of naturalistic acting in both theater and film has been to make the language of players seem less elitist, closer to speech on the street. As one indication of the relation between older forms of vocal training and conservative social values, consider the remarks of the stage actor Otis Skinner, who, in 1929, received an award for "good diction" from the American Academy of Arts and Letters. In his acceptance of the award, Skinner lamented the "polyglot American speech" and decried the "menace" of movies and radio: "Since the birth of our nation demoralizing verbal seepings from every part of the globe, civilized and savage, have muddied the clear stream of our mother tongue. . . . There was a time when the theater held up a standard of diction in America . . . before the invasion of the dialect play, the sports play, the crime play, the argot of the prize ring and the burlesque show—all written and spoken in the vernacular" (Cole and Chinoy, 588–89).

Actors continue to take speech instruction (even a naturalist like Montgomery Clift usually rehearsed his movie scenes with a voice coach), and there are famous cases where vocal exercises have contributed to a film star's appeal (for instance Lauren Bacall's smoky trombone sound in the Hawks pictures). Likewise, films often call attention to performing skill by means of long speeches: notice Edward G. Robinson's lightning-fast recitation of actuarial statistics in *Double Indemnity* (1944), Brando's famous soliloquy about being a "contender" in *On the Waterfront* (1954), or James Woods's frantic, dizzy talk on the telephone at the beginning of *Salvador* (1986). Nevertheless, since 1927 all forms of actorly expression—gestures, movements, facial grimaces, and especially voices—have been rendered in the tones of everyday conversation, more or less conforming to the usage of the movie audience. As a result, whereas the language of the screen has been democratized, and the speech of working-class or minority characters is often rendered in an unpatronizing style, the voices of the actors have become relatively transparent, less like expressive instruments.

In the silent cinema, by contrast, expression was somewhat more formalized and hierarchical, and "speech" required a special technique. One of the actors' jobs was to suggest ordinary conversation, and the best way of doing this was to speak occasionally, giving slightly exaggerated ostensiveness to tiny expressive movements of eyes, face, and hands. The circumstances were just the reverse of both conventional theater and everyday discourse, where movement is prompted by utterance, and where gestures either support speech or reveal latent meanings behind it; in silent movies, actors needed to make their few words rise out of their gestures, never forgetting that meaning lay in their eyes and at their fingertips.[8] Hence, as Charles Affron notes, the medium belongs to "the same category of style as pantomime, ballet, and opera. . . . The best silent films are not superficial, but they do pay homage to the fact that we perceive surface, not depth" (90).

Once sound was introduced, gestures became more like accessories. Editing and camera placement had fragmented the actor's body, and now the soundtrack furthered a movement toward invisible acting, inviting us beyond outward display, as if voices were letting us into private regions and revealing the "natural" traits of individuals. Ironically, when talking films wanted to emphasize performing skill, they sometimes made strategic reversions to melodramatic silence: either the actors played mute characters (*Johnny Belinda* [1948], *Children of a Lesser God* [1986]), or they employed the Method, which has always been suspicious of mere words.

Godard and Gorin were addressing this issue when they argued that "every actor of the silent film had his or her own expression . . . when cinema begins to speak like the New Deal, every actor begins to speak the same thing" (84). Where speech is concerned, however, this argument is only partly correct. True, the typical sound film tends to efface its production of meaning, creating what Stephen Heath describes as "a contract of thought . . . with the voice as the medium, the expression of a homogeneous thinking subject" (191). But the emphasis on naturalism preceded the talkies, growing at least partly out of a democratic, socially progressive impulse. Furthermore, anyone who is aware of American accents knows that at a certain level Holly-

---

8. Pudovkin cites this as one reason why people with theatrical training had difficulty working in early films: "In *The Postmaster,* Moskvin—an actor of undoubtedly big filmic possibilities—none the less tires one unpleasantly with his ever-moving mouth and with petty movements beating time to the rhythm of the unspoken words. Gesture-movement accompanying speech is unthinkable in the film . . . Moskvin speaks a great deal and obviously, while at the same time, quite automatically and naturally, like a man accustomed to spoken business, he accompanies every word with one and the same movement of the hand. During the shooting, when words were audible, the scene was effective, and even very effective; but on the screen it resulted in a painful and often ridiculous shuffling about on one spot" (142–43).

wood talking films made actors seem *more* rather than less heterogeneous. When sound was introduced, the studios hired elocutionists, trying to establish a mid-Atlantic accent for leading players; nevertheless, the stars of vaudeville quickly prospered in movies, and the thirties cycle of gangster films, some of them prompted by social-realist Broadway theater, made certain types of ethnic speech romantically attractive.[9] The successive waves of realist acting therefore had complex social and aesthetic implications. On the one hand, as Brecht and his successors have pointed out, naturalistic representation narrows the instrumental range of performance; by concealing the fact that actors produce *signs,* it disguises the workings of ideology. On the other hand, as Brecht also recognized, certain kinds of naturalistic expression are important to a committed theater, helping to rid acting of arty, stylized gentility.

This double-edged argument applies not only to voices but to gestures, faces, and bodies, which were once subject to a strict elocutionary control. Modern drama and the movies, in response to larger social changes, have in some ways broken the hold of an elitist expressive technique; but they have also tended to mask their conventions, rationalizing them in terms of "doing nothing," thus making us think of the actor's speech, posture, or gesture as relatively "organic" phenomena. The truth is, all forms of actorly behavior have formal, artistic purposes and ideological determinants. Only the frightened amateur, suffering from robotic stiffness and a lack of affect, is truly "alienated" from these purposes (which is precisely why Brecht was interested in amateur actors). Everyone else in public situations is taught to adopt a "proper" theatrical voice, stance, and movement style—whether she or he emotes in grand fashion or in quiet, everyday tones.

It is therefore important to emphasize that professional players—even the most natural-looking—have learned to master both the performing space and every aspect of their physical presence. For example, they often use posture in the service of characterization (as in any of Robert De Niro's roles); more fundamentally, they are taught or they intuitively grasp the art of standing and executing simple, appropriately dramatic movements in effortless fashion. These movements usually originate from standardized, culturally determined

9. By contrast, the English cinema retained its Olivier-like enunciation until the late fifties, when neorealism and a growing economic dependence on Hollywood helped to produce stars like Albert Finney, Richard Harris, and Sean Connery. Michael Caine has recalled what the situation was like before that period: "In American pictures, you had working-class heroes, and your actors came from the working class. Even the ones from society families, like Bogart, looked and talked like they were from the working class. . . . In English films, . . . someone came on and said, 'Hello, Bundy's having a party,' and they were all floating through the French windows and playing tennis in flannels, and the maid would come on just like in plays. We used to hoot with laughter at the way they spoke. Then when someone who was supposed to be a Cockney came on, one of those from the Royal Academy of Dramatic Art doing an accent, we'd roll under the seats in hysterics" (Demaris, 5).

positions. From the late Renaissance until the eighteenth century, leading actors worked from what was known as the "teapot" stance—a position influenced by Greco-Roman statuary, in which the male figure is posed with one foot forward, one hand on the hip, and the other lifted in gesture. (Laurence Olivier deliberately imitates this posture in the early scenes of *Henry V* [1944] when he is trying to indicate what Shakespearean acting might have looked like in the days of the Globe theater.) In the nineteenth century, actors were taught balance and movement by dancing masters, so that a good deal of silent-film behavior—with its air of grace and refinement, its flexibility and sentimental lyricism—seems vaguely related to classical ballet; thus Gish has an erect posture and a quality of delicacy mixed with strength that might have been learned in a dancing class, and Chaplin is the most balletic of actors.

Circus acrobatics, vaudeville comedy, and jazz music have all contributed to the way people stand and move in films, and various twentieth-century schools of acting have fostered their own styles. Meyerhold and the Soviet avant-garde of the twenties, under the influence of Marxism, Taylorism, and early Hollywood,[10] tried to create gymnastic actors who would evoke "the skilled worker in action" (see the discussion in Higson, 16–17). Meanwhile the Stanislavskians felt that players should be relaxed and open to sensation, as loose as animals in the wild. Sometimes they supported their instruction with Rousseauistic appeals to the "natural man," as when Richard Boleslavsky contrasts the ideal actor with people in the street:

> Let us take a look back at our childhood: on the way we were taught to carry ourselves, the conventionality of our clothes and shoes; on the unnatural way of our modern locomotion compared to the one indicated by nature itself. Think of rush hour in streetcars or subways, when we travel for hours suspended like grapes, . . . and you'll understand how much energy we are wasting and how far we are removed from the free body of an ancient Roman or an animal. Compare the free stride of a savage with the walk of a modern girl. (Cole and Chinoy, 513)

The Meyerholdian actor and the Stanislavskian actor therefore worked from different physical assumptions, and they could look as opposite from one another, even in repose, as Buster Keaton and Marlon Brando.

A still more crucial influence on the physical quality of acting in this

---

10. Frederick Winslow Taylor was the first American efficiency expert, and his studies of industrial movement were imitated to a certain degree in the Soviet Union during the period of the NEP. A satiric biography of Taylor ("The American Plan") can be found in John Dos Passos's *The Big Money* (1935). On the influence of Hollywood in early Soviet avant-garde acting, see Sergei Gerassimov, "Out of the Factory of the Eccentric Actor": "Grigori Kozintsev taught the principal matter, called 'cine-gesture.' It was based on the mathematical precision of American comic and detective films. The actor was required not to 'feel.' The very word 'feeling' was only ever pronounced with derisive grimaces accompanied by scornful laughter from the whole troupe" (Schnitzer and Martin, 114).

century relates to two broadly different techniques for producing expressions. At one extreme, the actor develops the body as an instrument, learning a kinesics, or movement vocabulary; at the other, he or she is encouraged to behave more or less normally, letting gesture or facial expression rise "naturally" out of deeply felt emotion. Professional players have always spoken about the value of both skills, but as I have indicated, modern dramatic literature strongly favors the second. To explain the difference between the two, critics and players usually resort to an inside/outside antithesis fundamental to Western thinking. Thus Olivier, who defines acting as "the art of persuasion," has remarked almost apologetically, "I'm afraid I do work mostly from the outside in . . . I think personally that most film players are interior people" (Cole and Chinoy, 410–11).

The modern stress on "interior" work becomes especially evident in English theater around 1890, in the debates over Diderot's paradox that broke out when the playwright William Archer published *Masks or Faces? A Study in the Psychology of Acting* (1888). Attempting to overturn Diderot's famous argument that actors are unaffected by the emotions they portray, Archer interviewed a number of professional thespians and found that nearly all of them were quite emotional, "living the part" to some degree. The real significance of Archer's research, however, was not its attack on neoclassical "reserve," or its proof of a relatively unimportant point. Actors have always been caught up in the passions of drama, and there is every reason to suppose that they felt their emotions as deeply in the nineteenth century as they do today. At bottom, Archer was concerned less with emotionalism than with what theater historians now call the mimetic or "pantomime" tradition—a performance technique that relies on conventionalized poses to help the actor indicate "fear," "sorrow," "hope," "confusion," and so forth.

"Pantomime" in this sense has something in common with the techniques of silent performance, but it is a much broader concept, indicating a whole attitude toward the mechanics of gesture. As Benjamin McArthur has pointed out, for most actors in the nineteenth century, "each emotion had its appropriate gesture and facial expression, which were passed down from one generation to the next. . . . Books were written analyzing, classifying, and breaking down gestures and expressions into their component parts" (171). Until fairly recently, the old "cookbook" tradition seemed almost to define acting. "The fundamental concept of codified pantomime," John Delman has remarked, "is several thousand years old, while the modern tendency to laugh off all codes and conventions is younger than the memory of living men" (241).

In place of pantomime, Archer was tentatively, almost covertly proposing a naturalistic style; inspired by Ibsen and a new wave of European dramatists, he was promoting the notion that acting should be less flamboyant and contrived, more attuned to the psychological dynamic of everyday life. Repeatedly, he insists that actorly emotions should not be "imitated": "We weep our own tears, we laugh our own laughter. . . . Therefore I think there is a clear distinction between mimicking tricks or habits and yielding to emotion or contagion. Roughly speaking, one is an affair of the surface, the other of the centers" (Cole and Chinoy, 364–65).

Archer is symptomatic of a so-called revolutionary trend, a shift from a semiotic to a psychological conception of performance that began with the rise of drawing-room dramas in the 1850s but that can be localized in the period between 1880 and 1920. The development of this more or less subjective approach was uneven; it left certain marks on Griffith and the movies (Griffith had in fact acted Ibsen on the stage before becoming a film director), but its full-scale arrival in America was delayed. Louise Brooks recalls how it affected her contemporaries in New York theater:

> In the twenties, under the supervision of old producers like David Belasco, stage direction dated back to the feverish technique of the English theatre before the plays of Ibsen, Chekhov, and Bernard Shaw revolutionized it, introducing what Lytton Strachey called "a new quiet and subtle style of acting, a prose style." In New York, we began to realize how bad our directors and actors were when the new young English stars began to appear on Broadway. There was Lynne Fontaine in *Pygmalion,* Roland Young in *The Last of Mrs. Cheney,* Leslie Howard in *Berkeley Square,* and Gertrude Lawrence and Noel Coward in *Private Lives.* These marvelous actors of realism spoke their lines as if they had just thought of them. They moved about the stage with ease. And they paid attention to—they actually heard—what other actors were saying. (61)

The single most important exponent of the new, "quiet" naturalism is of course Stanislavsky, who was not conscientiously studied in America until the late twenties, but who, in the very year that William Archer's book was published, had begun his work at the Moscow Art and Literary Society. It is difficult to find a single individual of comparable importance who stands for the older, pantomime tradition, but a leading candidate is François Delsarte (1811–71), a Parisian elocutionist who made one of the earliest attempts to codify expressive gestures for actors and public speakers. Even though Delsarte's fragmentary writing is now virtually unknown, his way of thinking about "performance signs" helped determine American acting at the beginning of the century. His influence persisted alongside psychological realism during the period of silent cinema, and in some ways he deserves reconsideration in our own time.

Delsarte paid a good deal of attention to what he himself called the semiotic function of gesture (a term he took from Locke, and used well in advance of either Peirce or Saussure). His work led to prescriptive, formulaic descriptions of actorly poses, as when he tells us that "conscious menace—that of a master to his subordinates—is expressed by a movement of the head carried from above downward," or when he claims that "any interrogation made with crossed arms must partake of a threat" (Cole and Chinoy, 189–90). Rules such as these are based on a crude faculty psychology, and they ignore the contextual determinants of meaning; nevertheless, most writers on acting in the nineteenth century adopted a similar approach. (Two important manuals in English were Henry Siddon's *Practical Illustrations of Rhetorical Gesture and Action* and Gustave Garcia's *Actor's Art,* both published in 1882 and filled with pictures of typical poses and gestures.) Furthermore, Delsarte had a significant impact on public life at the turn of the century—especially in the United States, where his disciples enjoyed a tremendous vogue.

Delsarte's teaching had been imported to America by Steele MacKaye (1844–94), the manager of New York's Madison Square Theater and the immediate predecessor of David Belasco. The elaborate melodramas MacKaye staged in his specially constructed "Spectatorium" prefigured the silent epics of Griffith (Vardac, 151), and his Delsarte-inspired technique of "Harmonic Gymnastics" became the principal method of formal instruction for American actors between 1870 and 1895. In 1877 he established a conservatory called the New York School of Expression; in 1884, together with Franklin Sargent, he founded the Lyceum Theatre School, which evolved into the American Academy of Dramatic Arts. Soon afterward, similar conservatories began to spring up in major cities as far west as St. Louis (McArthur, 100–101), and a "Delsarte System" of public speaking was in wide popular use from then until the 1920s. Throughout that period, advertisements called upon "every elocutionist, every singer, every teacher, and every other cultured person" to use Delsarte "recitation books" as a means "of acquiring grace, dignity, and fine bearing for society people" (quoted by Cole and Chinoy, 187). Ultimately, the "Delsarte Movement" was so deeply embedded in the culture that a good many actors could be described as Delsartean whether or not they ever studied him—just as middle-class Americans once behaved according to Emily Post whether or not they actually read her advice.

At its best, this tradition could produce dazzling results. I would argue, for example, that the expressive behavior of the entire cast in *The Phantom of the Opera* (1925) owes to Delsarte's vision of the theater. David Thomson has observed that Lon Chaney "moves with a stunning languor, as if he knew of Conrad Veidt in *Caligari*" (94). But an even more likely influence on both Chaney and his co-star, Mary Philbin, is the supple, demonstrative, highly codified style of pantomime that dominated the previous century and remained in use to a greater or lesser degree throughout silent movies.

Despite its frequent beauties, however, the pantomime style was linked with attempts to perpetuate bourgeois "deportment," and the recommendations of its teachers could frequently lead to stilted, pretentious behavior. To appreciate how bad the technique could become, one need only glance at *Lessons in the Art of Acting* (1889) by Edmund Shaftesbury, one of Delsarte's

86th Attitude: Triumph.
This attitude is made by stepping back with the weight up-
on the right foot, the right index hand raised over the head.
Triumph.
" Justice is satisfied, and Rome is free'! "
Brutus, Act V, Scene I.

From Edmund Shaftesbury, Lessons in the Art of Acting *(1889).*

87th ATTITUDE: AGONY.

This attitude is made by retiring the weight upon the left foot; placing the tips of the fingers of both hands back of the neck, the head falling back upon the left shoulders.

AGONY.

"O Antony! Antony! Antony!"
Antony and Cleopatra, Act IV, Scene I.

many American imitators. On his title page Shaftesbury announces "a Practical and Thorough work for all persons who aim to become Professional Actors, and for all Readers and Orators who desire to make use of the power of Dramatic Expression, which is the True Element of Success in the Pulpit, at the Bar, and on the Platform." In his introductory remarks, he comments on the "Delsarte Method," which he says was "accompanied by an irrational craze some years ago, and is still advocated by persons who spent large amounts of money to acquire it, for the purpose of afterward teaching it" (11). Announcing that he has studied Delsarte himself and found "many excellences, and some defects," he proceeds to offer his own guide, which includes 106 illustrations of "Dramatic Attitudes" for the actor. (See the figures on the preceding pages; all of Shaftesbury's pictures involve the same portly, mustachioed male.)

A more interesting writer of this sort is the Frenchman Charles Aubert, whose training manual, *The Art of Pantomime,* was translated into English in 1927. Aubert occasionally addresses himself to silent film actors; he never mentions Delsarte, but he draws heavily on the semiotic approach, producing an illustrated list of positions for the legs, the shoulders, the chest, the abdomen, the arms, the hands, and the facial muscles—each attitude signifying a range of possible meanings. Thus if a man stands with his weight on both feet, his thumbs hooked into the armholes of a vest, the pose indicates "Assurance, Independence, Gay Humor, and Self-content" (41). If he folds his arms across his chest, one supporting the other, he suggests "Expectancy, Reflection" (42). If he grasps both hands to his head, the possible meanings are "What shall I do? All is lost; My head hurts: Despair. It will drive me crazy" (45).

Aubert gives almost as much attention to the face as to the rest of the body combined, dividing it into separate expressive components that he analyzes in structuralist terms. For instance, he argues that all expressions of the forehead can be understood as two simple operations: the brow can be leveled, raised, or lowered, and the eyebrows can be separated, drawn together, or left at rest. These basic moves lead to nine different combinations, then to a vastly greater number of permutations, depending on how much the forehead muscles are bunched together, how far the eyebrows are separated, and at what rhythm the movements are timed. Every variation is assigned a set of meanings, but the entire system is founded on a single binary opposition:

> All expressions which are stamped by will and intelligence, . . . such as covetousness, anxiety, reflection, intellectual effort, scorn, disgust, horror, anger, defiance . . . etc., are always characterized by a drawing of the eyebrows down and together, forming at the base of the forehead vertical wrinkles, and are also accompanied by a tension of the limbs and whole body.

Paroxysm of physical pain.   To weep.   To burst into tears.

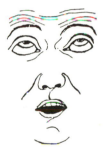

Ecstasy.   Rapture.   Fright.   Terrifying sight.

From Charles Aubert, The Art of Pantomime *(1927).*

Expressions where intelligence and will are inactive . . . such as hesitation, ignorance, admiration, stupefication [sic], fear, extreme physical suffering, gayety . . . are always characterized by extreme elevation of the eyebrows which causes horizontal lines on the forehead. They are also accompanied by relaxation of the muscles and flexion of the limbs. (7)

On the following pages I have provided a few of Aubert's illustrations, which are rather more abstract than Shaftesbury's, using a skeletal figure instead of a fully-clothed, gentleman actor. He claims to be describing a "natural" language, and to some extent behavioral science might support his

The attitude of carrying the body on the forward leg conveys the following emotions:

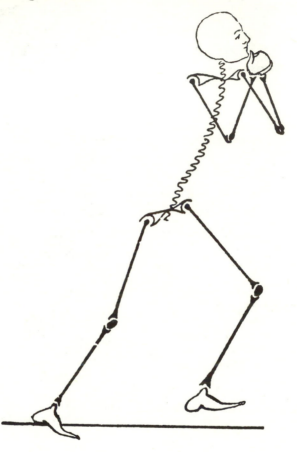

To struggle.	To admire.	To supplicate.	To promise.
To order.	To desire.	To wish.	To observe.
To threaten.	To ask.	To affirm.	To persuade.

In general, all expressions controlled by will.

From Charles Aubert, The Art of Pantomime *(1927).*

Throwing the body's weight on the backward leg
gives postures which more properly express passive sensations
or indecision, such as:

Ignorance.	Stupefaction.	Doubt.	Meditation.
Anxiety.	Hesitation.	Negation.	Repugnance.
Astonishment.	Fear.	Scorn.	Terror.

claim.[11] But it becomes quickly apparent that most of his expressive postures
and gestures are socially specific, signaling attributes of social class or gender. For instance, "A comic bow is executed by a series of backward kicks
. . . This is the countryman's bow and a peasant woman may use it also. Still
if she is young and pretty, she had better use the soubrette's curtsey" (30–
31). Almost any position with the legs spread is forbidden to women, unless
they want to suggest extreme coarseness; and seated postures are a good indication of upbringing: "To sit, with body twisted, legs wide apart, indicates
Vulgarity, Don't Care, Impudence; to sit, legs wide apart, chest forward, and
elbows resting on your knees, gives the picture of a rough person without
education" (26–27).

By the time Aubert's book was published, the theoretical commitment to
pantomime was disappearing from American theater and films; even Chaplin
had often parodied Delsartean gestures for comic effect (see the subsequent
discussion of *The Gold Rush*). Clearly, a massive cultural change had been
wrought by the postwar economy, by the proliferation of naturalistic literature, and by the growing interest in various psychological determinants of
behavior. Nietzsche, Freud, Bergson, and William James had influenced social thought, and dramatic literature as a whole was becoming increasingly
introspective. Now more than ever the emphasis in training performers fell
on *being* instead of mimicking; the gestures of the actor were supposed to
grow out of his or her feelings rather than the other way around. Mae Marsh,
who published a short book entitled *Screen Acting* in the early twenties, helps
to illustrate the trend:

> While we were playing *Intolerance* . . . I had to do a scene where, in the big
> city's slums, my father dies.
>   The night before I did this scene I went to the theater—something, by the
> way, I seldom do when working—to see Marjorie Rambeau in *Kindling*.

11. Modern scientific interest in this issue dates back to Charles Darwin's *The Expression of
Emotions in Man and Animals,* first published in 1873 (reprinted by University of Chicago,
1965). Darwin claimed that "the same state of mind is expressed throughout the world with
remarkable uniformity; and this fact is in itself interesting as evidence of the close similarity in
bodily structure and mental disposition of all the races of mankind" (17). One hundred years
later, in *Darwin and Facial Expression* (New York: Academic Press, 1973), clinical psychologist
Paul Ekman assembled a series of papers by contemporary researchers, who mostly supported
the view that "some facial expressions of emotion are universally characteristic of the human
species" (258). See also *Emotion in the Human Face,* ed. Ekman (Cambridge University Press,
1982). As Ekman notes, however, there is a tricky problem in defining emotion and giving labels
to its various manifestations. Indeed, the major weakness of behaviorist empirical research on
expression is that it tends to rely upon a faculty psychology that reifies both gestures and feelings
in much the same fashion as Delsartian theories of stage performance. (Not surprisingly, Darwin's
original work was filled with illustrations similar to the nineteenth-century texts on acting.) An
interesting paper which addresses this problem is "Emotion and Act," by Theodore R. Starbin,
in *The Social Construction of Emotion,* edited by Rom Harre (London: Basil Blackwell, 1986),
83–87. Starbin stresses the need to think of human subjects in a social context, as Erving Goffman has done. When we name an emotion in the abstract, he points out, we are making an
ideological judgment.

> To my surprise and gratification she had to do a scene in this play which was somewhat similar to the one I was scheduled to play in *Intolerance*. It made a deep impression on me.
>
> As a consequence, the next day before the camera . . . I began to cry with the memory of Marjorie Rambeau's performance uppermost in my mind. . . .
>
> Mr. Griffith, who was closely studying [the rushes], finally turned in his seat and said:
>
> "I don't know what you were thinking about when you did that, but it is evident that it was not about the death of your father." . . .
>
> We began immediately upon the scene again. This time I thought of the death of my own father and the big tragedy to our little home, then in Texas. I could recall the deep sorrow of my mother, my sisters, my brother, and myself.
>
> This scene is said to be one of the most effective in "The Mother and the Law." (76–79)

A rudimentary form of "affective memory" had long been used by actors, but movies and the new literature made it seem essential. And because players ceased to think in terms of a repertory of gesture, the various nineteenth-century guides to acting gradually took on a merely historical interest, ultimately constituting what Richard Dyer calls a "record of melodramatic performance practice" (*Stars*, 156).

Certain aspects of the pantomime tradition were of course sustained by silent film, but its last flowering is probably in German expressionism, which devised an approximately Delsartean technique via a different, modernist aesthetic. "The melody of a great gesture," Paul Kornfield wrote in his *Nachwort an den Schauspieler* (1921), "says more than the highest consummation of what is called naturalness." This credo is evident in *Metropolis* (1926), where the gestures of the various characters are intended to support a political allegory in the boldest, most elemental way. On the next page, I have assembled a few images which indicate the stark, highly choreographed effect of the acting. Alfred Abel, as the industrialist's liberal son, beats his breast, looks heavenward in "feminized" spiritual agony, and crucifies himself on a factory machine; Rudolph Klein-Rogge, as the mad scientist, leans forward threateningly and swoops his talonlike hands in triumphant arcs; Brigitte Helm, as the "good" and "bad" Maria, alternates between prayerful entreaties and sinewy, erotic enticements. Of all the characters, Gustave Froelich, the master of Metropolis, is the most inexpressive; nevertheless, he occasionally raises a hand to give a sinister order, and by the end of the film we see him in anguish, clasping both hands to his head.

Very few actors in talking movies worked along such lines (Dietrich and perhaps Garbo are qualified instances, and a film like *Grand Hotel* [1932] seems highly pantomimic by contemporary standards); occasionally, however, the old "histrionic" style was revived for ironic purposes. Gloria Swanson's flamboyant behavior in *Sunset Boulevard* (1950) comes immediately to mind, but notice also the expressive mannerisms of the female characters in

Expressionist gesture in Metropolis.

The Heiress, who use stereotypical nineteenth-century gestures to help establish a cultural code. Among these later allusions to pantomime acting, Robert Mitchum's performance in *Night of the Hunter* (1955) deserves special mention: as Harry Powell, a demented backwoods preacher who might have learned his mannerisms from a vulgarized Delsartean textbook, Mitchum is both comical and terrifying; his honeyed charm and crocodile tears, his booming voice and almost dancerly poses—all these things are a clever fusion of melodrama and expressionism, keyed to a Freudian vision of childhood. For me at least, there are few more startling moments in American cinema than the climactic scenes of that film, when Mitchum harmonizes with Lillian Gish in a rendition of "Leaning on the Everlasting Arm."

In general, the manuals on nineteenth-century pantomime continue to have an ethnologic interest, and even though they have been abandoned by acting students, many of the positions and gestures they describe can be seen throughout the history of cinema. Leafing through these books, one quickly recognizes that at some level actors have always employed basic, culturally transmitted gestures to "write" characters; the standard postures change slightly over time, but they are easily noticed, especially in comedy, where stereotypical expression is foregrounded. Thus, despite the fact that film acting has usually been explained in roughly Stanislavskian terms, the players in classic Hollywood frequently relied upon an untutored application of principles Delsarte and Aubert tried to systematize.[12] Notice, for example, the image on the next page, from Joan Fontaine's Academy-Award-winning performance in *Suspicion* (1941). Having learned a secret Cary Grant has been keeping from her, she grasps her head and registers fear that she is being driven mad.

In most films, actors need to produce vivid expressions in brief shots which are photographed out of sequence, and when asked to register "fear" or "pain" in close-up they look rather like one of Aubert's drawings. Peter Lorre was roughly correct when he described the work of movie acting as "face-making." For example, Hitchcock's most "cinematic" montages—the shower murder in *Psycho* (1960), the cropdusting sequence in *North by Northwest*—elicit grimaces, postures, and movements that function like elemental signs. In fact, as I shall argue later, no less a movie star than Cary Grant could be described as a consummate modern practitioner of vaguely Delsartean technique; more specifically, Grant was the sort of actor Kuleshov had in mind when he devised pantomimic "études" for students, training them to render simple, crisp expressions for the camera.

All of which suggests that the nature of acting may have changed less than

12. There has always been a fundamental similarity between acting and cartooning. At the turn of the century, actors imitated line drawings; in 1938, the Disney animators copied the movements of the young dancer Marge Champion, using her to create the "lifelike" figure of Snow White.

Joan Fontaine in Suspicion.

we think. John Delman comments, "No doubt the nineteenth century, in its eagerness to perfect the traditional language of pantomime, reduced it to absurdity; but that does not lessen the truth that bodily action, simplified by selection, moderately exaggerated, provides a language of expression more universally intelligible than words" (241). In fact, actors continue to practice the rhetoric of conventionalized expression; most of them simply explain their craft in a different way, exchanging new gestures for old. Recognizing this phenomenon at the turn of the century, Yeats joked that when "educated modern people" are deeply moved, "they look silently into the fireplace." Theater historian Michael Goldman makes a similar point when he writes, "The inner space that Ibsen and his successors were concerned with had to be charted by a repertory of pauses and indirection, by small details of gesture and expression. . . . The construction of plays, the technique of the actors, the age's growing interest in psychological science and detection of all sorts, invited the audience to listen for movements beneath the characters' public performance" (102).

The result is not only a slightly different set of poses and small gestures, but a greater emphasis on the idiolect of the performer. James Stewart, for example, is an expert pantomimist, but whenever he wants to register "anguish" in close-up he relies on a personal habit rather than a standardized expressive vocabulary. Inevitably, at the point of his greatest trauma, he will raise a trembling hand to his open mouth, sometimes biting at the flesh. On the next page are two instances of the technique, one from *Rear Window* and one from *Vertigo* (1958).

Individual mannerisms aside, a book rather like the ones by Shaftesbury and Aubert could be written to illustrate the standard expressions in contemporary naturalistic cinema. Consider Meryl Streep's close-ups in *Sophie's Choice* (1983), which are filled with lip biting, sidelong glances, and halting speech delivered in an almost whispered register. Doubtless Streep works mostly from the "inside," employing a Stanislavskian method; nevertheless, her movements are carefully orchestrated, consisting mainly of the readable formulas of twentieth-century interpretation, raised to the level of old-fashioned melodramatic eloquence. At the same time, we can make two rather tentative formal distinctions between her practice and the older tradition. Unlike the typical nineteenth-century performers, who tended to arrange their faces in a picture to indicate "grief," Streep tries to register a repressed emotion, so that her look communicates something more like "grief held in check by an attempt to remain calm." In addition, she signals a good deal of what William Archer called "emotional contagion," chiefly by means of blushes and a visibly pulsating blood vessel in her neck—a purely biological language, intended to convince us that she is not simply imitating passion, but responding from her central nervous system. (Because biological symptoms are important to naturalism, film actors have often submitted their bodies to their roles in quite fundamental ways: Agnes Morehead's hysterical breakdown near the end of *The Magnificent Ambersons* owes its power partly to Orson Welles's having shot the scene over and over, until Morehead was truly exhausted; and Ingmar Bergman has claimed that during Bibi Andersson's description of an "orgy" in *Persona* [1966], he wanted the audience to see Liv Ullmann's lips distending with desire.)

We make an error, therefore, if we assume that theorists like Delsarte and Aubert are relevant only in the realm of arcane histrionics. Ironically, Delsarte's writings have exerted two sorts of influence—one on the theater and oratory of his own day, and the other on training techniques for the twentieth-century avant-garde. Kuleshov remarked that "for the work of the face and all the parts of a human being, the system of Delsarte is very useful, but only as an inventory of the possible changes in the human mechanism, and not as a method of acting" (107). In the same qualified way, Delsarte's studies of gesture and expression helped to shape Ruth St. Denis's choreography, indirectly fostering modern dance, and were acknowledged as a source for the "physical theater" of Artaud and Grotowski. Although Delsarte was very much a part of the romantic movement, he had foreshadowed the modernist

James Stewart expresses anguish in two films.

dehumanization of art; and if we put aside certain uses of his teaching, particularly the American attempt to instruct public speakers in genteel manners, he seems curiously advanced (see Kirby, 55–56).

Perhaps not surprisingly, the most unorthodox filmmakers have intentionally drawn from the mimetic tradition, departing from it chiefly in their attempt to divest performance of emotional and rhetorical unity. Thus Robert Bresson, a radical idealist, devotes much of his *Notes sur le cinématographe* to advocating a form of "automatism." As Mirella Affron has noted, Bresson thinks of his largely amateur players as "models," and he never makes upon them "the conventional demands of dramatic expression; that they cry, for example. He asks them instead . . . to wipe away nonexistent tears, to find not the gesture through the feeling, but the feeling through the simplest and most stylized of gestures" (124). Repeatedly, Bresson emphasizes that acting should be seen as a simple labor: "Let people feel the soul and heart in your film, but let it be made like a work of the hands" (quoted by Affron, 125). An attitude such as this is both old and new. It runs strongly against the grain of mainstream performance, but it has something in common with an earlier era, when actors were regarded as rhetoricians and interpreters, building character out of expressive movement. There is a sense, therefore, in which old-fashioned pantomime can feed our thinking about newer performance techniques, broadening the potential of dramatic films and helping us to understand the complex language of emotion.

4

Expressive Coherence and Performance within Performance

I now see thinking as just a way of behaving, and behaving socially at that. It's something that the whole body takes part in, with all its senses.
—the Actor in Brecht's *Messingkauf Dialogues*, 1940

There's an old rule in Hollywood that when your face is up there on the screen in a close-up, if you don't believe the line you're speaking, the audience will know it, and they won't believe it either.
—Ronald Reagan, quoted in *Time* magazine, 1986

At one level, an informal conversation between friends can allow for a good deal of incoherence, inconsistency, or irrelevance: speeches may overlap, persons may glance away from one another, insignificant movements or interruptions may occur. At another level, however, the situation is quite different. Most of the people we meet at close quarters are quick to spot affective discrepancies: the smallest signs of distraction, weariness, or irritation can stand out in the midst of an ostensibly friendly exchange, and inappropriate degrees of sympathy, interest, or amusement can easily be detected. The flicker of an eyelid, the hint of a smile, the movement of a hand—any muscular tension or minor fluctuation of tone can threaten to disrupt the emotional unity of an everyday performance. As a result, intimate social behavior follows a rule of expressive coherence, a formal logic that operates as rigorously in ordinary life as in professional theater.

As exchanges become more public, they grow increasingly theatrical, so that players are required to observe what Erving Goffmann describes as "synecdochic responsibility" (*The Presentation of Self,* 51), maintaining not only a coherence of manner but also a fit between setting, costume, and behavior. The movies often exploit this situation for comic or dramatic effect: princesses are not supposed to remove their shoes in court, as Audrey Hepburn tries to do in *Roman Holiday* (1953), and the former British Vice-Consul in Mexico is not supposed to attend a formal dinner without socks, as Albert Finney discovers in *Under the Volcano* (1984). In maintaining this sense of expressive coherence, we are all actors, and our performances are judged at nearly every moment of our lives. We prove our expertise whenever we participate in rituals, whenever we carry off lies, or whenever we do our jobs competently in the midst of personal grief or pain. In fact we often employ Stanislavskian techniques on these occasions, learning emotional recall, imaginatively projecting ourselves into a role, using the "creative *if*" (Stanislavsky, 467) to make ourselves partly believe what we do. Even when our presentation is utterly sincere, we remain actors because the expression of "true" feeling is itself a socially conditioned behavior. As Brecht has written:

> One easily forgets that human education proceeds along theatrical lines. In a quite theatrical manner the child is taught how to behave; logical arguments only come later. When such-and-such occurs, it is told (or sees), one must laugh . . . In the same way it joins in shedding tears, not only weeping because the grown-ups do so but also feeling genuine sorrow. This can be seen at funerals, whose meaning escapes children entirely. These are theatrical events which form the character. The human being copies gesture, miming, tones of voice. And weeping arises from sorrow, but sorrow also arises from weeping. (152)

Our manner of expression is so deeply embedded in the process of socialization that it becomes spontaneous, instinctive, a part of thinking itself. In this regard it is ironic that various schools of psychotherapy (especially in America) have put so much emphasis on emotional sincerity, using techniques of role-playing to make subjects dramatize past experience. Whatever success this therapy might have, it resembles nothing so much as a clinical version of the Actors' Studio. The fact is, all our feelings are wedded to a behavioral *langue* that we have mastered and turned into an idiolect. Regression to a childlike state of "natural" emotion would probably result in an undramatic, incoherent performance, less like primal screams and more like amateur acting—for the simple reason that a child has not yet learned to theatricalize a self. We might say, with Terry Eagleton, that the child begins as a "Brechtian actor, performing what he does not truly feel, and by dint of doing so ends up as a professional or Aristotelian one, fully at home with his forms of life" (635).

In either case, we are always copying other actors, never arriving at an unacted emotional essence, even though we become increasingly adept at noticing strains or inconsistencies in the performances of others. For that reason, professional acting could be regarded as part of an unending process—a copy of everyday performances that are themselves copies. In turn, it induces members of the audience to add to the chain of representation by copying what *they* see, adopting mannerisms for a personal repertory. Perhaps Hollywood movies give us pleasure and a sense of identification simply because they enable us to recognize and adapt to the "acted" quality of everyday life: they place us safely outside dramatic events, a position from which we can observe people lying, concealing emotions, or staging performances for one another.

Notice, however, that these performances-within-performance create a major formal difference between professional acting and the presentation of self in society. Ordinary living usually requires us to maintain expressive coherence, assuring others of our sincerity; theater and movies work according to a more complex principle, frequently demanding that actors dramatize situations in which the expressive coherence of a character either breaks down or is revealed as a mere "act." As one example, consider the many occasions where characters either succeed or fail at maintaining expressive coherence in *Double Indemnity* (1944): near the beginning of the film we see Walter Neff (Fred MacMurray) violate the decorum of his role as insurance salesman by engaging in sexy repartee with Phyllis Dietrichson (Barbara Stanwyck), the wife of a prospective client. The wife encourages his "improper" performance, matching him in the exchange of double-entendre, showing off an ankle-braceleted leg as if she were a chorus girl instead of a lady interested in life insurance for her husband. Later, having helped Dietrichson commit murder, Neff has to behave with poker-faced calm, putting on a show of professional competence while a man who might identify him as a killer is brought to the insurance office for questioning. Dietrichson must behave with equal cool, acting the role of bereaved widow while under the scrutiny of an ace investigator; in fact she is the best actor of all, because we discover at the end of the film that her passion for Neff, concealed so cleverly from the law, is itself a pretense, the device of a *femme fatale*.

Sometimes we are as much taken in by these performances as the characters in the drama; sometimes we know that a character is behaving falsely because the plot has given us that information; and sometimes we can see indications of deception in a player's expression even when these signs are invisible to others. Thus Stanwyck's work in *Double Indemnity* is somewhat different from her earlier appearance in *Stella Dallas* (1934), where she is given many opportunities to display expressive incoherence quite openly. Phyllis Dietrichson is a cool and skillful performer who seldom steps out of character, but the whole point about Stella Dallas is that she never successfully manages the roles she has chosen. In the crucial scene where she offers to give up her beloved daughter to wealthy Helen Morrison, she tries to behave with polite calm, but all the while we can see her torment in the way she picks nervously at the arm of a chair and twists a pair of gloves she holds in her lap.[1]

Such films give us models of human behavior, emphasizing certain of the characters' lies or misrepresentations while showing us how "true" emotions are expressed. "In this exceedingly serious sphere," Brecht wrote, "the stage is virtually functioning as a fashion show, parading not only the latest dresses but the latest ways of behaving: not only what is being worn but what is being done" (151). As a result, the movies seldom foreground their own techniques of representation, nor do they venture very far into philosophical questioning of so-called natural human expression. In other words, the rule of expressive coherence is broken only at the level of characterization, where we see persons in the drama trying to conceal or repress their "sincere" feelings. At the level of professional acting itself, the film requires an absolute coherence, so that everyone plays *in character,* never disrupting the unified front of their job. MacMurray can show Walter Neff concealing anxiety behind a mask of aplomb, but he cannot deconstruct his performance of that performance; Stanwyck can reveal that her character is faking, but she cannot drop the persona she has adopted for the story. All the actors must "live the part" at the moment of its realization, in much the same way as we do in everyday life; in fact, the closeness and magnification of movie images seem to require them to draw upon the very thought process of the character, creating a seamless fit between emotion and expression. Lawrence Shaffer has described the phenomenon quite accurately:

> We squirm when an actor [in a film] puts on his character's face à la Marcel Marceau. We are transfixed when he simply appears to be "economizing" by using his own face in a kind of transmigratory transference. . . . The faces of certain actors—Brando, Gielgud, Clift, March, Tracy, Bogart—seem to be acutely inner-reflective. These actors seem to be doing a good deal of thinking. Their faces look preoccupied, as if attending to some inner voice, or memory. (6)

The "inner voice" of which Shaffer speaks is a product of that roughly Stanislavskian technique we all use occasionally—an imaginative absorption that turns acting into a form of affective thinking. As I have suggested, however, it is wrong to assume that expression in films is equivalent to behavior

---

1. Stanwyck's films often gave her the opportunity to show off acting skill by displaying two aspects of character. Besides the examples I have cited, consider her dual role in *The Lady Eve* (1941): as Jean Harrington, she is a seductive cardsharp, leaning against a trunkful of high-heeled shoes, revealing her ribcage, and asking Henry Fonda if he sees anything he likes. As Eve Sidwich, she is an equally seductive aristocrat, fluttering an ostrich fan, batting her eyes, and making a fool of nearly every male in sight. Only William Demarest remains skeptical; throughout, we hear him muttering, "It's gotta be the same dame!"

in daily life. For one thing, most film actors are acutely sensitive to the purely rhetorical need to make their "thought" visible to the camera. Moreover, they must sometimes signal that they *act persons who are acting*. In these moments when deception or repression are indicated, the drama becomes a metaperformance, imposing contrary demands on the players: the need to maintain a unified narrative image, a coherent persona, is matched by an equally strong need to exhibit dissonance or expressive incoherence within the characterization. Thus, we could say that realist acting amounts to an effort at sustaining opposing attitudes toward the self, on the one hand trying to create the illusion of unified, individualized personality, but on the other suggesting that character is subject to division or dissolution into a variety of social roles.[2]

These two contrary demands on expressive behavior are worth examining more closely, beginning with the actor's need to maintain a consistent persona. To appreciate the virtually obsessive importance of this problem in conventional moviemaking, one need only observe that Pudovkin's classical text, *The Technique of Film Acting,* devotes more space to the "unity of the acted image" than to any other topic. I have already quoted enough from Pudovkin to make clear that his remarks on this and other subjects are symptomatic of mainstream practice. Pudovkin, a Stanislavskian conservative whose attitude toward acting differed considerably from that of the first generation of Soviet avant-garde filmmakers, often worked with players from the Moscow Art Theater, and his advice was addressed to them. It applies equally well to professional thespians in the Hollywood system, or to anyone who thinks in terms of traditional realism.

Pudovkin begins his study by remarking on a "basic contradiction" between the fragmentary process of shooting and the unified look of the character in the finished product (22). His use of the word "contradiction," however, is misleading. It seems to establish his credentials as a Marxist-Hegelian, whereas his real concern is not to expose conflict at all; at bottom,

2. The Italian director Elio Petri has remarked, "within us there's the possibility of having many 'I's.' . . . In a way, coherence is a word you apply to a state of madness, incoherence to a state of normality" (Oumano, 143). By attempting to preserve the illusion of a unified self, by maintaining coherence in the face of multiple possibilities, most acting on the screen (as in life) is ideologically conservative or "mad" in Petri's sense. At this juncture Goffman's studies of role playing have something tentatively in common with postmodern psychoanalytic theory. Realist types of performance might even be said to conspire in what contemporary writers call a fundamental "misrecognition" upon which the Ego is founded. Hence, the analysis of acting can be linked to Jean-Louis Baudry's familiar argument about the paranoid structure of cinema spectatorship. Baudry, following suggestions offered by Lacan and Althusser, has described the cinema as a "mirror" in which the "fragmented body" of the viewer is brought together by "a sort of imaginary integration of the self"; the apparatus, he says, helps to foster the illusion of a "transcendental subject" and imposes meaning on "discontinuous fragments of phenomena" (45). For a similar argument, elaborated in greater detail, see Christian Metz's *The Imaginary Signifier.*

he is a romantic idealist, and he badly wants to smooth over potential incongruities or disruptions. Thus his entire discussion is grounded in metaphors of organic unity:

> Here let us reaffirm our principal desideratum for acting on both stage and screen. *The aim and object of the technique of the actor is his struggle for unity, for an organic wholeness in the lifelike image he creates.*
>
> But the technical conditions of work on the stage and for the screen impose a number of demands on the actor that perpetually tend to destroy his unity and continuity in the role.
>
> The splitting-up of the performance on the stage into acts, scenes, episodes, the still more subdivided splitting-up of the actor's work in the shooting of a film, set up a corresponding series of obstacles through and over which the entire creative collaborative . . . must combine to carry the organic unity of line of the actor's image. (25)

Pudovkin knows that continuity editing can help overcome "obstacles," but he emphasizes the degree to which actors themselves contribute to the illusion of wholeness. As he suggests, the players in naturalist theater have always worked along similar lines. Both film and theater actors need to be aware of the difference between "plot time" and "story time," and they need to convey the sense of *change* so important to classic narrative; as a result, they usually try to construct a mental bridge across gaps, "living" the part at the level of the story itself, so that, for example, a soldier who has gone away to war in act one and returned in act two will seem properly and logically different. Stanislavsky was especially concerned with this effect and attempted to assist actors by instituting long periods of "table work" prior to rehearsal, during which everyone discussed and analyzed the full experience of the characters. When the drama itself was presented, he advised everyone to remain partly in character even while they were offstage, feeling their way into events that were elided or not shown; for example, a butler who might leave a scene briefly and come back with a serving tray was encouraged to imagine the process of going to the kitchen and returning.

Pudovkin recognizes, however, that film is qualitatively different from theater—its narratives are more elliptical, and the circumstances of production pose an additional threat to actorly coherence. On stage, he notes, three minutes is a relatively short piece of performance time, but in movies it is almost the longest period a camera runs; furthermore, the temporal order of shooting is usually quite different from the temporal order of the plot, so that characterizations are not only broken but scattered, like pieces of a puzzle. Even when the glances and movements of the players are fitted together perfectly in the cutting room, the "acted image" is subject to variations in expressive quality, rhythm, or intensity. For example, in the famous taxicab sequence in *On the Waterfront*, Marlon Brando and Rod Steiger occupy a shared, almost static, position for several minutes of screen time, maintaining coherence across three or four camera setups. Here the work of matching movements from one shot to the next is minimal; the real difficulty lies in the actors' attempt to sustain emotional "flow" and preserve analog changes of mood despite Elia Kazan's busy camerawork. In an interview about this sequence, Steiger claimed that his own job was made especially tough because Brando behaved like a prima donna: "I don't like Mr. Brando. I'll never forget, or forgive, what he did to me. . . . I did the take with him, when the camera was on him, but when it came for the camera to be on me—he went home! I had to speak my lines to an assistant director" (Leyda, 440–41).

Pudovkin believed that carefully shaded, intimate acting, which poses a great many potential conflicts between the rhetoric of the camera and the expression of the players, would require detailed rehearsal and close collaboration between actors and director. He wanted the entire story to be performed first like a stage play, so that everyone concerned could bring a Stanislavskian "organic" vision to the process of shooting; he even suggested an "actor's script," as distinct from a "shooting script," that would enable the players to study their scenes in chronological order and form a complete mental image of the characters. Few filmmakers before or since—with the qualified exception of D. W. Griffith—have resorted to such elaborate and costly methods, but almost every narrative movie has shown a similar concern for unity, employing some technique to maintain expressive coherence across shots. Occasionally a director photographs a scene "around the clock," using multiple cameras (Robert Rossen experimented with this device for some of the more delicate moments in *Lilith* [1963]), but usually the actors must accommodate themselves to long periods of waiting between short bursts of performance, learning to render characters in no logical order.

When the continuity of the "acted image" breaks down, the results can be striking. For example, in a later chapter on Lillian Gish, I note an unintentional mismatch near the beginning of *True Heart Susie* (1919) that momentarily transforms the central character from a Victorian innocent into a sophisticate. The mistake is caused chiefly by a sudden, unmotivated change in Gish's posture and facial expression; in other words, she breaks expressive coherence at the level of the persona, so that Susie's entire personality threatens to fragment before our eyes. The change is visible only briefly, but it illustrates how much the effect of wholeness depends on the actor's emotional attitude at any given moment. The work of maintaining this wholeness is more difficult than it might appear, because neither the actor nor the character is a simple image. Both are made up of a bundle of traits, different faces and "semes" that have special functions; both tend to change over time, and all changes in appearance and manner must be kept under the control of narrative cause-and-effect. Hence the "error" in Griffith's film makes it seem as if the woman Gish plays at the end of the story—an experienced, maternal type— had suddenly been mixed up with the child she plays at the beginning.

Ironically, however, a second common feature of an actor's job in realist films is to split the character visibly into different aspects. Thus the brief lapse in continuity near the beginning of *True Heart Susie* makes an interesting contrast with many occasions in the same film where Gish is actually *required* to exhibit expressive incoherence, and where the audience accepts her duality as a perfectly natural event. For instance, an emotional scene midway through the picture shows Susie attending an engagement party to help celebrate the forthcoming marriage between the man she loves and another woman. In close-up, we see Gish seated in a parlor, fanning herself gently and smiling at the happy couple. After a moment she raises the fan to the side of her face, shielding herself from the room but giving us a privileged view; in this presumably hidden position, she lowers her glance to the floor and weeps. For a while she alternates between smiles and tears, dropping the fan to glance offscreen left at the other characters, then raising it to show her "true" feeling.

This behavior has a double importance, allowing us to see the difference between Susie's public and private faces but at the same time showing off the emotional range of the actor. A similar effect, involving a slightly different rhetoric, is achieved in a well-known scene from *Camille* (1938), when Garbo lies to Robert Taylor. She pretends that she does not love him, and all the while the viewers in the theater (who already know her motives) can see clearly that she is faking, alternating between the imperious, coolly amused disdain we normally associate with a figure like Dietrich and a wilting, passionate ardor typical of Victorian melodrama. Throughout, Taylor seems completely fooled, partly because Garbo's emotional anguish is registered out of his sight—as when he briefly turns his back and she leans weakly against a table or when she pulls him toward her and makes a tortured face over his shoulder. Even if we grant that her technique is skillful, however, the scene requires a certain suspension of disbelief. Charles Affron has written that Garbo "shifts radically from insincerity to passion, then to renunciation and grief" (199). Shouldn't we therefore expect that her lover, holding her in his arms, might notice some tremor of vulnerability, some vague alteration in tone? The answer of course is yes, but audiences in the late thirties did not mind; they were used to seeing high degrees of what Erving Goffman describes as "disclosive compensation" (*Frame Analysis,* 142)—a common theatrical convention whereby players are allowed to reveal information to the audience without much regard to the other characters. In its oldest, "presentational," form the convention can be seen in Shakespearean asides, but in classic Hollywood movies it has a more realistically motivated, representational quality, allowing actors to register conflicting emotions as if they were only *thinking* to themselves, outside anyone's view.

Another, somewhat more plausible form of "acting" within the diegesis can be seen in the exchanges between Bogart and Mary Astor in *The Maltese Falcon* (1941). In this case, the man recognizes that the woman is putting on a front, but the plot has made her motives ambiguous. Astor behaves like a sheltered innocent, casting demure glances down at the floor, wringing her hands and touching her brow in an appeal for sympathy. "You're good," Bogart says at one point, admiring her performance. "You're very, very good." And in fact she is good, even though she lets us see that she is slightly overplaying, registering what Lawrence Shaffer has called "appliquéd" expressions; indeed the wit of the scene derives from the way she gives her ostensible innocence a somewhat knowing, flirtatious twist, as if she were acknowledging a lie to charm Bogart. When he calls attention to her ruse, she adopts the pose of a weary but frightened woman of the world, her head tossed back on a couch in seductive fashion, so that Bogart's amused interest gives way to a more serious, cautious study of her contradictory attitudes.

These examples should indicate that any film becomes a good showcase for professional acting skill if it provides moments when the characters are clearly shown to be wearing masks—in other words, exhibiting high degrees of expressive incoherence. In such moments the player demonstrates virtuosity by sending out dual signs, and the vivid contrast between facial expressions gives the "acted image" an emotional richness, a strong sense of dramatic irony. Certain character types or fictional situations are particularly apt to foster this type of incoherence: villainy is a favorite subject for actors because it usually takes the form of an insincere or duplicitous performance; the emotional anguish of the "women's picture" requires the central character to struggle against a spontaneous overflow of powerful feelings—thus she not only cries but attempts to hide her tears from others; and movies about drunkenness or addiction provide excellent opportunities to show a character losing expressive control, so that many celebrated actors, from Chaplin in *One A.M.* (1916) to Jack Lemmon in *Days of Wine and Roses* (1962), have played alcoholics.[3]

Having mentioned Chaplin, I should add that broadly comic films, which often provoke alienated styles of performance, depend on exaggerated forms of *bodily* incoherence, often resulting in a sort of expressive anarchy. Jerry

3. In "Genre and Performance: An Overview" (Grant, 129–39) Richard De Cordova has observed that "acting" within the diegesis occurs often in thrillers, where characters are deceptive. In "women's melodrama," as Laura Mulvey has noted, "there is a delicate balance between the protagonists' self-consciousness and the actresses' mastery over a self-conscious performance" ("Melodrama In and Out of the Home," 97). Actually, the breakdown of repressive constraints on behavior—the "failure" of performance—is a telling moment in any sort of theater and can have especially powerful effect in a documentary. For example, in *Shoah* (1985) we see a barber, in the process of cutting a man's hair, being interviewed about the job he once had in a Nazi death camp. At first, he matter-of-factly recalls how naked women were brought before him to have their heads shorn. He claims to have felt nothing, but then he remarks that some of the women were the wives, mothers, and daughters of people he knew. As he speaks, he has a good deal of difficulty maintaining his "mask": ultimately, his throat begins constricting; he rolls his tongue around in his mouth and seizes a towel, wiping sweat from his face and trying to hide his tears.

Lewis is perhaps the most obvious example, but consider a typical scene in *The Gold Rush,* when Chaplin meets Georgia Hale in a saloon. First he takes an opportunity to dance with her, establishing the "front" of a polite gentleman by tipping his hat, holding her at a slight distance, and waltzing around the floor with a finesse that contrasts nicely with the rowdy crowd in the background. Then, midway through the dance, his beltless pants start to slip, causing him to gyrate wildly with his legs and hips while desperately trying to maintain decorum with his face and arms. Steve Martin's *All of Me* (1984) creates similar chaos, casting Martin as a lawyer who has been magically possessed by the spirit of a dead woman. Through most of the film, the lawyer's body is at war with itself, his arm swishing out in an effeminate gesture while his face looks on with panic; at one point, in the midst of a speech before a crowded courtroom, the woman inside him tries to collaborate in the manufacture of a coherent illusion, breaking into flamboyantly macho poses that leave the jurors staring in openmouthed incomprehension. Notice also the famous moment at the end of *Dr. Strangelove* (1963) when Peter Sellers tries to keep one arm from breaking into a Nazi salute. Strangelove's gloved fist, reminiscent of Rotwang's in *Metropolis,* keeps flying up in the air at a radical angle, only to be caught by the other hand and wrestled back into place; trying to keep the offensive body part out of sight, he pounds it down into his lap, but then it jumps up and grabs him by the throat.

Comic acting of this sort brings us very close to the spirit of radical deconstruction—hence *Dr. Strangelove* is able to exaggerate the melodramatic convention of the dual role, turning it into the multiple impersonations of postwar British farce. The film allows Sellers to play three wildly different characters whom the audience clearly perceives as one actor, sometimes doing scenes in which he has dialog with "himself." There is, of course, nothing especially new in this practice. Vaudeville-style comedy has always relied on similar tactics, threatening to disrupt coherence at every level of the performance, deriving laughter not only from the foolish inconsistency of the characters but from a split between actor and role. The comedians who worked in skits during the days of live television knew they could get a big response from the studio audience if something went wrong, and a few of them even began to structure "spontaneous" breakdowns into their act. Long after videotape was developed, Red Skelton tried to compensate for weak jokes by cracking up in the midst of a scene, and in its later days "The Carol Burnett Show" featured elaborate parodies of old movies in which Harvey Korman struggled to keep a straight face while playing opposite Tim Conway. The same technique can be seen in the nondramatic context of talk shows, where a figure like Johnny Carson can redeem a failed monologue by suddenly commenting on the writers or where "Late Night With David Letterman" can build an entire program around the host's strategic loss of control. Thus comedy is usually a step removed from realist acting; it lets an incoherence in the "acted image" become almost as visible as the divisions within the character.

Radical theater takes the process of fragmentation even further, indicating a more complete break in the mask or experimenting with performance styles that denaturalize expression. For example, a favorite acting exercise of the Open Theater required the ensemble to practice walking "sad" while making "happy" sounds. In cinema, however, the mechanical apparatus can disrupt continuity in another, perhaps more fundamental, way, as *Dr. Strangelove* suggests. Even more unconventional is Luis Buñuel's surrealist comedy, *That Obscure Object of Desire* (1977), which neatly reverses the old practice of having a single actor play multiple roles. Here is Buñuel's account of how he came upon the idea:

> If I had to list all the benefits derived from alcohol, it would be endless. In 1977, in Madrid, when I was in despair after a tempestuous argument with an actress who'd brought the shooting of *That Obscure Object of Desire* to a halt, the producer, Serge Silberman, decided to abandon the film altogether. The considerable financial loss was depressing us both until one evening, when we were drowning our sorrows in a bar, I suddenly had the idea (after two dry martinis) of using two actresses in the same role, a tactic that had never been tried before. Although I made the suggestion as a joke, Silberman loved it, and the film was saved. Once again, the combination of bar and gin proved unbeatable. (46)

Buñuel chose Angelia Molina and Carole Bouquet to embody Conchita, the young temptress who makes a fool of a middle-aged businessman played by Fernando Rey. (The film is derived from Pierre Louÿs's *La femme et le pantin,* which Sternberg and Dietrich had used as the source for *The Devil Is a Woman* in 1935.) What seems particularly important about the casting is that the two women are utterly different physical types—one of them an earthy, bosomy Spaniard, the other a tall, willowy Parisian. Buñuel takes care to make them completely interchangeable, sometimes having them play alternate sequences, occasionally substituting them for one another in the midst of a continuous action, as when Molina goes into a bathroom and a seminude Bouquet comes out. Furthermore, he never allows the audience to explain this inconsistency as a sign of Fernando Rey's distorted imagination; unlike the realist filmmaker, who gives every distortion or incoherence a psychological motive, he simply lays bare his technique, foregrounding the arbitrariness of his choice and making a joke of it. (Even so, as he wryly noted in his memoirs, many spectators have watched the film without ever noticing his capriciousness; accustomed to a coherence in the "acted image," they respond exactly like the central character, assuming that the two relatively unfamiliar women who play the "obscure object" are a single person.)

Buñuel's device is empty of the usual narrative significance, but it is none-theless meaningful, commenting on the arbitrary, fetishistic structure of desire and at the same time exposing a technique by which classical cinema usually supports that structure. As I have previously noted, movies are the only medium in which several actors are *typically* used to play one role: a voice is dubbed, a body double represents a torso, a hand model manipulates objects in close-up, a stunt man performs dangerous action in long shot, etc. All these different figures are merged in the editing and mixing, appearing on the screen as a single characterization, an "object" of fascination tied together by the name of a character and the face of a star. By reminding us of such a phenomenon, Buñuel playfully attacks the very foundation of "organic," Stanislavskian aesthetics.

A similar effect, produced by Brechtian methods, may be seen in Godard's *Breathless,* where the principal actors repeatedly fracture realistic illusion with direct address to the camera—as when Belmondo turns to the lens and tells the viewer to "go hang yourself." These unpredictable shifts between representational and presentational rhetoric are in keeping with a certain "amateurish" quality of the production as a whole, which not only permits unstable camera movements, jump cuts, and 180-degree violations but also toys with the continuity of the acted image. At one point, for example, Godard cuts from a long shot of Belmondo to a close-up of his profile; suddenly the actor turns and glances into the camera, revealing that one eyepiece of his sunglasses is inexplicably missing, as if he had dropped half of his mask.

In other ways, however, *Breathless* is a model of naturalistic performance, and its central characters have become virtual icons of existentialist fiction, easily adapted to Hollywood. (The American remake, starring Richard Gere, was able to employ the same technique of direct address as the original, adapting it to a somewhat more symbolic approach.) It was only later, as Godard's work grew increasingly politicized, that he departed utterly from the established conventions, filming *Lehrstücke* in a flat presentational style—a technique that virtually prohibited the actors from developing psychologically "rounded" personae. Although he continued to employ famous professionals, he required them to adopt a relatively one-dimensional manner, exactly reversing the structure of bourgeois performance: in other words, the characterizations seldom involved a display of expressive incoherence, and the split between actor and role was foregrounded.

The contrast between Godard's films in the early and late sixties is so vivid that it can be used to illustrate the formal logic of actorly expression. As an instance of the lifelike naturalism to which most film acting aspires, consider a shot that occurs midway through *Breathless,* when a police inspector tracks down Patricia Franchini (Jean Seberg) in the Paris offices of the *International Herald Tribune* and thrusts a newspaper in front of her face, asking, "Do you know this man?" In close-up, we see Patricia taking the newspaper and glancing down at the front page, which contains a large photo and an article announcing that her lover, Michel, is a cop killer. She is positioned in the three-quarter, "open," profile of standard movie rhetoric, with the camera looking just over the edge of the newspaper at her face. Until this point in the narrative, she has not known the full extent of Michel's criminal activity, and she tries to conceal her profound shock from the detective. Seberg's reactions seem remarkably understated compared to the ostentatious theatricality of an old-fashioned player like Lillian Gish, but they are no different in kind; in fact, the edge of the newspaper functions much like the fan Gish manipulates during the engagement-party sequence in *True Heart Susie*, forming a boundary between "private" and "public" expressions. Beyond the paper, we can see a small tightening around her mouth and a deepening seriousness in her eyes, followed by subtle indications of anger and hurt as she intently scans the article. When she looks up over the paper's edge at the offscreen detective, her face changes, adopting the mask of a sweetly pretty Midwestern girl. Her eyes widen slightly and her lips almost smile as she shapes them into a lie: "No," she says, shaking her head, at the same time allowing a shadow of unease to break her calm.

Seberg's performance-within-performance in this shot depends on a fundamental trope of realist film acting: the player assumes a representational stance, her gaze turned slightly away from the lens, and then makes at least two different faces, both clearly visible to the audience, one coded as "suppressed," the other as "ostensive." Maurice Merleau-Ponty's comments on the phenomenology of character (which Godard subsequently read) are strikingly relevant to such moments. As he suggests, there is probably no such thing as an "inner" emotion, either in life or on film: "Anger, shame, hate, and love are not psychic facts hidden at the bottom of another's consciousness: they are types of behavior or styles of conduct which are visible from the outside. They exist *on* this face or *in* those gestures, not hidden behind them" (52–53). The same argument could be made in semiotic terms, forcing us to abandon the notion of a Stanislavskian "subtext." The fact is, all actorly emotion is equally manifest. Audiences have simply learned to read certain types of expressive incoherence as a sign of psychological complexity, so that the dual faces of the actor function much like irony or ambiguity in written language.

Only a few years later, Godard abandoned this style, eschewing "depth" in both staging and expression. The multiple faces of Jean Seberg in *Breathless* are quite different from those of a player who appears near the beginning of *Two or Three Things I Know about Her* (1967). In this case we are presented with a Techniscope color image of a woman in close-up, standing against an urban cityscape and looking directly into the lens: "This is Marina Vlady," Godard's voice whispers on the sound track; "she is an actress." Vlady, her expression cool and impassive, quotes Brecht: "Yes, speak as if quoting truths. Old Brecht said that. That actors should quote." She then turns her head to the right of the screen, assuming the three-quarter profile of ordinary movie acting. "But that isn't important," Godard whispers. Suddenly a jump cut takes us to another image of the same woman, framed exactly as before, the cityscape behind her seen from a slightly different angle. "This is Juliette Janson," Godard says. "She lives here." Once again the woman looks at us, her face shaped into an impassive stare. "It was two years ago in Martinique," she says, and begins describing her character in cryptic, disjointed sentences. She stops and turns her head to the left. "Now she has turned her head to the left," Godard announces, "but that isn't important."

The offscreen commentary, the speeches, and the slight mismatch of shots all serve to drive a wedge between two conceptions of the human figure on the screen. Meanwhile the performer seems alienated, distanced from both of her roles. The images are paradoxical because we cannot distinguish between Vlady and Janson on the basis of the player's appearance, rhetoric, or expression. Throughout, she remains essentially the same figure, with the same sweater and the same hairstyle, speaking her lines like a Brechtian actor who is "quoting the truth" rather than "living the part." As "herself," she gazes back at the lens with the compliant yet slightly cynical air of a woman who has been photographed many times, avoiding the ingratiating warmth of a typical narrator or guide, as if she were acknowledging that she speaks to an apparatus. As Janson, she has much the same attitude—a cool, almost lobotomized manner that might be regarded as an emotional response to life in working-class Paris but that gives the audience very little opportunity to feel empathy. Even when she turns her head to the profile position of representational theater, she indicates no special emotion, and Godard tells us that her movement is unimportant.

By subordinating the expressive aspect of Vlady's performance to a rational, "epic" address, the film gives us little indication of a difference between a social mask and a private identity. Godard is less interested in the psychology of people than in how they function as workers or images, and as a result he shows us the split between actor and persona rather than the divided self of a character. Vlady's overt statements and her actions during the film's intermittent narrative take precedence over her ability to render complex emotions; much like Brecht, who remarked that a photograph of a factory would tell us very little about its meaning, she seems almost contemptuous of the phenomenology of expression. As she says later in the film, "something can make me cry; but the cause of the tears is not to be found in . . . their traces on my cheeks; . . . one can describe everything that is produced when I do something without indicating, for all that, what makes me do it."

The technique here is exactly opposed to the close-up in *Breathless*, which uses an Iowa schoolgirl made famous by Otto Preminger to embody an American in Paris. Rather like the classic cinema to which it alludes, the early film melds a celebrity into the character she plays, making the audience feel a subtle *glissement* between star and role. Both emerge as a single, psychologically complete personality—a dangerously attractive contemporary version of Daisy Miller, born of a union between the New Wave and *film noir*. By contrast, *Two or Three Things* disturbs the coherence of the acted image, suggesting a different structural relation between actor and character: both Vlady and Janson, according to Godard, are workers, and like all workers under postindustrial capitalism, they are engaged in a type of prostitution. (At one point, Vlady / Janson removes her clothes and puts an airline bag on her head while a photographer who strongly resembles Godard "directs" her movements.)

Partly for this reason, we cannot always tell whether Vlady is addressing the camera as "herself" or as the character. In one sense, however, the problem is academic, because she is never fully merged into her role. Godard's commentary and her own somewhat flat, emotionless style make us continually aware of a double aspect to her image, as if we were always watching someone going through motions. Hence the film reverses the formal priorities of conventional cinema, becoming its dialectical opposite. It collapses private into public expression, at the same time creating divisions where we expect unity. By this means, it points to the fundamentally "two-faced" quality of most performance and reveals the process by which both theater and social life create the illusion of a unified subject. *Two or Three Things* remains a theatrical spectacle, but its players might be said to operate at the very margins of acting.

5

Accessories

*The fetishes and cult images of early cultures . . .
were bathed, anointed, clothed, and carried in pro-
cession. What wonder that illusion settled on them
and that the faithful saw them smiling, frowning, or
nodding behind the clouds of incense.*
　　　　　　　　　—E. H. Gombrich, *Art and Illusion*

A recent textbook on acting refers to props, costuming, and makeup as the "externals" of performance (as if anything were "internal" in a public show).[1] My remarks on this theme are grouped under the vague rubric of "accessories," but my real concern is with the ways persons and inanimate materials interact, so that we cannot tell where a face or body leaves off and a mask begins.

Expressive Objects

As every impressionist knows, Katharine Hepburn once said "the calla lilies are in bloom"—first in a Broadway flop entitled *The Lake* (1934) and then again a few years later, when the opening scene from that production was used for *Enchanted April,* the play-within-the-movie in *Stage Door* (1937). I mention this bit of trivia not because I am interested in Hepburn's idiosyncratic voice but because she happens to be carrying a bunch of lilies when she speaks her famous words. I want to call attention to the flowers themselves—and, by extension, to any object an actor touches.

Stage Door casts Hepburn as Terry Randall, a sheltered but likeable heir-ess who forsakes her father's millions and pursues a career on the stage. Believing that acting requires no special training ("It's just common sense"), she takes up residence in a theatrical boarding house and begins making the

---

1. See Bruder, et al., *A Practical Handbook for the Actor* (New York: Vintage, 1986), 48–54.

rounds of New York auditions. Without her knowledge, her father gets her a leading role by paying money to a producer. Meanwhile, back at the boarding house, we see a struggling thespian (Andrea Leeds) who was born to play the part Hepburn has been given and who suffers the loss of her most cherished dream.

During rehearsals of the play, Hepburn is comically inept. The "calla lilies" line is supposed to represent grief, but she speaks it like a bored announcer in a railway station. She can't understand why the producer keeps tearing his hair, and as opening night draws near she shows no improvement. The women at the boarding house are largely unsympathetic; even though Hepburn is innocent of wrongdoing, her upper-class manner, her naivete, and her easy rise to stardom have made her an outcast. Only Leeds is helpful, generously offering advice on how to play the role. Unfortunately, Leeds grows increasingly despondent and commits suicide on the play's opening night. Hepburn receives word of the death in her dressing room just before the curtain is about to rise. At first she refuses to go on, but then, in the best tradition of show business, she musters all her strength and makes an entrance. She is able to use Leeds's advice, but more important, she "lives the part," allowing her own shock, grief, and guilt to inform her interpretation of the character. When she speaks her line about lilies, everyone in the theater can feel the depth of her pain. The audience goes wild, and out of tragedy a star is born.

Hepburn's reading of the play's opening speech functions both as a joking allusion to her own recent stage fiasco and as an important plot device, marking the "progress" of Terry Randall from a Brechtian amateur to a Stanislavskian professional. It is important to note, however, that when the character begins rehearsals for her Broadway debut, her handling of the lilies is as awkward as her reading of the line. When Andrea Leeds offers to help, her first suggestion is that the flowers ought to be carried differently. "I think I would hold them like this," she says, cradling the lilies in her arms like a mother carrying a child. The blossoms, which had previously seemed as ludicrous as a stalk of celery, now become a sign of ethereal, rather maternal, sadness.

The lesson Hepburn's character has been taught is that feelings or psychological states are communicated by the way one handles things—an obvious fact that amateurs frequently overlook because they think of objects in the *mise-en-scène* as static, inert materials. As Jiří Veltruský has pointed out, however, "the sphere of the live human being and that of the object are interpenetrated, and no exact limit can be drawn between them" (86). This phenomenon is so crucial to most kinds of theater that objects alone, in the absence of human beings, can become agents of narrative and therefore actors. When they do, they are not so much personified as raised to the level of what Jan Mukařovský called "action in the proper sense of the word, based on the unlimited initiative of the subject" (quoted in Veltrusky, 89). Pudovkin

Hepburn drinks champagne in Holiday.

has made a similar argument, citing the following example of an "active" object from film: "In *The Battleship Potemkin,* the battleship itself is an image so powerfully and clearly shown that the men on board are resolved into it. . . . the shooting down of the crowd is answered not by the sailors standing to the guns, but by the steel battleship itself, breathing from a hundred mouths. . . . the steel driving-rods of the engine incarnate in themselves the hearts of its crew, furiously beating in tenseness of expectation" (144).

Pudovkin called this category of things "expressive objects," and I should like to appropriate his term here, using it in a narrower sense than he intended. My aim is to focus on moments when the human subject and the theatrical object come into contact in that indefinite realm Veltrusky describes, where "no exact limit can be drawn between them." Prior to the moment of contact, of course, the object already has a meaning—a dagger in *Macbeth* is a sign of danger even if it merely rests upon a table. Once the object is picked up, however, its significance is inflected by the stance and behavior of the person holding it. In *Holiday,* for example, when Katharine Hepburn grows depressed and contemplates getting drunk, she grasps the stem of a champagne glass tightly, wrapping her hand around it and making a fist; thus the prop helps her to signal "repressed" anger.

Perhaps the best-known and most brilliantly employed expressive object in the history of movies is Chaplin's cane. A virtual part of Charlie's anatomy, it can be used to signal an astonishing range of character traits and emotional responses. At one moment he twirls it nonchalantly, showing off his cheerful dandyism; at the next, it becomes a fragile support for heartbreak. Depending on how he waves it about, it expresses anger, aggressiveness, politeness, surprise, anxiety, and even the state of the Tramp's health. In *The Gold Rush,* for example, the prospector Hank Curtis steps out of his door and finds Charlie frozen stiff in the snow. Hank picks up the body and carries it inside to thaw, propping it against a wall like a department store dummy. All the while Chaplin keeps himself as rigid as a plank, holding the cane crosswise in front of his body; the normally animate object now seems dead, exactly like one of his frozen arms and legs.

Every form of theatricality, on or off the stage, tends to use objects in this way: cavalry officers brandish swords, orchestra conductors flourish batons, and striptease dancers toy with bits of clothing. In each case, the object transmits both a symbolic and a "personal" message; hence the crown and the scepter stand in metonymic relation to kingship, but when a specific king in a particular dramatic setting wields the scepter, we induce something about his strength and capacity to play his role. Even when the handling of objects is not motivated by the setting or the narrative, actors need things to touch. Mae Marsh wrote, "I look over [the sets] very carefully in the hope that some article of furniture, etc., will suggest some attractive piece of business. An odd fan, a pillow, a door, in fact, anything may prove valuable" (54). Certain objects are especially handy—for instance, those ubiquitous cigarettes in *film noir,* which not only provide *Stimmung* but also give the players a repertory of dramatic gestures. And when an actor finds an excuse to manipulate an unusual prop, he or she will inevitably steal the scene. In *Giant* (1956), one of James Dean's best moments occurs when he converses with a group of Texas oilmen while tossing a weighted rope around in his hand; at the climactic moment, just as he is indicating his contempt for everyone in the room, he flicks one end of the rope in the air so that it ties into a knot as it drops.

Sometimes an entire sequence is built around what an actor does with an object. The silent comedies of Keaton and Chaplin provide numerous instances, but notice the function of a small plastic bottle of nose spray in a scene from *The Apartment* (1960). Jack Lemmon is summoned to his boss's office at an inopportune moment: Lemmon's character is suffering from a head cold, and throughout the interview he has to squirt liquid up his nostril so that he can talk clearly. At first, the bottle conveys his nervousness and ineptitude (all the more so when he tries to be nonchalant), but then it suddenly changes function. The boss (Fred MacMurray) announces that Lemmon is about to be promoted, and Lemmon registers surprise and excitement by involuntarily squeezing the spray, sending a stream of decongestant across the room. Regaining composure, he completes the interview and walks cheer-fully out of the office, expressing joy by spraying a flower in his lapel with the medicine and tossing the empty bottle into a wastebasket. In this case a single prop has helped to chart what Stanislavskians would call the emotional "through line" of the scene; elsewhere in the same film, one can find many other less elaborate but equally amusing uses of a similar technique—as when Lemmon prepares a humble meal for Shirley MacLaine, draining spa-ghetti with a tennis raquet and then happily flopping it onto a plate with a backhand.

Part of the actor's job, therefore, is to keep objects under expressive con-trol, letting them become signifiers of feeling. Sometimes the player's dex-terity is foregrounded (as when Chaplin does a "dance" with dinner rolls); but more often it is hardly noticeable, lending emotional resonance to the simplest behavior. As an example of such "invisible" technique, consider the famous tear-jerking climax of the Barbara Stanwyck version of *Stella Dallas*. "My favorite scene in the movie," Stanwyck has said, "was the one where Stella Dallas stands by a rail outside [the Morrison house] as Laurel is being married to her well-born fiancee. I had to indicate to audiences, through the emotions shown by my face, that for Stella joy ultimately triumphed over the heartache she had felt" (Smith, 99). The expressions on Stanwyck's face are in fact important, but in recollecting the scene she forgets that her perfor-mance was enhanced by the use of a white pocket handkerchief. When she watches the ceremony, she brings the handkerchief slowly to her face as if she were going to weep; then she pauses, slightly openmouthed, and begins to bite and suck at the white cloth in childlike absorption. Cut to a shot of Laurel kissing her new husband. Cut back to Stanwyck, standing outside in the rain; she smiles blissfully, still biting on the handkerchief, grasping at the other end and pulling it taut. In medium shot, she turns dreamily away from the gate, looking downward as if lost in her thoughts, all the while continuing to bite and pull at the cloth (see next page). The camera tracks backward as she walks toward us and away from the house; she has tears in her eyes and a smile on her face, but her mounting joy is signaled most clearly by the way she tugs at one end of the handkerchief, swinging it back and forth in rhythm with her happy walk. At last she releases it from her mouth and bunches it up in her fist. Beaming with satisfaction, she quickens her stride, proudly straightens her head, and stuffs the handkerchief in her pocket as "The End" appears on the screen.

Virtually every modern theorist of acting—from Kuleshov to Strasberg—has believed that players ought to be trained in how to execute such elemen-tary actions as Stanwyck illustrates here. After all, only the most vulgar em-piricism regards the objects around us as inanimate. Once those objects have entered into social relations and narrative actions, they are imbued with the same "spirit" as the humans who touch them.

Barbara Stanwyck with an "expressive object."

Costume

The expressive dialectic between people and things extends to the clothing actors wear. Costumes serve as indicators of gender and social status, but they also shape bodies and behavior. "[We] may make them take the mould of arm or breast," Virginia Woolf wrote in *Orlando*, "but they mould our hearts, our brains, our tongues to their liking. . . . The man has his hand free to seize his sword, the woman must use hers to keep the satins from slipping from her shoulders. The man looks the world full in the face, as if it were made for his uses and fashioned to his liking. The woman takes a sidelong glance at it, full of subtlety, even of suspicion. Had they both worn the same clothes, it is possible their outlook might have been the same." The principle that clothes determine movement and character can be applied with equal force to theatrical costumes. Who shall say how much the lumbering walk of Frankenstein's monster was created by Karloff and how much by a pair of weighted boots? We even have Chaplin's word that the Tramp grew out of the costume, not *vice versa:* "I had no idea of the character. But the moment I was dressed, the clothes and make-up made me feel the person he was" (144). As Richard Crenna puts it in *The Flamingo Kid* (1985), "You are what you wear."

Quite ordinary costuming provides actors with expressive objects: male characters typically doff their hats, finger their lapels, or toy with their watch chains; females adjust their skirts, grasp their purses, or worry their necklaces. When a costume is laden with accessories—vests, suspenders, handkerchiefs, and so on—the opportunities for gesture are considerably enhanced; hence the "dressy" figures in films are always the most expressive ones. A particularly vivid illustration of this phenomenon can be seen if we turn once again to the Barbara Stanwyck version of *Stella Dallas,* in which the characterization depends to a great extent on Stella's gaudily inappropriate finery. During a moonlit walk with Stephen Dallas early in the film, she carries a wide straw hat in her hands, hiding her face behind it when she blushes or shyly biting the hatbrim; later, having married Dallas, she wears a dress with a long chiffon scarf that she nervously runs through her fingers; still later, when she visits a country club and tries to impress her daughter Laurel's rich friends, she flings an absurd foxfur around her neck in a pathetic attempt at regal dignity. Throughout, Stella's frilled or beribboned dresses, feathery hats, and clunky jewelry (designed by Omar Kiam) have been turned into veritable flags for her emotion.

In her comprehensive study of Hollywood androgyny, Rebecca Bell-Metereau notes that women players or males who cross dress are allowed a broader range of both accessories and clothing styles and hence a larger emotional vocabulary. Extreme forms of "masculinity," in both theater and daily life, seem to involve a relatively stoic, deadpan manner and a serious attitude, so that dress seems rather like a plain utilitarian skin. Compare Dana Andrews or William Holden with any of Hollywood's male comedians or with "feminine" matinee idols such as Valentino, Errol Flynn, or Tony Curtis, who wear visible, changeable costumes and as a result exhibit a much greater degree of "expression and flexibility" (Bell-Metereau, 10–11). At this level of characterization, dress and its accessories have other uses besides giving the actors something to touch. When cloth molds or drapes the human figure, it helps determine certain poses or gestures; thus the grand leaps and swoops of swashbuckling "costume" pictures virtually require capes and tights; and the famous image of Henry Fonda in *My Darling Clementine* (1948), tilted back in his chair while shifting from one leg to another on a post, must have been partly inspired by Fonda's tailored Western attire.

In fact, any clothing not intended purely for physical labor tends to promote "fashions" in both postures and bodies. For that reason, nudity in painting, photography, and film can usually be regarded as what Stephen Heath calls the "final adornment" (188). Compare Hedy Lamarr in *Ecstasy* (1933) and Maria Schneider in *The Last Tango in Paris* (1973)—not only do we see more of Schneider's flesh, but the nude poses and movements in the latter film belong to a culture where young women wear blue jeans, miniskirts, and high-heeled boots.[2]

The hidden relationship between our bodies and the cultural norms of dress is made obvious in a film like *Pumping Iron II: The Women* (1984); but to get an even better sense of how much nude figures and clothing work in tandem, conforming to the same patterns, one need only glance at nineteenth-century "French postcard" photos of women. The models nearly always look as plump as Molly Bloom, and they often stand in postures that emphasize their arched backs, their heavy thighs, and their large outthrust buttocks. In effect, they are *corseted* figures, assuming the shape of late Victorian garments. Interestingly, the "modern" female begins to appear in the same period, most clearly in the work of fin-de-siècle painters who reject plumpness in favor of a sinewy, sometimes tubercular, look and costume their figures in straight, pseudomedieval dresses. Edward Burne-Jones's portrait of Ellen Terry in *Macbeth* is a classic instance, but see also John Singer Sargent's flattering portraits of turn-of-the-century aristocrats, in which bodies are elongated and the bulky, constraining look of feminine attire is de-emphasized.

The ideal of slimness does not become dominant until after World War I, at the moment when the classic Hollywood cinema is being institutionalized. It quickly manifests itself in changes of everyday dress—first in the abandonment of the corset and then, more important, in the shortening of skirts, so that for the first time in Western history the lower extremities of women's bodies are visible in everyday life. By the thirties, fashionable female movie stars are even wearing trousers, which, together with the short skirts, lead to new postures and styles of movement.[3] Women now have two legs, and the coy, bent-knee stance of classical art gives way to another image, in which

---

2. Clothing styles and gestural cues of gender are likely to change over time, but society usually expects that movements will conform to clothing. One of the most famous comments on this expectation is a scene from Mark Twain's *Huckleberry Finn*, when Huck puts on a dress to disguise himself. He is quickly spotted by a woman, who notes that he doesn't know the "feminine" way to throw a rock or catch an object tossed in his lap.

3. According to Anne Hollander (214–15), men have been wearing trousers since the Greco-Roman period, but the garmets did not become "normal" attire for European males until around 1820. Women, on the other hand, seldom appeared in any sort of costume that separated their legs; in the mid-nineteenth century, they were regarded as lascivious or perverse if they so much as wore panties beneath their long skirts.

the bodies of the "weaker sex" are supported by separate, independent pillars, their feet spread expressively.

The emancipation movement and the postwar economy were the chief determinants of this new image, but the movies helped it to proliferate. Summarizing the twentieth-century's design for women, Anne Hollander writes:

> Feminine sexuality had to abandon the suggestion of plump, hidden softness and find expression in exposed, lean hardness. Women strove for the erotic appeal inherent in the racehorse and the sports car, which might be summed up as mettlesome challenge: a vibrant, somewhat unaccountable readiness for action but only under expert guidance. This was naturally best offered in a self-contained, sleekly composed physical format: a thin body, with few layers of covering. Immanent sexuality, best expressed in a condition of stasis, was no longer the foundation of physical allure. The look of possible movement became a necessary element in fashionable female beauty, and all women's clothing, whatever other messages it offered, consistently incorporated visible legs and feet into the total female image. Women, once thought to glide, were seen to walk. . . . The various dance crazes of the first quarter of the century undoubtedly were an expression of this restless spirit, but its most important vehicle was the movies. (152–53)

Hollander's description evokes the quintessentially glamorous women of classic Hollywood—Hepburn striding across a room, Dietrich cocking her foot up on a chair, Lombard displaying leggy fashions for screwball comedy, and Bacall comparing herself to a racehorse in a famous exchange with Bogart in *The Big Sleep* (1946). There are, of course, other fashions embodied in movie stars, as one can see from the soft roundness of Harlow and Monroe; even these women, however, are strikingly sleek and modern compared with the Victorian popular ideal, whose last surviving representative is the comic Mae West.

Precisely because bodies are *fashionable,* or shaped by a specific culture and circumstance, the clothes in historical movies are adjusted in subtle, almost unconscious ways to contemporary taste. Hollywood directors from Griffith and DeMille onward have operated according to historicist assumptions, much like nineteenth-century painters, who thought the past was accessible to direct representation. (The Hollywood approach, which never attempts a radical disjunction between dress and setting, is challenged in Straub and Huillet's *History Lessons* [1972], where people garbed in Roman togas appear against modern backgrounds.) Nevertheless, the bodies and mannerisms of actors in the average "costume" film seem influenced by present-day clothing styles. Douglas Fairbanks was the essence of twenties energy, whether he played Robin Hood or a modern urban male; and as Hollander points out, "Bette Davis behaved and dressed quite differently in her two versions of Queen Elizabeth, one in 1939 and one in 1955; both were in 'authentic' period dress and naturalistically acted, although neither much resembled the clothes and gestures in Queen Elizabeth's actual portraits. Each looked correctly dressed and naturally behaved for its own time" (297).

In films that take place in modern-day settings, the situation is somewhat different. Some of these pictures turn clothes into spectacle—especially musicals or dramas involving upper-class characters; nevertheless, the actors "fit" their clothing and seldom seem to be costumed in a purely theatrical sense. Cary Grant or Humphrey Bogart, for example, must have worn much the same clothes on screen and off. This is a relatively new phenomenon, born of Western bourgeois society. Actors in most periods and cultures have dressed in fashions specific to the performance—a tradition that survives for us mainly in circus, certain types of mime, and classical ballet. And yet Cary Grant's dress changed remarkably little during his long career in the movies, partly because his style of movement was predicated on a two or three-piece suit, a cleverly designed, invisibly theatrical costume out of which he developed a series of characteristic poses and gestures.

Bourgeois realism in theatrical decor and dress, which took root in the eighteenth century, has had a complex effect both on drama and on society at large. Because actors in modern Western culture are allowed to wear anything or nothing, our films can involve a much greater variety of expressive movement. Then, too, the blurring of boundaries between theatrical and everyday costume has enabled us to represent class divisions in vividly accurate detail, making direct political comments about the way we live. (As late as the 1880s, according to Oscar Wilde, authorities in London complained when actors in certain plays wore real military uniforms onstage, claiming that authentic garb might breed disrespect for public institutions.) At the same time, however, realism has enabled movie actors to serve as fashion models, stimulating other areas of the capitalist economy. The most ordinary apparel becomes extraordinary by association with a star, and it is probably no exaggeration to say that the Levi Strauss company profited greatly when James Dean wore blue jeans.

But Dean is a comparatively minor example of the influence of media costumes on clothes in society. As Charles Eckert has noted, Hollywood became deeply involved in advertising sometime during the early thirties; as a result, "the many fine sensibilities of Hollywood's designers, artists, cameramen, lighting men, directors, and composers had lent themselves, even if coincidentally, to the establishment of powerful bonds between the emotional fantasy-generating substance of films and the material objects those films contained" (20). Actors were as deeply implicated in this process as photographers and other craftspeople; indeed, they were the figures who endorsed the products and put them brilliantly into motion on the screen. Thus Eckert can imagine a typical consumer of 1934—a nineteen-year-old store clerk, female, Anglo-Saxon, somewhat resembling Janet Gaynor—setting off on a shopping errand that will make her more like the people in movies: after adorning herself with various cosmetics and undergarmets advertised by the stars, she dresses herself in a Bonnie Bright frock (the kind worn by Francis Dee in *Of Human Bondage*), a Wittnauer watch ("Watches of the Stars"), and a simple necklace (a Tecla was used by Barbara Stanwyck in *Gambling Lady*). As she window-shops, she encounters a forty-dollar copy of the Travis Banton gown designed for Carole Lombard in the just-released *Rumba,* co-starring George Raft. Purchasing the gown, she rushes off to catch the matinee showing of the film; there, the fabric is transmogrified: "Back-lit, descending a stair, . . . it whisper[s] and sigh[s] its way into George Raft's roguish arms" (Eckert 11–12).

The vaguely theatrical nature of everyday costume and the libidinal urges it can provoke have worked to Hollywood's advantage. (Macy's once had a department of "Cinema Fashions," and as of this writing it features a whole line of "Dynasty" products.) Indeed the movies have shown Madison Avenue how to make television commercials—thirty-second dramas that distill the slickest techniques of cinema, sometimes pitching garments outright, sometimes using them to showcase other accoutrements of "good living." The consumer toward whom all this energy is directed may have changed somewhat since the thirties (today the audience might be male or female, aged somewhere between eleven and twenty-one, as can be seen from the colorful costuming on MTV or in movies with teenaged protagonists); nevertheless, the commercial intent is the same, and the interaction between people and things continues to be reciprocal. Clothes bestow form, vitality, and traits of character on the actors' movements, but the bodies of actors bestow exchange value on the clothes, and give sex appeal to the costumes we acquire for everyday performances.

Makeup

Clothing and makeup are closely related, although the wearing of visible rouge or paint is the most theatrical thing we can do in an offstage encounter. The very sign of theater, makeup is the vestige of a mask. The design of the face can also provide actors with still another expressive object. Consider the way hairstyles function as sources of gesture: melodramatic villains stroke their mustaches, and seductive women toss long tresses out of their eyes. (Stanwyck rejected the idea of wearing a wig in *Stella Dallas* because "I couldn't do anything with my hands, like running them through my hair"

[Smith, 100].)[4] Nevertheless, modern actors—particularly males—often hide these tricks, conforming to the politics of cosmetics in society at large.

Like many other forms of expression, the rules for the use of makeup in Western culture have long been grounded in an opposition between nature and artifice. In the Renaissance these terms had flexible meanings, but during the Romantic period they became quasi-moral categories, with nature linked to "truth" or "godliness," and artifice to "lies" or any attempt to conceal imperfection. The Baudelairian aesthetes and decadents of the late nineteenth century tried to reverse these values, making artifice the highest good. As long as the basic opposition existed, however, it could be used to enforce any number of deeply-embedded social attitudes, including a pervasive misogyny. Hence, from the age of Victoria onward, visible makeup in everyday life has been sanctioned chiefly for women, who are alternately praised for their alluring charms and attacked for their deceptive paint and powder.[5] The romantic stance toward cosmetics, which prevails in most public life even today, helped foster the image of woman as a dangerously protean figure—a Lamia or a *belle dame sans merci*—or, more contemptuously, as a vain, pathetically aging creature who hides behind a mask.

Such attitudes, endlessly acted out in movies, usually by made-up stars, can be seen in their most naive, puritanical form in Griffith's *True Heart Susie* (1919), where the central character's goodness and honesty are associated with her refusal to use cosmetics to capture a husband. The Stanwyck version of *Stella Dallas* offers a more sophisticated, ironic variant, in which we see the pathetic Stella applying cold creams and peroxide while her daughter Laurel speaks with glowing ardor about the rich Helen Morrison, who looks "natural," like a "goddess." By contrast, the Sternberg films with Dietrich are the best examples of pure aestheticism in Hollywood; in them the star becomes a hymn to every kind of artifice, even as she is identified with the traditional vamp or the "devil as a woman." Later, as the glamour queens of the twenties and thirties began to age, they lent themselves to horror, tragedy,

4. In this regard, it seems appropriate to cite an advertisement that appeared in the window of a Philadelphia hairdresser in 1802: "Ross respectfully informs the ladies that he has on exhibition a most elegant and whimsical head-dress, calculated either for mask balls, full dress, or undress, and may be worn instead of a veil, having the peculiar quality of changing its shape, occasionally covering the whole face, yet capable of being disposed in wandering ringlets; as a mask the disguise is complete without oppression; as a veil it protects without the dull uniformity of drapery, and may be scented to the perfume of any flower" (quoted in McClellan, *The History of American Costume*, 293–94).

5. "Men may well be less aware that gender is created since man, and hence masculinity, has always been the norm, the generic—and woman/feminity is defined by how it differs from that standard. Masculine is the unadorned face, the uncontorted form, the uncontrolled appetite, and raw emotion. The necessary artifice and self control of femininity has helped create among women a greater awareness that our 'natural' gender role is more or less elaborate disguise." (Wendy Chapkis, *Beauty Secrets: Women and the Politics of Appearance*, 130.)

and satire—as in the ludicrously painted and harshly lit closeups of Swanson, Davis, and Crawford in *Sunset Boulevard* and *What Ever Happened to Baby Jane?* (1962). In the Faye Dunaway imitation of Joan Crawford in *Mommie Dearest* (1981), the character's madness is suggested by her garish makeup, and during one of her most outrageous attacks on her child, her face and costume have been designed to resemble those of a player in a Kabuki drama.

It is hardly surprising that movies should replay such familiar patterns, for the entire practice of twentieth-century drama is grounded in the philosophy of romantic realism. Thus Pudovkin attacks the early silent cinema's use of "theatrical" makeup:

> In the cinema the quality of make-up, where this be necessary at all, is estimated by its efficaciousness in preserving all the finest complexities of the given human face. An artificial expression—a cheek pasted on, a line drawn to represent a non-existent furrow—are simply idiotic in the cinema, inasmuch as, deprived of their theatrical purpose of helping the actor to establish an expression at a distance, they simply become a hindrance damaging that expression, particularly destructive in close-up. (321–22)

Most people would agree with Pudovkin, who relied on *typage* rather than on false noses or wigs to create the faces of his characters. It should be pointed out, however, that there is no such thing as a "natural" face and that theatrical makeup in older cultures evolved for reasons other than the need to make expression "visible at a distance." The first actors wore literal masks, and paint was applied to flesh to mark off performers from the audience. Theatrical makeup, like costume, was originally intended as a sign of ritual drama; it was only after the romantic revolution that players sought to hide such things, always appealing to naturalness and "sincerity."

In modern theater, makeup has usually been regarded as an "aid" to performance, and male actors in movies seem vaguely guilty about using too much of it. John Barrymore was proud of having played his silent version of *Dr. Jekyll and Mr. Hyde* (1920) without the assistance of disguise, so that the transformation from man to beast was effected by his own grimaces and changes of posture (Spencer Tracy wanted to do the same thing for the forties adaptation but was overruled by MGM). Despite this preference for the "natural" face and body, however, the movie factories have always maintained huge makeup departments. Before the invention of panchromatic film stock, actors were usually painted white because the pinkish-gray flesh of Anglo-Saxons registered black on the screen. Later, the classic stars who were famous for playing "themselves" relied on toupees and corsets as well as plastic surgery, lights, and lenses, to give structure and texture to their faces. Certain forms of makeup have therefore become the most truly invisible of movie crafts. Even when a film seems to be giving us the actor unadorned, the effect can be deceiving: Orson Welles was as elaborately designed when he played the young Charles Foster Kane as when he played the dying old man; and Barbara Stanwyck wears as much makeup at the end of *Stella Dallas*, when she is ostensibly plain, as she does in the earlier parts of the film, when she is ostensibly gaudy.

Sometimes, of course, actors make a great show of abandoning artifice: Walter Huston removed his false teeth and went unshaved to play the prospector in *The Treasure of the Sierra Madre* (1946). But Huston's looks in that film are no less artful than usual—in fact, his short beard had to be trimmed regularly to maintain continuity from shot to shot. Likewise, Humphrey Bogart had to wear a full wig throughout the picture because a vitamin deficiency was causing him to temporarily lose his hair. There is, in other words, no such thing as an uncontrived face in the movies. The features of the typical film actor are a regulated, controlled variant of the features we encounter in society—a field of signs prepared for a viewer, so conventionalized as to become a "mythology" or an invisible ideology. That is why the most unorthodox players have not been those who abandon makeup but those who make it visible. Examples range from comics like Chaplin and Groucho Marx, whose faces suggest painted clowns, to the young Cary Grant and James Cagney, who were fond of evident eyeliner and lip rouge. A still more unusual case is the later work of Orson Welles, who deliberately chose stage makeup for his role in *Mr. Arkadin* (1955), so that we cannot tell whether he or the character is wearing a disguise.

In more conventional films, the actor's face is usually taken as the ultimate guarantee of reality—the very seat of emotions that are meant to be truthful even if everything else is fake. For example, in the concluding shot of Preminger's *Bonjour Tristesse* (1958), Jean Seberg applies cold cream to her cheeks and suddenly breaks into tears, revealing the character's buried sadness. Perhaps the only exception to this rule occurs in the horror or fantasy genres or in pictures where the actor is supposed to age. Even in these stories, however, makeup operates rather like a "special effect" and is supposed to remain at least partly invisible. Thus when the camera tracks in for an enormous close-up of F. Murray Abraham at the end of *Amadeus* (1984), we maintain a fetishistic splitting of belief that classic realism always encourages. Technicians have aged Abraham so much that he is no longer recognizable, and yet we seem to see every pore of his skin; we know he wears a mask (as all actors do), but nonetheless we want to accept it as a face.

Part Two

Star Performances

6

Lillian Gish in
True Heart Susie (1919)

Griffith's *True Heart Susie* opens in a one-room Indiana schoolhouse, where a teacher is conducting a spelling bee. The students are standing in a row around the walls of the room, arranged according to their ages. The camera isolates two students—William and Susie (Robert Harron and Lillian Gish)—showing them facing the camera as if in a police lineup. Susie stands on the left, holding herself at attention with her arms stiffly at her sides; her head is cocked slightly, her eyes opened wide, her brows raised in an exaggeratedly cute, almost dopey, innocence. Next to her William stands more awkwardly, rocking from one foot to the other in discomfort over the teacher's impending question. Although a title card prior to the shot identifies Susie as "plain," the girl we see is quite pretty. Her tiny nose and rosebud mouth are set off against her large eyes, and her pale face is surrounded by wispy blonde hair gathered into pigtails. A simple plaid frock conceals her body, but obviously she is slender and well proportioned.

Griffith now cuts to the teacher, who quizzes the younger students and turns to glance offscreen in the direction of William and Susie. "Anonymous," she asks, and we return to a shot that appears identical to the previous one; at any rate the camera angle is the same, the clothing and the relative positions of the players are the same, and Robert Harron still looks like the same clumsy boy. Gish, however, might be a different person. One reason for the change is a subtle, unmotivated alteration in the lighting, which makes her hair seem much darker; but she also wears the hair differently, so that bangs fall over her forehead and her curls are less evident. Moreover, her posture and her facial expression suggest that she has totally revised her conception of the role. Her arms are relaxed, her hands are clasped calmly in

Two versions of Lillian Gish.

front of her, and she glances sidelong up at William; gone is the kewpie-doll innocence, replaced by a quite mature face, less self-consciously pretty and more knowing.

Suddenly, a jump cut returns us to the first image of the couple, as if Griffith had discovered an error, partly erased it, and restored the original shot. William raises his hand for another chance at answering the question. Susie, looking rather dotty, her eyes wide with fake innocence and her head wobbling from side to side, seems to say, "I know!" She spells the word, ending her recitation with a self-satisfied smile.

When the sequence is slowed down with an analyzing projector or when a single frame is isolated from the two shots, the transformation in Gish is remarkable. During an ordinary viewing, however, the error in continuity goes by almost unnoticed. I mention it chiefly because the two images of Gish indicate a polar opposition that she keeps in balance throughout the film. Her performance ranges between innocence and experience, between stereo-typical girlishness and wry, sophisticated maturity—the latter quality giving *True Heart Susie* much of its continuing interest. In other ways, too, Gish adopts a variety of expressive attitudes for the role. As the narrative develops, she exhibits distinct personae that mark the growth of the character; and within individual sequences, her performance involves multiple faces that the audience is *supposed* to notice—especially when Susie is shown masking her feelings around others. If we look at her work more closely, we can see that it also entails a variety of acting styles, creating a complex emotional tone within Griffith's otherwise simple story. Thus, although Susie may be a "true heart," her identity (much like Gish's public identity as a star) is created out of disparate, sometimes contradictory, moments, all held together by a name, a narrative, and a gift for mimicry. The minor disturbance of illusion in the sequence I have described helps call attention to the way Gish normally keeps differing elements of the characterization in harmonious relation, maintaining a sense of unity across scores of shots.

I want to emphasize Gish's variety because *True Heart Susie* requires a good deal more actorly invention than is usually recognized. Then, too, I hope to counter the misleading notion that good movie acting consists of *being* rather than *meaning*. In certain ways, of course, we hardly need to be reminded that Gish was a player who contributed artistic labor to her films; her scenarios were constructed to highlight her emotive talents, and the silent medium made her seem an artist by definition, a "poet" who suggested char-acter through pantomime. Even so, the dominant theory of movie acting after 1914 was articulated in terms of "natural," transparent, behavior. "We are forced to develop a new technique of acting before the camera," Griffith wrote. "People who come to me from the theater use the quick broad gestures and movements which they have employed on the stage. I am trying to de-velop realism in pictures by teaching the value of deliberation and repose" (quoted in Gish, 88).[1] As a result, performers like Gish were frequently praised for their authenticity, a quality that transcended mere art.

The star system contributed to an increasingly antimimetic conception of acting because it made some of the links between actors and roles seem inevitable. Almost from the beginning, movie stars were regarded as aesthetic objects rather than as artists, or as personalities who had a documentary reality. Griffith and many other directors strengthened the "organic" effect by inserting details from an actor's real life into the fiction. In *True Heart Susie*, for example, when Susie carries on imaginary conversations with the photograph of her dead mother, the picture she looks at shows Lillian Gish's own mother, cradling the infant Lillian in her arms. When William later tells Susie that men flirt with "painted and powdered" women but marry the "plain and simple ones," the joke is partly on Robert Harron, who said the same thing during his offscreen courtship with Dorothy Gish. It hardly matters whether anyone in the audience recognized these details, since the deepest purpose of biographical material was to facilitate performance, helping players to merge with their parts. The emphasis on personal relevance and sincerity was further enforced by the early critical discourse on stars, which helped shape the attitudes of viewers and moviemakers alike. Thus Edward Wagenknecht, who in 1927 wrote the first extended appreciation of Gish, remarked that "she always claims the right to make her roles over to suit Lillian Gish." He praised her for expressing "her own point of view, a distinctive something which is Lillian Gish and nobody else on earth." "The part and the actress are one," he wrote. "In a very deep and very true sense, she is the profoundest kind of actress: that is to say she does not 'act' at all; she *is*" (249–50).[2]

At first glance, *True Heart Susie* lends additional support to such romantic-realist attitudes. It contains a virtual sermon on the theme of Art versus Nature, and its central character is valued precisely because she is what she

1. Gish recalled that one of Griffith's favorite mottos was "Expression without distortion," and Mack Sennett once claimed that when he tried acting for Griffith he was congratulated by the director for simply standing in front of the camera.

2. Wagenknecht's rapturous mystification of Gish is understandable, given her charm, and is no different from countless other essays about actors. Compare, for example, George Bernard Shaw's comments in the English *Saturday Review* of the 1880s, on the stage performances of Mrs. Patrick Campbell: "Who wants her to act? Who cares twopence whether she possesses that or any other second-rate accomplishment? On the highest plane one does not act, one is. Go and see her move, stand, speak, look, kneel—go and breathe the magic atmosphere that is created by the grace of all those deeds. . . ."

Interestingly, although Hollywood promulgated similar ideas, it sometimes tried to create counterillusions that would selectively dispel them. Hence, the typical fan magazine story that showed an actor like Edward G. Robinson at home among his paintings and children, a happy bourgeois rather than a Little Caesar. Dorothy Gish once joked about how her sister was confused with her screen persona: "The popular conception of Lillian as soft and dreamy makes me think of the gag used too often in the comic strips. A hat lies upon the sidewalk; some person kicks it enthusiastically and finds to his astonishment and pain that there is hidden inside it a brick" (*The Movies, Mr. Griffith, and Me*, 96).

seems. "Is real life interesting?" Griffith asks in the first title card, and the story, as it develops, becomes a parable about craft and deception in conflict with simple, artless goodness. Susie, the true-hearted country girl, is contrasted at every point with Bettina (Clarine Seymour), the scheming milliner from Chicago: Bettina drives around in "Sporty" Malone's flashy car, dances the Charleston, and engages in loose sex; meanwhile Susie embraces her cow, does spontaneous dances of joy, and lives in single-minded devotion to William. Bettina spends a good deal of time in front of a mirror, fashioning an image, whereas Susie is shown hoeing the fields or sitting by the hearth. Bettina "acts" in flamboyant style, deceiving men with her paint and powder, but when Susie tries to follow suit, daubing her face with cornstarch (a homelier, more "honest" substance that is all she can afford), her puritanical aunt berates her: "Do you think you can improve on the Lord's work?" The equation seems exact: if Art is as bad as Bettina, then Nature is as good as Susie— hence, by a process of association, we might argue that Gish is profound to the degree that she rejects old-fashioned theatrical mimesis, letting her moral "self" shine through the fiction.

But when we examine Griffith's parable more closely, it doesn't work out so neatly. All three major characters aspire to middle-class respectability, and this desire involves them in various degrees of "acting." *True Heart Susie* is therefore filled with performances-within-performance: Bettina is the most obviously theatricalized figure, batting her eyes seductively at William, playing a carefully contrived role that enables her to capture the town's most eligible bachelor. Prior to her entry on the scene, however, William has also developed an image for himself. When he returns from college, he no longer behaves like a rube; grandly stroking a new mustache, he parades the streets and practices a sermon, using Susie as his enraptured audience. As for Susie herself, she is in one sense as much a schemer and actor as Bettina. She decides early in the film that she will change William from a bumpkin into an educated pillar of the community ("I must marry a smart man!"). She sells her farm animals in order to pay William's college tuition, and then keeps the source of the money secret, playing the innocent companion. From the first we see that she is more clever than William; unable, because she is a woman, to become a Horatio Alger, she determines to create one and marry him. And although she is less sophisticated than Bettina, she seems no less sexually and romantically driven, ready at any moment to dress up for William. Bettina is in fact Susie's doppelgänger, as Susie inadvertently acknowledges in the scene where, overcome with pity, she holds her ailing rival in her arms. The real difference between the two is that Susie is wiser and more self-sufficient, and her craftiness is benign; William is her work of art.

It is difficult to say exactly how much Griffith wants the film to be interpreted in this ironic fashion. Like the novelist Samuel Richardson, he is too didactic to be described as a formal realist, and too realistic to be described as a "primitive" or a wish-fulfilling fantasist. Terry Eagleton's remarks on Richardson's *Pamela* could be applied with little qualification to *Susie:* "Do we laugh with Pamela at the novel's solemn moralizing of her 'baser' motives, or laugh with the novel at her . . . self-apologies? Do we have the edge over both the novel and Pamela, or does the novel have the edge over us all?" The problem confounds us because Richardson's writing (like Griffith's direction and Gish's performance) seems compounded of two voices, neither having absolute priority. The result is what Eagleton describes as an uneasy relation between "the metalanguage of bourgeois morality" and a "still resilient popular speech" (*The Rape of Clarissa,* 32–33).

The film seems only partly aware of the discrepancy, and its plot goes through a series of improbable twists in order to achieve a happy ending. Bettina steals William from Susie, marries him, and becomes a philandering wife. One evening, she finds herself accidentally locked outdoors during a rainstorm. Her exposure to the elements gives her pneumonia, and even though Susie nurses her, she dies. Later, one of Bettina's friends tells William the truth about his dead wife's infidelity, and at nearly the same moment he learns that Susie paid for his education. Soon afterward, in an especially coy scene, we see him proposing marriage to Susie from outside her flower-bedecked window. They consummate a long-deferred kiss, and to make the ending still more rosy the film transforms Susie—now a mature woman who has suffered rejection—back into a girlish innocent: Griffith closes with a reprise of an image we saw near the opening, showing William and Susie *as children,* walking together down a country road. The soft focus shot is bathed in a nostalgic light, and a title card asks us to imagine the two "as they once were." Thus, using plot conventions of nineteenth-century melodrama, together with certain events from Dickens's *David Copperfield* and *Great Expectations,* Griffith has awkwardly smoothed over the many contradictions that sustain an ideology of the natural self.

As Thomas Elsaesser and others have pointed out, this sort of plot has a long history; where *Susie* is concerned, the ancestry of the narrative can be traced back not only to Richardson's novels but also to the eighteenth-century dramatic genre known in England as "sentimental" or "weeping comedy." Literature for the stage in the eighteenth century was designed to challenge the cynical attitudes of Restoration drama (much as Griffith denounces flappers and city slickers), showing bourgeois life in its best light. Leading characters were admired for their sincerity or "sentiment"—a term that suggested "virtuous or moral emotion"—and the chief acting style, made famous by the tragedian David Garrick, involved painterly *tableaux,* in which the players struck elaborate poses (Todd, 34). The typical plot formula combined pathetic and comic situations, resolving all conflict in the fifth act and confirming marriage and sensitive fellow-feeling as the ultimate good. Oliver Goldsmith joked about the form, noting its hypocritical tendency to forgive any fault or reprieve any character "in consideration of the goodness of their hearts." Nevertheless, sentimental comedies multiplied, directly influencing Victorian literature and, indirectly, the Hollywood narrative. The leading characters of such dramas also helped to form the style of early movie stars. Gish, for example, repeatedly played women whose emotions were "spiritualized," motivated by a simple goodness of heart. Charles Chaplin is a more complex, refined version of the same type. As David Thomson notes, "Chaplin's persona is often very close to eighteenth-century sentimentality: a beautifully mannered dreamer who has trained himself into the emotional sensibility that will sometimes shame a woman" (98).

Variants of bourgeois sentimental comedy can still be found in modern theater and films, disguised somewhat by naturalistic conventions and inflected by the Freudian "family drama." Critics nearly always treat Griffith's uses of the form with condescension, but the survival of the basic plot indicates that we have not moved far from his values—especially as they are expressed in marriage, family life, and charity toward the weak. Raymond Williams has cautioned historians not to take these values lightly:

> The wider basis of sentimental comedy, and of a main tradition in the novel, was the particular kind of humanitarian feeling, the strong if inarticulate appeal to a fundamental "goodness of heart"; the sense of every individual's closeness to vice and folly, so that pity for their exemplars is the most relevant emotion, and recovery and rehabilitation must be believed in; the sense, finally, that there are few absolute values, and that tolerance and kindness are major virtues. In rebuking the sentimental comedy, as in both its early examples and its subsequent history it seems necessary to do, we should be prepared to recognize that in point of moral assumptions, and of a whole consequent feeling about life, most of us are its blood relations. (*The Long Revolution*, 288).

Seen in Williams's terms, one of Lillian Gish's achievements was to embody a "feeling about life"—making "good heartedness" plausible, conveying sweetness and moral sentiment without making us doubt her sincerity. The somewhat Cavalier ethos of American life after World War I, when a good many important stars were beginning to resemble college boys or flappers, made this job especially difficult; Gish was able to maintain her stardom into the middle twenties (when L. B. Mayer tried to talk her into having an "affair" that the studio could publicize) only because she was a master at expressing believable contradictions within her old-fashioned characters, hinting at sensuality and sophistication even in a purely bucolic role like that of Susie.

Gish's ability both to play comic scenes and to give a relatively complex tone to pathos also suggests that she was far from being a "natural" personality whom Griffith employed in appropriate fictional contexts. True, she had physical characteristics well suited for Griffith's fantasies of delicate, idealized girls tormented by brutish males. Never an extraordinarily beautiful or striking woman, she had a china doll's complexion and an ability to look young (which she retains even today). To a degree, however, her physical appearance was the product of design. Her features seem petite and regular— the perfect incarnation of WASP beauty—but she has said that she never laughed in her early films because her mouth, which is so tiny on the screen, was oversized in relation to her eyes.[3] She is usually described as "frail," but her softness was an illusion, like Chaplin's. She was small but strong, as anyone can see from her erect carriage, which in some contexts made her look prim. She had an iron constitution, a highly conditioned and flexible body, a cheerful and attractive face, and a capacity for delicate gestures. Out of this raw material, aided by her intelligence and apparently Spartan devotion to her job, she made herself into a memorable character type and an expressive instrument with more range than is immediately apparent.

Gish specialized in child-women with a strong maternal streak—a description that already suggests some of the oppositions she was able to contain. Despite the cloyingly sweet roles she was given, she was able to seduce the audience and redeem the movie, sometimes with such skill that her art was invisible. Thus Charles Affron, who recognizes her inventiveness in other contexts, finds her merely "adorable" in *True Heart Susie,* a film he describes as a "personal" and "original" Griffith work in which Gish is "never asked to be anything more than cutesy-pie." Her performance, he claims, is "simplistic" and "shackled by sweetness" (48–47). The trouble with this conclusion is that if the film works—and virtually everyone seems to agree that it does— it must do so largely because of Gish, who contributed to its most compelling imagery and who completes what one might call the "writing out" of the plot through action. In fact Gish is asked to do a great deal in the course of the film. Not only must she convey Susie's growth from innocence to experience, charting the turns of the narrative; she must also provide a lively charm that will countervail self-sacrificing goodness. As she herself once put it, "Virgins are the hardest roles to play. Those dear little girls—to make them interesting takes great vitality." At every moment, therefore, she suggests a duality in her character, making us feel cleverness beneath youth, strength beneath fragility, humor beneath spirituality, and sexual warmth beneath propriety. To do all this, she has to call upon a variety of skills and a number of possible "selves." In the following brief analysis, I try to point out some of them,

3. Griffith's racist imagination prompted him to turn Gish into an Aryan ideal, but he was not alone in such attitudes. Throughout the silent period, the faces of "spiritualized" characters were supposed to have small, delicate features. As late as the thirties, Humphrey Bogart was typed as a villain partly because executives at Warner Brothers thought his lips were too large to play a sympathetic leading man; ironically, as Louise Brooks has pointed out, Bogart's mouth was quite beautiful, and once he became a star, it turned into his most expressive feature: "Bogey practiced all kinds of lip gymnastics . . . Only Eric von Stroheim was his superior at lip-twitching" (*Lulu in Hollywood,* 60).

illustrating the range of tasks she accomplishes in the course of what might seem one of her simplest performances.

Gish was influenced by the pantomime, or mimetic, form of acting she had learned in turn-of-the-century theater. But in Griffith's films, even at this relatively late period, players could swing back and forth between radically different kinds of behavior. At one extreme, especially in comic episodes, his characters used a rudimentary gestural "signing." Notice, for instance, the scene in *True Heart Susie* where Susie shares her bed with the ailing Bettina: first Gish purses her lips, squints, and doubles up her fist as if she were going to sock her rival in the jaw; then she virtually wipes away the angry expression and registers ostentatious pity, tenderly putting her arm around the sick woman. At another extreme, Griffith inherited some of the performing conventions of eighteenth-century sentimental drama. In close-ups, his actors could sometimes behave with remarkable naturalism, but they were also required to model for artfully posed moments of gestureless "restraint." The style was influenced by late Victorian portrait photography and painting, which meant that Gish had to serve not only as Griffith's Little Nell, but also as his Elizabeth Sidall and his Jane Burden. She seems to have been eager and skillful at turning herself into a pictorial representation, an object of desire; she selected her own clothes with fastidious care, she persuaded Griffith to hire Hendrick Sartov because of his ability to light her hair, and she was able to pose for virtually still, "painterly" imagery without appearing as rigid as a figure in a *tableau vivant*. *Susie* is full of these images, largely because the central character spends so much time "waiting" for her man. It is worth considering some of them to illustrate how even as a photographic model Gish appears in a variety of guises.

At one point, for example, she is Susie the rural maid, patting her cow on the neck and kissing it farewell; the dumb animal nuzzles her, its broad, hairy face in vivid contrast to her own, which is childlike, pigtailed, sad, and very pretty beneath a flat little hat. Later, preparing herself to be a "fitting mate" for her hero, she is posed like a young Lincoln, reading books by firelight, her hair gathered in a bun and a look of eager studiousness on her face. Still later, in a shot titled "Susie's Diary," we see her in her room at night, her hair down to its full Pre-Raphaelite length, as in an illustration for a pseudo-Arthurian romance. Wearing a loose dressing gown, she is seated on a stool at the right of the frame, her knees toward us and her upper body twisted slightly to the right as she leans forward on a desk to write—an unnatural position that creates a languid, graceful line and contributes to the sublimated eroticism of the image. An unmotivated keylight falls from the upper left, making her skin glow white, and backlighting halos her fine hair, which spills in ringlets down her cheeks; her lashes are lowered to the paper, her slender hand holds a pencil, and her features are relaxed and aristocratically serene.

By contrast, toward the end of the film she is depicted as a "single-track heart" and is seated more naturally at the same desk, her hair gathered in a spinsterish bun and romantically backlit; two white, furry kittens are perched on her shoulders, making her look like an angelic *Venus im Peltz*.

In shots like these Gish is virtually a piece of statuary, but in the more dynamic portions of the film she employs a wide vocabulary of movement. The demands on her in this regard would have been great in any film, but Griffith's rehearsal methods gave the leading players an especially important function in the "writing" of his stories. He seldom used a script, preferring to start with a vague outline and develop the action by positioning the players on a bare stage. Sometimes he demonstrated all the parts himself, but by 1919 Gish had become so sensitive to his methods that she was allowed to create the details of her behavior and appearance. Much of her activity in *Susie* consists of variations and sudden departures from a simple graphic set of movements: she holds her head straight and high, squarely topped by a flat, narrow-brimmed hat, keeping her arms stiff at her sides, so that when she walks her upper body seems disassociated from her legs. In the first part of the film the posture and walk are comically stylized and exaggerated; in context with the rest of the action, they suggest various things about Susie: her naive innocence, her puritanism, her directness, her single-minded devotion to a man, her almost soldierly courage, her sense of duty, and her "unaffected" country truthfulness. Her movements make an amusing contrast to Bettina's swiveling hips and butterfly gestures, especially in the scene where the two women are brought together at the ice-cream social in the local church; and although Gish modulates her behavior slightly as the character grows older and gains dignity, she often duplicates the best work of the silent comedians. Her doggedness as she paces along behind her lover is much like Keaton's; her slump-shouldered movement away from Bettina's flirtations with William is pure Chaplin; and her innocent, level-headed gaze whenever she enters or exits a scene makes her resemble no one so much as Harry Langdon.

Susie's wide-eyed face and fairly rigid upper body become a character "tag" and a recurrent joke (at one point, delighted to discover that Bettina is showing interest in another man, she skips across the floor of her room and spins in a joyful circle without moving her arms and head), but they also establish a pattern that can be broken in interesting ways. Because her posture suggests the idealism, determination, and restraint bred into her by an aunt who tells her, "Deport yourself," her moments of letting go have a special force, like emotions breaking through repression. Sometimes they also reveal new aspects to the character, as if a mask had been dropped briefly.

One of the best examples of the latter effect occurs in Gish's pantomime during the comic sequence when Susie and William walk through a lovely, almost expressionist, bower of trees on their way home from school. Susie is in an adoring trance, walking about one step behind William but occasionally brushing his arm. Each time he moves, she follows. He pauses, turns, and paces toward the camera with her immediately behind him. Awkwardly pretending that his mind is on something other than the girl at his side, he turns again and walks toward the trees; she wheels and turns with him, patiently waiting for his attention but not demanding it. Griffith cuts to a closer view as they come to a stop before a tree, showing them from the waist up, looking at each other in a shared composition. Susie stares straight up at William from beneath her flat bonnet, her eyes no longer adoring nor quite so innocent; in fact, the look has a great deal of frankly knowing sexual desire behind it, so that it tempts William and flusters him at the same time. He bends slightly to her; suddenly she leans forward on tiptoe most of the way toward his face, closing her eyes in a comic gesture of passivity. At the crucial moment he hesitates, backs off, and turns his head toward the tree so that his back is to the camera. For just an instant Gish makes a gesture that almost breaks the representational surface of the fiction: she turns her own face away from William for the first time, showing it to the camera but not quite looking into the lens. She registers frustration and sad disappointment, but she also seems to comment on William, taking the audience into Susie's confidence as if she were a roguish character in a farce. Almost immediately her expression turns back into the sad look of a little girl, but not before it has told us that her character is more clever and self-aware, more of an "actor" than we had thought.

Gish also changes the basic pattern of her behavior when she expresses hysteria or inconsolable grief. Her pantomime when she receives William's first letter from college is silly (she wrote that she had a "constant argument" with Griffith because he wanted her to play little girls as if they had "St. Vitus's dance" [99]), but her moments of pain are among the most effective in the film. At one point, wearing the flat hat and a frilly, beribboned dress that makes her look as old-fashioned as ever, she prepares for an "overwhelming assault" on William. Marching to his house, she arrives only to find him embracing Bettina, and she instantly shrinks back against a door to hide herself, holding a small black fan like a shield in front of her body. As she leaves the scene, she is hunched over and hobbling slightly, shaking with ironic laughter and tears. Later in the film, her spunky, straight-backed posture gives way completely. After the wedding of William and Bettina, she waves goodbye to the married couple, backs away into the garden behind her house, walks slowly and weak-kneed toward a fence, holds it briefly for support, and then suddenly collapses to the ground, her body curling into a fetal position. It is one of many occasions in Gish's career when she is subjected to overwhelming torment; yet here there are no bullies, no ice floes, no blasts of wind or ravages of disease—only the force of the character's emotions and a sudden release of stiff muscles.

Gish's most impressive moments, however, involve her face alone. I am referring not only to the relatively crowded middle-distance shots, which she usually dominates by her position in the frame and the animation of her features, but also to the several instances when she is given large, lengthy close-ups. Here, virtually unaided by *mise-en-scène* or expressive objects, she reduces theatrical pantomime to its most microscopic form, displaying a stream of emotions, conjoining her movements so gracefully and inventively that we hardly notice how various they are.

One of the most protracted examples of the technique is the scene in which Susie, hoeing in a garden, overhears William and Bettina conversing on the other side of a hedge. The scene serves both to illustrate how much emotion Gish could gather into a single close-up and to rebut oversimplified interpretations of the Kuleshov effect. In one sense, of course, Kuleshov was correct: the various muscular arrangements of a human face (which are "coded" differently in different cultures) have little force or meaning outside a specific narrative context. We are able to "read" the lengthy succession of emotions in this scene—tension, pain, worry, grief, numbness, anger, fear, suspicion, curiosity, confusion, shame, and so forth—partly because of Griffith's repeated crosscutting between Susie and the couple on the other side of the hedge. Once a general context has been established, however, we are able to make clear distinctions between the emotions by reference to Gish's face alone.

Later in the film—in what must be one of the more complex reaction shots in the history of movies—Gish employs the same close-up pantomime without benefit of crosscutting, using only her face and her left hand to speak to the audience. After Susie accidentally discovers that William and Bettina are engaged, she backs out of William's doorway and leans against a wall. Unseen by the couple in the next room, she tries to recover from the shock and assess her new situation. In close-up, Gish makes Susie waver between shock, grief, fear, and a sense of ironic detachment that keeps her from falling into self pity. In fact, Gish elicits more emotion from the audience than she herself shows—although there are tears in her eyes at one point, she demonstrates how the close view of the camera enables the actor to use smaller and less extreme emotional gestures. At no time is she the wilting, suffering heroine who gives way to hysterics. She laughs ironically more often than she cries, creating a drama out of Susie's precarious balance between strength and pain.

The images on the facing page represent only a few of the many faces she gives us during this crucial close-up. As still photos, they give the impression of expressive gymnastics, but in the shot itself they are linked together with such fluid transitions that Gish seems to be doing hardly anything. Turning her head away from the scene she has just witnessed, she faces the camera and looks abstractedly downward, her lids half lowered. She seems dazed or

Susie reacts to the loss of William.

lost in thought, and her left hand rises to finger the dark choker around her neck. (This movement echoes a gesture from earlier in the film when William sits on her front porch and asks if she thinks he should get married. Trying to conceal her emotions, Susie smiles pleasantly and lifts her hand involuntarily, somewhat nervously, to stroke her neck and cheek.) There is just a hint of crazed numbness in her face, an effect that owes chiefly to the unfocused look in her eye, and to a tiny wisp of hair sticking wildly out from under her bonnet. Her fingers rise slowly from the choker, moving up her throat and cheek to pluck at her right earlobe. Her head tilts and she "thinks," a sad, faraway look in her eyes. Her half-closed lids blink, her head straightens almost imperceptibly, and the corners of her eyes turn down more; she blinks again, looks up a bit, and a wry little smile breaks over her mouth. For a moment Gish allows herself a half-suppressed laugh that seems to block her tears, her hand moving down from her ear to cradle her chin. She lowers her eyelids again and purses her lips slightly, continuing to smile. Turning her head, she glances toward the room where she has just seen William and Bettina; still holding her hand to her cheek, she smiles more openly, presumably amused by the foolishness of everyone concerned in the love triangle. (At this point she looks older than at any time in the film and evokes the same sort of saddened, tolerant, maternal amusement she uses in Laughton's *Night of the Hunter* thirty years later.) Her smile fading a bit, she turns her head back toward the camera, her eyes cast to her left, looking at nothing in particular. Her head then turns to the left, and she brings her hand from her cheek to her chin. Cradling the chin once more, she brushes her lips thoughtfully with her extended little finger. Her smile has faded almost completely, and her mouth parts while her finger moves gently, pensively, back and forth across her lower lip; maternal only a moment ago, she now looks sexual and childlike, her lips forming into a moue. Her eyes blink again and glass over, as if she were in a trance. Her little finger plucks more roughly at her lip, rubs it, and then plucks it again. She turns her head back toward the room and inserts the tip of her finger between her lips, nibbling it thoughtfully. Her other fingers, spread across her cheek, clutch slightly at her face, the nails digging into her flesh in a way that suggests a sudden painful surge of emotion. She holds this position for a moment and then relaxes, moving her hand away; a slack, heavy-lidded look passes over her, and her head bobs. She seems on the verge of fainting, but then rights herself, raising her head. Her mouth opens slightly and her eyes widen in fear, her brow furrowing. She tilts her head to the right, her hand touches the choker again, and she softly rubs her neck to dispel the fearful thought.

I have dwelled upon this shot because it shows various articulations of Gish's face and also because shots of its type occur in modified form in virtually all "women's melodrama"—a genre that *True Heart Susie* prefigures. The full close-up of a woman suffering for love is the very centerpiece of such films, the image to which they all gravitate. But the actor is seldom called upon to register suffering alone. Usually, the film wants the woman to express some delicate, "restrained" mixture of pain, renunciation, and spiritual goodness—a smiling through tears that leads up to a kind of acquiescence in suffering. Barbara Stanwyck's *Stella Dallas* is a classic example, and it is interesting to compare Gish's long close-up to the one of Stanwyck described in the previous chapter. In both cases, the actor's job involves *combining* conventional expressions (anger or indignation are the only emotions the genre seems to rule out), so that the shot has a slightly ambiguous effect.

Where Gish is concerned, the close-up is especially notable on technical grounds, giving her an opportunity for straightforward, bravura pantomime, showing the remarkable range of effects she could achieve within the limits of a formula and without the aid of props, editing, or expressive photography. Her carefully modulated changes of expression also reveal something about the structure of her performances in general. She was a superb instrument for Griffith's obsessive "visions" of maidenhood crushed like a flower, and she was also good at suggesting other qualities—maternal care, sexuality, intelligence, and a prim courage and resolve that embodied elements of the pioneer ideal. In some ways, she was a more sophisticated artist than the director she always referred to in public as "Mr. Griffith"; in both the comic and pathetic episodes of this film, she gives her character an ironic self-awareness, cutting against the grain of Griffith's pastoral allegory, as if she were constantly tending toward the more plausible version of Susie that can be seen in the second image at the beginning of this chapter. Whatever her personal motives, however, her success depended on the way she collaborated with and complicated Griffith's sentimental fictions; ultimately, her different faces and gestures were organized into the illusion of a "personality," and her mime took on the power of myth.

7

Charles Chaplin in
The Gold Rush (1925)

Gish's performances were designed to harmonize the various potentialities of her roles and acting skills; but Chaplin, who worked in a different mode, sometimes created vividly antirealistic dissonances or disjunctions. In fact, Brecht once wrote that "the actor Chaplin . . . would in many ways come closer to the epic than to the dramatic theater's requirements" (56). The idea is not surprising, partly because of the social criticism in Chaplin's films, but chiefly because the *Verfremdungseffekt* has a good deal in common with the standard techniques of comic alienation. To cite an example from an un-Brechtian context, Cary Grant refers to "Archie Leach" in two of his screwball comedies, and in *His Girl Friday* (1940) he remarks that the character played by Ralph Bellamy looks like Ralph Bellamy. By its very nature, comedy undermines our involvement with the characters, barely maintaining a dramatic illusion. It might depict violent or deadly action, but it does so in a way that invites us to observe plot machinery *as* machinery. Every comic actor is therefore something of a deconstructionist, calling attention to the way we manufacture our socialized selves; this is especially true of "crazy" comedians like Chaplin, who are prone to what I have already described as "expressive anarchy." They lose control, tripping, stumbling, or behaving inappropriately; they become nervous or emotional, reacting without proper decorum; they enter or exit a little too soon or too late, slipping on banana peels at the very moments when they are most concerned to maintain dignity.

Chaplin, however, was apt to pass from comic exposure of performance to the expression of "honest" sentiment in the space of a breath, veering sharply between lyric pantomime, music hall mugging, and Stanislavskian revelation of psychological "depth." As a result, Brecht was qualified in his praise:

"Chaplin is perfectly aware that he must be 'human,' i.e., vulgar, if he is to achieve anything more, and to this end he will alter his style in a pretty unscrupulous way (viz. the famous close-up of the doggy look which concludes *City Lights*)" (50).[1]

Chaplin was indeed a sentimentalist, drawing on a tradition of sad clowns at least as old as Pierrot; but within that style his characterizations were complex, mixing sweetness and satire, switching rapidly from moments when he was the butt of a joke to moments when he was a joke's cause. Ultimately, the Tramp evolved into a mixture of waif and prankster, wit and fool—a comic everyman who exerted considerable influence on the literary imagination. Beckett used him as one of the models for Vladimir and Estragon; Hart Crane and the Brazilian Carlos Drummond de Andrade made him the subject of lyric poetry; Edmund Wilson wrote a ballet libretto for him, although it was never produced; and Brecht himself may have paid the ultimate compliment, borrowing most of the plot from *City Lights* (1931) for his play, *Mister Puntila and His Valet Matti.*

The vivid emotional and cultural contrasts out of which Chaplin built his fame are evident in every aspect of his physical style. He was an exquisite player, a "sensitive plant" whose agility and strength came as a surprise. His slight figure and delicate, unusually small hands (about which, in private, he was almost neurotically self-conscious) gave him an air of sensibility, even when his comedy was at its most coarse. He executed ordinary pratfalls with élan: he would kick both feet high in the air and hold them extended in a perfect line as he came down square on his seat; then he would absorb the shock by quickly rolling backward on his spine, legs stretching gracefully over his head while they wiggled in bug-like abandon. W. C. Fields's well-known description of him—"the best damned ballet dancer who ever lived"—was not far from the mark. Like Keaton, Chaplin could do breathtaking stunts, but his chief concern was with an incongruous mix of romantic pantomime and Rabelasian farce. Sometimes his body language had the squirmy, prissy look of effeminate British gentility; at other times, it made him seem childlike and sweet in the midst of gruff American types. Whatever the situation, he was the most cultivated comic in the movies.

Chaplin also had an extremely intelligent sense of the way his idiolect, embodied in the gradually evolving character of the Tramp, could be adjusted to different contexts and to an increasingly open social satire. *The Great Dic-*

1. More to Brecht's liking was the Bavarian comic Karl Valentin (1882–1948), a live performer in the Munich cabaret. Brecht actually co-directed one of Valentin's short films, *Mysteries of a Barbershop* (1922), which contains enough cruelty jokes to have made W. C. Fields envious. On the affinity between comic satire, deconstruction, and radical Marxism, see Walter Benjamin's comments on "Satire and Marx." Marx, Benjamin writes, "was the first to bring back the relations between people from their debasement and obfuscation in capitalist economics into the light of criticism," and in so doing he became "a teacher of satire who was not far from being a master of it. Brecht was his pupil" (*Illuminations,* 202).

tator (1940) makes it impossible to look at newsreels of Hitler's jerky, hyperbolic behavior without thinking of the Führer as the Tramp's perverse clone. And as André Bazin once pointed out, the beloved Charlie repeatedly peeps through the role of the bourgeois killer in *Monsieur Verdoux* (1947): Verdoux's moustache is trim and pointed upright at a jaunty angle, but he sometimes gives it a familiar, purse-lipped wiggle. He has Charlie's widely blinking eyes and bobbing brows, his "feminine" hand poised on the hip, and his coy chuckle accompanied by shrugged shoulders and an embarrassed, under-the-lashes look. He even carries a cane-like furled umbrella and incessantly tips his hat to the ladies, making dainty little gestures with his fingers before he jumps into frenzied action. This deliberate evocation of the Tramp gives the film its pervasive, bitter irony. For instance, at one point Verdoux is shown with his back to us, looking dreamily out a French window at a painted moon in a pose reminiscent of Charlie's most sentimental moments; sighing for Endymion, he turns and steps through a bedroom door to murder his ugly bride.

The Verdoux character is all the more disturbing when he is read as the Tramp's "unconscious" (or perhaps, as others have noted, as the flip side of the idealization of women that runs throughout the Chaplin oeuvre); but then Chaplin had always played something more than a charming comedian or a poetic vagabond. Whether he was the amoral ragamuffin of the Sennett shorts, the innocent loner of the silent features, or the morally ambiguous Verdoux, his performances inevitably gave a sense of rarified beauty amid ugliness, sorrow, and various kinds of social or psychological anger. To study his technique is therefore to learn a great deal about the entire range of acting effects; even when he takes on the role of the endearing prospector in *The Gold Rush*, he enables us to study those moments when a performer moves from comedy to pathos and to observe the artful blending of wit, sentiment, and pain.

The Gold Rush is an ingenious dramatic construction, with a double plot that mixes humorous, sentimental, and angst-ridden situations. On the one hand, it tells about the companionship between Charlie and Big Jim (Mack Swain)—a rags-to-riches tale set in the dreary but hilarious mountain cabin amid the snowy wastes, symbolizing the hardships of man versus nature. On the other hand, it tells about the romance between Charlie and Georgia (Georgia Hale)—a boy-meets-girl story set in the warmly crowded dance hall in the mining town, symbolizing the conflicts of man versus woman. The film neatly weaves together the two plot lines by linking them to the idea of loneliness: in the Mack Swain sections, the tiny figure of the Tramp is isolated against a barren whiteness; in the Georgia Hale sections, he is isolated against the social gaiety of a saloon. Sometimes a motif from the first part is brought over into the second, where it is cleverly transformed: the falling snow inside the mountain cabin is a sign of comic horror, but the "snowstorm" of pillow feathers inside Charlie's town dwelling is a sign of comic delight. Finally, the double plot is brought together when Big Jim discovers Charlie (thus recovering his lost mountain of gold) at the same moment that Charlie discovers a note from Georgia (thus, he imagines, recovering his lost love). Title cards indicate that the twin goals have been achieved simultaneously: "THE CABIN! THE CABIN!" Jim shouts, and Charlie yells "GEORGIA! GEORGIA!"—gigantic letters flashing across the screen like themes in a symphony.

But all this is a matter of words, which are the dramatist's medium. Silent film actors used movement and physical inflection; and despite Chaplin's evident powers as a dramatist, it is impossible to forget his greatness as an actor. His work in *The Gold Rush* is a model of bodily eloquence and invention from which we can derive an elementary poetics of performance.

We might begin by noting a few of the comic techniques by which Chaplin "alienates" his audience. For example, his behavior and his familiar costume are in many ways inappropriate to the conventionally realistic world established elsewhere in the film. *The Gold Rush* opens with documentary-style footage of hundreds of prospectors struggling over the Chilkoot Pass; but then Chaplin's sudden appearance introduces a note of absurdity. In long shot we see the Tramp skittering across a studio set designed to represent an icy mountain ledge, hopping around a corner on upturned shoes, holding his hat and using his cane for balance. Trying to maintain his savoir faire, he pauses and twirls the cane, oblivious to the bear that is trailing him. In the next shot (now a real exterior), he comes off the mountain by accident, sliding along a snowbank on the seat of his pants and tipping his hat to us as he bumps downward.

The gesture with the hat makes for still another type of comic estrangement. Like many clowns, Chaplin is allowed to address his audience directly, disrupting the imaginary hold that realist performance tries to secure. (Contrast a noncomic use of the same device in *The Great Dictator* when, still wearing the costume of the Führer, he steps out of his role and delivers an antifascist speech to the camera.) Even when he isn't looking at us, he frequently seems aware that someone is watching, so that his gestures are those of a character who is self-consciously borrowing from a set of nineteenth-century stage conventions. In the snowbank scene, for example, he behaves like someone who has lost his dignity in public and who tries to cover his embarrassment with exaggerated nonchalance. Rising, he does his best to look unconcerned, lifting his chin and turning his profile to the horizon in the pose of an explorer. He puts one hand on his hip and leans casually on the cane, but it sinks straight as a shot into the snowbank and he falls flat, legs bouncing in the air. Righting himself, he yanks the cane out of the snow and frowns at it as if it were the cause of the problem. He then stands up and saunters off into the blank whiteness.

Extending to everything Chaplin does in the early scenes, this sense of putting on an inappropriate act produces a comic gestural "diction" that establishes him as the classic fool. Within this image, however, there is always its opposite—a sense of Chaplin the enunciator, moving with such quick grace and falling with such abandon that the audience can always appreciate the difficulty and the clever theatricality of the show. In the next shot, for example, his silly waddle becomes a determined march, feet turned out, cane held in front of his body with both hands, elbows swinging from right to left. No longer behaving like a dandy out for a stroll, he now thinks of himself as a seasoned military guide. Pausing to find his bearings in the white limbo, he briskly snaps his cane under one arm and pulls out a map, popping it open with a flourish. An insert shows a crude drawing indicating the points of the compass. Shading his brow like an Indian scout, he looks "north," clasps the paper with both hands, and then, holding it securely, hops around to the side that points him in the right direction.

In these opening shots Chaplin is like an inky cartoon, an abstraction against the snow; elsewhere, he and Mack Swain (a well-known comic from the Sennett films) make a vivid contrast with the realistic *typage* of the people in the saloon or with the typical Hollywood glamor of Georgia and Jack. In fact, Chaplin's particular behavioral style marks him off from every other player he encounters. His entire manner is derived from classical mime and the imitative tradition of melodrama, so that he looks more like a singer or a dancer than like an ordinary movie actor. For example, while everyone else gestures and moves their lips in a fashion appropriate to naturalistic cinema, the Tramp seldom communicates with speech. Caught gnawing a bone in Black Larson's cabin, he indicates his hunger by rubbing his tummy in childlike circles; denying that he has eaten one of Larson's candles, he makes a cross over his heart. His comradeship with Big Jim is formed on the basis of cooking a shoe, and his love for Georgia is expressed by servile looks and tips of the hat. In the rare moments when he "speaks," a title card appears just as his lips are about to move. Consider the New Year's dream: the women around the table applaud fiercely, begging him to give an after-dinner talk. He stands to acknowledge them. His lips part, but suddenly a title card breaks in: "Oh I'm so happy—I can't," it says, and we return to the Tramp, who scrunches up his shoulders and grins in embarrassment. In lieu of oratory, he presents the dance of the dinner rolls.

Chaplin repeatedly foregrounds the performed quality of social behavior, using abstracted techniques like dance rather than quotidian gesture; and for the greater part of the film, the camera participates in the distanciation of his work by holding us away from him. As a director, he eschewed complex photographic effects; nevertheless, he was intensely concerned with the distance between actors and camera: "I found that the placing of a camera was not only psychological but articulated a scene," he wrote. "If the camera is a little too near, or too far, it can enhance or spoil an effect" (151). As a result, he avoided tight close-ups or compositions in depth when he performed gags; usually he put the camera at chest level, far enough away to show the Tramp's entire body, and he blocked his entrances and exits from the sides of the frame, using the flat, presentational framing of the earliest cinema. In fact, if lateral tracking movements were added to certain of Chaplin's scenes, the result would be something like the "non-bourgeois style" Brian Henderson has described in Godard. (Not coincidentally, many of Godard's compositions were derived from silent comics like Keaton or Laurel and Hardy.)

This is not to say that Chaplin was a radical artist. On the contrary, he was a theatrical conservative who preferred realistic, mainstream theater, and who thought Brechtian rhetoric was pretentious.[2] For that reason, his early, more anarchic and presentational, films with Sennett look a good deal more modernist than his later features. Even so, he recognized that slapstick comedy required visibly geometrical blocking, so that actors would seem a bit like puppets moving against a flat space. One of the most obvious instances of this technique in *The Gold Rush* occurs near the beginning of the film, when Charlie is blown by a storm to Larson's cabin. Much of the sequence is photographed with the cabin set outlined like a proscenium stage, its "fourth wall" represented by the screen. As if to emphasize the squareness of the composition, Chaplin's movements become precise, quick, and rigid, like the undercranked, slightly robotic action in the Sennett comedies. At the same time, the action is blocked so that the characters make a zany series of entrances and exits parallel to the camera, whizzing through open doors on each side of the cabin, which has become a sort of wind tunnel.

Panning movements or close-ups would have spoiled the comic, nearly abstract, geometry of this scene, just as they would spoil the antics near the end of the film when the cabin itself has been blown to the edge of a precipice. Probably the most brilliant sight gag in all of Chaplin's work, this climactic episode might have delighted Hitchcock (who would have shot it using montage and "subjective" angles to heighten our involvement with the players). Chaplin and Swain perform most of the action in a proscenium-style master shot, with the contrasting bodies of Charlie and Jim at either side of the frame balancing both the composition and the cabin.

On the morning after a gigantic storm, we see the primitive shack neatly

2. Chaplin outlines his attitudes toward theater in *My Autobiography:* "I dislike Shakespearian themes . . . I cannot identify myself with a prince's problems. Hamlet's mother could have slept with everyone at court and I would still feel indifferent to the hurt it would have inflicted on Hamlet. . . . As for my preference in presenting a play, I like conventional theatre, with its proscenium that separates the audience from the world of make-believe. . . . I dislike plays that come over the footlights and participate with an audience, in which a character leans against the proscenium and explains the plot. . . . In stage decor I prefer that which contributes reality to the scene and nothing more. If it is a modern play of everyday life, I do not want geometric design" (257).

"Geometric" performance.

poised between safe ground and a sickening chasm. A title card announces that the two men inside are in "blissful ignorance." While Jim continues to sleep, Charlie wakes and begins preparing breakfast. He crosses to the right to hang an oil lamp on the wall, and the entire cabin tilts slightly. Then he crosses to the left, and the place returns to level. Staggering a bit, he tries to shake the early morning cobwebs from his brain. As he drags a heavy breakfast table across the floor, the cabin leans; he turns the table a bit, walks around it "uphill," and the room balances. The gentle sway of the cabin causes Jim to wake up, but at first both men assume they have a hangover. Suspense is prolonged and milked for comedy by having them remain for a time at opposite sides of the room. Jim rises and crosses left to get his coat at the same moment as Charlie goes right, where he stands on a box and plucks icicles off the rafters to make boiling water; they recross, Jim now standing at the right and brushing off his coat. Suddenly Charlie moves to Jim's side and the cabin starts to pitch; but Jim walks left just in time to rock it back in place. Jim's enormous weight makes the room crash down so hard that the walls shudder, and for the first time the two men suspect that they are not having stomach trouble. Standing at either side of the screen, they look at each other. Charlie tests the floor by jumping up and down. Then they each walk in little circles, Charlie jumping with Ariel speed and Jim with Caliban heaviness. Nothing budges. Charlie shrugs everything off and goes about his business, but as he walks over to Jim's side of the room the building sways again and he collapses into the big man's arms. They both scramble wildly to the left as the breakfast table slides toward them, ultimately managing to shift everything back to level. Holding one another, they try a cautious experiment: easing to the center of the room, each man puts his weight on his left foot. The cabin sways dizzily, and Charlie begins running up the incline, his feet spinning but his body staying in place, just as it did in the earlier, "wind-tunnel," sequence. At last he inches forward enough to rock the place level, but as it falls his momentum pitches him forward into a hot stove, which sends him zinging back across the room, starting the process over again.

Throughout most of this action, the camera is positioned as it must be, like the axis of a teeter-totter. The initial sequence has already established that there are doors at either side of the room, and Chaplin occasionally cross-cuts to the outside, letting the audience know that one door opens to safety, the other to an abyss. Sometimes, too, he switches to a relatively close reaction shot of one of the panicked prospectors; but as the sequence builds to a harrowing climax, with the cabin suspended by a rope at forty-five degrees over the cliff's edge and the two men climbing on one another's shoulders to escape, he keeps returning to the proscenium view, building laughter out of the silly right-left pattern of movement. The distance of his camera also allows us to witness the acrobatic skill of the actors, who perform a complex choreography without much help from the cutting, and who get laughs from the smallest business. When Chaplin tests the floor, he makes a baggy-pants plié and then does a series of quick hops, bending his legs at the knees like a cricket. When he opens the wrong door and finds himself dangling over the precipice, he scrambles back inside and stands there, his entire body weaving in graceful concentric circles. Leaning against the door for support, he flies out again and has to struggle back; he then neatly tilts on his heels, balances for a moment, and flops over in a dead-out faint.

As the sequence develops, Chaplin's facial expressions range from woolly-brained incomprehension to outright terror, and they usually involve some comic exaggeration of old-fashioned, "stagy" postures. At one moment he is the wilting heroine of melodrama, chin tossed back, eyes closed, hand grasping his forehead; later he is a comic ironist, frozen in a belly crawl on the deeply tilted floor, glaring out the door at Jim (who has finally escaped), and signaling with his forefinger like a man summoning a waiter. Some of his funniest looks are minimal. Realizing that the slightest movement could send the cabin slithering down the mountain, his normally animated features lock into a stupified mask, and he communicates with Jim by a series of eye blinks; suddenly he tries to repress a coughing fit, eyes boggling and then growing woozy from stiff-necked desperation.

Swain's face is no less comic, but he is inherently funny-looking. His dour, almost primitive reactions and the sheer ridiculousness of his physiognomy, which James Agee described as "a hairy mushroom," make him the perfect foil to the Tramp's delicate frenzy. Earlier in the film, when Chaplin crosscuts between himself and Swain as they dine on a shoe, Swain hardly needs to bat an eye; we can imagine what an appetite he must have, and his slightly ravaged but exasperated expression is balanced perfectly between disbelief and a mounting what-the-hell willingness to taste Chaplin's boot. By contrast, Chaplin's features are spiritual and articulate. Unlike the more American and "monosyllabic" Keaton (who was also pretty and soulful), Chaplin is a "talkative" mime, his arpeggios of expression serving as a defense against brutes.

The mercurial changes of Chaplin's face are well suited to comedy. The genre serves to remind us that we are chameleons in everyday life, acting out different roles in different situations, and Chaplin's Tramp makes this quality especially apparent. In the course of *The Gold Rush*, he behaves like an explorer, a headwaiter, a manservant, a millionaire, a tango dancer, a lover, and a host of other things. One reason he is a comic hero is that there is usually a disparity between his grand actions and his humble "essence."[3] In every

3. In comedy, the distance between essence and reality is usually established by context. (In Chaplin's case, his clothing and the whole plot of the film signify that he is a tramp foolishly behaving like a lover.) But it is also reinforced by gesture. The actor's job is to single out certain conventions of performance and exaggerate them, signalling that the character is pretending

Chaplin and Georgia Hale "quote" melodrama.

way he is what Leo Braudy describes as a "theatrical character"—a figure who *acts* and who lets us see the artificiality of his performance. For example, he lapses into grand sweeps and flourishes of Delsartean rhetoric when he bids goodby to Georgia and sets off with Jim to claim the gold mine: he first embraces Georgia and then does a kind of waltz step out from her arms, holding her extended hand. She leans one arm back on a nearby table, extending the other toward him in a graceful line. He throws his head back, lifts his free hand over his head in a triumphant pose, and rises on his toes to his full height. Proclaiming victory like a man on a soap box, he releases Georgia, tosses his head back even more, and puts a hand over his heart to signify eternal love. Then he extends both arms, waltzes forward to her on his toes, bends, and kisses her extravagantly on the hand. Stepping back to an "upstage" position, his face glowing with idealistic ardor, he puts both hands on his bosom. He then flings his right arm out and sweeps it across his chest, pointing offscreen left to indicate the direction of his journey. (See p. 123.) He rises on his toes again to declare that he will remain true, but he is interrupted by a comic reversal: Big Jim's arm comes in from offscreen, grabs his pointing hand by the wrist, and yanks him out of the scene like a floppy towel.

The humor of the scene comes partly from Charlie's resemblance to a ham actor who gets the hook. *The Gold Rush* contains many superb illustrations of such exaggerated performance-within-performance, all of them dependent on Chaplin's mimic skill. For example, when the tramp cooks his shoe for Thanksgiving dinner and pretends it is an elaborate meal, the situation *per se* is not funny. Prospectors in the Yukon did in fact starve or turn to cannibalism, and according to Jack London they sometimes made an edible mush out of their moccasins. Chaplin's routine, however, would be humorous even if he were eating real food, chiefly because of the way he caricatures a man with extravagant table manners. He is "acting" the meal, improvising various culinary possibilities out of inedible material, and at the same time transforming himself into a series of stock characters—from chef, to waiter, to gourmet. Throughout, his behavior calls attention to comic phenomenon that

---

rather than being. For instance in Shakespeare's *Henry IV, Part I* (a play that figures in my later discussion of *Holiday*), Falstaff is funny because he is a fat wastrel who tries to behave like a chivalrous knight. The prince might have been funny, too—like Zorro playing a fop or Superman playing Clark Kent—if Shakespeare had given him a sillier, less convincing type to impersonate or if the character were supposed to give a less convincing performance. The most amusing scene between the two is a play-within-the-play, where they exchange roles and act out an imaginary interview between Hal and the king (an interview that the play later shows us seriously, "in reality"). Notice how Orson Welles conveys Falstaff's make-believe in *Chimes at Midnight* (1967): perched fat and filthy on a makeshift throne, a pot on his head to represent Henry's crown, he gives a brilliant parody of John Gielgud's fastidious voice. (Or perhaps it is Gielgud himself whom we hear, dubbed in place of Welles.) A moment later, we see Gielgud as Henry, playing his role with such tragic dignity that we take his representation as truth.

Tasting a shoe nail.

Sartre observed in society at large: "The child," Sartre wrote, "plays with his body in order to explore it, to take inventory of it; the waiter in a café [much like the chef or the diner] plays with his condition in order to *realize* it" (quoted by Goffman, *The Performance of Self* 75–76).

And yet even though this famous scene can be used as a definition of comedy, it has another quality as well. The situation is pitched near to real horror, and the camera watches Chaplin from a relatively close vantage, framing his spot at the table and bringing us near to the character's suffering. His makeup is a visible, chalky pancake with heavy black circles beneath the eyes, but there is an authentically glassy, hallucinated look on his face. It would be wrong to say that his performance resembles the "black comedy" of Kafka or the absurdists, but he never lets us forget the ugly details of privation, and he creates a chilling pathos beneath the laughter.

The mixed effect is basic to Chaplin's work. Although he seldom invites the audience to identify with his character in the same way they would with the protagonists of realistic drama, he involves them in a more complex way than the other silent comics. *The Gold Rush* can be read not only as a slapstick comedy but also as an allegory of Capital, full of symbolic implications about Greed, Fate, and the *condition humaine;* hence the Tramp is designed to elicit the audience's sympathy more directly than the typical clown. The essential comic disparity in his behavior, as Raymond Durgnat has pointed out, is that he is like "a child trying to be an adult" (*The Crazy Mirror,* 78). Given the barren environment and the stark conflicts of this film, he becomes a fantasy object, a symbol of elemental, infantile anxieties. Besides the fear of poverty and starvation, he enacts the fear of abandonment and isolation, to say nothing of the fear of being surrounded by bigger, intimidating "adults." Of course he is also, in Durgnat's phrase, "a tramp trying to be a dandy," and is the most self-consciously artistic or aestheticized hero in American cinema, so close to a familiar literary type—the fin-de-siècle poet caught in the gutter—that it is intriguing to imagine how the young Chaplin would have played Stephen Dedalus.

The various strands in Chaplin's work—clownishness, grace, pity, and fear—are perfectly blended in the "Oceana Roll" dance, which derives its name from a popular tune published by Lucien Denni and Roger Lewis in 1911. The routine is an old gag from the Sennett days (Fatty Arbuckle did something like it in *The Cook* [1918]), but it has been transformed utterly by a new context and by Chaplin's mime. As with the Thanksgiving dinner sequence, the comedy derives from performance-within-performance, in this case the Tramp's imitation of a dancer, using forks inserted into dinner rolls which he manipulates on a table top. As usual, there is a comic distance between his shabby appearance and his grand theatrical manner, but more specifically, he gets laughs out of the contrast between the high seriousness of his face and the jazzy, cartoonish look of his dancing "feet." Besides foolishness, there is considerable wit in the performance, which contains a number of clever reversals or sudden changes of dancing style, all of them executed with graceful dexterity. Underneath all this, however, there is an atmosphere of pathos, partly because of the way the dance is situated in the plot. It is part of the dream in which Charlie imagines he is entertaining Georgia and her friends, and the image at the close of the sequence—a gaggle of women in finery and paper hats, laughing and applauding—is almost sinister in its implications: Georgia is flirtatious and manipulative, and the fat woman seated at the right of the frame is as much an evil caricature as the bloated capitalists in Eisenstein. (In the terms of Bazin's argument, we could say that somewhere within the Tramp there was always a latent Verdoux.)

Most of all, the scene derives its pathos from Chaplin's saddened, highly sensitive visage above the dancing forks. It sets him against a dark limbo that functions like the background of a puppet theater, with his head spotlighted by a circle of light so that his face becomes a central part of the drama. We see him holding the forks just below the point where his jacket closes over his tie, the dinner rolls poised on the table like turned-out feet and the handles of the forks looking like tiny bowed legs. The difference in proportion between the parts of his "anatomy" is comic, and the effect is heightened by his lofty attitude. His face is theatrically serene and serious, the eyelids lowered

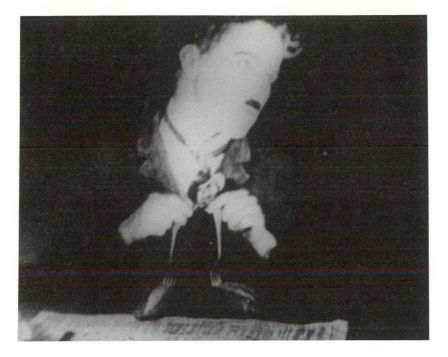

The dance of the rolls.

demurely, the lips closed and slightly pursed. He begins by ever so gently moving his body to imagined music, lifting his shoulders, swaying to the left, and turning his head in a three-quarter profile to the right. Suddenly he lifts both "feet," stomping them rhythmically and kicking one "toe" up to his nose. For a while he repeats this step, turning his head to one side and then the other, his upper body remaining as soulful as a ballet dancer's, his puppet legs moving in vaudeville style. He then adds flourishes to the routine, making a little twirl with each foot before kicking it up to his nose, quickly skipping to the side. The right foot crosses over the left, the head scrunches down to the level of the hands and looks like a doll's, gazing wide-eyed and blankly out at us while the shoulders and legs sway from side to side. Kick right, cross, sway. The feet quickly turn profile, pointing right, and execute a little "run," the head glancing down and bobbing with each step; then a turn front, a crossover step, and a sudden buck-and-wing to the left. As if captivated by his own skill, Chaplin makes a few more twirls of each foot, his eyebrows raised, his lips pursed, and his eyes rolled up to the sky. After a shuffle to the right and left, he does a slow split, the toes pointed straight up, the head bowing ceremoniously toward each foot, chin touching the toes. The feet then slide together, lift the body upright, shuffle a bit to the left, and stop. The dancer smiles, modestly acknowledging everyone's applause.

The dance is performed in a single shot that brings us closer to Chaplin's face than we have been at any point. Looked at closely, his expressions have an ambiguous effect. In one sense, he is Charles Chaplin "himself"—an exquisite personality spotlighted and set apart from the onward movement of the narrative, showing off for the audience of the film. In another sense he is a clownish character who is playing a dancer, sometimes glancing upward with graceful aplomb, sometimes peering down with childlike concentration. Still again he is a shy, slightly nervous young man, looking wan and ethereal in his shabby garb, who is seeking the approval of the film's diegetic audience. In other words, his face functions partly as a "personal appearance," partly as a mask determined by the performance-within-performance, and partly as the "genuine" look of the character. It is as if Chaplin were simultaneously putting on an act and revealing the essence of his soul.

Within this ambiguity, we can see two exactly opposite functions of theatrical gesture. The actor of comedy lets his movement seem foolish, exaggerated, or marked in some way as an act; he performs in a double sense, making his work visible to us as a socially determined code or ritual. In contrast, the actor of Aristotelian pathos uses gesture as an indication of sincerity; his movement becomes an expression of the character's essential self, a window onto being. The difference between these two functions is not a matter of how stylized or foregrounded the gestures might become, since highly conventionalized or expressionist acting can seem quite serious. The key to traditional comedy lies not in the form of movement itself but in the revelation of a disparity between character and sign.

The mixed effect of the "Oceana Roll" dance has to do both with its context and with its intimacy. It would be absurd to say that any camera angle is inherently either comic or serious; nevertheless, most American comedy, from the silents of Chaplin and Keaton to the most talkative films of Hawks and Lubitsch, has been relatively sparing in its use of close-ups. The general notion is that a tight shot should be reserved for moments of intense psychological emphasis. In *The Gold Rush,* therefore, close-ups nearly always involve non-comic acting or sudden intrusions of indeterminacy and ambiguity into scenes of comic melodrama. Early in the film, for example, there is a quite unexpected tight shot of "Black" Larson (played by ex-vaudeville comic Tom Murray) that briefly transforms him from a stock villain into a beleaguered prospector. Notice also that the montage of faces in the saloon during the singing of "Auld Lang Syne" seems almost like a documentary of suffering. As for Chaplin's own close-ups, they function like a microscope or X-ray, de-emphasizing makeup, costume, and gesture—everything, in fact, that normally constitutes theatrical performance—while seeking out his "true" expression.

An important instance is the largest close-up of the film: the moment when Charlie wakes from his New Year's dream and finds that no guests have come

Chaplin's "doggy look."

to his party. The image of laughing women dissolves to show him at an empty candlelit table, his head bent over in sleep; he wakes, goes to his door, and looks out, remaining in that position while the film crosscuts between him and the activity at the "Monte Carlo." The shot has an almost candid effect, making the lines and ridges of Chaplin's face visible, denying him the distance that comedy or even theater seem to require. From this vantage, and in this context, his expression vaguely resembles that of the suffering women in Griffith. He is shown in profile, head bent in dejection, hair slightly rumpled from sleep, face lit with a hard light that throws very little shadow. There is a wilted flower in his lapel—a rose like the one that appeared in the corner of a title card when Georgia was introduced to the audience—and he is posed against the black void beyond the open door. He wears no visible makeup and does not contort the muscles of his face, relying on slack flesh and a single pouch or seam beneath the right eye to give him a haggard, faded look. He "performs" slightly more than some actors might have, blinking his eyes once and making a tiny movement of his lips, as if he wanted to smile but could not make the edges of his mouth turn up. Finally he closes the door and turns toward the camera, gaze downcast, looking teary-eyed. Then he heaves a sigh and steps out of the frame.

If there is any important difference between what actors typically do in comedy and what they typically do in dramatic movies, it is exemplified in this "gestureless moment," when Chaplin no longer creates his character with the broad, projected mimicry of a stage performer or a dancer. His half smile, his blinking eye, his downturned head—all these are conventional signs of pathos, indications of an outward display; nevertheless, the primary impression left by the shot is of a man *thinking,* observed by no one at all. The player's feelings, the thoughts that flit through his eyes as he inserts himself into the role, have become the stuff of the performance. We can easily recognize that the scene is fictional, but the actor strikes us as no longer "representing" a self; his close-up becomes a minimalist art, bordering on no art at all.

At least since the time of Griffith, close-ups have been used in this way, to make the cinema's gestures transparent, evoking a sense of emotional truth. In Chaplin's case, however, we have an especially clear instance of an actor who employs the entire range of performance effects, rapidly manipulating the relationship an audience has with a character. Perhaps that is why—as if to indicate his skill—he chooses to end *The Gold Rush* on a more self-reflexive note: the comic terror in the mountain cabin is now over, and he and Jim are millionaires sailing out of Alaska on a liner. Charlie agrees to pose for a newsman's "before and after" photograph, and momentarily dons his old costume as the Tramp. By comic accident, he encounters Georgia, who is hiding on the boat as a stowaway. They kiss, posing in close-up for the cameraman. A title card shows Charlie remarking, "Don't spoil the picture." The line bestows a genial irony on the typical Hollywood happy ending, but it also reminds us that the intimate gestures of love, however transparent they seem, are as much a matter of performance signs as the distanced, "acted" gestures of a clown.

8

Marlene Dietrich in
Morocco (1930)

Dietrich's work with Josef von Sternberg involves what Freud, in another context, called a "transvaluation of values." Neither a realist nor a comic, she inhabits a realm where visible artifice becomes the sign of authenticity. She also challenges our ability to judge her acting skill, because her image is unusually dependent on a controlled, artful *mise-en-scène*. In fact, to hear Sternberg tell it, she was little more than his masochistic slave. In his curious autobiography, *Fun in a Chinese Laundry,* Sternberg treats her with a mixture of cool admiration and catty, paranoid contempt—exactly the tone of a spurned, neurotically proud lover. His frequent comments on movie acting are equally scathing: "The more I ponder on the problems of the artist, the less they resemble the problems of the actor" (97). "An actor is turned on and off like a spigot, and like a spigot, is not the source of the liquid that flows through him" (165). "To study acting is one thing, but to study the actor and the female of the acting species is something else again. There would be no need to study them at all were it not that [films are] dominated by them, and it is necessary to become familiar with the material one is compelled to use" (122).

Dietrich herself has not contradicted these judgements. In the documentary *Marlene* (1986), she describes her early Hollywood films as "kitsch," makes condescending remarks about the intellectual powers of women, and seems reluctant to acknowledge that she ever paid much attention to what she was doing. A number of critics have explicitly or implicitly agreed, often noting that Dietrich's work after the dissolution of her partnership with Sternberg is relatively disappointing.[1] It is well to remember, however, that Sternberg's

---

1. As one example, consider David Thomson's commentary in *The Biographical Encyclopedia of Film*, 153–55.

own reputation would be slight had he not "discovered" her. Perhaps the balance of the equation between them can be restored if we study her acting technique more closely.

Admittedly, Maria Magdalena Dietrich von Losch (her real name seems more appropriate than the one she adopted) was a player who required a special setting, and in the highly decorated world of Paramount in the thirties she found it. In most of her subsequent work she is like a celebrity guest on loan, undermining or deflecting the film's ostensible project—for example in *Seven Sinners* (1940), where she serenades John Wayne, dressed in a naval officer's uniform exactly like his own. Among her later directors, only Orson Welles cast her brilliantly, as Tana, the gypsy prostitute in *Touch of Evil* (1958). For once, she appeared in a movie that rivaled Sternberg for stylistic audacity, and she blended perfectly with the Wellesian atmosphere of self-reflexive jokes and overheated theatricalism. Otherwise, she was most effective when she played the person she appeared to be in the public mind: a grand and still beautiful star from the old days who never suffered the torments of Norma Desmond—as in *Stage Fright* (1950) and *No Highway in the Sky* (1951).

No matter what the ambiance of her Hollywood films, Dietrich nearly always took the role of a gilded, extravagant figure on a stage. She became a star who *acted* stardom, an exotic European who was rarely "naturalized" or brought down to earth. In her early days with Sternberg, she was also provocative and controversial. Her costuming, makeup, and lighting were fore-grounded to a remarkable degree, like mannerism in painting, and her style was slower, much more expressionistic than talking pictures encouraged. As a result, many viewers found her pretentious. For example, John Grierson complained that Sternberg had become a mere photographer, bent on picturing Dietrich ad nauseam: "Her pose of mystery I find too studied, her makeup too artificial, her every gesture and word too deliberate for any issue in drama save the gravest. Sternberg is perhaps still after that ancient intensity. When themes are thin it is a hankering that can bring one very close to the ridiculous" (59).

Apparently Grierson did not appreciate the humor in Dietrich's performances or the possibility that her nearly ridiculous posing was intended to challenge the normal canons of taste and decorum. David Selznick was aware of her oddity and was expressing a fairly typical industry opinion when in 1931 he remarked that Sternberg's films dealt with "completely fake people in wholly fake situations. He has forced audiences to swallow things that their intelligence would normally reject, by a series of brilliant tricks" (28). In fact, the Sternberg films with Dietrich were a baffling mixture of commercial melodrama and extreme aestheticism, of dime-novel clichés and worldly irony; even at their most self-consciously artistic, they were poised in a zone somewhere between romantic idealism, camp, and modernism, as if a certain tendency of Hollywood and late-nineteenth-century art had been pushed to such extremes that it began to deconstruct. Any commentary on Dietrich needs to acknowledge this bewildering melange of effects. The trouble is that some of the best writing devoted to her seems unable to capture the contestatory implications of her performances and the paradoxes of the Sternberg films.

The problem becomes evident when we reflect on the considerable differences among three of the most influential approaches to Dietrich, beginning with Laura Mulvey's "Visual Pleasure and Narrative Cinema," the most widely-debated essay on Hollywood in the past two decades. Mulvey makes brilliantly radical use of Freudian/Lacanian psychology, leaving a hypostasized masculine audience suspended between two mutually misogynistic avenues to pleasure: Sternberg's "fetishistic scopophilia" and Hitchcock's sadistic voyeurism. Both alternatives are phallocentric: both depend on "the image of the castrated woman" (6) and support the patriarchal values of mainstream culture. Unfortunately, as Mulvey and others have subsequently noted, such a reading offers little possibility for countercultural play; it not only suggests that female viewers are passively molded by Hollywood but also oversimplifies Sternberg and Hitchcock, both of whom anticipate and even encourage psychoanalytic interpretation.[2] And where Dietrich is concerned, Mulvey seems only to confirm Sternberg's notion that she was a sort of wax dummy or canvas upon which he painted, doubtless using the *camera stylo* as a substitute penis.

A quite different view is suggested by Susan Sontag's earlier "Notes on Camp," which briefly comments on Sternberg's links with gay subcultural style. "The two pioneering forces of modern sensibility," Sontag writes, "are Jewish moral seriousness and homosexual aestheticism and irony" (290). She associates Sternberg with the second category, but she mentions the Dietrich films only in passing, commenting on their breathtaking decorative excess. Actually, her interest is much broader; she wants to define an apolitical, decadent, but potentially subversive attitude—produced by a distinctly male imagination—that operates intermittently in Western art between the seventeenth century and the present. In the last analysis, she leaves it up to us (as camp often does) to decide exactly which products of the aesthetic tradition merit "serious admiration and study" (278).

2. There have been a great many qualifications and critiques of Mulvey's original position. See, for example, Mulvey's "Afterthoughts on 'Visual Pleasure and Narrative Cinema' Inspired by *Duel in the Sun*," *Framework* 15 / 16 / 17 (Summer 1981); D. N. Rodowick, "The Difficulty of Difference," *Wide Angle* 5, no. 1 (1982); Gaylyn Studlar, "Masochism and the Perverse Pleasures of the Cinema," *Quarterly Review of Film Studies* 9, no. 4 (Fall 1984); Florence Jacobowitz, "Feminist Film Theory and Social Reality," *Cineaction* 3–4 (Winter 1986); E. Ann Kaplan, *Women and Film: Both Sides of the Camera* (New York: Methuen, 1983), 50–52. See also Janet Bergstrom, "Sexuality at a Loss: The Films of F. W. Murnau," in Susan Suleiman, ed., *The Female Body in Western Culture* (Cambridge, Mass.: Harvard University Press, 1986).

Between Sontag's Hellenic and Mulvey's Hebraic views are the liberal-humanist readings of Andrew Sarris (*The Films of Joseph von Sternberg*) and Molly Haskell (*From Reverence to Rape*), which acknowledge a dialectic between director and star. Sarris and Haskell are well attuned to the ambiguities of the Sternberg-Dietrich collaboration and to the realpolitik of the star system. But even though Sarris recognizes Dietrich's importance, he is chiefly concerned with Sternberg's "emotional autobiography," arguing that directorial style cannot be opposed to "serious" content: "there is nothing trivial about the size of Sternberg's emotions, and nothing disproportionate in the means to express them, critics from John Grierson to Susan Sontag notwithstanding" (8). Haskell, meanwhile, is more interested in the complex implications of Dietrich's image than in the specific details of her performances.[3]

Dietrich's performing mannerisms aside, these three approaches seem equally convincing—proof of the contradictory, dialogic force of the films.[4] My own discussion has drawn freely from each of them; I would justify my pluralism by arguing that the Dietrich-Sternberg collaboration is a meeting point of at least three distinct cultural and subcultural strains:

(1) The Hollywood narrative, with its strong emphasis on heterosexual love and conflict, its patriarchal norms, and its classical form—although here we need to be more specific, noting that several of the Dietrich-Sternberg films were made before the Production Code and in the wake of silent cinema, when Hollywood was just passing out of a vogue for titillating "women's" romance derived from writers like Belasco Ibañez and Elinor Glyn. This is the aspect Sarris and Haskell emphasize, and it follows that their best observations concern things that happen at the manifest level of plot, in the conflict between male and female characters.

(2) The decadent, largely male homosexual art of the eighteen-nineties. Sternberg, one of the last dandies, might have adopted a statement by Oscar Wilde as his motto: "What the paradox was to me in the sphere of thought, perversity became to me in the sphere of passion." Dietrich's persona clearly derives from the cruel women imagined by Victorian aesthetes—Swinburne's

3. I should point out that Haskell's classic study prefigures Mulvey, since reverence and rape can be easily related to fetishistic scopophilia and sadistic voyeurism. But having suggested this crucial point, Haskell never oversimplifies Hollywood narrative pleasure and never implies that women are passive viewing subjects.

4. Here and in a few other places the reader will notice an allusion to the work of Mikhail Bakhtin. Some of my arguments have an affinity with his, chiefly because throughout this book I have stressed the heteroglossia or polysemia in roles, star personae, and films. I should like to emphasize, however, that I have not tried to apply Bakhtin in a systematic way. In fact, it seems to me ironic that Bakhtin, who privileges the novel as a literary mode, has drawn much of his important terminology—"dialogic," "carnivalistic," and so on—from the world of theater. His comments on the theme of the mask in Renaissance and Romantic literature (*Rabelais and His World*, 36–41) are nonetheless strikingly relevant to film directors like Sternberg and Welles.

Dolores, Pater's Mona Lisa, Wilde's Salome, and Sacher-Masoch's Venus.[5] At this level, psychoanalysis has an important explanatory value, even suggesting that a strong social prohibition against homosexuality gives rise to certain types of fetishistic imagination. Susan Sontag's essay on camp, however, does not employ Freud, probably because she has chosen not to use "Jewish moral seriousness" to explicate an ideologically opposed tradition.

(3) The military glamour and whips-and-bondage display of the Kurfürstendamm. This style, to which Dietrich's name tends to adhere as much as Sternberg's, is not entirely different from camp, but its tone is arch and sardonic, reminiscent of Berlin during the Weimar republic. Sternberg has described the sexual confusion of Weimar nightlife in his autobiography: "At night, when I went out to dine, it was not unusual for something that sat next to me, dressed as a woman, to powder its nose with a large puff that a moment ago had seemed to be a breast. . . . Not only did men masquerade as women, but the woods were full of females who looked and functioned like men. . . . To raise an eyebrow at all this branded one as a tourist" (228–29). Berlin in 1929, he wrote, "was an evocation by Goya, Beardsley, Marquis de Bayros, Zille, Baudelaire, and Huysmans." When he first noticed Dietrich, leaning against the wings of a stage with "a cold buffoonery, . . . indifferent to my presence," she seemed "a model who had been designed by Rops, but Toulouse-Lautrec would have turned a couple of handsprings had he laid eyes upon her" (232). Such attitudes, embodied in his films, undoubtedly provoke Laura Mulvey's analysis of "fetishistic scopophilia" and her revulsion against a sexist, latently pornographic meaning.

None of these cultural strains can be separated neatly from the others. The Hollywood norms tend to hold the potentially subversive, subcultural meanings in check, but that only serves to heighten the fetishistic playfulness, the tone of sexual humiliation, the threat of deconstruction. In effect, the dominant cultural voice causes the subcultural voices to "collaborate" in the making of a suspended, almost ruptured illusion. The resulting sexual and ideological ambiguity has been well described by Bill Nichols, who notes that Sternberg "promises pleasure in a context of presence and absence, hide and seek. . . . He stresses the tenuous alliance between our belief in the illusion and our belief in its reality. He threatens to unveil a scandal before our very eyes; he invites us to play in the gap, the wedgelike opening that his style unveils. . . . Like Yasujiro Ozu, Sternberg can be read as a modernist but, like Ozu, that decisive step toward Brecht and a political modernism is only

5. The blatancy with which Dietrich's films allude to sadomasochism is remarkable. Her introductory scene in Fritz Lang's *Rancho Notorious* (1952) shows her in a dancehall outfit, astride the back of a paunchy cowboy, riding him across a barroom floor and lashing him with a whip. The image is like something out of the Nighttown episode of Joyce's *Ulysses*, but the narrative makes it seem as if the characters were just having innocent fun.

threatened, never taken." Moreover, Sternberg's method is homologous with Dietrich's performing style, which is dependent upon "signifying that she seems to be something she is not, and that *she* is in control of the difference." In this way, "the fetish remains triumphant. What is guaranteed is the delicious, tantalizing fullness of waiting for what is promised but neither revealed nor exposed" (125–26).

Such observations could perhaps be made about Hollywood performance in general, because the stars appear before us in the form of gigantic photographs projected on a screen; the "absent" presence of actors as images, together with the images' size and the fact that they cut off and isolate parts of the body, all contribute to a fetishistic aura. But Sternberg's films with Dietrich are an extreme manifestation, raised to an unusual level of self-consciousness. They enact the drama of the fetish in all its aspects—in the form of commodity-fetishism, using Paramount's luxurious costumes for a spectacular display; in the form of aestheticism, turning Dietrich into a creature of pure art who always signals her artificiality; and in the form of Freudian psychology, making Dietrich's body an ambiguous field of sexual symbols. There is, moreover, every reason to believe that Dietrich knowingly contributed to these effects, cleverly manipulating her performances. Even in *Marlene* she finds a correlative to her early work, insisting that director Maximillian Schell never photograph her or her surroundings, so that she "appears" as nothing but a voice, speaking over old photographs; hence she remains tantalizingly present and absent, stimulating curiosity and continuing to signify mystery.

Sternberg's films insist on the same kind of paradox, and they always openly confess their obsessiveness, disarming their more sophisticated viewers. His *mise-en-scène* is fairly littered with fetishistic paraphernalia, as if Dietrich's style had prompted him to stretch the codes of Hollywood glamour farther than usual, ultimately creating a world that was too playfully perverse, too exquisite for a popular audience. His private taste for highbrow pornography, his infatuation with his star, his dandified contempt for mass taste— all these attitudes seemed to fuel his need to subvert convention, producing views of Dietrich that were finely balanced between irony and idealization. The process is evident as early as *Morocco*, before the obvious excess of *The Scarlet Empress* (1934) or *The Devil Is a Woman* (1935). In one sense *Morocco* seems to take its faintly absurd situations seriously, expressing all sorts of romantic notions about love, about the instinctual self, and about the director as a gifted individual; in another sense it makes everything a fabrication, hinting that sex is most interesting when it is slightly perverse, that the self is a masquerade, and—by means of the artistic fusion between Dietrich and Sternberg—that there is no such thing as an individual artist.

This atmosphere of double or even triple *entendre* has an effect on everything we can say about Dietrich. It extends even to Sternberg's well-known

Flaubertian boast, "I am Marlene—Marlene is me." The words function both as an assertion that he designed her image, basing it on what he saw in her and her culture, and as confession that she was his projection; at the same time, they suggest that she was an active agent, gazing back at Sternberg and determining his attitude. As a result she becomes simultaneously a sex object, an ego ideal with which he identified, and a partial shaper of his fictions. Like Sternberg himself, she is an independent character, capable of grand romantic (or masochistic) behavior, ready to shock her audience or thrill them by flouting convention. The films enforce this parallel by taking the leading metaphor of *Morocco*—"there is a foreign legion of women, too"—and combining it with the traditional themes of the vamp or the sexually domineering woman, allowing Dietrich, often wearing pants, to adopt the postures of men, standing or sitting with legs spread, arms akimbo. Occasionally during these moments, the director and star are so closely allied that we cannot tell whether Dietrich is playing a man or Sternberg is playing a woman; identity becomes costume, and in Andrew Sarris's words, "surfaces become essences."

Furthermore, while Dietrich helps to foster the psychopathology of Sternberg's "vision," her acting style and the plots of the films offer a simultaneous critique of patriarchal convention. Her slowed-down, expressionistic manner, her ambiguous gestures and illocutionary acts,[6] her evident sense of humor— these things involve a special disavowal, less like the fetishistic dynamic described by Mulvey and more like a social irony. For this reason, Dietrich's most interesting performances have opened up a marginal space for liberal or radically alternative readings, exemplified by the reactions of such diverse critics as Molly Haskell, Robin Wood, Ann Kaplan, Rebecca Bell-Metereau, and Judith Mayne.

Whatever its various effects, the Dietrich-Sternberg collaboration was anything but typical, and its success did not last for long. Although Dietrich's salary in the mid thirties was enormous, she was never listed among the top ten box-office attractions, and depression-era audiences often felt she was preposterously exotic. Paramount had begun its publicity campaign for *Morocco* by describing her as "the woman all *women* want to see" (Baxter, 75); by the end of the decade, however, Hollywood was attempting to make her more "ordinary," casting her as a saloon entertainer in *Destry Rides Again* (1939), where James Stewart tells her, "I bet you've got a lovely face under all that paint. Why don't you wipe it off some day and have a good look?"

6. Linguists often analyze utterances in terms of three "performance" functions: each statement is simultaneously a *locutionary* act (the formation of a correct sentence); an *illocutionary* act (a statement directed toward some purpose, such as asking a question, issuing a command, making an assertion); and a *perlocutionary* act (a statement that has a particular effect on a listener). A theatrical performer's interpretation of a role is largely a matter of choosing among the various illocutionary possibilities of a given sentence. See Elam, 156–66.

Over the years her primary appeal has been to aesthetes, male gays, intellectuals, and some feminist critics who see her as an emblem of assertiveness. Only in the late phase of her career, as an aging but "eternally" glamorous woman (and as a German who had entertained GI's during the war), did she become an object of nostalgia and popular affection. The old-world "military code" that Alexander Walker detects in her screen character—her apparent contempt for bourgeois comfort, her tendency to dress in soldiers' clothes, her jaunty salutes and cocked hats—was poignant in these later appearances, making her sustained beauty into something heroic, worn like a badge.

The complex implications of Dietrich's persona can be illustrated best if we turn to a specific example: her early, youthful work in *Morocco*, which was designed to make her a star. The least spectacular of her pictures with Sternberg, this film is played slowly even by her usual standard (a pacing that is partly due to the young Dietrich's awkwardness with English); nevertheless, it is one of her legendary performances, establishing her fame with Americans and influencing her subsequent appearances. Based loosely on a play by Benno Vigny, it tells the story of Amy Jolly, a cabaret singer who leaves Europe after a failed romance and takes a job in a tough Mogador nightclub. Amy's profession makes her a potential Shanghai Lily, but she is not the embittered, imperious manipulator we find in some of the later Sternberg films. Although courted by LaBessière (Adolphe Menjou), a wealthy "citizen of the world" and a Sternberg lookalike, she is clearly drawn to Tom Brown (Gary Cooper), a beautiful legionnaire. Brown, who has had affairs with everyone from the local prostitutes to the commandant's wife, cynically refuses to commit himself to the relationship. As a result, Amy accepts LaBessière's invitation, her attitude suggesting neither contempt nor any special gratitude; he, in turn, treats her with a polite restraint that barely masks his obsessive desire. Unfortunately, she cannot endure the suspense when the man she loves is sent off to battle. At an elegant dinner party, she hears drums announcing the return of troops from the desert; leaping up from the table, she breaks a pearl necklace LaBessière has given her, ignoring the beads that spill across the marble floor. When she locates Brown in a dingy, exotic bar and discovers he has been concealing his true feelings from her, she chooses passion over security. As the soldiers are about to depart once more, LaBessière drives her to the city gates; she watches the band of legionnaires marching over the horizon and impulsively rushes after them. Garbed in a fashionable white dress, she discards her high-heeled shoes in the sand and joins a motley group of camp followers. In the distance, we see her take the leash of a goat from one of the women and trudge off over a dune. Faintly, we hear a bell attached to the goat's collar, mixed with the sound of arid wind and military drums.

The absurdity of this conclusion is worthy of the surrealists. One of the great images of *l'amour fou* in the movies, its delirious mixture of romantic excess, psychological realism, and satire cannot be conveyed in a summary. The only way to do justice to such a film, and to Dietrich's performance, is to study a few important scenes more closely, using them as a microcosm of the Sternberg-Dietrich "touch."

A convenient place to start is with Dietrich's opening sequence. Realizing that this was her introduction to an American audience, Sternberg took care to make her tasks relatively undemanding. Dietrich's English was a bit clumsy, so she was given only four short lines to speak, no more than one in any single shot: "*Merci, monsieur,* you are very kind," "Yes," "I won't need any help," and "*Merci, monsieur.*" (Even at this, Sternberg later wrote that she had difficulty pronouncing "help.") Her movements, too, were kept simple: she did little more than walk up to a mark and stand there while another player approached—a staging that heightened her aura of mystery and importance, making her an object of worship. Nevertheless, the sequence must have been difficult because the camera was fixed on her at virtually every moment, and her tiniest reactions are the most important elements of the drama.

The scene begins as she materializes out of a fog on the deck of a studio-manufactured ship, dressed in a black coat and a skullcap, carrying a suitcase. She walks forward into focus with a loping, weary stride, her coat hanging open to reveal a suggestion of her body, a "masculine" independence in the sway of her arm. (The slow determination in her walk and her arm is calculated to express a sexy androgyny and a soldierly courage—she will repeat these movements in the last shot when she goes marching over the sand dune, dragging the goat behind her.) Pausing, she glances around, the figures on the deck behind her barely visible, a bleating foghorn on the soundtrack.

Here as everywhere else in the Sternberg films, Dietrich's performance consists largely of an ability to strike poses that would be almost as effective in a painting, a still photograph, or a contemporary advertisement. Her stance and her tentative glance establish her as a beautiful woman who is slightly jaded and long-suffering, still romantically stylish and independent but also melancholy and vulnerable; at the same time the technique is more than simply instrumental to the narrative. In everything Dietrich does, there is a quality similar to what the Prague structuralists, referring to literary language, described as *aktualisace*—an ostensiveness that makes us more than usually aware that we are watching a performance. Her slightly self-conscious attitudes, drawn from a recognizable lexicon of pantomimic representations, make her seem rather like a character in an old-fashioned melodrama. In certain ways she resembles the silent actors, except that her artificiality is a tease, used in the context of an impressively sophisticated visual setting; it is a deliberate "showing off" rather than a transparent "being there"—a toying with illusion that serves in part to heighten the viewer's desire.

Dietrich's style is an instance of what Roland Barthes has called the "tableau" effect, a form of drama he labels "fetishistic" because it communicates by means of static, composed, "cut-out" pictures (*Image/Music/Text*, 69–78). The entire tradition of Delsartean and expressionist theater, discussed in part one, has something of this feeling—a slowing down and drawing out of the actor's movements, a reduction of the performance to a series of *gests,* or moments when the body pauses in a slightly exaggerated posture so that the audience can contemplate the figure. But the *gest* can have different effects, depending on its context. Eisenstein, despite an aesthetic temperament comparable to Sternberg's, turned each frozen moment into a political or historical poster—consider the angry sailors in *Potemkin* or Cherkasov's elaborate poses as Ivan. (Notice also the conclusion to Haile Gerima's *Bush Mama* [1976], where a woman is caught in a freeze frame, set off against a poster on the wall behind her.) In the case of Dietrich or Sternberg, the postures are charged with sexual implication, derived from the style of cabaret and *art nouveau*.

The sexual implications of the opening sequence in *Morocco* are developed when the weight of Dietrich's bag becomes too much and she drops it to the deck, its contents spilling out. A gentleman dressed immaculately in white (Menjou) steps to her side, kneels, and begins to assist her. In close-up, he works carefully, restoring her clothes to the bag, while behind him we see her nicely stockinged legs and black high heels. The image of Menjou at Dietrich's feet, replacing the intimate articles of clothing in her bag, is an echo of those moments in *The Blue Angel* (1930) when Emil Jannings crawls about on the floor beneath her skirts or when he stands at the bottom of a stairway looking up her dress. In both films a dignified man is shown worshipping a woman from below, next to her spiky heels; she momentarily becomes a dominatrix, and the framing of the shot alludes to that primal male curiosity that in Freudian psychology is the very basis of the fetish. Considered in relation to the film as a whole, the shot also helps to illustrate how Dietrich's image was being adjusted to the requirements of Hollywood stardom. As Lola Lola in *The Blue Angel*—released after *Morocco* in the United States—she plays a working-class entertainer who is momentarily intrigued by the paternal strength of a grammar-school professor; Lola marries the professor and then watches calmly as he is humiliated and destroyed by her attraction to a cabaret muscle man. By contrast, Amy Jolly has an aristocratic manner and is made to seem "heroic" because she will ultimately give up everything for a straightforward American type like Gary Cooper.

In her own closeup Dietrich is shown gazing off into space as if to ignore the man at her feet—a striking introductory vision of her face that owes to Lee Garmes's "north light" photography and to Sternberg's growing obsession with an impressionist visual technique he shares with the nineties aes-

Dietrich's introductory close-up.

thetes. Dietrich's head is a milky-white, three-quarter profile (in her early work it was always the right profile), framed by her dark hat and the surrounding shadow and fog. Diffusion on the lens makes her softly romantic, barely revealing that her hat has a veil that covers her radiant features with dark flecks. The shot is therefore "veiled" in at least four ways—by the "Rembrandt" light, by the fog, by the lens, and by the diaphanous fabric. It is almost a signature of Sternberg, who, when he does not shroud Dietrich's face, tends to obscure it somehow, looking at it through blurred glass, through smoky air, or from behind gauzy curtains. In *The Scarlet Empress* the camera brings the curtain itself into sharp focus, Dietrich's image behind it becoming a vague digital outline.

Dietrich's slightly covered face became the most pervasive motif in these films, and the fake North-African setting of *Morocco* allows Sternberg to celebrate its meaning.[7] For example, in the opening sequence of the film, just prior to Dietrich's appearance, we see Gary Cooper and a troop of legion-

7. In his autobiography, Sternberg says that the Pasha of Marrakesh mistook the California desert for the real Morocco. If so, the Pasha knew his country even less than the Paramount artisans. From the opening shots of the film, when we hear a sort of hoochy-coochy dance and see a bespangled woman, it is clear that Sternberg is mixing his cultural stereotypes in a fairly casual way.

naires marching into the streets of Mogador, where they halt and are dismissed; Cooper puts down his rifle, lights a cigarette, and glances up at a Moroccan girl standing on a balcony, her face covered with a white veil. Eyeing Cooper, the girl brazenly lifts the covering and smiles at him. The whiteness of the image, the traditional garb, and the open flirtation all contrast neatly with Dietrich's initial appearance in darkness, her face covered with a suggestion of a European net veil, her attitude vaguely contemptuous. In both cases, the veil functions as a sexual lure, stimulating the curiosity of the male and heightening the game of hide-and-seek.

But the tease of concealment and display is only one aspect of fetishistic pleasure. Another is a sense of ambiguity, and Dietrich's performance has that quality in abundance. Her postures often create a playful confusion of both gender and other, more general, significations. Her voice and facial expressions are difficult to read, capable of sending out two messages at once or no clear message at all. Consider the famous scene near the end of *The Blue Angel* where she watches over the shoulder of her new lover as Jannings goes mad on the stage: is she awed, frightened, merely fascinated, or what? Consider also the sequence I have been describing. Once Adolph Menjou has restored her clothes to the bag and fastened it, he stands and speaks to her: "There you are. I hope I haven't forgotten anything." Dietrich pauses for a very long time, allowing the audience to study her face and wonder what the expression contains. Boredom? Contempt? Sadness? Fatigue? Perhaps all these things, together with the most typical of all Dietrich reactions—a small, slightly crooked smile that acknowledges that everything is a charade.

All this lends irony to her simple reply: "*Merci, monsieur,* you are very kind." The force of her words, their purpose as what J. R. Austin calls a "speech act," is still more ambiguous. She speaks in a low register that adds to the vaguely "masculine" aura of her personality and with a slow, neutral style that is meant to seem pregnant with meaning: "You are polite," she suggests, "but I have played this scene often, and although I am on a boat to nowhere I do not wish you to approach me any further." Having spoken, she turns and looks away. We know that she is sad and alone and also that she is ironically amused and uninterested. Menjou gracefully responds to her rebuke, as he does throughout the film, and her face becomes a mask. Ever the gentleman, he gives her his card. She saunters over to an isolated spot on the rail of the ship and there, in a medium close-up, ends the sequence with a nicely timed gesture: slowly tearing the card into pieces, she smiles to herself, places the fragments on her palm, and flicks the paper overboard.

Intriguing as this introduction is, the full import of Dietrich's style does not register until the next few sequences, which show her performing for the clientele of a Mogador nightclub. She is perhaps best remembered for such moments, but of course it is impossible to imagine her in any sort of musical comedy. Unlike the stars of American musicals, who behaved like "ordinary" folk until they leapt into a number, Dietrich was the same character onstage and in a dressing room. Her singing and dancing abilities were actually rather slight; essentially a *diseuse,* as she herself called it, she specialized in *Sprechtstimme.* Her typical "act" was to play a spectacular woman of the world working in some low dive, singing half-heartedly, almost contemptuously. The laziest gal in town, she was sexy precisely because of the way she threatened to expose the illusion of her performance. In effect, her songs gave a perfect motivation for all the acting techniques I have been describing. Her deliberate pace, her ironic smile, her tendency to exhibit herself to the camera in dramatically lit, ostentatious poses—all these seemed quite natural when she was depicted as a showgirl and when the camera photographed her in a theater of some kind. Her grand, self-referential manner was in danger of looking too "performed" in the context of Hollywood realism, but it could be normalized when it was surrounded by various recognizable *signs* of performance—a stage, an orchestra, and an audience within the film.

The songs made Dietrich into an object of pure display, and at the same time she was depicted as a woman who dominated her audience, singing as if to acknowledge that they had paid for the pleasure of fantasizing about her. In Sternberg's fin-de-siècle imagination she resembled what the Mona Lisa had been for Walter Pater—a tantalizing, enigmatic woman framed by a decadent gloom, whose face hinted at delicious perversities.[8] Throughout *Morocco,* therefore, she is delicately made up and lit so as to conceal her rounded nose, heighten the sharpness of her cheekbones, and give her a sultry, sexually "experienced" classicism. But her performance lends another quality to the traditionally aloof, fetishistic temptress of Pater's description. To grasp its ideological potential, one need only compare Dietrich with a "hot" sex star like the American Louise Brooks, who played emasculating women in Germany for G. W. Pabst. For all Dietrich's evident physical charm, she is no Stanislavskian caught up in the moment, her flesh radiating the pleasure of taunting men. As Raymond Durgnat has remarked, her "humor is kindly," as if she were displaying "musicianly control, not of gestures merely, but of an emotional facade" ("Six Films," 98). Always a little more sophisticated than the plot she has been given, she seems to enjoy her job in an intellectual sense, gently satirizing her masquerade.

Dietrich's musical numbers also institute another sort of playacting: they suggest a Paterian "malady" and joke about unchecked female desire even while they remain within heterosexual bounds. Her first appearance as an

8. Pater's empurpled description of Leonardo's painting might have been composed by a breathless movie critic enamored of a Dietrich close-up: "Hers is the head upon which all of the ends of the world are come, and the eyelids are a little weary. It is a beauty wrought out from within upon the flesh, the deposit, little cell by cell, of strange thoughts and fantastic reveries and exquisite passions. Set it for a moment beside one of those white Greek goddesses or beautiful women of antiquity [or beside most Hollywood actresses from Gish to Harlow] and how would they be troubled by that beauty, into which the soul with all its maladies has passed!"

Dietrich prepares for her act.

entertainer in *Morocco* is the most famous example. She is shown in her dressing room, wearing a man's white tie, looking at herself in a hand mirror, quietly singing the French song she will perform in her act ("Elle est jolie"). Despite the mirror and the words, she gazes at herself coolly, like a dandyish male who is also a tough guy, explicitly rejecting feminine accoutrements by picking up a Moroccan lady's fan—a prop left behind by the previous *chanteuse*—and smiling ironically before tossing it aside. A busy, nervous manager (Ulrich Haupt) suddenly bursts in to tell her that the house is packed. She stands, putting a hand in the pocket of her tuxedo trousers, and casually lights a cigarette, blowing plumes of smoke into the beam of light around her head. Then she takes a top hat from the dressing table, using it as an expressive object: as the manager says, "My house is patronized by the finest society in Morocco," she pops the hat open with a contemptuous flick. Ignoring her jabbering employer (who is exoticized by a gigantic ring in his right ear), she crosses and picks up her coat. He helps her put it on, so that she is now fully costumed as an Astaire-like male.

Dietrich's "performance" on stage is an elaboration of these same gestures, played in a more grandly stylized way before an audience within the film.

The technical demands of her number are considerable, however, because the narrative does not simply come to a halt while she sings. She must not only captivate the movie audience with her song but also convey emotional changes in the character she is playing, suggesting Amy Jolly's gradual conquest of the rowdy audience in the nightclub, her growing self-confidence, and her developing interest in Gary Cooper, whom she meets for the first time. She must do all this without the aid of dialogue and without much help from editing; she is "onstage" at every moment, her behavior telling the story.

Just before Dietrich goes into her act, we are shown two important areas of the house: at a reserved table in the distance, Menjou is seated with the "best society." Among his party is the wife of the Foreign Legion commandant, who signals across the room. From a low-priced seat near the foot of the stage, Gary Cooper secretly acknowledges her greeting. At virtually the same moment, a peasant girl with jiggling breasts runs up to Cooper, who treats her almost as contemptuously as Dietrich has just treated the manager of the club, suffering her to sit down. Much of Dietrich's performance will be directed toward these two groups. She is costumed exactly like Menjou, and her introductory number can be seen as a parody of or mocking commentary on his masculine urbanity; sometimes, in fact, Sternberg draws explicit visual parallels between them. (See the following page.) Meanwhile she is also paralleled in important ways with Cooper, who will not only become her lover but her soul mate: both Amy and Tom Brown are "foreign legionnaires," equally arrogant and cynical, their behavior and postures almost identical at certain points in the film. During this early scene, Sternberg makes them seem like two sides of the same coin, comparing their actions and subtly confusing their sexual identities. Dietrich dresses and behaves like a man, whereas Cooper will take a flower offered by Dietrich during the song and wear it behind his ear, ultimately flirting with her from behind a lady's fan like the one she has tossed aside in the dressing room. As Sarris has noted, the film is in some ways more audacious for the way it "feminizes" Cooper than for the way it "masculinizes" Dietrich, and one could hardly say which of the two is more erotically costumed or more exhibitionistically posed for the camera.

Andrew Britton has observed that Dietrich's first number onstage is partly about the social conventions of gender, showing us a woman who "affirm[s] her active sexuality not by becoming 'masculine' but through an ironic commentary on a cultural image of male sexual prowess" (*Katharine Hepburn*, 42). But the sequence also threatens to violate sexual taboos at a more basic level. It explicitly introduces the theme of lesbianism, eroticizing Dietrich's approach to women while devising fetishistic strategies to reassure the movie audience that she is safely heterosexual. In this context, the fetish serves both

Two of a kind.

Gary Cooper wears a flower.

as a defense and as a subversive device, allowing Sternberg and Dietrich to preserve the boy-meets-girl plot required by Hollywood narrative even as they create an atmosphere of sexual ambiguity.

A close study of Dietrich's singing number reveals the process at work. First we see her standing in the wings of the stage, blowing cigarette smoke, her head tossed back; then she strolls out to face her audience, one hand in the pocket of her trousers. A close-up shows her reaction to the jeers of the crowd: for an instant there is a frightened look in her eye, but she goes ahead with her act. She sits on the arm of a Moroccan chair, one hand extended to balance her weight on the opposite side, and strikes a profile, her leg extended in a languid pose. Cut to Gary Cooper, who forces the noisy groundlings to quiet down. Another close-up of Dietrich, again backlit, as she looks at him in her typically ambiguous way; she seems amused and surprised, heartened by the support she is getting and mildly intrigued. She puffs her cigarette slowly, lets out smoke with a little smile, and crosses to sit on a railing near the good seats. There, with one hand in her pocket and the other on her thigh, she begins her song.

Throughout, Dietrich's clothing and behavior function to combine obvious femininity with signifiers of phallic power. In *The Blue Angel,* her frilly costumes were designed to call attention to her bare legs and the hidden area of her genitals even while her swaggering posture and high heels suggested other meanings.[9] Here, she is patently a beautiful woman costumed as a man, and heterosexual male viewers (both in the story and in the movie audience) are invited to respond in a vaguely sadomasochistic way, reading the performance as the fetishist in classic Freudian psychology is supposed to read the object of his desire.

I say "his" because according to Freud, the clinical definition of fetishism applies only to heterosexual males who are fascinated with certain objects that carry two mutually exclusive sexual connotations. For example, the first, overt, connotation of a high-heeled shoe (a meaning established by contiguity or metonymy) is feminine. But the second, latent, connotation (established by resemblance or metaphor) is masculine, since the heel can act as a substitute for a missing phallus. The value of such an object for the fetishist resides in a semiotic confusion that allows him to have things both ways, so that he retains heterosexuality by unconsciously bestowing a phallus upon a woman. To explain the phenomenon, Freud resorted to the idea of an *Ichspaltung* that serves as a defense against the fear of castration. In other words, a primal male anxiety about female sexual difference, which Freud claims can sometimes result in homosexuality, is here alleviated by an unconscious denial or "disavowal" (xxi, 149–57).

We do not have to adopt Freudian ego psychology (or suggest that it describes the way specific persons react to Dietrich) to see that satire of gender conventions in *Morocco* works in a roughly similar way, with the first musical number depending on a fetishistic style of double communication. Dietrich's costume is masculine, and she sometimes conveys an attitude of tough, casual disdain; at the same time, she takes care to send out heterosexual messages, largely through her fashionably made-up face, her backlit hair, her milky complexion, and the glances she bestows on Gary Cooper. For every "masculine" gesture or seductive look she aims at women, she makes an overriding counter-gesture, never allowing the fully subversive implications of the performance to take hold.

At first she seems hardly interested in men at all. When a crude fellow in her audience tries to reach out and touch her, she stands and walks to a new position, fondling a distinctly phallic newel-post as she crosses. She sits near a woman but glances at Cooper as she sings. Gazing at him and his increasingly jealous girlfriend, she smiles, flicking her hat back to the crown of her head like a male who has just made a conquest. An ugly man nearby offers her a glass of champagne. She steps over a railing, swinging up her trousered leg, takes the glass, and drinks it down as the audience applauds. Then she

---

9. For a close analysis of this phenomenon in terms of the most famous still photograph of Dietrich's career, see Peter Baxter, "On the Naked Thighs of Miss Dietrich," *Wide Angle* 2, no. 2 (1978).

The Sapphic kiss.

boldly eyes a pretty girl at a man's table. "May I have this?" she asks, taking a flower from behind the girl's ear. Hesitating for a moment while she sniffs the flower and gazes at its owner, she considers her next move and finally takes a daring step: cupping the girl's chin in her hand, she bends down, hesitates once again, and kisses her full in the mouth. She then steps back, smiling, while the audience (including the "cuckolded" man at the table) mutters in astonishment and applauds wildly. Dietrich now taps the hat on her head to a jaunty angle and smiles more broadly, strolling over to where Cooper leads a standing ovation. Given new confidence by the handsome young legionnaire in the low-priced seats, she tosses him the flower she has taken from the girl. The gesture marks Dietrich and Cooper as potential lovers, restoring the drag act to heterosexual norms; at the same time, it playfully transforms her into a tuxedoed "man," seducing Cooper by throwing out a posy.

This opening number is so stunning that viewers usually forget that Dietrich sings two songs in succession. The second is less remarkable but is a complete structural parallel with the first, accentuating her "womanliness," suggesting her sly appropriation of "manliness." Once again we see her in the dressing room with the babbling manager, but now we are given a glimpse of flesh. She wears a dark-belted camisole, high heels, and a long fur-and-feather boa that she will manipulate like a phallus. Sacher-Masoch might have fancied her costume, and her sexual allure is heightened by the light beaming down from the left, which models her long, bare legs. She leans against a doorway in a pose rather like the one Sternberg described in his autobiography, her hipshot stance and demurely bent knee typical of both classical art and early cheesecake, her cocked elbow signaling contempt of "buffoonery," a cigarette held insolently in her hand.

Onstage in the new costume, she again approaches the Moroccan chair, but this time she props one foot on it, showing her leg and loosely holding a basket of apples across her knee. The position neatly contrasts with that of her opening number, when she was costumed like a man but posed languidly; here, dressed as a showgirl, she leans over the chair in an aggressive, vaguely "masculine" way. (The same stance is repeated several times by Gary Cooper during the film, and later, when Dietrich finds Cooper drowning his sorrows in a bar, she herself repeats it, this time wearing trousers.)

A close-up shows Dietrich adjusting the feather boa around her shoulders, its whiteness glowing from a rimlight. Crossing her arms over the handle of the basket, she looks knowingly around the room, asks, "What am I bid for my apples?" and begins singing about female promiscuity. ("An apple a day, they say / Keeps the doctor away / While his pretty young wife / Has the time of her life / With the butcher, the baker, / The candlestick maker.") Her movements throughout are brazen, more in the vein of Lola Lola than anything else she does in the film—as when she walks through the crowd, a hand

The prelude to the second act.

on her hip, occasionally pausing to stand with her legs spread wide and locked at the knees. Repeatedly, she seems to offer her body to the viewer: for example, she leans over a banister to hand out an apple, extending a leg behind her in a dancer's attitude. At the same time, she puts men in their place. As she passes a rather sinister, sensual-looking man in a white tie, he grabs the boa and runs it through his fingers; stopping her song, she gives him a haughty look and pulls the boa away. The fellow is castrated by her glance, hunching up sheepishly while the audience applauds.

Borrowing words from Susan Sontag, we could say that both of Dietrich's performances-within-the-performance employ a "mode of seduction—one which employs flamboyant mannerisms susceptible to a double interpretation, with a witty meaning for the cognoscenti." They also draw upon "a mostly unacknowledged truth of taste: the most refined form of sexual attractiveness . . . consists in going against the grain of one's sex. What is most beautiful in virile men is something feminine; what is most beautiful in feminine women is something masculine" (281). The same effect could be explained in terms of the Freudian fetish, which constantly plays with "unacknowledged truth," preserving social norms and theatrical illusion while threatening to expose them; but the technique also functions in a more socially positive way, establishing Dietrich as a satirist, a woman who can defy convention and partly get away with it.

A similar strategy may be found in the initial love scene between Dietrich and Cooper, which is choreographed in the same playful way as the cabaret sequences. During her show in the club, Dietrich gives Cooper the key to her room. He arrives late in the evening, tosses the key on a chair, picks up a lady's fan, and helps himself to a seat. He is familiar with the room, having known the woman who occupied it before, and is nonchalant, still wearing the flower behind his ear. Once again Sternberg promotes a feeling of sexual ambiguity, using cues in the actors' behavior—languidness, insolence, narcissism—to make Cooper and Dietrich seem two of a kind. He also allows modest violations of continuity, so that Dietrich's makeup, lighting, and dress subtly change from one shot to the next in rhythm with the emotional progress of the scene. At the beginning she appears to be wearing almost no makeup (except for the thinly penciled brows that became one of her trademarks), as if she had just emerged from a bath after her singing duties; meanwhile, the light on her face is strong, balanced almost equally between fill and key, and she wraps her dark clothing about her body like a robe. At midpoint, just before she and Cooper kiss for the first time, her lips and eyes seem painted; she now has elaborate false lashes, and her wrap falls away to reveal both décolleté and a silky flash of legs. At the end, she looks slightly ravaged, makeup giving hollows to her eyes and a touch of shadow to her cheeks; she stands in a doorway, backlit, with only a soft fill on her face, grasping her dress around her shoulders like someone cold and forlorn, running a hand through her hair, a disheveled lock falling over her brow.

Despite this almost painterly *mise-en-scène*, most of the erotic power of the sequence depends on Dietrich's behavior. There is no background music other than some distant drums that can be heard out a window; Cooper is rather wooden, and everything is played in a slow, studied pace with a minimum of dialogue. Dietrich has only one speech of any length, so that all the excitement derives from the way she responds with her eyes and body to Cooper's monosyllabic comments or seductive advances. Once again she strikes a series of expressive poses, inflecting them with tiny movements that convey Amy Jolly's feelings. Each pose has the ostensive quality I have already noted, which in form is similar to the heightened theatricality of her singing numbers in the club; in fact, by 1937, according to the photographer Harry Stradling, Dietrich had become so attuned to the mannered technique of the Sternberg films that "while each shot is being lined up she [had] a full-length mirror set up beside the camera" (quoted by Whitehall, 20). This was no simple narcissism, but a precise understanding of the nature of her work. Her performance depended almost completely on a stylized display of her body and a rejection of transparency or "sincerity"; it was acting aestheticized to the point that it consisted of little more than meaningful stances, carefully selected gestures, and light that modeled her figure just so.

Within this simplified, ostentatious rhetoric, however, Dietrich's expression is usually ambiguous. Thus in this scene when she gives Cooper an arrogant smile, her pose has the forced bravado of a woman who is holding up her head through adversity. Repeatedly she hints at Amy's exhaustion and anxiety, as in the way she puts a bottle of gin and a glass on a table or in the way she avoids Cooper's stare. Having provided him with a drink and a cigarette, she crosses the room to a window, turns with a hand on her hip, and sits down, looking toward the floor. Cooper walks over behind her and tosses his cigarette out the window. "You can smell the desert tonight," he says, sitting on the arm of her chair and gently fanning her hair with the memento left behind by the previous singer. A vulnerable, passionate expression crosses Dietrich's face, and a close-up shows her eyes cast down, a deep shadow along her right cheekbone. As Cooper continues to fan her hair, she looks profoundly sad and tense, until she suddenly turns and looks up, her profile to the camera, her face pointed at the keylight, her long neck become a line of white flesh. "Hot, isn't it?" Cooper says from offscreen, and she gives him an ironic half smile. She turns to look back at the floor but almost immediately she glances up again, raises her hand, and takes the flower from behind his ear. She sniffs it, smiles, and tosses it away. "Faded," she says, with just the right blend of cynicism and passion.

Cooper bends down and kisses her, and the staging of the kiss is characteristic of the performance as a whole. As he takes Dietrich in one arm, he holds the fan over their faces, so that it comes between them and the camera—a gesture so coy it would be funny in a world less "performed" and sophisticated than Sternberg's. Meanwhile, Dietrich conveys a sense of sexual heat with a single movement of her hand. (Compare her seduction of John Lodge in *The Scarlet Empress*, when she pulls a veil over their reclining bodies and clenches it in her fist.) She reaches up with her fingers spread wide, pressing against Cooper with her wrist, as if she were half yielding and half trying to push him away.

The moment deserves comparison with Ernst Lubitsch's work at Paramount in the same period: whereas Lubitsch made leering jokes out of closed bedroom doors, Sternberg and Dietrich—more rarified cosmopolitans—partly concealed a Hollywood kiss behind a lady's fan, recalling the most sentimental gestures of romantic art.[10] The artful staging also makes an interesting contrast with Garbo's typical performances. Like Dietrich, Garbo was an exotic star who was photographed in elaborately atmospheric ways and

---

10. Andrew Sarris makes an interesting comparison between this scene and a moment in *The Shanghai Gesture* (1941), when Sternberg photographs Victor Mature and Gene Tierney from an opposite angle, so that a kiss they conceal from others is shown to the movie audience. The dramatic situation, he notes, is just the opposite from the one in *Morocco* and hence does not require a fetishistic playfulness. In the early film, the camera angle implies "that there was something genuine to conceal in the Dietrich-Cooper relationship. It follows with poetic logic that the ridiculousness of the Tierney-Mature relationship is revealed rather than concealed" (*The Films of Josef von Sternberg*, 50).

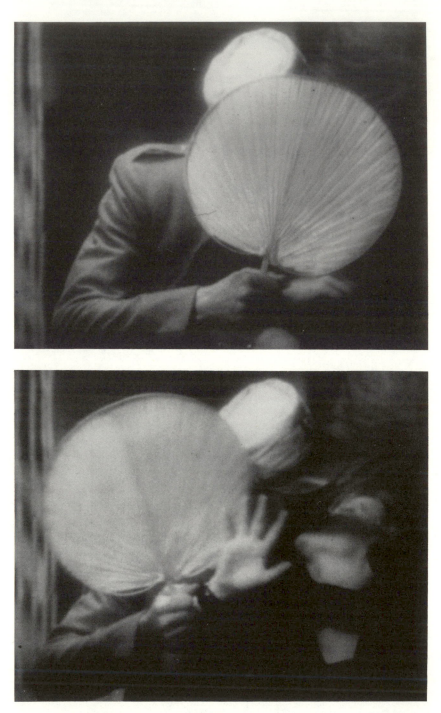

Cooper kisses Dietrich.

who behaved in the tradition of *la Divine*. Garbo's kisses, however, were a key ingredient of her image; they were usually played with daring naturalistic fervor, making her abilities as a lover clearly evident. By contrast, Dietrich tends to *imitate* sexual contact, her love scenes becoming as artificial as everything else.

Of course, *Morocco* entirely depends on innuendo and displacement, on suggestive decoration and highlights visible in darkness. In making this strategy evident, the demure fan tends to mock conventions even as it preserves them. Significantly, the aftermath of the kiss is played as if the lovers had consummated their passion. Dietrich crosses to a piano on the other side of the room, runs her fingers along the keyboard, and turns, her arms hanging loosely at her sides. "You can go now, soldier," she says. Cooper moves toward her, puts a foot confidently on the piano bench, and leans an elbow on his knee, echoing the pose Dietrich used at the beginning of her second number in the club. Avoiding him, she goes to get a cigarette, crossing to the French windows that open onto her balcony; there, in an elaborate series of poses that convey both toughness and pathos, she makes her biggest speech almost as if it were one of her songs, punctuating the lines with long pauses.

"There is a foreign legion of women, too," she says, flicking her lit cigarette out into the studio night, turning to look at him, crossing an arm over her chest: "But we have no uniforms, no flags." She steps forward to meet Cooper, who has joined her near the window, and she grasps a medal on his tunic: "And no medals when we are brave." She puts a hand on her hip and leans back in the doorway, suggesting a gallant and slightly fatigued defiance. She pauses, steps forward again, and gives Cooper's cheek a maternal touch, turning away to mask her emotion by looking outside. Another pause, and then she turns back to him: "No wound stripes when we are hurt." Cut to a close-up, lit so that Dietrich's face looks, in Yeats's phrase, as if she had eaten a mess of shadows. Cooper exits and she sinks down to a couch, running a hand through her hair uneasily, giving him a small two-fingered salute.

The choreographed, lyrical, teasing presentation of sex in this scene is in one sense typical of theater itself, which usually suggests more than it shows. Dietrich's performance, however, is unusual for the combination of meanings she produces and for the skill with which she balances contrary feelings; her poses and gestures mix abandon with restraint, irony with intensity, glowing sex appeal with an irony that blurs the boundaries of gender. Sternberg orchestrates this mixture skillfully, investing a twenties-style popular romance with a tone that is extremely difficult to describe. On the one hand, it is laughable to think we could accept the scene as taking place in a real Morocco, or that Dietrich and Cooper could be anything more than beautiful people lit and photographed by Garmes. The dialogue is too "poetic," and Dietrich speaks it with a shade of amusement in her voice. (There is a particularly ironic effect in her reference to "wound stripes when we are hurt" when one considers the many allusions to flagellation in Sternberg's films.) The costumes, makeup, and studio decor (some of it consisting of Dietrich's personal mementos and photographs) are too theatrical by far, as if they were being used as an arty pretext for seductive poses; surely, one thinks, to take all this seriously would be to become a "tourist" in a city like Berlin. And yet the delicacy and occasional seriousness of Dietrich's face seems to *ask* us to take things in earnest. As a result the scene partakes simultaneously of a deep romanticism and of a more avant-garde attitude that, to quote Sontag again, perceives "Being-as-Playing-a-Role." In every way, it is the "farthest extention . . . of the metaphor of life as theater" (280).

Throughout, Dietrich plays her part with an alternating conviction and irony that few American actors then or now would attempt, never allowing it to lapse into travesty. Consequently, as she says to Orson Welles at one point in *Touch of Evil,* her work seems "so old it's new." Like all actors, she allows the audience to indulge in illusion, but she widens the splitting of belief a little more than movies usually allow. She is the most extravagant of the shimmering women in thirties Hollywood, her "presence" dependent on something veiled and suggested, always promised and forever deferred. She is a goddess, but if we look for an essence or plenitude in her image, we shall never find it; she knows that she is all makeup and gauzy light, the glossy surface of a photograph, and her performance relies on that fact. We might describe her collaboration with Sternberg as relatively passive and masochistic, especially since it left her sadly imprisoned in the role of glamorous woman; but it also has modernist implications, making her one of the most paradoxical figures in the history of movies. Repeatedly, she frustrates our ability to make easy generalizations about her meaning or to decide exactly where the director leaves off and the star begins.

9

James Cagney in *Angels with Dirty Faces* (1938)

Like many viewers, I often have difficulty recalling or even registering the names of the dramatis personae in old Hollywood movies. For me at least, it is usually John Wayne getting on a horse, seldom the Ringo Kid or Ethan Edwards. But then who is John Wayne? In a very real sense he is as much a character as anyone else in a story, the product of publicity and various film roles, represented by a fellow whose original name was Marion Morrison. I think of him as real (Marion Morrison may have thought so, too), but he is just a construction, an image that has an ideological or totemic function.

This is one of several paradoxes about characterization and performance in films, and it raises some interesting problems for analysis. In Hollywood, as sometimes in our lived relations, we may ask where the actor leaves off and the character begins. How much does performance actually "write" or constitute the character? How much is performance itself an illusion, created by technical trickery, fame, and our fascination with actors? I doubt that these questions have definitive answers, and in one sense the Hollywood film is designed to prohibit them. The performer, the character, and the star are joined in a single, apparently intact, image, so that many viewers regard people in movies as little more than spectacular human beings, like found objects or dada art, magnified by the camera. Some may believe that the movie is simply happening at the behest of the stars. As Joe Gillis/William Holden says at one point in *Sunset Boulevard,* "People don't know that somebody actually *writes* the picture. They think the actors make it up as they go along." But even if the actors *do* make it up, even if they contribute some kind of work to produce characters, how can we identify this work, grounded as it is in their own bodies? In the illusionistic, Aristotelian drama of Hollywood movies, how can we separate the dancer from the dance?

I have been confronting such issues throughout this book; in this chapter I deal with them more systematically, through the work of James Cagney in *Angels with Dirty Faces*. I write in praise of Cagney, who is generally agreed to be one of the most compelling Hollywood performers, but I also try to show the complex, many-leveled process that constructs a familiar movie character and to demonstrate something about that character's ideological meaning.

Before turning to the analysis itself, however, it may be useful to distinguish among three elements of characterization that make up all star performances. First, there is the *role:* a character in the literary sense, a proper name attached to certain adjectives and predicates (or character "traits") in a narrative. The role may be written down in a script, or it may be revised or improvised during production (as Cagney claims to have done with the role of Rocky Sullivan in *Angels with Dirty Faces*), but it is essentially a prefilmic development, established before the cameras turn. Second, there is the *actor,* a person whose body and performing skills bring other important traits to the role. The actor is already a character in some sense, a "subject" formed by various codes in the culture, whose stature, accent, physical abilities, and performing habits imply a range of meanings and influence the way she or he will be cast. Finally, there is a *star image,* also a character, that begins as a product of the other two categories (for example, Cagney's famous performance as Tom Powers in *The Public Enemy* [1931]) but subsequently determines them (Cagney was often cast as a gangster). The star image is a complex, intertextual matter, owing not only to the actor and her or his previous roles, but to the filmic qualities of microphones, cameras, editing and projection; it derives as well from narratives written about the actor in publicity and biography and thus becomes a global category.

These three aspects of character are roughly similar to the triad listed in the earlier discussion of *Kid's Auto Race,* where I argued that people on the screen can be regarded as documentary evidence, as fictional persons, or as celebrities playing "themselves." Actually, none of the three concepts is entirely distinct from the others. In any given film, they are part of what Stephen Heath has called a "circuit of exchange," and might be thought of as points in a circular continuum.[1] In my discussion of Cagney, I will not try to make neat distinctions between them and will not be able to elaborate all their relations; nevertheless, I hope to show how a single film intermittently fore-

---

1. See Stephen Heath, "Body, Voice," in *Questions of Cinema* (178–93). Heath's theoretical discussion is more ambitious and uses a more elaborate deconstructive terminology: "agent," "character," "person," "image," and "figure." Along similar lines, John Ellis has described the commercial cinema as a dramatic text intersected by the text of a star; hence many stars "offer a supplementary signification: they are there as star; they are there as fictional role; but they are also there as actor, saying, 'Look at me, I can perform'" (105). The most detailed treatments of the evolution of star images in Hollywood have been Richard Dyer's two books, *Stars* (1979) and *Heavenly Bodies* (1986).

grounds each of Cagney's functions, sometimes making use of his established stardom, sometimes exploiting his specific performing skills, and sometimes requiring him to behave more like "Rocky Sullivan" than like "James Cagney." But first, because *Angels with Dirty Faces* is a vehicle from Cagney's middle period, I need to preface the analysis with a brief description of the actor and the star, showing how they relate to the specific role.

Cagney the actor brought two especially important qualities to early talking films. First was his reedy, nasal voice, which, although it was neither strong nor versatile, had an eccentric and ethnic sound, redolent of the streets. Even in supporting roles he would have been unusual because he spoke without the stage Irishman's brogue and without the "deeze-dem-doze" accents of Hollywood's ersatz lower class. As a leading man he was remarkable. Compare his speech with any of the leading actors in the transitional period—John Barrymore, Paul Muni, Lew Ayres, William Powell—and you have a good sense of how much he differs from the established theatrical mode. His second important quality was the lightning speed and acrobatic force of everything he did. Before him, the talkies had a leaden pace, perhaps because directors were not sure how much the audience could absorb, or perhaps because they were still following the rhythms of silent drama. Cagney was one of the first actors to show Hollywood how to give movies a truly big-city energy and tempo. For example, he saves *The Public Enemy* from William Wellman's excruciatingly slow direction: when he makes an entrance, the film changes from canned theater into sinister vaudeville.

Cagney always thought of himself as a comic song-and-dance man, and that is why he seems to engage with the audience more than other actors, as if he were trying to overcome the boundary between the screen and the auditorium. To watch him is to be aware of how much he combines ordinary realist acting skills with an older tradition that influenced the silent comics—the tradition of circus, of clowning, of improvised dance, and of slapstick violence. Because of this influence, he became one of the most mannered of the classic Hollywood stars, so busy with stylized movement that everyone can do a reasonable imitation of him. "Never relax," he is supposed to have advised a younger player—a strange idea in a profession where one of the chief technical problems is to be able to relax at all. Most amateur actors are overly tense, whereas professionals have the opposite problem, relaxing too much, resting when they ought to be poised to react. Cagney was special because he controlled the screen with the aggressive tactics of a vaudevillian or a small man in a fight: be cocky and get in the first blow; stay on the balls of your feet; always think ahead of your opponent; whatever happens, keep moving. No other actor in the frenetic thirties (with the qualified exception of Mickey Rooney) was able to do these things as effectively. When he was simply listening to somebody, Cagney drilled holes with his stare, and even when he was standing still, he seemed on the point of dancing; in fact, he actually broke into dance steps in the midst of non-musical pictures: both *Smart Money* (1931) and *Taxi* (1932) have charming moments when he makes an entrance with a soft shoe completely unmotivated by the script.

Cagney had begun his career as a vaudeville hoofer (Barishnikov was once approached to play him in a biopic), and he always liked to remind his publicists that his first theatrical performance was in drag. This background helps explain his unusual impact in violent melodrama. He was the most graceful of the pug-ugly Warners gangsters, smiling slightly when he threw a punch or pulled a gat, and the makeup he wore in some of his thirties publicity stills made him look decidedly androgynous. Hence the opening shot of *A Clockwork Orange* (1971), in which Malcolm McDowell leers into the camera, one eye painted with extravagant feminine lashes, seems derived from Cagney's face at its most troubling. There is an image remarkably like it in *The Public Enemy*, when Cagney stands under a streetlamp and grins back at us; the eyes are heavy-lidded, shaded with thick lashes and tilted up at the corners with Satanic points; the mouth is dainty, the cheeks dimpled and cherubic; the aggressive, phallic stare and the knowing smile are perverse, mocking the illusion of innocence, charming the audience as they threaten it.

There was never anything narcissistic or even self-conscious about Cagney's strutting toughness (as there is, for example, in the more neurotic performances of an actor like Richard Dreyfuss); nevertheless, he was the perfect boy sadist, small and amusing enough not to seem a monster, and it is no accident that he became a star at the moment when he rubbed a half grapefruit into Mae Clarke's nose. When he was called upon to be an actual lover, he was relatively ineffectual. He was obviously more at home in the world of Irish male bravado, where he and Pat O'Brien became buddies in film after film; in the majority of his pictures, however, he was an almost asexual figure. Middle age gave him a slight paunch, and his dancing movements were always pushed toward the grotesque; he became a mixture of urban leprechaun, stevedore, and tiny gorilla, evoking litheness and strength rather than the apish dullness of Muni's Scarface. He often stood with his feet in a dancer's turnout, his torso slightly forward, his thick arms bowed in front of his body, his stubby hands curled as if ready to make a fist. When he wore the dapper suits and snap-brim hats of crime movies, he subliminally suggested a monkey in a tuxedo, and David Thomson has made the amusing suggestion that he would have been the ideal Hyde next to Fred Astaire's Dr. Jekyll. Indeed, to appreciate just how simian Cagney could look, one has only to watch him climb the oil storage tank at the conclusion of *White Heat* (1949), muttering and giggling lowly to himself as his arms sway and his rear end juts out.

Cagney never played several roles to which he was ideally suited: Studs Lonigan, the eponymous hero of James Farrell's novels (James Agee once suggested that Cagney ought to be paired with Mickey Rooney as the young and old Lonigan); Christy Mahon in *Playboy of the Western World* (in the thirties he came close to appearing in the play, which he was going to produce himself); and Hildy Johnson, the star reporter of *The Front Page* (O'Brien got the part in the original movie version, although in 1940 Cagney, playing opposite O'Brien, portrayed someone loosely based on the character in *Torrid Zone,* an embarrassingly imperialistic and racist movie that Cagney liked to call *Hildy Johnson among the Bananas*).

As his own producer, he developed a gentle, philosophical streak, attempting a kind of populist whimsy in *Johnny Come Lately* (1943) and *The Time of Your Life* (1948). He played a blind, armless, legless war veteran in the radio adaptation of Trumbo's *Johnny Got His Gun;* he was a plausible, if miscast, Bottom in Reinhardt's *Midsummer Night's Dream* (1935); he was superb as a small-town dentist in Walsh's *The Strawberry Blonde* (1941); and in certain brash, eccentric musical comedies he was unique. Despite his range, however, he never shook off the image of a tough hustler. Like all the Hollywood stars of his period, he is remembered chiefly as a vivid type, equal to any of the great figures of melodramatic Dickensian fiction.

Nevertheless his particular image brought with it certain meanings that needed to be altered or kept under control. The sexual violence and amoral charm he gave Tom Powers in *The Public Enemy* tended to subvert the film's earnest sociology; the producers had claimed that their purpose was "to depict an environment rather than to glorify the hoodlum," but Cagney's performance immediately established him as a star villain. Forever afterward, his publicity and biography informed his more naive fans that he was an *actor—* a shy recluse (with a farm, no less) who was married only once and who liked to write Deeds-style verses as a hobby. Furthermore, his screen roles underwent significant changes during the thirties. At first Warners capitalized on his reputation by casting him in films where he roughed up women, but the formula grew stale and Cagney himself wearied of the typecasting. At the same time, the industry was under increasing pressure from the Catholic Legion of Decency. In 1934, the year when the Legion was helping to write the Motion Picture Production Code, Richard Watts, Jr., of the *New York Herald Tribune* wryly noted that Cagney was "sometimes alleged to be one of the cinema's subversive moral influences," and Regina Crewe of the *New York American* expressed fears that his work in *Jimmy the Gent* was "too swift to be followed in the sticks" (quoted in Dickens, 84–85). In 1935, when the Code went into effect, Cagney was promptly inserted into a series of films that put him in the service of the government: in quick succession, he was a sailor in *Here Comes the Navy,* a marine flyer in *Devil Dogs of the Air,* and an FBI agent in *G-Men.* By the time he returned to gangsterdom in *Angels with Dirty Faces,* he had become a more lovable character with a slightly understated technique; even more important, he was cast in the role of a man whose criminal reputation has made him potentially dangerous to children.

*   *   *

Angels with Dirty Faces is a rapidly-produced, assembly-line movie with no pretensions to art, but it is memorable partly because of the clever way it exploits the interaction between Cagney's star image and his ability to vary his characterizations. The filmmakers and Cagney himself built upon the public's affectionate recognition of the star's persona, using it to create some of their best effects and bending it to an ideological purpose. Such a process was typical of Hollywood under the star system, but to understand how it works in this particular instance, we must recognize how much *Angels* differs from earlier Cagney vehicles—despite its having the same urban milieu, the same general costuming and body language. *Angels* clearly belongs to the sumptuous, middle-class Warner Brothers of the late thirties rather than to the brash, cynical world of the studio's early sound period; Cagney is older, his image already somewhat altered, and is a perfect instrument for the lachrymose dramas of self-sacrifice in which director Michael Curtiz began to specialize.

Curtiz, who is not normally regarded as an *auteur,* seemed to discover in the late thirties and early forties a story he used again and again, probably because it was suited to his romanticism and to the prewar, Production Code years of the late New Deal, when personal sacrifice for the common good was a major theme in American mass culture. The story was Christian in its implications, and its agent was inevitably a hard-boiled Warners star who gave up everything for an ideal. In its early phase, this sacrifice was more pathetic than purely ennobling, as with Edward G. Robinson's performance in *Kid Galahad* (1937) or John Garfield's in *Four Daughters* (1938). In its late phase it was treated ironically, as with Joan Crawford in *Mildred Pierce* (1945). Cagney's role in *Angels* is one of the more straightforward and "tragic" expressions of the idea, which was to reach its perfect form in *Casablanca* (1942)—a film whose ending was probably determined as much by the formula Curtiz and Warners had discovered as by the temper of the times. *Angels* differs from *Casablanca* partly because its sacrificial character is not a disillusioned liberal but a true racketeer named Rocky Sullivan, a survivor of a Hell's Kitchen childhood, who screams and whimpers like a coward as he is dragged to the electric chair. The film's most interesting touch is that we never know whether Rocky has truly lost control or whether he is giving up his last moment of dignity for a higher cause. We know only that he has a heart of gold, that he begs for mercy before he dies, and that his behavior helps a priest back in the old neighborhood to divert the Dead End Kids from a life of crime.

Cagney's ambiguous death scene is so effective that it helps disguise some of the contradictions and absurdities of the screenplay, which begins on a note of liberal social consciousness, pointing to slums and reform schools as causes of crime, and then shifts emphasis toward the criminals themselves. (One of the authors of the script was John Wexley, who belonged to the radicalized Worker's Theater earlier in the decade.) Ultimately the viewer is asked to believe that if only Father Jerry (Pat O'Brien) could get rid of the Dead End Kids' criminal role models, he could move them out of the pool hall and onto the church-sponsored basketball court. *Casablanca,* a film with an equally absurd plot, was able to avoid this sort of reversal because World War II provided Warners with less problematic villains and an easier way to reconcile politics with melodrama. In *Angels,* however, Cagney must perform the tricky role of mediator between the underworld and the church. The film completely absorbs whatever positive values the state might have into the figure of the priest, who seems "naturally" good and who asserts moral control over every encounter between characters. The police are shown to be corrupt and cruel throughout, one of them even taking sadistic pleasure in Rocky's electrocution; but Father Jerry can act as their agent without having his role questioned. Whenever a social contradiction is raised, it is evaded by appeals to a Higher Law.

And yet the priest alone cannot entirely validate this Law, despite his having risen from the slums and despite Pat O'Brien's proletarian qualities as an actor. At one point he is allowed to assert his full-bloodedness by punching out a crook in a saloon (an almost imperative gesture for the heroes of American action cinema), but essentially he is a figure of abstract goodness, requiring help from "below" in the person of Cagney. Cagney's star image is of considerable importance to this project. After all, he is as much an ego ideal for the audience as for the neighborhood boys in the story. At the same time, he uses his actor's skill to modulate the old formula, signifying new traits and new meanings that can be read against the earlier image. Like most of the Hollywood stars, in a tradition that runs from the late thirties onward, he is able to exploit his celebrity status to create both empathy and subtle nostalgia.

Cagney's stardom is evoked by the film even before he makes his first appearance. *Angels* resembles many of the Warners crime films in having a sort of prologue describing the protagonist's youth; but this prologue is different from the one in *The Public Enemy* because the audience can so clearly recognize the boy actor (Frankie Burke) who will "grow up" to be Cagney. (*The Public Enemy* has a somewhat confusing opening. Cagney was promoted to the leading role in the midst of filming, after the prologue was completed, and the actor who most resembles him as a youth seems to be playing the wrong part.) By this point in his career, Cagney had become so well known that the boy in the first scenes seems to be impersonating him, almost in the style of a nightclub comic, by using a nasal, Lower-East-Side Irish voice ("Me old man's got troubles enough"), rapid-fire delivery, and characteristic gestures like hitching up his trousers with his wrists. He even plays out a typical Cagney incident, pulling a girl's hat down over her head and sneering at her.

This is a curious and quite interesting phenomenon—an actor portraying somebody who has already been determined by the image of another actor, as if Rocky Sullivan's characterization had been completely swallowed up by a star. Actually, however, a good many details in the boy's performance were the product not of a star image but of Cagney's specific design of the Sullivan role. In his autobiography, Cagney says that he partly modeled the character on a "hophead and pimp" he had known in New York, who would "hitch up his trousers, twist his neck and move his necktie, lift his shoulders, snap his fingers, then bring his hands together in a soft smack. His invariable greeting was 'Whadda ya hear? Whadda ya say?' . . . I did that gesturing maybe six times in the picture . . . and the impressionists are still doing me doing him" (73–74).

When Cagney himself enters the picture, in a brief montage sequence showing his adult criminal activity, we are on such familiar ground that we hardly have to see him in the rapidly passing images of bootlegging and gambling to have an illusion of a full presence. If the star system did nothing else, it enabled the classic Hollywood film to establish elements of character in a single instance, which accounts for some of the remarkable narrative economy of the better movies. We know what Rocky Sullivan will sound like before he has spoken a word, and we are prepared to be fascinated by him before the writers have invented a single speech; all the variation and development of the character will occur within the frame of a genre and a set of performing mannerisms that most of the audience can predict, and the emotional effect of the film depends on this fact.

Once Cagney has established the stereotype, however, his performance becomes nuanced. Many of his familiar touches are there, together with the special movements of Rocky Sullivan (he hitches his trousers only once, at a crucial moment I discuss later), but the tone is muted, the energy level turned down a few notches. For example, in his first dialogue scene, where he is interviewed in prison by crooked lawyer James Frazier (Humphrey Bogart), the camera moves in on his round cupid's face as he squints and wrinkles his nose: "I know you're a smart lawyer," he says, broadening the "a" in "smart" and pausing for a beat. He winks and gives a tiny left-right shake of the head, adding "very smart." His stubby hand lifts into view and a finger points off-screen toward Bogart. "But don't get smart with me." He appears to be the same sly, dangerous little guy the audience has always known, but at the same time the routine is underplayed; there is no gleeful smile, no perverse joy in the threatening gesture, no underlying sense of a criminal madman. The line and the movements are delivered with a brisk, clipped speed typical of Cagney, but the voice is quiet and rational, the actor mellowed.

Cagney is visibly older (he was already thirty-two when he played Tom Powers in *The Public Enemy*), and his maturity adds to the pathos of Rocky Sullivan's life. The film emphasizes this pathos by establishing that Rocky is a gangster because of his poor background and a stroke of bad luck: as a boy he is sent up to reform school for petty theft, refusing to squeal on his friend Jerry, whom he has saved from the pursuing police. In the opening scenes, his misfortune and his role as scapegoat are made relentlessly clear. After the talk with the lawyer, we see him returning to the old neighborhood, having just served a three-year sentence on behalf of his gang (throughout the movie he makes sacrifices, first for the crooks and then for the church). Before tracking down Frazier to claim the money he has been promised, he pays a visit to his old friend Jerry, now a priest. In a rapid, wordless, Kuleshovian sequence, Curtiz and Cagney poise the character neatly between sin and sainthood, transforming the ambiguous, potentially anarchic Cagney of old into a doomed figure in a moral allegory.

First we see a dark, low-angle view as Rocky enters the church during a boys' choir rehearsal. Wearing a dark suit and tie, he looks pencil straight, a strong backlight gleaming off his wavy, highly tonsured hair and almost no fill light on the camera side of his face. The camera tracks in and looks up at his shadowy, rather sinister, profile; he pauses, rapidly shrugs his shoulders, flexes his neck and chin, and then stands very straight, poised, glancing around cautiously. Cut to an innocent-looking choirboy singing a solo in the loft above. Cut back to a new angle on Cagney, shown full face as he looks up toward the loft; a fill light now softens the dark areas of his face, and his offscreen glance is in the direction of a diffused, religious "north light." He begins silently mouthing the words of the choirboy, as if he has heard them a thousand times before, and for a moment he seems to become one of the pretty children in the church, an Irish boy soprano. Cut back to the loft where Father Jerry conducts the rehearsal. Cut to a low angle behind Cagney's dark shoulder as he looks up at the choir and again makes a nervous shrug. Cut to the loft as the song ends and we see the soloist leaving, suddenly breaking into an unholy scuffle with one of the other boys. Return to the previous close-up of Cagney, who now laughs silently in recognition, his heavy-lidded, dark-browed eyes slanting up like a cat's. His amusement seems benign, but there is mischief in his smile. (See next page.)

These shots illustrate how the film separates out some of the range of meanings in Cagney's face, depicting him first as a dapper gangster, then as an innocent, then as an aging Puck. But what is even more interesting is the way Cagney himself seems to have achieved structural command of a familiar repertory of gestures and tics we associate with his screen performances. He "writes" the character not only by inventing new mannerisms but by controlling the old ones in systematic ways and linking them together in new combinations. For example, one of the most frequent gestures he has adopted for Rocky Sullivan is a light shrug of the shoulders, accompanied by a more typical Cagneyesque setting of the body, the feet spread slightly and the knees flexing. He repeats the shrug and the stance often, but always

Three faces of James Cagney.

when Rocky is uncomfortable, and always connecting it with movements of the head and mouth—stretching the neck, jutting the chin forward and pulling it back, scraping the upper lip with the lower teeth, running the tongue around the cheek. In every case these movements, accompanied by quick uneasy glances, convey Rocky's efforts to keep his cool in changed surroundings, his determination to fight against odds, his struggle to maintain dignity.

I should emphasize that Cagney is never as overstated as this description may indicate; his pace is so rapid, his gestures so brief, that he maintains his poise. Nevertheless his discomfort is one of the central issues of the film. As Andrew Bergman has pointed out, Rocky is "not only a criminal but an unsuccessful one, a man caught and sentenced time and again" (74). The key to Cagney's interpretation up until the end is in the way he subtly discloses the character's plight, using a great many movements but refusing to milk his scenes for their blatant emotional content. He consistently gives Rocky a surface buoyancy, barely suggesting loneliness; for example, his tag line, "Whadda ya hear, whadda ya say," is beautifully rendered, showing Rocky's attempt to be his old self, but registering the exact distance between the man he once was and the man he now is. In Cagney's hands, Rocky seems slightly weary from experience but unapologetic for his past. Never neurotic, he may be the only mentally healthy figure in the actor's gallery of mobsters and sharpies. Hence all of Cagney's potential for derisive glee is held in check, and his busy movements are keyed to Rocky's tense integrity.

Rocky's shrug occurs often during the first encounter with Jerry in the church, where the subtext has to do with a wary, embarrassed reunion of two old friends. (Once again the star system contributes to the effect because Cagney and O'Brien *are* old friends from previous movies and from studio publicity.) Rocky seems happy to see Jerry, but he is a bit reserved and uneasy, as we can see from Cagney's forced cheerfulness. Normally Cagney laughs a great deal—so often that a sort of nasal chuckle becomes part of his speech, punctuating his jokes, giving his words a threatening or ironic twist. Here, however, his amusement is self-depreciating and lacking in affect, almost grimacing. His relative physical distance from O'Brien is also significant, because as a rule Cagney touches other players quite often. In most of his films, he is constantly reaching out to pat a shoulder, grasp a lapel, or poke somebody with a forefinger. One of the reasons for the frightening unexpectedness of some of his performances is that he makes his contact as ambiguous as his smile, mixing affection with aggression—for instance his habit in this film of gently brushing someone's chin with a closed fist (a gesture he took from his father and used as a motif in *The Public Enemy*). The very fact that he does not touch O'Brien much, except for handshakes, becomes an important element of the scene, revealing tension beneath apparent casualness.

The same principles are at work in the beginning of the next major sequence, where Rocky rents a room in the old neighborhood and meets the former "girl in pigtails," Laurie (Ann Sheridan). It would be wrong to say that his moves are completely subdued—for example, he does not simply reach up and push the rooming-house doorbell with a forefinger; he leans his body in toward the buzzer and springs gently back like a dancer. Nevertheless, he is unusually cautious and stoical, shrugging once or twice, glancing around the place in an expressionless, businesslike way, until the scene provides him a strategic opportunity to evoke the carnivalistic mood of his earlier performances. When Laurie reveals to him that she is the girl he used to tease, she slaps him and pulls his hat down over his ears, running out of the room and slamming the door behind her. Cagney stands there for a moment like a vaudevillian in a blackout sketch, then slowly turns toward the camera, the hat crumpled over his head. He breaks into a dimpled, open-mouthed smile and crosses to his newly rented bed, walking with bouncy steps, his arms held slightly up at his sides and his hands dangling from the wrists like a marionette's. The walk and the wicked, dreamy smile are not far from the manic impersonation he was later to give of George M. Cohan in *Yankee Doodle Dandy,* and he climaxes the movement with a pratfall when he sits on the bed and it collapses; he lands like an acrobat on a trampoline, registering surprise but keeping his hands gracefully in the air, riding with the bounce instead of trying to break it.

In most of his other scenes with O'Brien and Sheridan, Cagney is relatively quiet, playing a man who has to keep his distance. It is with the Dead End Kids that he becomes a dynamo. In fact, he introduces himself to them by doing a parody of a gangster. Walking slowly down the steps of their hideout, his hat brim slanted over one eye, he pokes a hand in his coat pocket and holds the other open and out at his side. "Say yer prayers, mugs," he snarls. (The line is ironic. Father Jerry will come down those same steps at the end of the film, asking the boys to "say a prayer for a kid who couldn't run as fast as I could.") In this underground world of adolescent misrule, Cagney's delicate machismo is allowed to express itself so vividly that he seems on the verge of breaking into another soft-shoe routine. Strolling around the hideout and pointing to a place on the wall where Rocky is supposed to have carved his initials, he pops a piece of gum in his mouth, cocks the hat back, and winks at the kids—the same knowing wink he used with the lawyer at the beginning of the film, but this time filled with delight, energy, and affection, punctuated by a wrinkle of his button nose and a quiet chuckle.

The business Cagney performs with these boys is obviously not the sort of thing that the writers or director dreamed up out of thin air. Even though Curtiz has blocked and shot it skillfully, with an incessantly tracking camera, it was obviously based on the idea of how Cagney, as actor and star, would interact with this particular group. The thirties had produced a generation of pint-sized toughs like Frankie Darrow and Leo Gorcey, all of whom worked in Cagney's shadow. The boys in this film had become famous because of their appearance a year earlier in William Wyler's adaptation of *Dead End,* and Warner Brothers must have seen the advantage of pairing them with Cagney, who is in a sense their "father" as an actor. (Bogart had played a gangster role model for the Kids in the earlier film, but he was swarthy and evil, still typed as a coward and loser; Cagney could easily play a more benign figure, a gangster with a heart of gold.) Hence when Cagney performs in scenes with the Kids, he is called upon to do his star "turn" in the vaudeville sense. The audience has the nostalgic pleasure of watching a familiar actor go through his paces; the result is a subtle parallel between the fictional and professional situations of the actors as well as a stronger bond between audience and star.[2]

As Cagney's star image is foregrounded, the film takes on a heightened energy. Most of what we see is played for comedy, and Cagney's gestures become acrobatic. Inviting the Kids to his room for lunch, he orchestrates their chaos into a kind of circus act. He holds up a pickle jar while he talks, and then claps his hands together, tossing the jar across the room into somebody's lap; before it has even landed, he wheels and walks away, his hands coming apart and gesticulating at each side of his body. He eats with his hat on, pitching a sandwich over his shoulder to one boy while he talks to another, rising suddenly to stride across the room. "I'll tell ya what," he yells over the Kids' racket, pointing a finger at arm's length, turning and looking sideways down the arm like a duelist aiming a pistol; bending his elbow, he draws the finger back and seems to throw it forward a couple of times, keeping the wrist loose and flexible so that the gesture becomes a flourish.

These same choreographics take a more violent form in the basketball game Rocky subsequently engineers between the Kids and a respectable church-going group of boys. Acting as "referee," he performs a kind of Three-Stooges slapstick, his moves so rapid that he has done three things before the audience can react to one: he slaps an unruly kid and uppercuts him with the back of the same hand; then he wheels, almost pirouetting away, pointing at another kid, his mouth curled in a sneer. Although the basketball game is somewhat unconvincing (the very idea of Cagney on a basketball court is silly), it exemplifies the way the film as a whole organizes the performer's typical "act," allowing him moments of dervish intensity, but making him a far less anarchic character than he had been in the early thirties. Indeed all of his behavior is more controlled after this episode because the melodramatic plot takes over completely. Father Jerry suddenly becomes a Father Coughlin-like radio commentator, crusading against the bad influence of gangsters; the gangsters in turn plan to bump off Jerry, and Rocky is caught between his loyalty to a friend and his desire to "never be a sucker." He chooses to shoot down his untrustworthy companions in crime, a decision that ironically precipitates his last confrontation with the police.

The last sections of the film require a different strategy of Cagney the actor, a return to understatement that contrasts vividly with Curtiz's treatment of camera and *mise-en-scène*. All the Curtiz films of the late thirties had flamboyantly expressive lighting, a moving camera, and ostentatious sym-

---

2. One feature of the star system, as I noted in the previous discussion of Lillian Gish, is that the filmmakers often found some parallel between life and fiction that made the performance seem to grow directly out of the players. In this case, Cagney has described the Dead End Kids as a bunch of wise-guy rowdies whom he needed to tame on the set, just as he does in the movie (75).

bolism. The bottle of Vichy water that Captain Renault drops into a waste basket at a climactic moment in *Casablanca* is one of the most famous examples of a Curtiz "touch" (always underlined with a close-up), but there are equally obvious cases in *Angels,* as when Cagney shoots a gangster who falls dead over a leaflet urging citizens to express their opposition to crime. In this atmosphere, the relative subtlety of Cagney's portrayal is remarkable, and it prevents much of the film from becoming mere kitsch.

Rocky's final shoot-out with the police, for example, is staged no differently from the same scene in a dozen other crime pictures, except that Curtiz romantically backlights the exploding tear gas. Like the typical movie crook, Cagney finds himself trapped in a high place, surrounded by all the armed might of the police. He goes through a familiar routine, smashing out windowpanes and yelling at the cops down below, although when he fires his gun he does it in a Cagneyesque way, biting his lower lip, wrinkling his nose and throwing his arm forward with every shot like a boxer delivering a body punch. Most of the time, however, his moves seem measured, even a bit mechanical, showing none of the apocalyptic frenzy that marks equivalent scenes in other crime movies like *Scarface* or *White Heat.*

The implication of Cagney's performance is that for Rocky Sullivan the scene *is* a bit mechanical—still another battle with the cops that might be terminal but that he seems determined to act out to the end. Cagney never uses close-ups or his brief dialogue for their histrionic possibilities, or even for that feeling of tragic exhaustion one can see in Bogart's Roy Earle at the end of *High Sierra* (1941). Rocky is stoic, self-possessed, and uncomplaining, so that even in his most desperate moments he seems efficient and calm. He is nothing like the "Gangster as Tragic Hero" described by Robert Warshow, primarily because he never gives the impression that he is standing back to look at himself as the agent of some Marlovian drama. Quite simply, he is a man ready to deal with or accept whatever happens, a trait that will make his "breakdown" at the end of the film all the more shocking.

Cagney nicely calculates the closing scenes, never giving any more energy to a line or a piece of business than is necessary. (Notice that Bogart has served as a foil, sniveling, cringing, and generally overacting before Cagney shoots him down; at the same time, Bogart's death scene foreshadows Cagney's wild act near the end, when Rocky is strapped into the chair.) During the shootout we see Rocky in a disheveled state, his eyes burning with tear gas, but Cagney plays everything with utter calm, his age alone giving his close-ups a certain pathos. When he is captured (after throwing an empty pistol at the pursuing police), he is lit in the most extravagant, implausible way Curtiz could have chosen, the light coming from a low, unmotivated source, throwing crazy shadows up over his face. Rocky taunts the police ("So's your thick skull, copper!"), but Cagney's performance runs directly counter to the writing or the staging. Purely with the tone of his voice, he suggests that he is no hellish gunman, only an underdog who will never show fear or remorse.

This tone is maintained with considerable skill right up to the film's climax, even though the situation is pregnant with fake emotional possibilities: Rocky is on death row, waiting to be led off to the chair, and Jerry pays him a visit, asking him to die like a coward so that the Dead End Kids will be disillusioned. Everything about the scene in Rocky's cell is designed to show his undaunted spirit and toughness. Calmly smoking a cigarette, he says that Jerry can come in, but "tell him none of that incense and holy water." He flicks the cigarette butt into a guard's face, and when Jerry proposes that he make a sacrifice for the Kids, he rejects the idea immediately: "I'd have to have a heart, and that got cut out of me years ago." He says that his electrocution will be like sitting in a "barber chair," and when a sadistic guard tries to handcuff him during the last mile, he snarls "Get away from me, screw," punching him in the face. (Because this is Warners in 1939, none of the police retaliates.) "So long, kid," he says to Jerry and then marches grimly to the chair, dramatically lit by a series of spotlights that throw circles of light on the floor and provide him with a theatrical exit.

The whole thing is potentially laughable, and it presents problems for Cagney the actor. The trick is to convey Rocky's courage without making it seem braggadocio; every line and movement has to express strength, but Cagney's typical cockiness has to be muted, replaced by a kind of stoicism. Throughout the scene, therefore, he is relatively quiet, reading his speeches as fast as ever, but keeping them very soft, never inflecting them to show distress. When he speaks the "incense and holy water" line, he gives it no emphasis and no anger, only a slightly weary desire to dispense with pompous ceremony, at the same time letting us know that he is still Jerry's friend. When he slugs the cop who has been taunting him, he does it with the style of a man who is using absolutely no more energy than he needs to keep fools at bay. Only one touch of the old Cagney remains, and it is masterfully timed, signaling to the audience that he is the star they have always known: just before he begins the walk to the chair, he hitches up his pants with his wrists—the only time in the film he has used the gesture.

Rocky has refused the priest's request that he become a coward in the moment before death, but in fact he breaks down in a horrible crescendo of screams and sobs, pleading for mercy. The strategy of the film at this point is to produce an exchange or synthesis of value between the priest and the gangster. On the one hand, the Dead End Kids will adopt a new father, transferring their loyalty to the tough, authoritative priest whom we have seen using a fist in an earlier scene. For the real audience, however, Cagney's death has a reciprocal function, transferring saintliness from Jerry to Rocky, the tough star becoming a Christ figure.

In this regard it is interesting that we do not actually see Rocky being strapped into the chair. Perhaps Curtiz had to avoid the grisly details—in any case, he represents the electrocution with a montage, never even showing the actor's face. We see only dramatic shadows on the wall, hands clutching a radiator and being pried loose, and Pat O'Brien looking teary-eyed up to heaven. Cagney has said in his autobiography that he played the scene for its ambiguity and that for a long time afterward children would come up and ask him if Rocky was really a coward (75). But the ambiguity rises more out of the way the scene is written and shot than the way it is played, and its power has relatively little to do with Cagney's acting per se. The blood-curdling screams and tearful pleading are shocking, but they would have been equally impressive if some other actor's cries had been dubbed in place of Cagney's. It is the *idea* of Cagney's star image breaking down that is disturbing, because of all the Hollywood personae, he is the one the audience least expects to crack. (In *13 Rue Madeleine* [1948], for example, he is captured by the gestapo and endures hours of torture, laughing in triumph as the U.S. Air Force bombs him and the building to rumble.)

The audience has been cleverly set up for the hysterical death scene by Cagney's theatrical, spotlighted walk to the chair, which shows the diminutive actor dressed all in black, looking younger than at any other point, going off to death as if he were on his way to a performance. These shots hint that Rocky is going to be "acting" at the same time that they confirm the star's image—a player of tough guys for whom the audience has considerable affection. Then suddenly the image is broken or qualified, and the audience cannot be sure—they are left in nearly the same confused, troubled state of mind as the Dead End Kids, who cannot believe the reports of Rocky's death that they read in the newspapers. (At another level, the terror and intensity of Cagney's screams before death may give the general public a chastened attitude toward the death penalty; for if a tough male star from Hollywood, a supposed "innocent," can break down in such a fashion, public execution must be truly horrible.)

I do not want to overstate the ambiguity of these last scenes, but the ambiguity is there, hovering subliminally behind the film's conclusion, sanctifying Rocky in the eyes of the priest and also resulting in some fine dramatic ironies. Like the group of boys who have idolized Rocky, we in the audience have watched the hero act an out-of-character death, and this provokes a dizzy swirl of problems in reading the performance. Have we seen an actor acting a character who is acting? Where does "performance" end and "reality" begin? We are then given strange comfort by Father Jerry, who pays a visit to the boys in their hideout. "Let's ask Father," the boys all say, rushing forward to learn the truth from the spokesman who is supposed to represent God. Father Jerry says that Rocky died just the way the newspapers have reported it. (Is the priest lying, or does it matter? The irony is bottomless.) He then leads everyone off toward the church, the voices of a youth choir swelling on the soundtrack. If there have been any doubts about Cagney's toughness, any rupture of his image, this ending tries to smooth over the problem, confirming his stardom at a higher level. Indeed the film as a whole is intent on devising new structural relations between Cagney's celebrity, his fictional role, and his acting skills; it hopes thus to transform him into nothing less than a heavenly character.

10

Katharine Hepburn in *Holiday* (1938)

Although the images of players like James Cagney and Marlene Dietrich were eventually adjusted to the demands of the Production Code, stardom for Katharine Hepburn involved a series of subtler, more complex negotiations. Throughout her career, her name connoted not only breeding, intelligence, and "theatah," but also New England austerity, athleticism, and feminine emancipation. Occasionally, she played tomboys or charmingly lost her dignity in screwball comedy, but screenwriters and publicists had trouble making her sufficiently ordinary—a quality successful movie actors need, because they function both as ego ideals and as common folk with whom the audience can identify. Hepburn was badly suited to such ends, at least in terms of the usual formulas. She would have been miscast as a housewife or a dance-hall girl, and she seldom played the suffering women of soap opera. The roles critics have suggested for her include Shakespeare's Rosalind (which she attempted once on stage without much success), Jane Austen's Emma Woodhouse, and Henry James's Isabel Archer. In effect, she was what Andrew Britton has described as a Jamesian "princess"—too privileged and controversial to be well liked—and it was not until her much-publicized relationship with Spencer Tracy that the public truly took her to heart.

On screen Hepburn was alert, idealistic, and active, living in wealthy or professionalized worlds. Rarely flirtatious (except to put comic quotation marks around it), she seemed too witty and willful for the average leading man. Inevitably, her films raised feminist issues, but this inclination, like her upper-class manner, had to be contained or controlled. In fact, her social class could be used as a weapon against her whenever she appeared too progressive. Like Vanessa Redgrave or Jane Fonda—her descendants in some

ways—she was frequently described as "spoiled." Her acting technique ex-
acerbated these tensions, because it was clearly associated with "legitimate"
theater. Vocally and expressively, she was too lofty for the populist mid thirties, when John Barrymore (the star of her first film) became a symbol of
hammyness, and when Garbo and Dietrich were increasingly regarded as vestiges of an older, elitist sensibility. As a result, the bulk of her films developed
strategies to lighten or normalize her highly ostensive, drama-school style,
and they usually found ways to tame or chastise the strong-willed, aristocratic
characters she played. Moreover, the extended narrative constituted by her
various roles tells the story of a retreat from assertiveness, a cautious adjust-
ment not unlike the plot resolutions in her individual pictures. Simon Watney
has remarked that she "stands for a certain type of 'free woman' in her early
films, until her persona is eventually overwhelmed by its very longevity,
transforming her into an icon of survival, yet another version of the American
dream which successfully represses the history which determines it" (61).
Andrew Sarris makes a similar point, describing her career in terms of a
"premature feminism" and observing that she was complicit in a move toward
more conservative roles after 1939 (quoted by Watney, 39).

Like many successful stars, Hepburn selected her own scripts and managed her image to a remarkable degree—abetted by money and a series of
friendships with writers. From the beginning, she was regarded as a combat-
ive, high-spirited androgyne, and not surprisingly, she achieved her first great
theatrical success in *The Warrior's Husband* (1932), a modernized version
of *Lysistrata*. Soon afterward, she signed a contract with RKO, where she
won an Academy Award in the following year for *Morning Glory* (1933).
Throughout the thirties, especially in collaboration with Cukor, Hawks, and
Grant, she challenged the dominant modes of Hollywood romance, and partly
for that reason, her relationship to the studio system was embattled, involving
periodic returns to Broadway. Her most popular film role of the decade was
Jo in *Little Women* (1933), which was followed by a disastrous failure on
Broadway in *The Lake* (1934), where she provoked Dorothy Parker's famous
comment that her performance "ran the gamut of emotions from A to B."
Back in California, she acquired a new voice coach and a new co-star, Cary
Grant, who appeared with her in *Sylvia Scarlett* (1936) and then in *Bringing
Up Baby* (1938). But despite the critical praise her films of the late thirties
received, only *Stage Door* was popular with audiences.[1] Indeed, the poor
showing of *Bringing Up Baby* led Harry Brandt, president of the Independent
Theater Owners of America, to pronounce Hepburn "Box Office Poison" (a

---

1. It may be worth noting how *Stage Door*—in some ways the most politically progressive
of Hepburn's movies—tends to foreground the "negative" traits of the star in order to defend
against them. When the picture was made, Hepburn was known to the public as an aristocratic,
feminist type who loved the stage and who often refused to give interviews for fan magazines.
Thus, the film depicts Tracy Randall as a New England blue-blood who wants to go on stage (in

label he also attached to Garbo, Dietrich, Crawford, and Fred Astaire). RKO then began treating Hepburn badly, at one point offering her a project entitled *Mother Carey's Chickens*. In response, she bought out her contract for almost a quarter-million late-Depression dollars and moved to Columbia, where Harry Cohn assembled an attractive package: a remake of Philip Barry's *Holiday*, with Grant as co-star, Cukor as director, and Donald Ogden Stewart as writer. Once again the film was excellent, but it did not arrest Hepburn's declining fortunes. Although Cukor advocated her for Scarlett O'Hara in *Gone With the Wind*, her career in Hollywood seemed virtually ended.[2]

A turning point came soon, however, and it involved Hepburn's active intervention. Her friendship with Philip Barry and her brief romance with Howard Hughes (who became a financial backer) enabled her to commission *The Philadelphia Story*, a play which, as Sarris has observed, "was about Katharine Hepburn *herself*, and what the American people thought about Katharine Hepburn in 1939, and what Katharine Hepburn realized she had to do in order to keep her career going" (quoted in Watney, 39). The result, as everyone knows, was a great stage success and a celebrated MGM adaptation. Although Cary Grant received top billing in the film version, the entire project had obviously been designed to recuperate Hepburn—not so much changing her image as dramatizing her full submission to patriarchal authority and foreshadowing her later attachment to the most conservative of American studios.[3] Grant, in fact, was much less important to *The Philadelphia Story* than James Stewart, who performed the same "service" for Hepburn as he had for Dietrich one year earlier in *Destry Rides Again*. John Kobal's rapt description of a crucial scene in the Hepburn film is a clear, if unwitting, indication of how Stewart functioned ideologically:

---

a play associated with Hepburn herself); the other characters joke about her snooty-sounding accent, Adolph Menjou describes her as a "militant," and at the end, having achieved stardom, she is shown walking out on a crowd of reporters. By way of mitigating against such problems, the picture establishes Randall as a good-hearted, unpretentious democrat; it gives her an excellent reason for skipping out on the interview, and it pairs her with Ginger Rogers, who functions in exactly the same way as she had with Fred Astaire. As Hepburn's "buddy" or displaced love-interest, Rogers provides a "down-to-earth" middle-classness, making Hepburn as Randall seem more ordinary.

2. David Selznick had been as important to the "discovery" of Hepburn as George Cukor and was the producer of her first film. During the casting of *GWTW*, however, he wrote the following memo to his associate, Daniel T. O'Shea: "I think Hepburn has two strikes against her—first, the unquestionable and very widespread intense public dislike of her at the moment, and second, the fact that she is yet to demonstrate that she possesses the sex qualities which are probably the most important of all the many requisites of Scarlett. . . ." (171).

3. L. B. Mayer was fond of Hepburn, although he ordered the sexist conclusion to *Woman of the Year* (1942), in which she dons an apron and tries to cook Spencer Tracy's breakfast (Higham, 103). At MGM, she also worked regularly with her friend Cukor, but scholars make an error when they describe him as an especially sensitive exponent of women's concerns; indeed, some of Cukor's typical films—such as *The Women* (1939) and *Les Girls* (1957)—are profoundly misogynistic.

Here the still feverishly overactive spoiled brat is brought down to earth. She is told by a man of the people (James Stewart) that she is not a creature of ice but a real woman. . . .At this moment, her transformation occurs. Stewart woos her on our behalf. Hepburn, dressed by Adrian, incandescently lit and photographed by Joseph Ruttenberg . . . sways, trembles, succumbs, and—with Stewart as our envoy—wins us. Her film career began in earnest. (32)

It was Grant, not Stewart, who "got" Hepburn at the end of the picture. Perhaps significantly, however, it was Stewart who received the Academy Award, and Hepburn and Grant never acted together again. One year later, Hepburn began her remarkable association with Spencer Tracy, an even more plain-spoken "man of the people," who provided a counterbalancing ordinariness for the extraordinary Hepburn persona. Their work together contains some of the finest pieces of comic acting in the history of American cinema, and films such as *State of the Union* (1948) and *Adam's Rib* (1949) still seem "advanced." Nevertheless, the Hepburn and Tracy performances were increasingly predicated on the audience's knowledge of an offscreen relationship, and as various critics have observed, they foster an image of "good old Kate"—a woman who might behave like a liberationist, but who is reassuringly, almost maternally, attached to Tracy and who will, in the last instance, subdue her rebellion for his sake. Increasingly, she became an emblem of safely domesticated feminism, until finally, as if in full payment for all those years of independence, she was cast as a spinster who declared admiration for aging symbols of virility like Humphrey Bogart and John Wayne.

Some of Hepburn's later appearances are outstanding—especially her interpretation of Mary Tyrone in *Long Day's Journey into Night* (1962)—but her most exhilarating work was done in the late thirties, at precisely the moment when her career was foundering. *Holiday* comes from that period (*The Philadelphia Story* might have been written in direct response to it), highlighting her unusual but ravishing beauty and giving full range to the dynamic of her acting. *Holiday* also had an important personal significance. Although Columbia advertised her as "the new Hepburn," she was in fact going back to her earliest theatrical experience. In 1928, just out of college, she had been the understudy for the lead role in Barry's play (written for the stage performer Hope Williams and starring Ann Harding in the 1930 movie version). Later, Hepburn had used one of its scenes as the basis for her original RKO screen test. She seems to have identified with the role, and she certainly knew that it was a good showcase for her technique.

In certain ways, *Holiday* was also an attempt to mollify the more threatening aspects of Hepburn's persona: it allows her to signify patrician manners but at the same time gives her an opportunity to seem unpretentious and even folksy; it lets her challenge the rule of an oppressive father (a typical Republican financier of thirties melodrama), but it also suggests that she will fulfill herself through fond obedience to a husband. As a social commentary, the film is badly compromised—not least because Philip Barry was enamoured of the class he had set out to criticize; nevertheless, in qualified fashion it enables Hepburn to act out an "ideal self," providing a safe outlet for mannerisms the audience may have disliked. In this way, *Holiday* hopes to make viewers love the star.

Holiday belongs to an always problematic and nowadays virtually extinct movie genre—the well-made "comedy of manners" that gently satirizes the *haute bourgeoisie*. Typically, such films are derived from theater pieces set in drawing rooms, and they are composed of neatly rounded, almost epigrammatic speeches. George Cukor has described Barry's language as a form of "singing" dialogue (Higham, 87), and Hepburn was attracted to it. She and the other players often try to underplay the evident theatricality of the speeches by overlapping or throwing away lines; stylistically and in most other ways, however, the film remains faithful to the original text, merely rearranging a few scenes, adding some topical references, and "opening out" the action. (The chief screenwriter, Donald Ogden Stewart, was probably as fond of the project as Hepburn, since he had acted in the play when she was an understudy.)

Barry founded his drama on an opposition between two sets of values, visualized quite early in the film by a contrast between the Potter household and the Seton household. On the one hand are Susan and Nick Potter (Jean Dixon and Edward Everett Horton, who repeats the role he played in the first film version), a middle-aged, childless pair of academics, representing freedom from possessions, spontaneity, and "life." On the other hand is Edward Seton (Henry Kolker), a widowed patriarch with three children, representing old wealth, capitalism, and joyless acquistion of power. At first glance, the contrast between these figures seems to be posed in terms of social class, since the Potters live in a shabby-genteel, almost bohemian apartment, whereas the Seton mansion looks as large as the Louvre. At bottom, however, the film is offering a choice between two life-styles within bourgeois democracy. The Potters are a distinguished couple with enough income to take a "holiday" from capitalism. If they were real persons instead of fictional characters, they would be members of what Marxist theory describes as a social *fraction*—made up in this case of educated, dissident members of a privileged class who criticize the dominant ethos (the same fraction, in fact, to which Hepburn, Barry, and Stewart belonged).

Individualists rather than political activists, the Potters see life in terms of friendships and humane, egalitarian relations. They are a distinctly American couple who sometimes seem more like comics than intellectuals (an effect produced by the casting of Horton and Dixon, who play their roles fairly straight). Nevertheless, they are also professional educators who in their social position and attitude could be compared with the members of the "Bloomsbury" circle in England during the twenties and thirties: thus they are sophisticated, disrespectful of unrestrained capitalism, and vaguely feminist. (The Hepburn character immediately recognizes Susan Eliot Potter as someone who "once gave a lecture at my school.") In more specific terms, the film presents them as unpretentious liberals whose chief weapon is wit, as when they give Nazi salutes to an especially pompous, right-wing couple at a party in the Seton home.

The plot of the picture involves a deepening friendship between Johnny Case (Grant), a virtual child of the Potters, and Linda Seton (Hepburn), a dissatisfied daughter of the capitalist. The relationship between these soulmates is complicated by two factors: first by Johnny's engagement to Linda's sister, Julia (Doris Nolan), and second, by the conflict between Johnny and Linda's father. The emotional center of the action, however, is Linda, who spends most of her time on the top floor of the mansion in a children's playroom, which her deceased mother once constructed as a "place to have fun." Not yet a madwoman in the attic, she is a vibrant character who describes herself as a "black sheep." From the beginning, it is clear that she must break completely from her father or else become a wasted personality like her brother Ned (Lew Ayres). But she must also cope with an emotional struggle between her love for Johnny and her love for her sister.

To its credit, *Holiday* does not work out a reconciliation between Linda and her father; instead, it shows Linda making an intense, heroic denunciation of the Seton values and going off to live on "holiday" with Johnny. The conclusion is a disappointment nonetheless. Linda's sister has a last-act speech in which she coolly announces that Johnny's unwillingness to adjust to the Seton way of life has made him an unworthy partner, thus leaving Linda conveniently free to fly into Johnny's arms without guilt. Moreover, the impending union between Johnny and Linda evades the central issues. Johnny Case comes from a wage-earning family, but he has worked his way through Harvard and acquired all the skills necessary to become a "young wizard of finance"; his objection to Edward Seton has less to do with capitalism than with the supposedly dreary process of making millions. The major alternatives of the plot are therefore posed in terms of a settling/wandering dichotomy typical of American popular fiction. As Andrew Britton has pointed out, the final scenes have a great deal in common with *Stagecoach* (1939), where the ideal couple simply ride off into the sunset, "free of the blessings of civilization" (Britton, 85). An even deeper evasion can be sensed in Linda's parting speech to her father, in which she declares her independence in terms of her subordination to another man and to another sort of capitalism. She is going to be with Johnny no matter what he wants to do. Even if he decides to sell peanuts, "oh, how I'll love those peanuts!"

Despite these awkward compromises and a few other problems I shall mention, *Holiday* contains a striking performance by Hepburn. In classic fashion, she enters several minutes into the action, creating a mild *coup de théâtre*. The opening sequence shows Johnny Case returning from a vacation and breathlessly announcing to the Potters that he has found his ideal mate. "It's love fellas. I've met the girl!" Given the star system, we know that Hepburn will be his choice, and we assume she is the woman to whom he refers. That assumption is reinforced in the next sequence, when Johnny goes to meet the girl's parents, only to discover that she lives in a mansion. We expect Hepburn to make an appearance when the butler announces Johnny's arrival to "Miss Julia," but Doris Nolan enters instead, and Grant rushes to embrace her. Hepburn shows up later, symbolically intruding on the two lovers as they kiss in the mansion elevator. A door slides open and there she stands, a mink-coated figure casting an ironic glance at the couple: "For shame, Julia!" she says. "Is this the way to spend Sunday morning? Who's your partner, anyone I know?"

Until this point, the film has been relatively disappointing. Grant plays everything with characteristic pep and comic eccentricity, but his dialogue is speechy and somewhat fey. There is an intriguing moment when Lew Ayres appears as Ned—a reserved, rather *triste* drunkard who ignores Grant and asks the butler to have a drink ready at the end of church services; otherwise, however, Hepburn creates all the dramatic tension and interest. She is, in fact, a slightly more dominating presence than Barry had intended. Compare her effect to the stage direction accompanying Linda's entrance in the play, written with Hope Williams in mind: "Linda is twenty-seven, and looks about twenty-two. She is slim, rather boyish, and exceedingly fresh. She is smart, she is pretty, but beside Julia . . . she seems a trifle gauche, and almost plain." Hepburn possesses many of these traits, but clearly she is a glamorous figure, a good deal more attractive than Nolan. When she enters, the acting takes on a discernible pace and heightened energy, partly because of the sexual vitality she brings into the frame; in fact, one of the weaknesses of the film is that it never gives a plausible reason why Johnny should be interested in Julia in the first place. (The 1930 version cast Mary Astor in the Nolan role—a more interesting choice that makes Johnny's behavior plausible. Probably Columbia did not want to set Hepburn against another star, although it did test the young Rita Hayworth for the part.)

Then, too, Hepburn tends to command the screen with her flamboyant theatrical rhetoric. For example, she offers to shake Johnny's hand in a fashion that immediately announces Linda's difference from the rest of the Seton family—a strong movement, the spread palm placed exactly at the center of the shared, three-figure composition, connoting a forthright, no-nonsense offer of friendship. She repeats the movement toward the end of the sequence, when she tells Julia "I like this man," and as a signifier of character it is no less vivid than Johnny's repeated somersaults. In conventional terms the gesture is "unladylike," in keeping with the easy way she looks Grant up and down when she requests him to "step out here in the light." It is never "gauche," however, nor does it resemble the aggressive sexual innuendo of a player like Dietrich; instead, it suggests mature, aristocratic self-confidence, together with the unaffected frankness of a woman who expects to meet a man on equal terms.

There is, in other words, a likable sexiness about Hepburn's performance, a quality reminiscent of the leading women in the films of Howard Hawks, who never act coy and who engage in banter like one of the boys. Cukor allows her to exhibit those qualities immediately, and, like Hawks, he gives her plenty of opportunity to walk. One of the chief pleasures of *Bringing Up Baby,* which exerts a subtle influence on this film, comes from watching Hepburn stride confidently across the screen while Grant struggles in her wake, awash in chaos; in *Holiday,* her introductory sequence is photographed in a tracking movement designed to show her wit and physical grace. Leading Grant and Nolan briskly down a hallway, she jokes with Grant, adopting the tone of a family elder—the first of several instances where Linda Seton will parody her father: "This modern generation! Well, young man, I hope you realize what you're getting yourself in for." She pauses briefly to chat, and then as she parts company the camera tilts, watching her jog easily up a long stairway.

Linda's run up the stairs helps establish an affinity with Johnny—a physical exuberance apparent later in the film, when she joins him in a somersault. But it also functions in excess of what the story needs, pointing to Hepburn's own body. She has the flexible, slender build of a tennis player, and she walks or jogs as forthrightly as she shakes hands—legs extended, arms moving in an arc, with no suggestion of a wiggle or sway. This quality, more than any other, led to her "tomboy" roles, and it placed her virtually alone among the glamorous women of her day in suggesting a romantic line and style of movement not based on dance.[4] In certain contexts, her body could evoke a spartan schoolmarm or a willowy fashion model; its compositon and musculature, however, were developed from sport, and for a time she resembled what Kenneth Tynan has called an "outdoor Garbo." Several of her films allude to her well-known athletic skill: in *Bringing Up Baby,* she exhibits her golf swing, and in *Pat and Mike* (1952), she plays a character based on Babe Dietrichson. Earlier in her career, her more candid photographs made her look rather like a Wildean youth, especially when she was shown in short hair and slacks or when she was caught in movement. Yet no one who has seen her wearing a

4. In *A Bill of Divorcement* (1932), Hepburn's first film, George Cukor had given her a moment that convinced David Selznick she would become a star: "Not until the preview was the staff convinced that we had a great screen personality. . . . But very early in the picture there was a scene in which Hepburn just walked across the room, stretched her arms, and then lay out on the floor before the fireplace. It sounds very simple, but you could almost feel, and you could definitely hear, the excitement in the audience" (43). The effect of this shot remains electric; the distant framing and the silence allow us to focus on her body, revealing the sex appeal she could give to apparently ordinary movement.

skin-tight, silver lamé jumpsuit in *Christopher Strong* (1933) could doubt her potential as an erotic female star.

Whenever *Holiday* wants to give Hepburn a typical glamor, it emphasizes her long hair and exquisite cheekbones—all the while garbing her in a floor-length black dress, backlighting her face, and photographing her through diffused light. Even at her most "feminine," however, she is unorthodox, and her style has troubled some critics. Charles Higham, for example, has praised Cukor for concealing her "powerful stride" (actually, Cukor does nothing of the kind), meanwhile regretting that her voice is "too harsh and strident," her body insufficiently "soft and yielding" (88). Throughout her career, reviewers and co-stars made similar complaints; often she was regarded as a skinny, rather plain woman who spoke with an odd voice and knew how to create the *illusion* of beauty.[5] The idea that she was not beautiful is, of course, absurd, revealing Hollywood's difficulty in appropriating her manner to conventional norms of femininity. Besides her aristocratic features and fabled "Bryn Mawr accent," she had a lean physique and an energetic, potentially aggressive attitude; in the words of Andrew Britton, she suggested a "too militant beauty whose confidence precisely isn't contingent on male approval" (13).

In spite of all this, Hepburn was a blessing to cameramen, who knew how to accent her remarkable bone structure and who drew out her love of extravagant posing. There was also truth in the theory that she knew how to act like a beautiful woman. "Now that girl there," she once said to John Kobal, pointing to one of her old studio photographs, "liked to show off. . . . I photographed better than I looked, so it was easy for me. . . . I let myself go in front of the camera. I mean you can't photograph a dead cat. . . . it's not how you look that's important but how you come across" (109). Hepburn's way of "coming across," however, could sometimes be as controversial as her appearance. Chaplin had relied on techniques of music hall and mime; Gish had gestured like a heroine of melodrama; Dietrich had stood and posed like a singer in cabaret; and Cagney had evoked a vaudeville dancer. In contrast to these, Hepburn reminded her audience of the legitimate stage—Broadway or West End drama inflected by the older romanticism of Terry, Duse, and Bernhardt. As a result, both theater and movie critics sometimes found her pretentious, like a prima donna who was imitating theatrical conventions rather than genuinely "feeling" the part.

One of Hollywood's solutions to the problem was to cast her as an actor, so that her behavior would be normalized by the role. Thus in *Morning Glory* and *Stage Door* she freely indulges her "actressy" tendencies, projecting her resonant voice as if she were aiming at the back row of an auditorium, ges-

---

5. Hepburn's voice was the chief thing critics complained about, especially in the disastrous production of *The Lake*. Oddly, theater reviewers found her a weak speaker, whereas in movies she seemed just the opposite. In mid career she underwent training with Isaac Van Grove, who tried to make her sound less "affected" (Higham, 95).

turing rather grandly, and visibly thinking about the camera. By the same token, her films often contain moments when she amusingly "quotes" old-fashioned performance. In *Desk Set* (1957), for example, she gives readings of "Hiawatha" and "The Curfew Shall Not Toll Tonight," dramatizing the latter piece with elaborate pantomime gestures. In the early thirties, publicists praised her "genius" and directors stressed the theme of theater, allowing her to play characters who adopt visible masks, as in *Sylvia Scarlett* and *Alice Adams* (1935). In such contexts, her technique looked like "fine art" (which may explain why she won three Oscars and was nominated more often than any other actor).

As an instance of Hepburn's rather histrionic effect, notice her vivid changes in posture and voice during the scene in *Holiday* when Linda Seton confronts her father during her sister's engagement party: first she adopts an almost military stance, looking him in the eye and making a ringing declaration: "Listen to me, Father. Tonight means a good deal to me." Trying to explain why she wants time alone with a few friends, she appeals to his feelings, first bending slightly to plead, then turning away, tossing her head back, and gazing along the walls as if she were searching for some remote ideal. "It has something to do with this room, and when I was a child," she says in a tremulous, "singing" voice. When Henry Kolker suggests that she leave ("Why don't you go away? . . . You distress me. You cause nothing but trouble and upset."), she becomes teary and distraught, barely hiding her emotion by turning her back as she promises to go away forever. "I can't bear it here any longer," she says. "It's doing terrible things to me!" Her playing is invested with a good deal of emotional "contagion," but it clearly involves a classy middlebrow variant of melodramatic technique—a series of rather conventional mannerisms well-suited to "coming across" on the proscenium stage.

This style is especially evident in *Holiday* whenever Hepburn is called upon to display expressive incoherence—that is, during scenes when her character tries to mask her deepest feelings. Consider the moment early in the film when she and Doris Nolan are sitting at the bottom of a staircase discussing the forthcoming wedding: Hepburn asks to give an engagement party up in the old "playroom," and she insists that "Father's to have nothing to do with it." As she makes the point, she turns away from Nolan and slightly toward us, as if to conceal emotion from her sister. Holding her head up proudly, she gazes down to the floor in tragic dignity: "No one's to touch my party but me, do you hear?" Suddenly there is a tearful crack in her voice and a hesitation in her speech, covered by an attempt to laugh: "No, if they do I . . . I won't come to it!" In a later scene, Hepburn asks Lew Ayres if her affection for Grant has been showing too much. She stands in profile to the left of the screen, hands resting atop a grand piano. "Ned?" she asks, turning her face as if to hide her expression from him—all the while showing it more clearly to us. She tosses her head up proudly for a moment and then indicates embarrassment by looking down to the floor. "Do you remember when we . . . New Year's Eve?" Raising her handsome shoulders and tucking in her chin, she looks downward even more, as if she were ashamed. Her voice begins to tremble. "Does it stand out all over me?" The answer of course is yes, chiefly because she is behaving so ostentatiously for the camera.

Critics were sometimes distressed by such visible tricks, regarding them as highbrow affectations; nevertheless, the same critics were quite happy when Hepburn played comedy. For instance, the *Time* magazine review of *Bringing Up Baby* in 1938 remarked that "the cinema audience will enjoy . . . seeing stagey Actress Hepburn get a proper mussing up." In fact, she was brilliant in the Hawks film—not only because she had the physical skill for slapstick but also because most forms of comedy are "stagey," relying on heightened expressiveness and crisp theatrical enunciation. For nearly the same reason, Hepburn and Spencer Tracy were a stunning combination whenever they had amusing material; like virtually all the great comic duos, they comprised what Fredric Jameson has called a "tandem" characterization: her slightly overstated elocution was set off against his dry, conversational tone; her quick, visibly rhetorical movement was played off against his slow, stolid reaction.

Holiday seems particularly well-suited to Hepburn's bravura style, not only because it contains a number of gently comic and even "screwball" scenes but also because it subtly valorizes the art of acting, turning Linda Seton into another variant of the "theatrical character" described by Leo Braudy.[6] A typical film for both Cukor and Hepburn, it uses the idea of performance thematically, contrasting the liberated antics in Linda's upstairs room with the hypocritical playacting elsewhere in the Seton household. During the engagement party, for example, the guests in the "playroom" do acrobatic stunts, stage Punch-and-Judy shows, engage in communal singing, and imitate various funny characters. The dead mother's room becomes a carnivalistic space where acting is a force of personal and social health; paradoxically, it is also the realm of authenticity, where characters regress to pre-Oedipal games or hold heart-to-heart talks that reveal "true" feelings. Meanwhile, in the paternalistic downstairs regions, people become players of a different kind and enact a stifling ritual that they take all too seriously; no joy comes from such behavior, and their staged selves are marked as deceptive or repressive.

This theme is a very old one, common to what C. L. Barber once termed "festive comedy." (Compare Shakespeare's *Henry IV, Part One*, which creates

---

6. Braudy has remarked that such characters in the 1930s are nearly always members of the upper class, "or, better, someone pretending to be upper class. . . . Whether the aristocrat is Cary Grant, Katharine Hepburn, or Pierre Fresnay's Boeldieu in *La Grande Illusion*, the sense of self as theater, as play, is paramount" (235).

a dialectic between the two forms of playacting, reminding us that "if all the year were playing holidays, / To sport would be as tedious as to work.") An excellent basis for drama, festivity makes us aware of the craft of acting, creating a pretext for "staginess." At the same time, it implicitly justifies theater as a profession, emphasizing the therapeutic value of play and associating the performers' virtuosity with the *joie de vivre* of the most sympathetic characters. Thus the playroom sequences in *Holiday* not only enhance Hepburn's charm, they also suggest that her love of theatrics (like Linda Seton's) is consistent with humane wit and progressive idealism.

Aspects of these scenes are worth considering in detail, both as evidence of Hepburn's mastery of a variety of acting skills and as an indication of how the film merges professional attributes of the star with moral attributes of the character. Consider, for example, the quiet moment early on, when the rest of the Seton family is away at church and Linda invites Johnny upstairs for a chat. Throughout this relatively uncomplicated sequence, Hepburn is very much the center of interest, controlling the changing moods of the conversation. She moves, gestures, and poses more vividly than Grant (who, like most leading men, is reserved and less obviously on display), and as the friendship between Linda and Johnny develops, she becomes increasingly theatrical, dominating the entire space.

When Grant enters, she is munching an apple. "Wanna bite?" she asks, holding it out in a friendly gesture. This ingenious piece of business has no precedent in Barry's text, but it serves to mock the Seton family values: while everyone else is stiffly putting on a front at Sunday services, Johnny and Linda behave with childlike informality, the apple evoking an Eden where women are healthy rather than sinful. Grant accepts the fruit and walks around, his back to us, while she stands chewing and regarding him. The dramatic pause gives her time to swallow, and because the scene involves polite dialogue and several camera setups, neither character tastes the apple again—Grant merely holds it, preoccupied with the room. After a moment Hepburn picks up a cigarette and thoughtfully taps it against a box, as if considering how to begin. She keeps the cigarette unlit, using the incompleted action to show Linda's pleased response to Johnny's interest in the surroundings. First she explains the significance of the place ("This was Mother's idea . . . she was marvelous."), and as she talks she sits at the right of the screen in a favored position, crossing her legs and propping her elbow on her knee with characteristic angularity.

Answering Grant's questions about various toys, she begins moving about the room, at one point holding a stuffed giraffe named Leopold next to her face, its long neck and equine features echoing her own. "Looks like me," she says, and a medium close-up makes us aware of the actor within the role, joking about herself. When Grant finds a childhood picture of Julia Seton and admires it, Hepburn's amused tone changes, and she makes a frank avowal

Hepburn poses with a toy giraffe.

of how much she loves her sister; squatting on the floor next to him, she adopts the first in a series of overtly theatrical voices, imitating a stereotypical cop in order to ask about his past: "What about these little jaunts to Placid? Come clean, Case!" Grant answers that the skiing vacation where he met Julia was his first holiday and then expresses curiosity about her own background. Rather wistfully she confesses that she once wanted to go on the stage. "Would you care to see me do the sleepwalking scene from *Macbeth?* 'Out, out, damned spot!'" Hepburn flings the line off in her grand Yankee accent, and then turns wryly reminiscent: "The teachers at Miss Porter's school thought it was very promising," she cracks, tapping the still unlit cigarette on her thumbnail.

After Johnny confesses his plans for a "holiday" (not "just to play," but to find out "why I'm working"), the private conversation gives way to frivolous action. Ned and Julia make an entrance, having returned from church. Ned doodles at the piano, reluctantly playing a few bars of a pseudo-Gershwinesque "Symphony in F Minor" that is supposed to indicate his latent talent as a composer, and Linda becomes gleeful, drawing Johnny into a rehearsal for his upcoming interview with Edward Seton. (Notice once again that the technique bears a resemblance to *Henry IV, Part One,* where characters parody scenes that are later played in earnest.) "Ned," she says to her brother, "I think we can give him some coaching." Lew Ayres picks up a banjo and Hepburn goes into an act, pretending to be a sour patriarch inquiring about his prospective son-in-law. Clearing her throat and folding her arms across her chest, she looks at Grant sternly: "Well, young man?" Grant smiles: "Well, sir, at the moment I have in my pocket exactly thirty-four dollars and a coupon for a bank night."

Julia insists that Johnny ought to take things more seriously, but Hepburn quickly tosses off a whole series of impersonations. "I'm afraid he won't do, Julia," she says in a male drawl. "He's a comely boy, but probably just another of the vast army of clock watchers." When Johnny admits his humble origins, she rears back in the mock astonishment of a society matron: "You mean to say that your mother wasn't even a *whosis?*" Ned interjects that Johnny may have a judge somewhere in the family. "Yes! That might help," she says, and as Ned strums a ditty on the banjo she transforms her act into a minstrel show. "Ol' Jedge Case's boy! Evenin', Massa!" Ned then suggests that a little namedropping would be useful, and Hepburn reverts to her parody of a socialite; standing tall, one hand on her hip, she sashays over to Grant: "Johnny, she says to me (she always calls me Johnny). . . ."[7]

Later in the film during the massive New Year's Eve engagement party Edward Seton arranges for Julia, the behavior in the upstairs room becomes even more theatrical, with everyone joining in the act. Soon after the Potters arrive and introduce themselves to Linda, Ned enters like the pied piper, playing on a whistle and leading a platoon of waiters with champagne. Linda organizes the group into a quartet for a rendition of "Camptown Races," and Nick Potter acts the balcony scene from *Romeo and Juliet* with hand puppets. Johnny, sent upstairs by Julia to persuade everyone to come to the reception below, pretends to be a butler delivering a message. As punishment for his stuffy behavior, the other four make him run the gauntlet. Nick makes a comic public speech, presenting Johnny with the toy giraffe from the earlier scene as a "trophy." Johnny stands on the couch and bows shyly to applause, and then offers to demonstrate his acrobatic skill, teaching Linda how to do a back flip.

Throughout this busy action, the players assume childlike attitudes, putting their feet on the furniture and sprawling on the floor—a device common to many of the thirties screwball comedies, in which wealthy characters are made to seem charmingly irresponsible and "human" by virtue of their posture. Despite the apparent abandon of the party, however, Hepburn is at the center of most of the compositions, and she has a good chance to display the

7. Some of this mockery seems a bit strained, since Grant and Hepburn embody all the traits of sophisticated society. The problem is especially evident in a previous scene, when Grant describes himself as a "plain man of the people." The self-deprecating, ironic twist he gives to his voice cannot save the line from absurdity.

Hepburn adopts a "casual" pose.

angular grace of her body. A lovely figure in a dark dress, she smiles radiantly
and moves with a kind of swashbuckling élan—as when she steps over the
back of a couch, plants one foot on the pillowcase, and snatches a champagne
bottle off a table. When the festivity is interrupted by the entrance of Seton
Cram and his wife (Henry Daniell and Binnie Barnes), she mutters "It's the
Witch and Dopey" in a stage whisper and perches atop the backrest of a chair.
Crossing her legs, she leans forward and props her elbow on her knee, resting
her chin in her hand in a pose that contrasts with the stuffy postures of Daniell
and Barnes, making her look as lanky and appealing as the young Stewart or
Fonda.

The scene also allows Hepburn to ad-lib an occasional line and behave
"amateurishly," as when she harmonizes with the other actors in the singing
of "Camptown Races." The result is a sense of the star as "real" person—as
if the process of acting silly candidly revealed her nonprofessional attributes,
making her seem less like a highbrow. *Bringing Up Baby* is filled with such
scenes; for instance, when Hepburn and Grant sing their famous duet of "I
Can't Give You Anything But Love, Baby," the humor derives partly from
our recognition of two remotely glamorous stars who are behaving a little
awkwardly, like people we might encounter at a party. The equivalent moment

Performance within performance.

in *Holiday* comes when Grant teaches Hepburn how to do a somersault—a piece of action devised especially for this film. It hardly matters that the double flip is actually executed by stunt people; the illusion is perfectly maintained, and the action leading up to the trick is both amusing and graceful, clearly alluding to the fact that Grant had begun his show business career as a tumbler.

The stunt begins as Hepburn and Grant step onto the back of a couch, pushing forward with their feet so that it tips and carries them into the air like dancers. They acknowledge the applause of the other characters, and Grant lifts Hepburn onto his shoulders, where she stands like a brave, giddy amateur, holding her long skirt in her hand. For a moment, the narrative and characterization become less interesting than the spectacle of the star, who seems relatively unguarded.

"In working with [Hepburn]," John Houseman wrote many years later, "I made a fascinating discovery about star quality in general and hers in particular. Kate had learned . . . that stardom is achieved through beauty, intelligence, courage and energy but, above all, through the bravura that an audience comes to expect from its favorite performers. In every star role there are one or more opportunities for such peaks. If not, they must be created—as

Hepburn and Grant prepare for a double somersault.

they were, in different ways, by Duse, Bernhardt, Terry and all the others" (87). The somersault with Grant is just such a "peak," designed to emphasize Hepburn's beauty and adventurousness, giving the spectators a moment of pure voyeurism, when they seem to glimpse the star enjoying herself.

But if the joyful performance-within-performance in the upstairs room allows Hepburn to show off in a charming way, subsequent developments give her an opportunity to behave like a straightforward dramatic actress. As I have already suggested, the film is filled with calculated displays of expressive incoherence—"actorly" moments that reveal the conflict between Linda Seton's public and private self. Sometimes her technique is localized in a line of dialogue, as when she wishes Johnny "Happy New Year" in a voice that quavers with *chagrin d'amour.* Or it can be seen in her gestures and movement, as in the climactic scene in the Seton drawing room, when Johnny breaks off with Julia and walks out. Hepburn clasps her arm along her stomach and sits down on the arm of a chair as if she had lost her breath. "I'll miss that man," she says, gallantly concealing her love from the family while making it plain to us.

An especially dynamic example of what I have described in chapter four as "disclosive compensation" occurs during Julia's engagement party. Deciding to put her sister's happiness first, Linda leaves the playroom and goes downstairs, where she must put on an insincere act for the guests and at the same time try to repair the strained relation between Johnny and Julia. In extreme long shot, Hepburn steps into a hallway, pauses to adjust her hair, and walks to a staircase. Another long shot, photographed from a crane, shows her moving downward in a curve as waltz music wells up from below. She pauses at a landing and glances at the party like a player about to enter a stage; then a second crane shot shows her quick descent of the next staircase. At the bottom, her rather intense expression breaks into a smile and she greets two figures in formal dress who rush up to her. "Isn't it divine?" one of them says. An elderly lady enters the shot to offer congratulations, mistaking Linda for Julia; Hepburn continues to smile, exchanging polite words, and then moves quickly to the left, the camera panning as she weaves through a crowd. During the movement, her expressions alternate systematically between cheerful responses to the guests and anxious little glances around the room in our direction, as if she were looking for Johnny and Julia. Her growing urgency is conveyed not only by the timing and placement of these glances but also by her erect, increasingly rapid walk; as the camera pans along the landing, her stride becomes longer, almost breaking into a run but masking tension as happy excitement.

At last she sees Doris Nolan and rushes to embrace her, making congratulatory remarks in a loud voice for the benefit of the party. Nolan whispers that Grant has disappeared, and Hepburn looks quickly, anxiously around the room. Moving Nolan toward a nearby doorway, she glances back over her shoulder, smiles, and makes a little joke with one of the guests. She and Nolan then enter a darkened, "backstage" area of the house and have a sotto voce conversation, after which Hepburn goes back out into the party once again, fraught with worry about her sister and desperately looking for Grant. A crane shot shows her descending a third staircase toward the ground floor; the waltz music swells and the crowd grows thick. Again the camera pans as she moves neatly across the ballroom, maneuvering past knots of people, her head tossed back in apparent gaiety. "Hello! How's Baltimore?" she says to one of the guests, as she quickens her long steps. Smiling broadly, she opens a doorway into another "backstage" room. A cut shows that she has entered the kitchen, where her smile falls completely away. She dashes across the room toward a servant's entrance, while the kitchen maid tells her that Grant has just left. A close-up shows her arriving at the open back door, where she stands looking out as the maid offers congratulations on the forthcoming marriage. The camera tracks toward her face and the noise of distant traffic flickers on the soundtrack. Wind softly blows her hair and scarf while she gazes out into the night, her expression a commingling of sadness, longing, and admiration for Grant's flight.

Hepburn's elaborate journey through the Seton mansion seems to me to encapsulate most of the issues I have been discussing. It is first of all a considerable technical achievement—a series of lengthy, complex shots in which she skillfully modulates between the character's "private" and "public" expressions, all the while timing her gestures and movements to accommodate the camera and the other players. But in the context of the narrative her technique takes on additional value. By a process of association rather than logic, our appreciation of Hepburn's graceful behavior in difficult circumstances becomes wedded to our admiration for Linda Seton's poise under duress, two forms of theatricality joining to support one another. The synthesis between star and character also functions to control the ideological tensions provoked by Hepburn's style: she walks with athletic, independent energy through a ballroom, acting as the prime agent of the narrative, but at the end of the sequence she expresses yearning for a man in the distance; she crosses the set and speaks her lines with arisocratic panache, but she plays a woman who wants to escape from "one of America's six best families"; her passionate, idealistic, grandly theatrical manner is given full rein, but it is motivated by Linda Seton's need to put on a mask at a formal gathering.

Clearly, *Holiday* has been designed to heighten and glamorize aspects of Hepburn's screen personality even while it guards against the radical or unpopular implications she brought to her performances. Like most star vehicles, it tries to foster a harmonious and undisturbing relationship between the three ways an actor may be regarded by audiences: as subject in the culture, as professional thespian, and as literary character. In Hepburn's case, however, this process was difficult: she was such a strong, unusual actor that she made contradictions or social conflicts beneath the script seem evident. Thus, despite the skill of her work in *Holiday,* and despite the film's attempt to construct her as a popular image, audiences and producers continued to regard her suspiciously as a patrician and a feminist. Perhaps the world of this particular film was too rarefied, even when the heiress character abandoned her father's house; perhaps the male lead was too extraordinary, even when he dressed in a rumpled suit and did circus tricks; perhaps Linda Seton seemed too liberated, even when she sailed off happily ever after with a husband. Whatever the reason, other narrative contexts and other collaborations were necessary before Hepburn could become an appealing object of consumption and a legend of the movies.

11

Marlon Brando in
On the Waterfront (1954)

Unlike the other stars I have been discussing, Marlon Brando is commonly associated with an innovative "school," a theoretical approach to acting that gives us an opportunity to compartmentalize him. The technical distinction between Brando and his predecessors, however, is sometimes more apparent than real. The more one studies Brando's work, the more one doubts that it can be explained as the result of a pedagogy or that the pedagogy itself can be neatly separated from the main tradition of American film acting.

Consider one of the most celebrated moments in Brando's career. Early in *On the Waterfront,* he and Eva Marie Saint are walking through a children's school yard. She accidentally drops one of her white gloves, and Brando picks it up. They pause, and he sits on a playground swing in the center of the composition; as they talk, he casually slips the glove over his hand. Critics frequently cite this piece of business as a locus classicus of Method technique (see, for example, Higson, 12). Director Elia Kazan once discussed it at length in response to an interviewer who asked how the work of the Actors' Studio had influenced his films; the incident, he suggested, was at least partly improvised, revealing an important psychological subtext:

> The glove was his way of holding her. Furthermore, whereas he couldn't, because of this tension about her brother being killed, demonstrate any sexual or loving feeling towards her, he could towards the glove. And he put his hand inside the glove, you remember, so that the glove was both his way of holding on to her against her will, and at the same time he was able to express through the glove something he couldn't express to her directly. So the object, in that sense, did it all. (Ciment, 45–46)

Brando with Eva Marie Saint's glove.

Brando's handling of the glove is clearly an impressive moment, a little more flirtatious than Kazan's description indicates. Why it should exemplify the Method, however, is not clear: the idea of a subtext was not new in Hollywood performances, and every form of realist acting (especially the older, silent, movie form) encourages the use of expressive objects.

I shall return to the problem of recognizing the Method in practice, but for now I would like to suggest that the truly striking aspect of the scene has more to do with Brando's persona than with the Actors' Studio. The fact is, few virile male leads before him (with the possible exception of Cagney) would so effortlessly have slipped on a woman's glove. Quite apart from its narrative implications or its presumptive sources in the Method, the gesture helps point up what Kazan has elsewhere described as the "bisexual" effect of Brando's image (Downing, 21). Even when he is playing a slightly punchy ex-boxer, there is something deeply sensual about him, an Olivier-like delicacy in the movement of his hands that makes an effective contrast with his weight-lifter's torso and his Roman head. (The same quality can be seen in his eyes and mouth, and it is interesting that the eye makeup he uses for the Terry Malloy character makes him look both punched-out and somewhat "feminine.") Consider also the pose on the swing, which establishes Malloy's childlike nature and at the same time typifies the star—a relaxed, "cool" posture, suggesting macho power mixed with sexy, graceful indolence. Brando creates the same feeling in later movies, well after he has grown heavy and middle aged. Watch him in *The Chase* (1966), when he saunters out on the front steps of his sheriff's office and pauses briefly to survey the town; his Stetson is slanted forward and he rests his weight on one leg, cocking his knee forward in a Michelangelo pose. Or notice the famous poster for *Last Tango in Paris* (1973), which shows his body in silhouette, seated in a reclining chair, his knees bent and his legs crossed like those of a gloomy decadent.

All of which may help to explain why Brando was so effective as the stud of Tennessee Williams's dramas (*A Streetcar Named Desire* [1951] and *The Fugitive Kind* [1959]), and why he has appeared so memorably in the roles of homosexual fantasy figures—a biker in *The Wild One* (1954) and an unusually dandified cowboy in *One-Eyed Jacks* (1961). Later he seemed to exaggerate this tendency, playing a foppish Mr. Christian in *Mutiny on the Bounty* (1962), a closet gay in *Reflections in a Golden Eye* (1967), and a polymorphously perverse villain who cross-dresses and talks seductively to his horse in *The Missouri Breaks* (1976). He also lends a frighteningly eroticized quality to violence; he is frequently depicted as a sadistic character (*Streetcar, Last Tango, The Nightcomers* [1972], and *The Missouri Breaks*), or he is shown being horribly maimed or beaten by people who take pleasure in giving out punishment (*Waterfront, The Chase,* and *One-Eyed Jacks*—the last a film in which he plays a young man named "Kid" who gets his fingers crushed in public by "Dad" Longworth.)

A high contrast to the utterly straight Waynes, Gables, and Pecks of the forties, Brando is symptomatic of the period that produced Montgomery Clift, James Dean, Elvis Presley, and Marilyn Monroe—all of them brooding, ostensibly inarticulate types who suggested a scandalous sexuality and who signaled American entertainment's drift toward adolescent audiences in the decades after the war. Indeed Brando's relation to this particular group of stars can be demonstrated more easily than his indebtedness to the Method. For example, the accent he uses in *One-Eyed Jacks* seems to have been modeled on Presley's, and he and Presley together virtually taught Dean how to play the quintessential sexy teenager of the fifties. Dean's performance in *Rebel without a Cause* (1955)—a far cry from Andy Hardy—contains several obvious "borrowings" from *Waterfront,* including a scene where he uses a girl's compact for much the same purpose as Brando had used a woman's glove. The equally important influence of Presley on *Rebel without a Cause* is only slightly less apparent, perhaps because Warner Brothers was nervous about the implications of rock and roll; whenever the rebellious kids turn on a radio, we hear a big band.

Among the "rebel" stars of his day Brando always seemed the most gifted and intelligent, the least inclined to romantic excess or self-destruction. He was, however, contemptuous of celebrity and increasingly guilty about acting. He has probably appeared in more bad pictures than any important thespian since Orson Welles, and his disdain for show business has given a somewhat veiled effect to his work. Even in *Last Tango,* the most "biographical" of his performances, there is a deliberate coyness about the way his body is presented to the camera. As Norman Mailer once pointed out, Brando had been a virtual walking phallus in his early pictures; yet here, where the role is to some extent parodic and where we expect to see him stripped down and demystified, he is photographed in a gauzy light with his back turned.[1]

Unlike the typical Stanislavskian, Brando has also tended to hide behind changes of accent and makeup. He has been a Mexican in *Viva Zapata* (1952), an Oriental in *Teahouse of the August Moon* (1956), a southerner in at least six pictures, and a white-haired Nazi officer in *The Young Lions* (1958). In the fifties he was Stanley Kowalski, Napoleon, Marc Antony, and Sky Masterson all within a few years of each other—as if he were trying to escape both a "realist" tag and the fixed image of a movie star. Ultimately he adopted the shaggy-dog manner of a theatrical ham, choosing pictures that allowed him to play stylized imperialist villains (*The Ugly American* [1963], *Burn!* [1969], *Apocalypse Now* [1979]) or that earned him large sums of money for campy performances (*Candy* [1968], *The Night of the Following Day* [1969], *Superman* [1978]). Somehow he was able to retain enough respect for his artistic ability to create interest simply by being a famous man who does a cotton-in-cheek act, donning funny clothes and speaking in strange voices. His reliance on mimicry is particularly ironic in the context of *The Godfather* (1972), Hollywood's most self-conscious tribute to the Method. The cast in both parts of that film consists largely of players from the Actors' Studio; Brando and Strasberg, separated by parts one and two, are given the roles of patriarchs, but Brando gives a stronger sense than anyone of "putting on" his characterization.

At the time of *On the Waterfront* Brando's ambivalence about his work and

---

1. Bertolucci allows Brando to improvise in a casual way, and he merges the character of Paul with the roles and biography of the star: "You know he was a boxer? That didn't work . . . so he became an actor, then a racketeer on the waterfront in New York . . . It didn't last long . . . played the bongo drums . . . revolutionary in South America . . . One day lands in Tahiti." This sometimes playful self-referentiality, however, does not result in a Brechtian distanciation. Like the Method teachers, Bertolucci is an idealist, hoping to fuse the actor and character, thereby arriving at a psychological truth. He has claimed that he was looking for the "roots of human behavior," and for "absolute authenticity"; Brando, meanwhile, has called his work in the film a "violation of my innermost self." Despite such mystic pronouncements, *Last Tango* tends to romanticize both Brando and Hollywood cinema. Bertolucci said that he could not reveal Brando's genitals because he felt so much identification with the character: "To show him naked would have been like showing myself naked." Apparently he had no such qualms about Maria Schneider, who is not only shown in full frontal nudity, but is also assigned the role of a typical *femme fatale.* (For a complete, more sympathetic account of the film in light of contemporary theory, see Yosefa Loshitsky, "The Radical Aspect of Self-Reflexive Cinema," Ph.D. diss., Indiana University, 1987. The quotations above are taken from this source.)

his rather playful theatricality were less apparent; he was a sensational, slightly scary sex object, and he quickly became known as what Andrew Sarris has called an "axiom of the Method." Although the first of these attributes is obvious, the second is problematic. Critics often invoke Brando's name as they do Picasso's, to denote both an individual style and an artistic movement; yet Brando himself has disclaimed any significant influence from the Actors' Studio, and no one has come forward with an explanation of Method acting that would allow us to recognize every instance of it on the screen. Undoubtedly Hollywood saw commercial value in associating stars with a new style (even one that fostered an image of "artistic" outsiders who disdained the usual publicity), but where criticism is concerned, the word Method has always been vague, capable of indicating a variety of phenomena. Thus in books on the subject, Brando is sometimes lumped together with such different people as Joanne Woodward, David Wayne, and Shelly Winters, all of whom worked extensively with Lee Strasberg.[2] The result, as Richard Dyer has remarked, is that "the formal differences between the Method and, say, the repertory/Broadway style are less clear than the known differences between how the performances were arrived at" (154). Given these problems, a study of Brando's work in *Waterfront* needs to be prefaced by a brief history of the Method, both as a practice and as a critical term.

Perhaps one reason why the Method has dubious value as a term denoting a style is that it was never intended to refer to a performing technique in the strict sense. It consisted of a series of quasi-theatrical exercises, often resembling psychological therapy, designed to "unblock" the actor and put him or her in touch with sensations and emotions. Most of all, it tried to develop an "affective" or "emotional memory" that functioned rather like an onion concealed in a handkerchief, producing real rather than artificial tears. Players who used the Method continued to work in their own emotional idiolect, but they learned to manipulate buried sensory recollections and the Stanislavskian "as if," thus appearing more natural and spontaneous. Technically, they were not "living the part," and they were warned against using emotional memories during actual performances (advice they did not always follow— hence the slightly abstracted look associated with some actors). The point of the training was simply to put performers in a receptive state, thereby facilitating what was *already* recognized as "good" realistic drama. Lee Strasberg's claims could sometimes sound quite modest: "The entire purpose of the 'Method' or our technique or whatever you want to call it," he wrote, "is to find a way to start in each of us [a] creative process so that a good deal of the things we know but are not aware of will be used on the stage to create what the author sets for us to do" (Cole and Chinoy, 629).

2. For a history of Method acting in the United States (though it makes somewhat broad claims for the Actors' Studio), see Foster Hirsch, *A Method to Their Madness: The History of the Actors' Studio* (New York: Norton, 1984).

Where film is concerned, we can speak of an intuitive Method that was at work from the beginning, helping to shape the classic narrative cinema. Consider the affinities between Stanislavsky and Griffith: both were part of a turn-of-the-century attempt to make proscenium framing and blocking seem less artificial; both were interested in a subtext of intimate, emotionally charged acting; and both were attracted to a mixture of local color and melodrama (one of Stanislavsky's favorite plays was *The Two Orphans*). Alla Nazimova, a Hollywood star in the years 1916–1920, had been one of Stanislavsky's pupils, and, as noted previously, Pudovkin's classic treatise on film acting had advocated an explicitly Stanislavskian technique. Hence there was a good deal of truth in Strasberg's well-known remark that Gary Cooper resembled a Method actor. Strasberg later qualified the statement, but aren't the movies the place above all others where actors have perfected the art of playing "themselves"? And couldn't *High Noon* (1952) be described as a Stanislavskian western?

The term "Method" became fashionable in American dramatic criticism during the thirties, with Lee Strasberg's adaptation of what was then called the "Stanislavsky System" to the productions of the Group Theater. The word appears in the subsequent writing of various members of the Group, including Robert Lewis, Stella Adler, and Elia Kazan; but above all it was nourished by Strasberg himself, who used it more than anyone else. When the Actors' Studio was established in 1947 by Kazan, Lewis, and Cheryl Crawford, Strasberg was given the job of full-time teacher or "moderator," and in that capacity he began to elaborate what was initially a *politique* into a kind of theory. By the mid fifties, he had turned the Studio into an institution that was related to Stanislavsky in roughly the same way that psychoanalysis is related to Freud. But even though the Studio was often associated with a new American style, its work was easily assimilated into the mainstream of expressive-realist acting, and its specific achievements are difficult to assess. For example, Brando and Marilyn Monroe are often singled out as two of the Studio's "pupils," but they barely qualify. Brando was trained chiefly at Erwin Piscator's Dramatic Workshop, where he encountered both Lewis and Strasberg but where he also learned about Brecht. His most influential teacher was the eclectic, politically committed Stella Adler (who must have been amused when he yelled "Stella!" every night on the stage in *A Streetcar Named Desire*). As for Monroe, she did little more than attend a few sessions at the Studio when she was already a star, sitting in the back row and helping Strasberg to become a celebrity.[3]

Strasberg's romanticism, his emphasis on ego psychology rather than on training for the voice and body, his courting of celebrities in his guise of

3. The list of movie stars who actually worked with Strasberg is impressive: James Dean, Paul Newman, Jack Nicholson, Bruce Dern, Al Pacino, Jane Fonda, etc. Nevertheless, the very fact that the Studio became an entry point for Hollywood is an indication of how far Strasberg had moved from the repertory ideals of the Moscow Art Theater and from his own original aims.

philosopher and therapist—all these things were retrograde developments in a richer, more productive Stanislavskian tradition that precedes him. The Master's own "theory" had been little more than a distillation of common-places that governed Western theater since the seventeenth century, combined with strictures against pantomime and a series of training aids adapted from behaviorist psychology. Unlike Strasberg, however, Stanislavsky was a brilliant director who codified techniques for producing naturalist ensembles and who influenced generations after him. In the rather parochial teaching of the Actors' Studio, Stanislavsky's approach had been narrowed down to a quasi-Freudian "inner work" fueled by an obsession with the "self." Strasberg claimed to be teaching outside the theatrical event, and yet his moderating sessions were themselves performances, theatricalized encounters played out before a coterie audience, with Strasberg taking on the role of analyst. They helped make him a cult figure, but a case could be made that they impoverished the theater—feeding the star system, promoting conventional realism at the expense of the avant-garde, and giving American drama a less forceful social purpose.[4]

In this regard, we need to distinguish between the Studio and the earlier Group Theater, which mixed realistic social plays such as *The House of Connelly* with agitational, semi-Brechtian productions of *1931, Waiting for Lefty,* and *Johnny Johnson* (the last directed by Strasberg). In later years Strasberg de-emphasized the political basis of the Method, and, like most Stanislavkians, he always undervalued performances in the alternative comic, modernist, or deconstructive modes. Furthermore, his rather analytic approach to the actor's "self" was different from the Group Theater's stress on the ensemble and on the relationship between individual players and society as a whole. Here is Stella Adler describing the first principle of acting for the Group:

[We] asked the actor to become aware of himself. Did he have any problems? Did he understand them in relation to his whole life? To society? Did he have a point of view in relation to these questions?

A point of view was necessary, he was told. The actor should begin to question and learn to understand a great many things. A better understanding of himself would inevitably result. It would be of great artistic use for the actors to have a common point of view which they could share with the other co-workers of the theater. The actor was told that it was necessary and important to convey this point of view through plays to audiences; that theatrical means and methods had to be found to do this in a truthful and artistic way. (Cole and Chinoy, 602–3)

4. In fact, Strasberg found himself in one of the most contradictory positions in American theater. The Studio had been established as a place where professional actors could work on their craft apart from the dictates of the marketplace; but the actors' lives were determined by a capitalist economy, and any school they attended could not help but become what D. H. Lawrence would have called an adjunct of the "factory."

By contrast, the Actors' Studio was much less interested in a "point of view," and its jargon had a familiar ring: "private moment," "freedom," "naturalness," "organic"—the keywords of romantic individualism.

Whatever the Studio's limitations, Strasberg was unquestionably a gifted teacher who inspired actors and provided ways of producing "lifelike" performances in contemporary settings. Furthermore, under his direction, the Studio never completely lost sight of its origins in the socially critical atmosphere of the 1930s. From the beginning Strasberg's teaching manifested a tendency toward the kind of theater for which Stanislavskian aesthetics had been originally designed, thus contributing to a proliferation of naturalistic social drama in the fifties. Because there was a recognizable look to the male stars of these dramas, the term Method soon acquired a critical life of its own, associated with a dramatic genre and an actorly "personality."

As a description of film acting, the Method therefore seems most useful when it points to something at once broader and more specific than either Brando or the teaching of the Actors' Studio—that is, when it indicates a stylistic or ideological leaning within fifties culture, which has left its traces on contemporary Hollywood. In the context of a discussion of *film noir*, David Bordwell has pointed out that most words denoting style function in this way. They usually begin as negative assertions, signaling the "repudiation of a norm," but when critics later use them as positive definitions, they become unwieldy, making sense only when they refer to "particular patterns of nonconformity" within a dominant mode (75). Hence when Brando is described as a "Method actor" in *Waterfront*, the term can be taken to mean—correctly—that he was exposed to ideas of the Group Theater and the Actors' Studio during the late forties and fifties; but it also implies some combination of the following nonconformist "patterns," each of which helps to describe his image:

(1) He appears in a naturalistic setting. *Waterfront* belongs in company with a series of "social problem" films, most of them shot on location and directed by Kazan, that began to appear in Hollywood after World War II. During the fifties, such films were usually produced independently, with black-and-white formats that resembled those of prestigious television shows rather than big-screen movies. They frequently involved Actors' Studio personnel (*A Face in the Crowd* [1957], *A Hatful of Rain* [1957], *The Strange One* [1958]), or they were based on scripts by writers like Odets and Chayefsky (*The Big Knife* [1955], *Marty* [1955], *The Sweet Smell of Success* [1957]). They had a good deal in common with a slightly later outpouring of British neorealism (*Room at the Top* [1959], *Saturday Night and Sunday Morning* [1960]), and despite their sometimes naive or compromised politics, they represented a turn toward what Raymond Williams has defined as "authentic naturalism" as opposed to mere "bourgeois physical representation." "Naturalism," Williams writes, "was always a critical movement, in which

the relation between men and their environments was not merely *represented* but *actively explored . . .* it is quite evidently a bourgeois form, [but] it is also, on its record, part of the critical and self-critical wing of the bourgeoise" (*Culture*, 170, my emphasis).

(2) He acts out the "existential paradigm." In certain ways, Brando's Terry Malloy is a typical fifties protagonist, resembling not only the three characters played by Dean but also such ostensibly different fellows as John Osborne's Jimmy Porter in *Look Back in Anger*. Thus he is an "outsider," resentful of bourgeois society and "existentially" rebellious. As Fredric Jameson remarks, this is a "middle-brow media usage" of existentialism, entailing the favorite liberal theme of "the inability to communicate." Whether the character is a laborer, an upwardly mobile son of a wage-earning family, or an affluent teenager, he has the same problem: an uneasiness with official language and no words for his love or rage. At the same time, he brims over with sensitivity and feeling, the intensity of his emotion giving him a slightly neurotic aspect. The Method's stress on "affective memory" probably fuels his emotionalism. "The agonies and exhalations of method acting," Jameson notes, "were perfectly calculated to render [an] asphyxiation of the spirit that cannot complete its sentence." Ironically, however (especially in second-generation graduates of the Actors' Studio like Al Pacino), inarticulateness becomes what Jameson calls "the highest form of expressiveness . . . and the agony over uncommunicability suddenly turns out to be everywhere fluently comprehensible" (80–81).

(3) He deviates from the norms of classical rhetoric. Looked at today, Brando hardly seems unusual, but at the time of *Waterfront*, he was known for his "slouch" and "mumble." Like Dean, he spoke softly, sometimes departed slightly from scripted dialogue, and used regional or "ethnic" accents (many of them never heard in movies except in comedy).[5] At the same time, his body was almost self-consciously loose, and many of the working-class or outlaw characters he played allowed him to mock the "good manners" of traditional theater. In *One-Eyed Jacks*, for example, he eats Sunday dinner with Karl Malden and makes a great show of talking with his mouth full; later in the same film, he keeps a matchstick in his mouth during a barroom con-

---

5. Some viewers took Brando's slur in *Streetcar* as the sign of an untutored primitive; later, in a move virtually designed to prove he was an actor, he played Shakespeare alongside Gielgud, and it became apparent that he was an accomplished mimic with a soft but quite musical voice. His films are filled with artful uses of dialect and playful turns of phrase. Like many of the best poets, he seems to have listened well to demotic speech. Sometimes his accent mocks the film— in *The Chase*, for example, he slyly calls the Robert Redford character "Bubber," even though everyone else pronounces it "Bubba." My favorite of his impersonations is *One-Eyed Jacks*, in which he speaks such insults as "Git up, you skum-suckin pig!" Calder Wallingham's script is keyed to the voices of players like Slim Pickens and Ben Johnson, and Brando's drawl is similar to theirs, as in the moment when he explains why he had to shoot a man in a bar: "He didn't gimme no selection."

versation, even drinking tequila around it; still later, in the midst of a romantic encounter with a young woman, he abstractedly cleans his ear with his finger. It should be stressed, however, that Brando's work is always fluently representational and "centered," in keeping with the basic demands of narrative cinema. He never breaks the illusion, he never departs radically from the script, and his movements are never as casual as they seem. For instance, in *Waterfront,* he makes an amusing and nicely calculated turn when one of the federal investigators (Martin Balsam) calls out to Terry Malloy amid a crowd of men on the docks: we see him reluctantly glance over his shoulder that is nearest the voice; he starts to move but then changes direction, slowly revolving the long way around to make his response look contemptuous. Here and in other places he is conscious of the way people "revise" actions in everyday life; even so, he takes care to observe the spatial dynamics of ordinary movie acting. If he seemed unusual in his day, it was chiefly because he often gazed downward or off into space during conversations and because his posture and speaking style made other actors look politely stiff.

Only the last of these three "patterns of nonconformity" is concerned exclusively with what Richard Dyer has called "performance signs," and only at this level can we speculate on the relation between Brando's work and the specifics of Method teaching. For example, the "truth" of emotions in Stanislavskian drama was frequently elicited by improvisational techniques, which brought a feeling of halting spontaneity and verisimilitude to performances. The exercises in "affective memory," which Robert Lewis and Lee Strasberg first discovered in the teachings of Stanislavsky's disciple Richard Boleslavsky, may have indirectly contributed to Brando's hipsterish posture: Lewis had emphasized that one of the essential means of inducing emotional recall was "complete physical relaxation" (Cole and Chinoy, 631). Boleslavsky (who was influenced by a nineteenth-century behavioral psychologist named Theodule Ribot) encouraged relaxation not only in the training exercises but also on the stage; he had even devised a formula for achieving the best results: "Think [of your muscles] constantly, to relax them as soon as you feel any tension . . . you must watch yourself all day long, at whatever you do, and be able to relax each superfluous tension" (Cole and Chinoy, 513).

In more general terms, Brando's emotionality and slight abstractedness has something in common with the Method's valuation of expression over rhetoric—an essentially romantic attitude that reaches its ultimate form in what Strasberg called the "private moment." In the Actors' Studio, Strasberg frequently requested professional actors to imagine or relive an experience for themselves alone, ignoring their audience. Paradoxically, this stress on inwardness sometimes resulted in a shrill, almost hysteric quality—for example, in the work of the entire cast of *Splendor in the Grass* (1961) or in any performance by Rod Steiger. It gave Hollywood acting an emotionalism not seen since the days of Griffith, but it reversed Griffith's priorities, viewing characters in somewhat clinical rather than purely moral terms and (in its first stages at least) centering on male rather than female stars. As Andrew Higson has observed, "In some ways you can read the Method as a reinvestment of emotionality into the narrative film, where emotionality is conventionally associated with the feminine" (19).

In fact, Method-trained players seemed to relish the opportunity to weep (partly, one suspects, because emotionality is associated with "fine acting"), and in the process they helped establish what Virginia Wexman describes as the selective "softness" of fifties male protagonists.[6] Except in *Last Tango,* Brando himself seldom sheds tears on screen—in *Waterfront,* for example, his deepest pain is registered off camera, during the scene where he mourns the death of his beloved pigeons. But as Peter Biskind has remarked, other Method stars of the decade seemed to adopt Johnny Ray's "Cry" as their theme song; James Dean's incessant tearfulness in *East of Eden* (1955) even forces a rebuke from Julie Harris: "Do you want to cry all your life?" The persistence of Method training into the seventies ultimately resulted in Jack Nicholson's traumatic weeping in *Five Easy Pieces* (1970)—a moment that Nicholson says he conceived himself, using personal associations with a speech the character makes to his father. "I think it was a breakthrough," he told a writer for the *New York Times.* "I don't think they'd had this level of emotion, really, in almost any male character until that point" (Rosenbaum, 19). By the seventies, a reemergent feminism and a relaxation of censorship had enabled women (who were always allowed tears) to use the same hesitant, potentially rebellious, neurotically intense expressiveness as the Method males. Ann-Margaret's slightly Monroe-like Bobbie in *Carnal Knowledge* (1971) is one qualified example, but consider also three female stars who were more systematically exposed to Actors' Studio teaching: Faye Dunaway, Jane Fonda, and Diane Keaton. They are as good as James Dean at using "affective memory," and like him they are fond of indicating a brooding, restless emotionalism that their characters struggle to repress.

All of which brings us back to Brando's indolent pose on the child's swing in *Waterfront* and to his manipulation of a woman's glove. We can never know if he is truly feeling the emotions he acts, and we have only Kazan's suggestion that some of his behavior was improvised. There is, in fact, good reason to doubt that the action was purely spontaneous; the whiteness of the garment and Brando's position at the exact center of the composition seem calculated

---

6. "Softness" in male performance often functions to persuade the audience of a virile player's belief in his role. On July 20, 1987, the *New Yorker* magazine quoted an anonymous foreign observer of Lt. Col. Oliver North's televised appearance before the congressional Iran-Contra hearings: "'He has the oblique, diagonal eyebrows of Lillian Gish, . . . and that same American quality of always seeming about to burst into tears'" (19).

to make his gestures especially visible. Nevertheless, the sequence contains readable attributes of Method cinema, including a *mise-en-scène* that is nearly indistinguishable from documentary, and—in the case of Brando—a relaxed, sexy, sensitive performance filled with sidelong glances and unverbalized emotion. The function of the glove as an expressive object is also somewhat different from what it would be in the typical movie. If George Raft flips a coin in *Scarface* (1932), it becomes a motif associated with his character. If Dana Andrews plays with a child's toy in *Laura* (1944), it is referred to in the dialogue and shown in an insert, becoming an obvious sign of the character's need to maintain control. If Cary Grant pulls a matchbook from his pocket or handles Eva Marie Saint's travel razor in *North by Northwest*, these objects are not only singled out by the camera but used later in the narrative. The glove in *Waterfront* also has a purpose, but one that seems relatively unmotivated, more like an actor's than a writer's choice; Brando's handling of the garment is not prompted by anything but accident, and for that reason it looks spontaneous, contributing to the naturalistic cinema's love of verisimilitude.[7]

This verisimilar quality is in many ways evident throughout *Waterfront*. An independent production featuring actors from the New York stage rather than movie stars, the film was shot in a New Jersey locale that cameraman Boris Kaufman never glamorizes. On the surface it resembles Italian neorealism and some of the Group Theater projects of the thirties, although in other ways it is quite typical, recalling melodramas like *Angels with Dirty Faces*. (Budd Schulberg's script is based on a real-life character, but many people have noted that a film about a dockworker who cooperates with a federal investigation was an expedient project for Kazan; not long before the making of the film, he had served as a "friendly" witness before the House Un-American Activities Committee.) Like most other Hollywood films about social problems, *Waterfront* declares an evil—in this case, gangsterism in the New York labor unions—but avoids systemic analysis. Partly because of difficulties Kazan encountered with censors, the political attitudes beneath the gritty surface of his film seem especially familiar: a sentimental Christian populism mixed with a longing for a strong male hero to guide the masses. What gives the story its real novelty and interest is Brando, who brings a feeling of troubled adolescence to the central character, an attitude that would influence movies for years afterward.

Surprisingly, Brando was not the chief contender to play Malloy. Frank Sinatra, having established himself in *From Here to Eternity* (1953) as an actor of scrappy urban types, was under strong consideration and was report-

---

7. Brando's decision to wear the glove may or may not have been prompted by Method teaching; it is nonetheless a good instance of his sheer cleverness. His career is filled with small, inventive, if less richly functional pieces of business—for instance, in a conversation during *The Chase*, he slowly rubs the bowl of a pipe along the side of his nose to oil the wood.

edly furious when Kazan chose Brando instead. Brando himself seems to have approached the movie with a certain truculence, even though he turned in a performance so technically adept and intense that it energized the film and affected whole generations of actors. It is difficult to watch Newman in *The Left-Handed Gun* (1958), Beatty in *All Fall Down* (1962), Pacino in *Serpico* (1973), Stallone in *Rocky* (1976), Travolta in *Saturday Night Fever* (1977), Gere in *Bloodbrothers* (1978), or indeed any of Hollywood's proletarian sex symbols down to the present day (a more recent example is Sean Penn in *At Close Range* [1985]), without being reminded in some way of Brando in this role. He is a decisive moment in American cinema, one of those actors who represents a type so forcefully that it becomes a persistent feature of the culture.

In effect, Brando gives his working-class character a sex appeal based on the same fantasy that would later make James Dean the hero of a young cult: in Brando's hands *Waterfront* becomes the study of a tough but confused and sensitive male who wins his way to adulthood by overcoming brutal or misguided parent figures in an indifferent society. True, Brando plays an overweight former boxer who is pushing thirty; nevertheless, he is also a character who has been patronized and manipulated by older men and who acts as a kind of big brother to a group of street kids called the Golden Warriors. Brando lends to this plot situation his introspective manner and a sensual delicacy and sweetness that are all the more attractive for the way they coexist with the stocky, almost burly power of his head and physique; he is thus able to generate a remarkable sense of adolescent beauty and pathos. His shy but streetwise remarks, the sway of his walk, the absent-minded look in his eye as he chews gum, the way he sprawls on a pile of gunnysacks and flips through the pages of a girlie magazine—all these things function to establish him as a sort of child, in appealing contrast to the stereotypical and sententious "adults" who surround him.

Brando's every look, movement, and gesture is keyed to the essentially adolescent confusion of the character. Throughout, he oscillates between violence and childlike bewilderment, making visible Terry's conflict between the Social Darwinism of his criminal father-substitutes and the ideals of community inculcated by Edie Doyle and Father Barry. The film's strategy is to make Terry a synthesis of these two groups: a hero virile and independent enough to beat up the mobsters yet sensitive and caring enough to win the heart of Edie. As a structural ploy, the characterization works to maintain traditional patriarchal values while softening the male image; but Brando's performance and the particular thematic of *Waterfront* also yield more socially progressive effects than the usual movie. In *Rebel without a Cause,* for instance, the delinquent boy comes to embody the norms of a bourgeois family. The Brando film puts the rebel character in a different context, showing him choosing between cut-throat capitalism and the ethic of cooperation; it poses the selfishness of the paternalistic gangster-businessmen against the communal values of industrial labor and the church; and it falters only slightly by suggesting that Terry's "manhood" is achieved through a toe-to-toe slugging match. (The original ending was to have been different. Rod Steiger has said in an interview that Kazan and Schulberg wanted to close with "a shot of the dead boy floating down the river" [Leyda, 441], but the Hays Office insisted that crime could not triumph.)

Brando helps the central dynamic of the film succeed by letting us see a play of conflicts in his behavior. He gives an ambiguous significance to nearly all the objects he touches—for example, in one scene he angrily brandishes a pistol and then cradles it sadly against his cheek, converting it suddenly from a phallus into a breast. Notice also the way he uses the short jacket he wears, which is as obviously symbolic as James Dean's red windbreaker in *Rebel*. Sometimes Brando turns up the collar, drapes a loading hook around the neck, and stuffs his hands in the pockets; this rough-trade style contrasts with other moments when the jacket becomes a sign of his vulnerability, a thin line of defense against cold air and psychological pain. As Leo Braudy has noted, one of the most effective images in the film is Brando's wounded, solitary walk at the conclusion, the jacket "zippered tightly to keep the blood invisible inside" (242).

Brando's love scenes with Eva Marie Saint have a similar but more threatening dynamic, ranging in psychological effect from the moment when he tries on her glove like a child to the moment when he breaks down her door like a rapist. As a result, she alternately mothers him and shrinks away in fear. When they meet he wrestles playfully with her until she slaps his face; then when he discovers she is the sister of the man he inadvertently fingered for the mob, he stops in his tracks and does a beautifully understated double take, his eyes confused and anxious. Later he takes her to a dockside bar, teaches her how to drink a boilermaker, and proudly announces the philosophy of life he has learned from Johnny Friendly: "Do it to him before he does it to you." Only a moment afterward the camera closes in on his face to catch a glimpse of uncertainty as he mutters "I'd like ta help." Frustrated, he raises a hand to his chin, holding the thumb stiffly, almost as if he were going to suck it; then he pinches the chin between thumb and forefinger, pulling at it like a goatee. The gesture is more important than anything he says, expressing in one fluid movement the anguish of a child trying to be "manly."

"Some people just got faces that stick in your mind," Brando tells Saint in one of the film's most touching scenes. His own face is a fascinating blend of the pug and the poet—slightly ducktailed hair combed back to reveal a high forehead, battered but eloquent eyes, and full sensual lips. His nose is too straight for a boxer, but the width of his jaw and his slightly flattened profile make him look imposing, larger than in fact he is. Especially when standing still, he has a dancer's instinct for line and space, and he is good at

Brando strokes his chin.

calling attention to himself by being slightly quieter than the other actors. Contrary to what was first written about him, he does not mumble or scratch his way through the role. His "Method" consists of a softly articulated, some- times repetitive speech, an abstracted stroking of his body as he talks, a troubled reluctance to look anyone in the eye, and a series of relaxed poses that imply athletic grace and sexuality.

Brando is less disassociated from his body than the typical leading man of his day, and his eyes are able to express a wide range of understated emotions in an instant of time. Like most male stars in Hollywood drama, however, he is required to be less animated than the secondary players, who are presented as vivid stereotypes. His occasional reserve helps to signify a power and stoicism similar to those of every action hero from John Wayne to Clint East- wood, but when his reluctance to speak is combined with his emotional glances and his particular body language, he seems to be working subtly against the grain—not only of Hollywood in general but of everyone else in the film. Indeed, as Virginia Wexman has remarked, early Method acting became so heavily associated with star images that a picture like *Waterfront* often deliberately accentuates Brando's low-key behavior, marking him off from the other players.

Consider, for example, the way Brando contrasts with Lee J. Cobb and the rest of the cast in an early scene in the Union Hall. Cobb is wildly overstated—stalking around a pool table at the center of the room, staring with Neanderthal fascination at a boxing match on TV, chewing great hunks of a sandwich, and complaining that "there's nobody tough anymore." Brando enters slowly, head slightly bowed, wearing a dark pullover that makes him look slim and subdued. He responds to Cobb's "Hiya, Slugger!" with slight embarrassment, shyly holding out a hand to shake. Cobb ducks the hand, feints, and begins a mock boxing match that foreshadows the real combat at the end of the film, circling behind Brando to lift him in a fatherly bear hug. Throughout all this, Brando's movements are half-hearted, his smile wan and forced. While Cobb tells how he fought his way to the top of the union, yanking his collar open to reveal his battle scars, Brando reacts as though he knows the story all too well. Then he turns his back to the camera and leans against the pool table, playing most of the scene from a "weak" position typical of naturalistic drama. His head droops like that of a child trying to avoid attention, but meanwhile he stands at the center of the composition, gazed at by the other players; light from above models his hunched shoulders, giving him the power-in-repose look of classical statuary.

Brando's one partly assertive moment comes later in the scene, when he complains about the Joey Doyle incident. "I just figure I shoulda been told," he says, eyebrows raised in mock innocence, eyes meeting Cobb's and then sliding off to a distant horizon, palms rubbing together slowly but nervously. "Here, kid, here's half a bill," Cobb says, stuffing money into the collar of the pullover. In a flash, several expressions cross Brando's face: defensive shock, a flinch as if the money were burning his skin, and nearly imperceptible nausea—communicated by a curl of his upper lip, which he quickly hides by turning his head from our view and Cobb's. He exits as quietly as he arrived, tossing a jacket over his shoulder and sauntering off into the smoky light of an anteroom.

The same naturalistic rhetoric and the same feeling of power and nobility hidden beneath a vulnerable, inarticulate surface, help to account for Brando's impact in the celebrated taxicab scene, which encapsulates the film's major themes in a single, virtually self-contained, episode and forever establishes one definition of the Method. On the level of classical plot structure, the encounter between Charlie and Terry Malloy has been perfectly written, with a strong "through line" and a series of emotional changes that mark a beginning, middle, and end. For his part, Steiger's character has a compelling dramatic purpose: he has been ordered to stop Brando from cooperating with a federal crime commission or else to kill him—an action that ultimately involves a choice between saving himself and saving his brother. Steiger therefore undergoes a variety of quick, apparently spontaneous changes as the scene progresses: at first he smiles nervously, trying to be paternalistic

Brando adopts a "weak" dramatic stance.

and manipulative; when this fails, he becomes by turns abusive, threatening, and distraught, at last falling back in guilt, exhaustion, and fear as he lets Brando go free. By contrast, Brando operates from a fairly secure position, largely *reacting* to events. Wise to Steiger's patronizing attitude, he tolerates everything until the scene provides him with what one contemporary manual of Stanislavskian acting calls a "beat change"—a sudden reversal of the action, motivated by the character's discovery of new information.[8] When Brando realizes that Steiger is "taking him for a ride," a close-up marks his shocked response. Painfully and almost gently, he begins lecturing Steiger, charging him with having betrayed their relationship years before. His quiet speech leads to a climactic moment of recognition, and the scene ends in silence as each man contemplates what has happened.

8. See Bruder, et al., *A Practical Handbook for the Actor,* 87. This text is derived from what is sometimes called the "Mamet method," or the teachings of playwright David Mamet. The "beat change" describes any emotional fluctuation in a dramatic scene. In movies, such changes are often marked by a close-up; for example, in Wyler's *Jezebel* (1938), when Bette Davis discovers that the man she loves has married someone else. The change can also occur within a long take; compare Wyler's *The Letter* (1940), when Bette Davis's lawyer visits her in prison and calmly tells her that a piece of evidence has been found that might convict her of murder. In long shot, we see a shadow of unease cross her face, and then her attempt to mask the emotion.

The physical and rhetorical requirements of this scene are minimal, with the two actors placed in relatively "gestureless" positions, so that inflections and tones of voice carry the meaning. In fact, Brando and Steiger are hunched together to the point where they can barely move, their every glance and twitch microscopically studied. Venetian blinds have been drawn over the car's rear window to heighten the feeling of claustrophobia, and Leonard Bernstein's over-insistent score keeps pounding away on the soundtrack; the result is a feeling of almost hallucinatory, over-heated naturalism, a sense of hysteria held in check by the tiny enclosure and the muttered New-Yorkese. Of the two performances, however, Brando's is noticably more recessive, calculated to gain strength in relation to Steiger's inherent shrillness.

At the beginning of the scene, Steiger sits bundled up in his topcoat, his snap-brim hat and beady eyes pointed intently at Brando, who slouches back, glancing away out the side window, his hands relaxed on his knees. The conversation starts in a fairly innocuous way, with Steiger's nervousness and Brando's slightly knowing smile revealing its subtext. Finally, in near panic over Brando's impending betrayal of the union gang, Steiger's voice begins to rise while Brando responds in a still, almost sleepy tone that gives his dialogue a poetic flavor. When Steiger calls him a "rubber-lipped ex-tanker" and warns him to change his mind before they reach 437 River Street, Brando reacts. We can see the new information registering, leading to a kind of shock. In medium shot, he frowns at Steiger, and then he begins slowly, quietly, and intently shaming him, characteristically repeating a line to make it seem a spontaneous sign of Terry's bewilderment and growing anger: "Before we get to *where*, Charlie? Before we get to *where?*" In desperation, Steiger pulls out a gun, holding it so ineptly that we immediately feel his lack of conviction. Brando's face modulates from disbelief to disgust, and then breaks into a weary, disappointed smile. "Oh, Charlie, *wow!*" he says—the last banal word, softly sighed, becoming an eloquent reproach.

The scene's climactic speeches derive much of their power from Brando's rhythms and gestures, which reveal tides of emotion running beneath Terry Malloy's supposedly clumsy talk. When he recalls how he was forced to take a dive, he reaches out and touches Steiger gently on the shoulder with the tips of his fingers, a shadow of bitterness and sarcasm crossing his eyes. "It was you," he says in a near whisper. "You was my brother, Charlie. You shoulda looked out for me a little bit." Then he glances away and raises his right hand in the air, palm toward his face, fingers spread and curled like those of an actor playing Hamlet. All of Brando's energy seems collected in that hand, the rest of his body held in languid abeyance. Turning to Steiger, he gives the gesture an angry inflection. "You don't understand!" he says in an urgent undertone. His puffy eyes look up toward some imagined ideal, and his mouth twists in pain at the memory of a wasted life. Again he whispers, turning the sentences into a litany: "I coulda had *class!* I coulda been a con-

Brando makes a passionate gesture.

tender! I coulda been somebody!" He savors the poetic, musicalized flavor of the three lines—not only the chanting repetition of "coulda," but the alliteration, internal rhyme, and subtle augmentation in "*coulda* bee*na* co*nte*n*da*." Then he expels breath and lets the rest of the speech out in a rapid, prosaic fall: ". . . instead of just a bum, which is what I am, let's face it."

At this point, the relationship between the two men has been partly reversed, and their postures indicate the change. Steiger, the well-heeled, guiltily protective older brother, is reduced to a child who squirms in his seat as Brando speaks a saddened adult truth. Finally Steiger clutches his gloved fingers together and slumps back almost tearfully, his hat pushed up from his forehead. On the opposite side of the screen, Brando rests his chin in his palm and turns his gaze out the window. Silence descends, marking the exchange as a touchstone of American film acting, and as one of the best-remembered moments in either player's career.

The taxicab scene eventually became a part of folklore, the "contender" speech being alluded to in other films. The sequence also contributed heavily to what Richard De Cordova, borrowing from Foucault, has called the "discourse on acting," partly because it was so neatly self-contained, so observant of classical unities, and so completely centered on the two players. In such a context, naturalistic inflections of performance—always consistent with an underlying logic of well-made theater—tended to stand out in sharp relief. The irony, of course, was that an apparent search for "truth" and "authenticity" had turned into a showcase for technique.

We should not be surprised at this phenomenon; any slight departure from well-established convention quickly becomes evident as a stylistic choice. Moreover, naturalistic social drama has always been faced with contrary demands. On the one hand, it wants to persuade us that "the world is like this," but on the other, it wants to make moral or ethical judgements about the world. As a result, such drama tends to undermine stage rhetoric selectively while adhering to melodramatic structures of character and action. *Waterfront*, for example, was conceived as a documentary-like expose but maintains the traditions of the gangster movie; in the case of Method acting, a system of training that aims to transcend mere playacting depends, at bottom, on a star system.

Looked at today, what seems distinctive about the taxicab scene between Brando and Steiger is not its underlying approach to cinema but its mannerisms, especially the timing and emotional "beat" of the conversation, which differs from the more regular give-and-take of forties Hollywood rhetoric. This—combined with the slouched postures, the quiet but intense emotionalism, and the "ethnic" accents—has always been the popular idea of the Method. Brando's own cleverness fostered such a definition. The Method was articulated in terms of "essences," but audiences looked at surfaces; for them, the much-talked-about new technique was associated with behavioral tics and a star image. Thus, while the Actors' Studio valued emotional freedom and individuality, it soon elevated Brando's work to an ideal. In subsequent years, a good many aspiring male actors approached the Studio like a shrine, hoping to make their performances more "real"; in practice, however, they often imitated the early Brando, who became godfather to several generations of players.

12

Cary Grant in *North by Northwest* (1959)

Cary Grant enters *North by Northwest* trailing clouds of glory from twenty-seven years of movie acting, and like Cagney in *Angels With Dirty Faces,* he asserts a star persona even before his character, Roger Thornhill, has emerged completely from the narrative. In his opening scene he strides across a crowded office building, issuing orders to a secretary and tossing a joke over his shoulder at an elevator operator; as he weaves between passersby, hunching over slightly to accommodate conversations with lesser mortals, he leaves in his wake familiar traces—a clipped and jovial, somewhat English, accent; a generous but rather shy smile; a polished health and handsomeness; a beautifully tailored suit worn with aristocratic ease; and a chipper, lighthearted amusement suitable to comedy.

The surge of recognition and pleasurable anticipation most viewers feel during this opening scene constitutes the most elemental form of identification, and it has an obvious value for the filmmakers. Given our initial attachment to the star, our involvement can easily be deepened by the camera, the blocking, and the mechanics of narrative—until that moment when, as Hitchcock described it, "you and Cary Grant are now—because you are identified with him—left alone. And then suddenly the airplane comes down and shoots at him all over the place" (LaValley, 23).

Hitchcock's remark implicitly acknowledges that his own clever montage is secondary to the effect of Grant's presence. If, in fact, a publicity photo based on the crop-dusting episode has become one of the most famous images of world cinema, that is partly because the mere idea of this particular man-about-town running across a prairie, garbed in the same clothing he has worn in countless movie drawing rooms, produces a charge of surrealist wit. In-

Grant in motion.

deed the film seems to be constructed around Grant (whose salary and profits were greater than Hitchcock's own), and once the initial excitement of the plot is over, each additional viewing allows us to become more aware of the star as spectacle.

Throughout the crop-dusting sequence, for example, I find myself enjoying Grant's smooth stride and the sprinter's pump in his arms, chiefly because I can see that despite his age, he still runs beautifully. My contemplation also extends to apparently mundane things. For example, I have always been fascinated with Grant's socks, flashing out elegantly from beneath the cuffs of his trousers as he dodges bullets from that low-flying plane. Some years ago, I was amused to discover that Raymond Durgnat had admitted to a similar preoccupation, and more recently Stewart Byron noticed the same detail. In 1985 Byron opened the *Village Voice*'s annual "World's Most Difficult Film Trivia Quiz" with a multiple-choice question: "In the crop-dusting sequence of *North by Northwest,* the color of Cary Grant's socks is a) blue, b) orange, c) red, d) yellow." (The correct choice is "a", although for accuracy the socks ought to be described as bluish gray, in keeping with Roger O. Thornhill's darker gray suit and gray silk tie.)

Of course had Hitchcock been a novelist, he never would have mentioned socks. They are present in the film because Thornhill is represented by a costumed actor, and their color is relatively unimportant, so long as it seems appropriate to a Madison Avenue executive. In the overall economy of the film, the visibility of such minor details is little more than an instance of how stardom, acting, and photographic imagery tend to "outrun" narrative; if I am subjectively aware of Grant's clothing, that is simply because fragments of colored fabric, in dialectical relation to flesh, constitute an elemental lure. "The body in films," Stephen Heath has written, "is also moments, intensities, outside a simple constant unity of the body as a whole; films [contain] bits of bodies, gestures, desirable traces, fetish points—if we take fetishism here as an investment in a bit, a fragment, for its own sake, as the end of the accomplishment of a desire." The "desirable traces"—which are present in life as in movies—may be seen not only in Hollywood's tendency to exaggerate certain physical aspects of a star, such as breasts or hair, but also in what Heath describes as the "more random elements that exist for me, that I catch as a trace of my history (the curve of an eyebrow, the fall of a neck . . .), and including too—fetishes exactly—the 'attributes' of bodies (the color of a dress, the knot of a scarf, a hat)" (183).

North by Northwest seems to me a veritable festival of such guilty pleasures—resembling the sleek commercial imagery an ad man like Roger Thornhill might have concocted. The effect is enhanced by Robert Burks's Technicolor, Vistavision photography, which has retained its vividness and resolution through many generations of prints; but it owes chiefly to Grant's ability to wear a rich man's clothing and move with a springy, idiosyncratic grace. Each time I see the film, I marvel at the drape of his trousers as he crosses a leg; at the loose, comfortable cut of his suit; at the soft curl of his white collar. The small changes of his costume are equally pleasurable. I enjoy the moment when he tries on "George Kaplan's" coat in an empty New York hotel room, and I am struck by how good his tanned face and lightly graying, fastidiously cut hair look in dark blue, even if his sleeves are too short. Much later in the film, when he is supposed to be imprisoned in a hospital room in Rapid City, South Dakota, I admire his body in almost nothing at all: he is seen in a beefcake pose, first reclining on a bed in a bath towel, then pacing the floor, combing his hair, and raising an arm to show off a bruise to Leo G. Carroll. Although Grant was in his mid fifties when the scene was shot, he was probably never in better shape, with a runner's physique that indicates he was well prepared for the crop-dusting sequence. When Carroll brings him something to wear, I am fascinated as he unfolds and puts on a shirt, together with dark slacks, a belt, light socks, and a pair of loafers that he stamps onto his feet. I observe the blousing of the shirt where he hastily tucks it into his pants, his unstraightened cuff, and the whole dynamic of the cloth as he leaps into action, first climbing out a window to

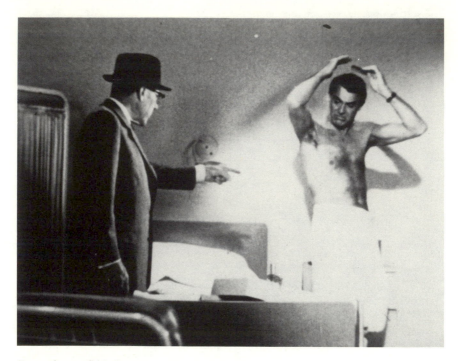

Grant shows off his form.

escape his captors and then scaling the sides of the villain's house as if he were a contemporary swashbuckler rescuing the Prisoner of Zenda.

In his interview with Truffaut, Hitchcock remarks that Grant's costume in those final scenes was selected for a utilitarian reason: the chase across Mount Rushmore was photographed largely in low-key long shots, and because Hitchcock wanted the audience to distinguish the distant figures on the screen, Grant was given a white shirt, Eva Marie Saint an orange dress, and the villains rather drab suits. But Grant's clothes accentuate his nimble movements, and *North by Northwest* shows off his sartorial elegance in other ways; it even makes a joke of the way he maintains unrumpled charm through a maelstrom of activity, his business suit serving at once as a Madison Avenue uniform, a symbol of grace under pressure, and a signature of the star. By this and other means, the film both supports and gently satirizes his persona, never completely absorbing his image into his role. Thus, although Truffaut was correct to say that *North by Northwest* "epitomizes" Hitchcock (190), it can also be viewed as a quintessential Cary Grant vehicle—or as a commentary on his stardom.

Clearly, *North by Northwest* has placed Grant in his "proper" setting, where he can display familiar mannerisms. He was always disappointing in historical pictures like *The Pride and the Passion* (1957) or in roles more in keeping with Archie Leach. *None but the Lonely Heart* (1944) was reputed to be his most personal project, but he was forgettable in that film, playing a character from the English working class; later, Grant claimed to enjoy going unshaved and wearing dirty shirts in *Father Goose* (1964), but the effect he created was rather like a star at a masquerade. Although he represented a variety of social types in the course of his career, the image of a debonair sophisticate clung to him. The business suit or the tuxedo became his "natural" attire, although he looked good in anything that reflected respectable urban taste: a cardigan, a naval officer's workaday uniform, or a plain shirt and slacks. Less rugged than Tom Selleck, less narcissistic than George Hamilton, Grant was the ideal male fashion model: he could be a smiling image in a rotogravure for Joan Fontaine to sigh over in *Suspicion,* and he could walk across a room in any of his pictures with energy and balance, giving contemporary tailoring "organic" style. He usually wore simple conservative clothing, but he also relied on touches that suggested a latent dandyism or theatricality: polished loafers with silk stockings, pleated or sharply creased trousers, carefully knotted ties, and so forth. What was most effective about his use of this costuming was the way he could suggest grooming without seeming especially concerned about it. Herbert Marshall, Adolph Menjou, William Powell, and Fred Astaire were flashy or dapper when they played light comedy; but Grant—who was once Mae West's "tall, dark, and handsome" companion and who wore drag in two of the Hawks comedies—was never dominated by his dress.

Perhaps the secret lay in Grant's posture and behavior, which implied both an unpretentious casualness and a lack of vanity.[1] There was a touch of diffidence in some of his reactions and a generous, almost stagy, cheerfulness in his smile. Unlike most theatrically trained actors, he frequently played scenes with both hands stuffed in his pockets, gesturing with his elbows or with slightly hunched shoulders—an unassuming, boyish stance that made him seem shy and unaffected. In farcical situations, he also had a taste for lowbrow exaggeration, his movements showing a deep indebtedness to the silent clowns: first he would squat like a man preparing to wheel and run; then he would cock his head, make a pop-eyed, openmouthed face, and punctuate his lines with quick little jerks of the neck. Taken all together, his behavior seemed to blend the traditions of Alfred Lunt, the American action hero, and the Chaplinesque music-hall comic.

The blending of traditions is evident also in his eccentric accent, which

---

1. Andrew Sarris has observed that Grant provided a "visual cue" for screwball comedy. He notes a seminal moment in *The Awful Truth* (1937): "Cary Grant is seen seated on the back of a luxurious sofa, his right elbow balanced casually on his right knee, which is bent over the sofa's arm-rest, while his left arm is extended to his left knee, which is bent over the seat cushions. His shoes are thereby pressing rudely on the upscale upholstery as part of a posture of infantile irresponsibility. . . . the one conspicuously askew element [in the shot] is Grant's unconventional pose in what would otherwise be a traditional Coward-Maugham-Barry-Behrman drawing room scene" ("Cary Grant's Antic Elegance," *The Village Voice* [December 16, 1986], 94).

was poised between two nationalities as well as between two social classes. Vestiges of the London streets could sometimes be heard in his speech, but they were muted by a crisp, rather studied pronunciation. (Tony Curtis's parody of Grant in *Some Like It Hot* [1959] catches this note perfectly, suggesting a middle-class Englishman who is trying hard to sound cultivated.) Grant never dropped a consonant and was so concerned about diction that he had a tendency to deliver lines in sing-song or slightly percussive rhythm. The technique worked nicely in comedy, although he seems to me slightly miscast as the fast-talking Walter Burns in *His Girl Friday;* his accent fit best in international settings, where audiences accepted him as a hybrid or a man of indefinite background. In Hitchcock productions, he was surrounded by foreign or patrician speakers—Ingrid Bergman, Claude Rains, Louis Calhern, Grace Kelly, James Mason, Jessie Royce Landis, and Leo G. Carroll—who made him seem relatively native to American ears. Then, too, actors like Rains and Mason provided an important structural contrast. Rains's epicene manner and Mason's deliberately stagy English-repertory accent served to heighten Grant's "Americanized" virility; thus in *North by Northwest,* Grant's speech is able to work in two ways: alongside Mason, he can seem a plausible Manhattan executive, but he can give an upper-class British whimsy to scenes involving a hotel maid, a midwestern farmer, and a series of cops.

Given the set of traits I have been describing, it is easier to understand Raymond Chandler's odd notion that Grant would have made the ideal Philip Marlowe. Grant was far too cheerful to have played the brooding loners of the *film noir* (even though Hitchcock was fond of suggesting that dark obsessions lay behind his charm), and his dialect was wrong for wisecracks; nevertheless, his stylistic achievement was in many ways similar to Chandler's. By combining the techniques and attitudes of sophisticated light comic acting with the looks of a matinee idol and the gestures of a vaudevillian, he managed to graft disparate worlds together. Like Chandler, he mediated between an aestheticized English public-school sensibility and an American idiom, projecting "gentlemanly" values but divesting them of what the mass audience might regard as too much elitist or homosexual implication. Also like Chandler, his work was devoted to a narrow range of popular fiction rather than to "serious" projects; as a result, film critics who admire Grant are fond of comparing him to Olivier (usually to Olivier's detriment), just as literary critics often compare Chandler to more academically respectable writers. The implication behind such comparisons is that Grant is an unpretentious "real man" who has worked his way up from lowly origins, whereas Olivier belongs to a sheltered, privileged, sissified caste. For example, David Thomson has written that "Grant had grown up in Archie's world of Empires, while Olivier had to be taken to the last active music halls to get a look at stand-up comedy" ("Charms and the Man," 58).

Grant's persona was therefore based on the familiar paradox that supports the careers of nearly all the great stars: he could seem both extrordinary and ordinary at the same time. He was at once a remote ego ideal and a "commoner" with whom large numbers of the audience could identify—a synthesis of "Cary" and "Archie." That his audience could think of him on roughly equal terms is evident from the number of times he was chosen to represent middle-class Americans. For example, in *Mr. Blandings Builds His Dream House* (1948), he and Myrna Loy were cast as an upwardly mobile couple born of a *Saturday Evening Post* fantasy ("We're just plain apple pie," Loy says at one point); and in *Penny Serenade* (1941) and *Room for One More* (1952) he played a small-town everyman, struggling to make ends meet while rearing adopted children. One need hardly add that whenever he was teamed with Irene Dunne, Jean Arthur, or Ginger Rogers, he made domestic settings glow with gentle amusement.

Grant took command of this image slowly, and it seemed to grow over time. He had worked in twenty films by 1935 and was still a relative nonentity. In the forties, he became an American citizen and a top box office attraction, but he did not reach the peak of his success with audiences until he was nearly sixty years old, after the studio system had broken down.[2] His almost legendary status from the mid-fifties onward is overdetermined, but it has something to do with his business acumen, the public memory of his long career, and his ripening looks and technique.

In youth, especially in the Mae West films, Grant had seemed too much like a parody of male beauty (Pauline Kael has described him as an "eight-by-ten glossy"); as he grew older, however, the face that had once suggested a slick Broadway type—suitable to characters Hollywood liked to call "Nick"—slowly became distinguished, a little sad behind its perfect mask of amusement. His once-pudgy cheeks took on hollows, his eyes developed squint lines, and his hair slowly greyed. Nevertheless, he retained most of the dark handsomeness of his earliest days. He appeared perpetually suntanned and trim, and although he was frequently described as "ageless," the real secret to his appeal lay in the quality of his maturity, which gave him "character." His advancing years and fame also induced a relaxed assurance and an understated style. He became the central attraction of his films, and as such he was required to be the still center around which the other players moved. In his earlier screwball comedies, he had performed everything with a slightly exaggerated zest, as if he were still in vaudeville or acrobatics. He was always excellent at reacting to someone else, but he was overstated and even a little uneasy when he made a joke or a long speech; in films like *Arsenic and Old Lace* (1941), for example, he mugs outrageously, reaching hysterics in the first reel. With a director like Hitchcock, who relied on montage and British understatement, he was held more in check, as he was in the dry, oblique dialogue scenes in some of the Hawks movies. In all his later

2. Throughout the classic studio period, Grant was an independent, and he was always a canny businessman. For a record of his popularity with audiences, see Cobbett Steinberg, *Reel Facts,* 57–61.

films, however, he cultivated an easy, laid-back quality typical of male stars, as if he were relying on the audience's affectionate response to his mere presence.

This is not to suggest that Grant's work involved any less acting than before. He simply modulated the ostensiveness of his behavior and slowed the pace of his reactions. For example, he had always been fond of the double take, but in his late films he resorted to comic pauses, holding some of them longer than anyone except Jack Benny. (The most famous instance is his response to Grace Kelly's kiss in *To Catch a Thief* [1955], where he seems to be thoughtfully sharing the fun of the shot with the movie audience.) As always, he performed small business superbly, but now it took on a calm, deadpan quality. In *Operation Petticoat* (1959), during a conversation with a frenetic Tony Curtis, he casually empties a champagne bottle into a sink, transforming the action into an unblinking off-color joke; in *Walk, Don't Run* (1966), his aptly-titled last film, he makes something ineffably funny out of a long slow-paced shot in which he does little more than move around a tiny Oriental kitchen trying to make a pot of coffee.

The mature Grant could also give a perfect imitation of an athletic hero who barely flinched at danger. Of all his films, *North by Northwest* shows that ability most clearly, allowing him to play the character in an urbane style that influenced the James Bond cycle and its countless variants. The film is equally typical of his comic work, especially in the ways it alludes to his stardom, allowing jokes about the familiar Grant image to structure both the role and the performance; in this, it goes even further than his other comedies, linking his celebrated persona to the themes of acting, impersonation, and the presentation of self.

Grant's performances often suggested a man who was simply having fun making a movie. Like most comics, he enjoyed peeking through the role, using an "alienating" disjunction as a source of humor. Howard Hawks allowed him to make autobiographical references to his offscreen self in both *Bringing Up Baby* and *His Girl Friday,* but at the peak of his success in the fifties and sixties, his stardom became the source of gags. At the beginning of *Monkey Business* (1952), we see him in a tuxedo, stepping out through the front door of a suburban house. "Not yet, Cary," Hawks's offscreen voice says, and Grant goes back into the house, mumbling abstractedly. The routine is repeated twice, until finally, after the film's credits have run by, Grant is allowed to make his proper entrance, acting his role as an absent-minded professor on his way to a party. As the plot develops, Hawks's otherwise rather slight film relies heavily on the audience's special fondness for Grant, so that most of the fun comes from watching the star rather than the character act silly, drinking a youth potion that makes him get a crew cut and regress mentally to childhood.

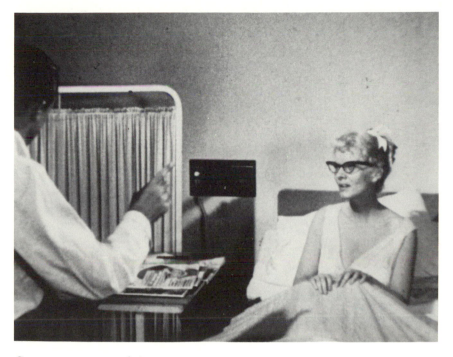

Grant encounters an admirer.

In a similar way, Grant's celebrity sometimes overwhelms the fictional circumstances in *North by Northwest*. At one point he removes a pair of Hollywoodish sunglasses and glances wryly across a table at Eva Marie Saint: "I know," he says, as if to voice what she is thinking. "I look *vaguely* familiar." The phenomenon here is similar to one that operates in many films, but in this case the recrudescence of the star is more vivid, more comically self-reflexive. "Cary Grant" is displayed not simply as a famous personality who is performing a role but as the very essence of stardom—that is, as a remote, glamorous object who emits a glorious light simply by being "himself." The film makes the same kind of reference to his aura when during his attempt to escape from government captors he accidentally steps into a lady's hospital room. "Stop!" the lady screams in fear; but when she puts on her glasses and sees Grant, her tone changes from alarm to a breathless plea: "Stop!"

Such jokes are as old as Hollywood. In *North by Northwest*, however, they have an especially ironic implication. Hitchcock and his writer, Ernest Lehman, not only refer to Grant's stardom, they also use him in a tongue-in-cheek story (compounded of ideas from *The Thirty-Nine Steps* [1935], *Saboteur* [1942], and *Notorious* [1946]) about the construction of a "person" out of nothing. "George Kaplan," the fake identity manufactured by government agents, is barely less substantial than "Roger O. Thornhill," a corporate executive who is the product of a bundle of stereotypical traits and a middle initial that stands for zero. By extension, both characters have something in common with "Cary Grant," who has been created by the actor and the entertainment industry out of a made-up proper name, a set of performing attributes, and a series of narrative functions. As a result, the film allows us to think of Grant in contradictory ways. On the one hand, it suggests that he is a presence rather than an actor (just as Roger Thornhill is sincere while most of the other characters pretend); on the other hand, it teases us with the possibility that Grant's stardom is itself an act, a calculated image built out of theatrical convention and the technical skill of a performer.

Hitchcock's formalist temperament and his lifelong attraction to themes of identity and theatricality doubtless contributed to this effect. The "wrong man" plot was one of his favorite devices, and the stage was one of the most frequent images of his British films. In his later Hollywood work, the familiar doppelgänger theme of Gothic fiction took on especially disturbing implications, threatening any notion of a transcendent, organic subjectivity. For example, at the end of *Psycho,* Anthony Perkins stares out at us and "thinks" with the voice of an old woman, as if character and sexual difference had dissolved altogether. *Vertigo,* too, contains a quicksand of shifting identities: the protagonist of that film, played by James Stewart, is an empiricist with the practical Scottish name of John Ferguson; but there is a deliberate irony in his being called Scotty by some people, John by others, and Johnny-O by his closest woman friend. Meanwhile the Kim Novak character has multiple personalities, so that we can never say with certainty which manifestation is real: is she Madeleine Elster (one of the film's many references to the work of Edgar Allan Poe), or Carlotta Valdez, or simply Judy Barton? Or does the question matter, given her death and the detective's state of mind at the end?

The two Cary Grant vehicles Hitchcock made during this period—*To Catch a Thief* and *North by Northwest*—are at least marginally concerned with the same issues, evoking them in a comic mode appropriate to Grant, often celebrating the theatrical qualities of selfhood instead of viewing them as a source of pure anguish. Of the two, *North by Northwest* is more clever at developing permutations of the theme, becoming a potentially dark satire on "image making" in general. Although it sweeps away much of our unease by a fairy-tale ending, it suggests that Madison Avenue, the CIA, and even the presidential monuments at Mount Rushmore are duplicitous "fronts" for a sinister game. Grant and the other actors partake of a similar duplicity, but their pretense is socially sanctioned, a function of art and "entertainment." Thus the film frequently calls attention to the people "behind" the roles, and even allows them to talk about their performance.

Early in the film, when Roger Thornhill has been abducted and brought to the Townsend estate, he encounters Townsend (actually Vandamm), played by the suave James Mason. "With such expert playacting," Mason says, "you make this very room a theater." For a moment we have a heightened sense of two stars who have certain features in common and who share the same dramatic space. Mason's velvety voice is itself theatrical, and we can see him relishing his part as he sits down on a couch, rubbing his forehead with a finger, holding a hand over his heart, and looking up at Grant with a dyspeptic stare. Later Mason encounters Grant at an art auction in Chicago and complains that all this "acting" is growing tiresome. "Has anyone ever told you that you overplay your various roles rather severely, Mr. Kaplan?" As he speaks, he transforms a pair of horn-rimmed glasses into an expressive object by twirling them nonchalantly in his hand; then he launches into a summary of the plot, sneering over certain words to make them drip with irony: "First you're the outraged Madison Avenue man who claims he has been mistaken for someone else. Then you play the fugitive from justice, supposedly trying to clear his name of a crime he knows he didn't commit. And now you play the peevish lover, stung by jealousy and betrayal. Seems to me you fellows could stand a little less training from the F.B.I. and a little more from the Actors' Studio!"

Of course it is Mason, not Grant, who is overacting, and the irony is repeated at the level of the narrative, where it is Vandamm, not Thornhill, who has consistently posed as someone else. A similar effect is created at other points in the film, especially when Lehman's script manipulates what Erving Goffman calls the "information state" of the plot (*Frame Analysis,* 149–155), not only shifting focalization or point of view, but repeatedly playing tricks with what the audience needs to know to determine whether a character is "acting" or behaving sincerely. Thus when the police take Thornhill to the Townsend estate to give him a chance to prove his improbable story about thugs who tried to kill him with "bourbon and sports car," they are confronted by a sweetly charming middle-aged lady who tells them that her husband is about to deliver an address to the United Nations. "What a performance!" Grant says, simultaneously admiring the player (Josephine Hutchinson) and commenting on what we know to be the character's duplicity.

When we meet Eve Kendall aboard the Twentieth-Century Limited, the plot situation is just the opposite. At first we take her at face value, assuming she is motivated by a mixture of kindness and lust; but later that evening we see her passing a note to Vandamm, unbeknownst to Thornhill. Here and in several other places we learn important information before the Grant character does; Eve Kendall becomes an actor within the narrative, and we wait to see Thornhill's reaction when he discovers the truth. Then, just when we have grown accustomed to this privileged view, the plot takes another twist: Grant meets Mason a third time in a cafeteria below Mount Rushmore. "What little drama are we here for today?" Mason asks and is shocked when Grant seizes

Eva Marie Saint by the arm, pulls her to one side of the room, and accuses her of betraying him. In apparent anger and desperation, Saint draws a gun from her purse and ends the lover's spat by shooting Grant in the stomach. Everyone in the cafeteria gasps, screams, or rushes for the exits as Grant staggers backward, curling his body and hunching his shoulders. He pauses, rises on his toes, and turns, one hand on his wound and the other grasping air. Then he falls toward the camera, his mouth open, his eyes bulging in horror. We perhaps expect that deception is involved here, because we and Grant have previously been informed of Saint's true identity; nevertheless, it is not until later that we learn the bullets are blanks and that the whole episode in the cafeteria has in fact been a "drama." In other words, Thornhill, too, is capable of putting on an act. When Grant and Saint meet afterward in a secluded spot in the woods, she admires his work: "You did it rather well, I thought." He smiles shyly but knowingly. "Yes. I thought I was quite graceful."

And in fact Grant *is* graceful. If he sometimes appears to be acting less than the other players, that is partly because *North by Northwest* exploits him as an image rather than a "thespian" and partly because the plot gives the supporting cast a slightly better opportunity to show off their histrionic abilities. The technique is fairly typical of Hollywood, where the hero is usually noble, honest, and relatively inexpressive, and where the star is often supposed to "behave" rather than merely pretend. Hitchcock seemed to be reinforcing this impression of the star as a relatively passive presence (as well as boasting of his own power) during his interview with Truffaut when he suggested that Grant was ignorant of his job: "Cary Grant came up to me and said, 'It's a terrible script. We've already done a third of the picture and I still can't make head or tail of it.' . . . without realizing it he was using a line of his own dialogue" (190).[3] Grant's work in the film, however, belies such notions.

For want of a better term, Grant might be called a Kuleshovian rather than a Stanislavskian actor. More concerned with mechanics than with feeling, he was especially effective in comedy or in the Hitchcock films, where everything depended on timing, athletic skill, and a mastery of small, isolated reactions. He seldom seemed preoccupied or thoughtful and rarely displayed intense emotionalism (*Penny Serenade,* in which he weeps and pleads before a judge who is trying to take his adopted child away, is a notable exception to this rule). Nevertheless, he is an expert at crisp expressiveness and movement, a player whose understanding of classical film rhetoric is equal to anyone's.

3. There is no line of dialogue in the film similar to the one Hitchcock quotes, and evidence suggests that Grant was an active collaborator in the production process as a whole. For a plausible explanation of Grant's complaint, see John Russell Taylor, *Hitch: The Life and Times of Alfred Hitchcock,* 255–56.

One of the important skills he brings to *North by Northwest* is the ability to walk, run, climb, or execute smaller, everyday actions in a graceful, clearly enunciated fashion. An extraordinary number of shots in the film require him to make crossing movements, either parallel or diagonal to the camera—as in the opening scenes, where he rapidly exits from an office building, leaps into a taxi, and walks through the lobby of the Park Plaza Hotel. His movement helps to establish a literal pace for the film, and at the same time it displays character traits, showing Thornhill both as a self-satisfied, charmingly manipulative executive and as a man in a perpetual hurry. Thornhill dashes his way through New York yet remains less harried-looking, more tanned and unperturbed than anyone else. Repeatedly he is shown hustling (or being hustled) in and out of cabs, using telephones, scribbling notes, and behaving with extemporized savoir faire (at one point he bribes his somewhat mercenary mother in the same style he would use to tip a headwaiter). In fact all of Grant's small actions in the opening scenes—swiping a cab, ordering a drink, glancing at his watch, signaling a messenger—become motifs central to the rhythm, the cultural codes, and the visual dynamic of the film.

Skills of this sort are not necessarily rare, but they are invaluable in the context of *North by Northwest,* which is not only an action piece but also at times a wordless example of Kuleshovian "pure cinema." "People performing organized, efficent work appear best on the screen," Kuleshov wrote. "Actors, having come to study our film work, cannot content themselves with such an elementary task as how to enter a room, take a chair. . . . Ordinarily, such a task is done with scornful derision—so easy does it seem. If you ask an actor to perform this task several times, you will see it is performed variously . . . sometimes better, sometimes worse" (101). To solve the problem, Kuleshov recommended a Delsarte-like training for screen actors, a series of exercises that would make all movement systematic. Most of all, the actor's behavior needed to become "exceptionally distinct, quickly and clearly comprehended by the viewer" (99). Significantly, the professionals he recommended for study were not the major theatrical players of the day but Chaplin, Fairbanks, and Pickford, all of whom possessed a quality of efficient vivacity.

Grant did not study Kuleshov, but he probably learned a good deal from the silent players Kuleshov admired. His early training as an acrobat and vaudeville performer enhanced this quality. He was an emotionally reserved actor whose work was engineered to fit the precise needs of a given sequence. He was so conscious of posture and ostensiveness that he could perform the same action again and again, looking good in the retakes and never spoiling the rhythm of a sequence. He effected small actions with absolute clarity, never complicating them with unnecessary movement. At the same time he had technical control over *degrees* of expression, so that he could produce a series of distinctly shaded reactions in close-up—little pieces of behavior that could be laid out on an editing table and used to structure a line of narrative.

Grant on the roadside.

As an instance, consider his technical contribution to the crop-dusting sequence, where he speaks only three lines of dialogue and is seldom required to project intense emotion. When the Greyhound bus deposits him on a barren roadside in the midst of the prairie, Grant stands there for a while, hands lightly touching in front of his body, eyes squinting against the sun. He looks around in both directions, motivating the camera's "subjective" view up and down the empty road, and pokes his hands casually in his pockets, watching in utter deadpan as a car approaches and passes. He gives a slight shrug, rocking back on his heels, then suddenly reacts with interest to something offscreen, his hands moving up as if he were about to remove them from the pockets. A dark limousine approaches and passes. Grant's hands relax into their former position, but after a moment he stiffens again as he looks down the road. We hear the sound of a heavy motor. A gigantic truck dopplers past, speeding off into the distance. Grant ducks his head to one side and squints, pulling his hands from his pockets and wiping dust from his eye. When the cloud of dust subsides, he shrugs and returns the hands to his pockets. After a pause, his body straightens slightly, becoming still and expectant, his eyes directed offscreen to a space behind the camera. We see an old car approaching from a side road. Grant bites his lip expectantly. Cut to the car stopping at the highway and a man getting out of the passenger door. Looking intent, Grant starts to take his hands out of his pockets, then pauses, his elbows lifted. We see the stranger (Edward Binns) walking to the opposite side of the roadway while the car backs up. Grant moves both hands to his sides, frowning. A long shot shows him and the stranger in a fifty-fifty composition, facing one another across the roadway. Grant unbuttons his jacket, puts his hands on his hips, frowns again, and bites his lower lip. He holds that position for a moment, then looks left down the road and back toward the stranger. He lowers his arms decisively and starts to cross the road. Stepping into

A stranger arrives.

a *plan américain* alongside the stranger, he speaks with forced casualness: "Hi. Hot day." "Seen worse," says the stranger (a farmer out of a Grant Wood painting, standing with hands in the hip pockets of a mail-order brown suit that contrasts neatly with Thornhill's big-city attire) Grant signals his nervousness by rubbing his palms together and clasping his hands, rocking back on his heels in an attempt at nonchalance. "Are you supposed to be meeting someone here?" he asks. When the farmer says no, Grant rubs his knuckles and bites his lip: "Then your name isn't Kaplan?"

Soon a bus arrives, and the farmer rides off (after noticing a plane dusting "where there ain't no crops"). We see Grant once more alone on the roadway, his hands on his hips. He stands for a while, drops his hands, clasps them rather forlornly in front of his body, and then checks his watch. He looks calmly off toward the direction of the plane, whose engine grows louder on the soundtrack. Cut to the approaching aircraft and then back to Grant's face, shown in a closer view. He stiffens and looks intently forward, frowning against the sun. Another view of the plane and then back to Grant, who is now framed in tight close-up, his eyes opening in surprise, his head pulling defensively into his shoulders, his body turning slightly. He makes a half turn of his shoulders as if to move away, but then catches himself, unsure of the pilot's intentions. A reverse angle shows the plane approaching head on, and we return to Grant, his eyes fixed in astonishment at an offscreen space, his body twisting and dropping out of sight. Cut to a low-level shot from behind him, as the plane swoops noisily overhead.

From this point onward, the performance depends on a combination of athletic and expressive skill—as when Grant breaks into a sprint toward the retreating camera while the plane is visible just beyond his shoulders. (See the series of shots on the next page.) For most of the sequence, however, Grant's emotional reactions and movements have been fairly low-keyed—

Grant attacked by the biplane.

chiefly a matter of frowns and astonished looks. He has been given no objects to manipulate, so that his chief expressive instruments are his elbows and shoulders, which he keeps raising and lowering as he moves his hands in and out of his pockets or as he buttons and unbuttons his jacket. His behavior consists largely of what theorists like Delsarte and Kuleshov would call a "coiling" and "uncoiling"—slightly extensive and intensive motions of the body that indicate degrees of tension or awareness. These are not complicated moves, but they hardly need to be. Grant's job is to find elemental postures and expressions that will fit neatly and clearly into the montage. In accomplishing this task, he employs a craft that is as important in its own way as any other type of acting; thus when Albert LaValley wrote a descriptive analysis of the crop-dusting sequence for his *Focus on Hitchcock,* he closed by remarking on "the perfect suiting of acting, timing, delivery of dialogue, gestures, *etc.,* of Cary Grant to the rhythms of Hitchcock's editing" (149).

Grant's work elsewhere in the film frequently involves a quiet, relaxed underplaying. This is particularly true of his appearances with James Mason, who, as we have seen, tends to overact—for example, when he flourishes a cigarette like a Hollywood Nazi while Grant simply stands still, his hands in his pockets, looking mildly angry. A roughly similar logic operates during the love scenes with Saint, who has been cast in the typical Hitchcock mold as an aggressive, upper-class blond. What is particularly important here, however, is Grant's comic inflection, which transcends the dialogue and makes Thornhill something more than an archetypal capitalist and chauvinist. When he bumps into Saint on the Twentieth-Century Limited, he does a sudden astonished take, jerking his head back characteristically and then leaning forward with a confidential air to explain why he is hiding from the police: "*Seven* parking tickets." "Oh," she skeptically comments, looking him over before she goes strolling off down the corridor. He looks after her, holding a deadpan pause of several beats; then he turns to address the movie audience, his eyes concealed by sunglasses, a hint of a smile on his face, nicely avoiding a leer.

In subsequent scenes, Grant's behavior lends an air of polite, ironic intelligence to sexual byplay. The effect he creates is crucial, because any misjudgment of tone could have reduced *North by Northwest* to the level of one of its debased imitations, such as the Matt Helm series played by Dean Martin in the sixties. The script establishes Thornhill as a boozing, smooth-talking playboy, some of whose witticisms are crude: for example, he tells Saint that she's "big in all the right places" and later remarks that he's "accustomed to having a load on." Grant's apparent modesty and polish somehow redeem this material, and he helps make the scene in the dining car one of the most sensual moments in Hitchcock's career.

The setting for the dining-car sequence is perfectly in keeping with what I have already described as an adman's fantasy: it gives us food, wine, and two beautiful, immaculately dressed people who stare at one another across a white tablecloth while a Vistavision landscape goes floating by. The writing, the photography, the scoring, and the mixing are all technically admirable (for example, just at the moment when Grant lights Saint's cigarette, the tinny diegetic music of the dining car is subtly replaced by Bernard Herrmann's romantic background orchestration), and everything is shot and edited with Hitchcock's customary feeling for classical syntax. Ultimately, however, the scene's effect depends crucially on Grant's behavior in close-ups. His job is chiefly to react to Saint's sexual aggressiveness, and the comedy of his performance is produced by small means—for example, the mildly knowing way he uses his eyes and voice when he sits down at the table and says "Well! Here we are again"; or the way he speaks when he writes out an order for the waiter: "Brook . . . Trout." Grant's handling of small objects—sunglasses, napkin, table fork, matches—gives the scene its quality of polished amenity, and at the same time his actions make a nice counterpoint to Saint, who speaks a good deal but remains almost motionless.

Grant's voice also contrasts with the subdued, breathy tones Hitchcock required of the heroine. When she tells him she knows he is Roger Thornhill, "wanted for murder on the front page of every paper in America," he has a delightful way of saying "oops" while chewing a mouthful of trout. As the conversation becomes more sexually explicit, he achieves a maximum of comic expressiveness from lines that are so simple they hardly seem like dialogue at all. Here is a key exchange:

> *She:* It's going to be a long night.
>
> *He:* True.
>
> *She:* And I don't particularly like the book I'm reading.
>
> *He:* Aaah.
>
> *She:* You know what I mean?
>
> *He:* Now let me think. . . .

Grant's slow drawing out of the syllables, as if the film were a musical and he were about to break into song, is impossible to capture on paper. Equally hard to illustrate is his tone, which in the hands of many actors would have been lascivious or vain. He understands the playfulness of the give-and-take, its status as a performance within the performance, and he has a way of registering amused anticipation or eagerness without seeming randy. For example, when Saint suggests that it seems "unfair" for him to have no place to sleep, he says "Yes, isn't it?" without resorting to drooling exaggeration; instead he bestows a witty discretion on the line, smiling and glancing shyly down at his plate.

Everywhere in the film, in fact, Grant's accent and enunciation tend to improve the humor in Lehman's writing. At one point, he protests to Leo G. Carroll that George Kaplan must be a real person: "I've been in his hotel room! I've tried on his clothes! He's got short sleeves and *dan-druff!*" The stress he gives to each syllable of the last word makes him seem like a whimsical aristocrat who has discovered a true oddity, but also like someone who is imitating Cary Grant. Earlier, he makes a similar protestation to James Mason, who has accused him of checking in and out of hotels under the name of Kaplan: "But I've never even *been* in Pittsburgh!" he says, giving a slightly English inflection to the line. (In much the same vein, Grant, Mason, and Leo G. Carroll all give a fastidious pronunciation to "Rapid City, South Dakota," amused by its American quaintness.)

Usually Grant plays Thornhill in such a relaxed style that he never seems in any true danger—even on Mount Rushmore, he is relatively calm, leaving Eva Marie Saint the job of expressing intense alarm. In perilous situations,

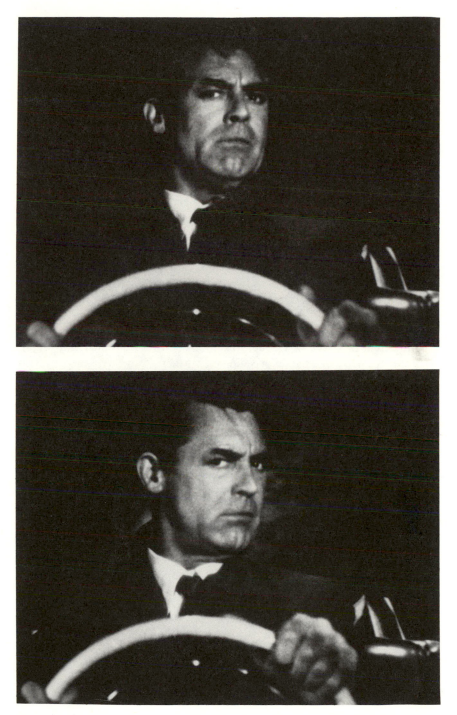

Grant "mugs" drunkenness.

however, he sometimes resorts to exaggerated facial gymnastics, recalling some of the farcical movies he made in his youth. When two men pour bourbon down his throat and load him into a Mercedes poised on the edge of a cliff, he mugs wildly. Looking drunkenly over the side of the car, he notices that the rear wheel is hanging in space and spinning; he pauses, head pointed straight down, and then glances up to stare cross-eyed at the movie audience. Holding that position for a moment, he frowns, mutters "oooh," and then turns to drive off, the car miraculously freed. In the next sequence, which shows Thornhill tooling down the highway, Hitchcock cuts subjectively back and forth between Grant and the road ahead, and Grant's overplayed reactions give the scene an atmosphere of purely comic anxiety, almost like a chase from a Sennett picture. Imagine James Stewart in an equivalent sequence, and it becomes apparent how little Grant tries to exploit intense, deeply felt emotions: a sleepy drunk, he narrows his mouth to a slit and tries to focus on the road, which is shown to us as two weaving, superimposed images running out in front of the car. Then he squints, blinks, and reacts with bug-eyed alarm when he notices obstacles ahead. Getting the car under control, he relaxes into a kind of ostentatious aplomb. A moment later, when he hears a police siren, he does a slow double take, looking over his shoulder, frowning, shaking his head, and then proceeding on his merry way.

Brought to a jailhouse by the police, Grant once again plays everything for broad physical comedy, getting laughs from the way he maintains an air of witty dignity even when he is practically falling on the floor. Judged by any realistic standards, he is a barely convincing drunkard, but he makes excellent use of slapstick conventions. Two officers are holding him up as he enters: "Somebody call the police," he says, turning to look nose-to-nose at the cop on his left. Led into the courtroom for a drunk test, he leans at a forty-five degree angle against the man who is supporting him, and then crawls up on a bench to lie down. Throughout, he behaves like a man who is falling asleep on his feet, all the while babbling away in a cheery confidence.

A great deal of Grant's humor in these sequences is vaguely reminiscent of Chaplin's, partly because it depends on a quality of sensitive politeness and wit amid farcical situations and partly because it uses the crisp, ostentatious expressiveness already described. Consider, for example, his way of playing a minor scene in the back seat of a Chicago police car just after Thornhill has deliberately gotten himself arrested. Most of the action is shot from a single camera position, with the driver of the car (Patrick McVey) seated at the right of the screen, Grant in the center of the composition on the back seat, and a second cop (Ken Lynch) hunched up next to him on the left. The symmetry and flatness of the image is itself comic, and Grant adds to the effect by behaving in the slightly exaggerated style of a silent mime. First he adjusts the knot in his tie and then pats the cop next to him on the shoulder. "Thank you, my friend, thank you," he says. The two policemen slouch in

their seats, looking ahead with weary, disgruntled expressions; in response Grant adopts a formal, straightbacked posture, occasionally turning his head at right angles to his body in an attempt to show his face to the man immediately next to him. His companion refuses to meet this glance, and Grant turns forward with a happy smile of anticipation: "Well!" he says, "Let's have some smiles and good cheer! Don't you know who I am?" He pauses, sitting back in a rigid, dignified pose. When he gets no reaction, he swivels his head once more to the left. Still no reaction. Moving his hand across an imaginary newspaper to indicate block capitals, Grant reads off a headline: "*'Chicago Police Capture United Nations Killer.'* Congratulations, men!" He sits back contentedly for one beat, and then swiftly turns his head to stare into the openmouthed face of the man next to him. When the driver calls headquarters for instructions, the car makes a sharp U-turn and Grant tilts, keeping his body geometrically rigid. "Where are we going? I want to be taken to police headquarters!" Getting no response, he jerks his head back in a little birdlike spasm and frowns. "I'm a *dangerous assassin!* I'm a *mad killer* on the loose!"

Another instance of the similarity between Grant and the silent comics may be seen in a short, wordless sequence, photographed in a single shot, showing him attempting to shave with a tiny lady's travel razor. Midway through the film, hiding in Eve Kendall's bathroom aboard the train, he notices the razor on her shelf, holding it up and staring at it in deadpan contemplation. A bit later, in the men's room of Chicago's Union Station, he conceals himself from the police by busily smearing lather over his face as he stands at a lavatory. Once the police exit the room, he decides to shave in earnest, pulling out the miniscule razor, making a quick swipe along a heavily-lathered cheek, and leaving a ridiculously tiny path through the foam. He does a slight "take," staring in the mirror with mild astonishment, and then notices that he is being observed by a fat man next to him who is also shaving. Holding up the razor as if to explain the strange pattern on his face, he opens his mouth to speak, but obviously can't come up with a plausible story. With a typical jerk of his head and a small crouch, he looks back in the mirror, studying the visual effect. Then he playfully swoops a clean little stripe down the center of his upper lip, leaving a Hitlerian or (more appropriately) a Chaplinesque "mustache." With placid calm, he leans back slightly, admiring his work. (See next page.)

This small joke underlines Grant's indebtedness to a comic tradition that produced some of the most important movie players—a tradition opposed to naturalism and dependant chiefly on physical dynamics. If the specific relation between him and an actor like Chaplin is not often clear, that is probably because Grant was also one of the most glamorous of screen lovers, who seldom reached for pathos. In the romantic passages of his films, he could serve as a polite, self-effacing object of beauty, simply letting the camera admire his handsome profile. He could also make a physically difficult love

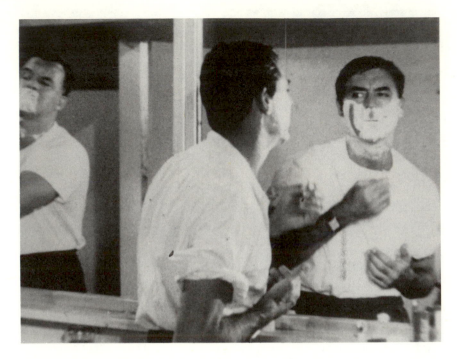

Grant's homage to Chaplin.

scene look fairly easy—as in this picture, where, in addition to speaking dialogue, he executes a slow, waltzlike turn with Saint in his arms, inducing a Hitchcockian feeling of sexual vertigo.

Viewers tend to forget that this sort of action involves actorly skill. Then, too, they lose sight of Grant's craft because his image, like that of most of the major stars, overshadows the technique that helped to create it. It is common to hear his admiring critics and even his fellow players speak of him as if he were a relatively natural phenomenon. One fairly typical judgment of his career can be summed up as follows: "Cary Grant, I think, is a personality functioning. . . .He can't play a serious part or, let me say, the public isn't interested in him in that way. . . .But he has a lovely sense of timing, an amusing face and a lovely voice" (quoted in Shipman, 254). That was Katharine Hepburn speaking, and she was certainly in a position to know. A film like *North by Northwest*, however, can lead us to different conclusions, suggesting that a vivid star personality is itself a theatrical construction and that comedy is no less artful than serious drama. After all, it takes as much acting to play "Cary Grant," adjusting him slightly to meet the requirements of "Roger Thornhill," as it does to perform any other movie role.

In fact, the more one studies Grant, the more he resembles what the early Soviet directors liked to call an "eccentric" actor—a highly stylized creation made up of peculiar movements and an interesting combination of expressive codes (a quality he shares with a great many Hollywood personalities, including such different players as James Stewart and Burt Lancaster). Ironically, the Hollywood star system and most of the other media strive to make obvious theatrical eccentricity seem invisible; the star's image is a valuable commodity, affecting her or his every public appearance, so that popular actors seem to become the figures they play, shading their fictional behavior into their celebrity appearances. We therefore need to remind ourselves that in creating "himself" Cary Grant employed a technique; ultimately, he evolved a character of no less resonance or cultural significance than Chaplin's Tramp, but it was a character just the same.

Part Three

Film as a Performance Text

13

Rear Window (1954)

Rear Window gives most of its collaborators a chance to show off their technical skill The script, adapted by John Michael Hayes from a Cornell Woolrich story, is an ingenious "claustrophobic" narrative, grounded firmly in the cinema's love of subjectivity and monocular vision; the set, designed by Hal Pereira and a team of Paramount craftsmen, is a charmingly detailed fantasy based on Greenwich Village architecture, like a doll's house backed by an ever-changing cyclorama; Robert Burks's color photography is richly sensual, filled with elaborate camera movements, delicate reframings, and tricky manipulations of focus—as in the opening panorama of the back wall of an apartment building, which ends with a gigantic close-up of a bead of sweat on James Stewart's forehead; the soundtrack, engineered by Harry Lindgren and John Cope, is a near symphony of effects and diegetic music, all of it edited and mixed to give the feeling of an echoing city courtyard on a hot summer's day and night. My concern, however, is with the work of the actors—not only the stars like Stewart and Grace Kelly but also the minor players who never speak a word. At this level, too, *Rear Window* is infused with an almost comic pleasure in its own technique, offering a virtual compendium of theatrical conventions that allows me to summarize many of the formal issues I have discussed.

It may seem strange to talk of acting and theatricality in this context, since *Rear Window* is widely regarded as a sustained exercise in "pure cinema." Nevertheless, when Hitchcock made the film he was preoccupied with relations and differences between the stage and movies—a point emphasized during the credits, as matchstick blinds slowly rise like a curtain and the camera tracks through a window. The plot also makes this concern apparent: the principal action is situated in one room and is structured exactly like a three-act proscenium drama. Except for the crucially "cinematic" device of Stewart's binoculars, the same events could be presented with a fair amount of suspense on Broadway. Thus when Hitchcock released the film, he gave an interview comparing it to his earlier experience with *Rope* (1948):

> A stage play is designed for a limited area of presentation, that is, the proscenium arch. Some years ago I tried to get around this problem when I made a film called *Rope*. . . . I tried to do it as if I were giving the audience all opera glasses to follow the action on the stage. . . . I think people make a dreadful error when they "open up" stage plays. (LaValley, 41)

Like André Bazin (but for different reasons), Hitchcock recognized that the key to filming well-made drama was not to spread the action over various settings or to invent pretexts for photographing scenes outdoors. After all, he reasoned, movies are not about landscapes or horses galloping; they are about the primal desire to watch other humans, stimulated by narrative, montage, and camera placement. *Rear Window* demonstrates this theory while dealing explicitly with the psychological dynamic of exhibitionism and voyeurism; moreover, it enables Hitchcock to place the opera glasses in the hands of a character, plausibly combining a novelistic point of view with a theatrical *mise-en-scène*.

The film also interested Hitchcock for what it seemed to demonstrate about a minimalist form of acting that is typical of movies:

> I think it was Pudovkin, the famous Russian director many years ago, who took a closeup and he put various objects in front of a woman's face [sic]. . . . For example if Mr. Stewart is looking out into a courtyard and—let's say—he sees a woman with a child in her arms. Well, the first cut is Mr. Stewart, then what he sees, and then his reaction. We'll see him smile. Now if you took away the center piece of film and substituted—we'll say—a shot of the girl Miss Torso in a bikini, instead of being a benevolent gentleman he's now a dirty old man. And you've only changed one piece of film, you haven't changed his look or his reaction. That is one of the reasons why I chose this film. (LaValley, 40–41)

Rear Window creates a set of circumstances that keep the James Stewart character utterly immobilized, simply watching other people put on a show. As virtually every critic has noticed, he is emblematic of the typical movie spectator; but as the quote above indicates, he is also a metaphor for the film actor—a figure Hitchcock had previously defined as "a man who can do nothing extremely well." What better illustration of this principle than to have the star imprisoned in a wheelchair throughout the movie, with a plaster cast encasing the entire lower half of his body and a thermometer poked in his mouth?

As a formal device, Hitchcock's idea is almost worthy of Beckett, who not only put actors in wheelchairs but sometimes planted them in gigantic vases, as if to reduce the human figure to an elementary sign. It would be wrong, however, to suggest that *Rear Window* is an avant-garde experiment or to imply that Stewart does nothing. On the contrary, the film is as much a *tour de force* for the star as for the director, heightening the cleverness of Stewart's performance by severely constraining him.[1] It would be equally wrong to accept Hitchcock's simplistic account of the Kuleshov effect or his glib descriptions of how the "best" acting in movies is achieved. A more accurate way of generalizing about the performances in *Rear Window* would be to say that the film involves three different acting tasks, each of them determined by the scale of the image and normalized or motivated by the plot. First is a method in which players "think" for the camera, projecting tiny reactions in close-up to events that are presumably occurring offscreen; next is a presentational form where players are viewed (as in the earliest silent movies) in a strong frontal position, executing large, vivid gestures in long shot and without benefit of dialogue; third is a more complex behavior that owes chiefly to the realistic proscenium stage, where players, framed at medium distance, move about on separate planes of a single room, participating in the give-and-take of dramatic dialogue, manipulating various objects, and making theatrical entrances and exits.

The first of these techniques attracted Hitchcock to the project, but what makes *Rear Window* especially interesting as a "performance text" is the way it makes structural contrasts out of the most extreme forms of acting, as if to comment on the historical development of screen rhetoric. Stewart, frozen in the wheelchair, his movement limited mainly to reaction shots and "gestureless moments," is an actor who works completely within the dominant contemporary mode, whereas the supporting players in the apartment windows have to gesticulate emphatically, performing with their full bodies and regressing to an earlier, almost nickelodeon, style. During the course of the film, our view of the action in Thorwald's apartment tends to recapitulate the "progress" of the medium, taking us from distant proscenium shots to close-ups, from presentational to representational technique, as if to demonstrate the classic cinema's longing for intimate, psychological accounts of character.

The little scenarios on display outside L. B. Jefferies's window are the very stuff of popular movies—all of them concerned with "human interest," sex, and violence. As Jefferies deciphers the narrative in Thorwald's rooms, he becomes a representative to the movie audience—caught up by the hermeneutic code, looking deeper into the image, trying to see the flicker of an expression that will reveal the true self of a character. For this reason one of the most formally intriguing performances in the film is that of Raymond

1. Stars sometimes delight in such roles. Consider Barbara Stanwyck's scene-chewing hysteria in *Sorry, Wrong Number* (1948), which allows her to play an invalid confined to a bed and a telephone.

Burr, who begins as a silent actor in the distance, then becomes a close-up image, and finally speaks whispered, intimate lines of dialogue. "What do you want of me?" he asks as he enters the fully realistic space of Stewart's room, at once challenging the audience and gratifying them, revealing the depths of a tortured soul.

Prior to the climactic scenes, Stewart and Burr are sometimes required to perform similar actions in different styles. When L. B. Jefferies grows drowsy from boredom, he simply nods his head a few millimeters and closes his eyes, drifting off to sleep in his chair; but when Lars Thorwald becomes weary after a long night of chopping up his wife, he sends a signal that can be read in the back gallery: he walks "downstage" center and makes a gigantic yawn, arching his back and stretching his arms high on either side of his body. By the same token, an argument between Jefferies and his lover is expressed through mild changes in tone and a few tiny gestures, such as a troubled glance into the depths of a wineglass or an irritated flick of the hand. Meanwhile a roughly parallel argument between Thorwald and his wife is staged like a melodramatic tableau: she sits on the edge of her bed, laughing while he scowls, ultimately collapsing in derisive hysteria as he waves his hand in disgust and stalks out of the room. If the film were to create a disjunction between acting and the other elements of *découpage*—that is, if the performance styles of Burr and Stewart remained the same while the camera and sound were centered in Burr's apartment—these contrasts would become especially vivid. The traveling salesman would spend most of the time standing in a window, flinging his arms about as if he were playing to a distant audience. Across the way, we could see a man with a broken leg getting a rub-down from a nurse, and later being served dinner by a blond in a Paris dress; in general, however, the behavior in the photographer's rooms would be almost unreadable, consisting mostly of unheard conversations between unidentified persons, accompanied by gestures too vague and indistinct to produce meaning.

But Thorwald's behavior is not always so vividly presentational. As the plot develops, it makes us want to see his hidden motives, and at that point his movements become more "private" or subtle. Midway through the film he turns his back to the camera as he wraps a knife in a package. Seizing a pair of binoculars, Jefferies converts our viewpoint from proscenium framing to a *plan américain,* so that we can see portions of what the package contains. When Thorwald completes the job, he crosses to the window and stands looking out into the courtyard, his expression indistinct. Frustrated, Jefferies puts the binoculars aside and snatches up the telephoto lens of a camera, changing the medium shot to a close-up, hoping to read the message in Thorwald's eyes. Somewhat later, Jeffries looks through the same lens and Hitchcock cheats the perspective, giving us a much larger close-up of Thorwald, who sits in a chair and takes his wife's wedding ring out of her purse. We watch his eyes as he contemplates the ring, and, like Jefferies, we search deep into the expression, trying to find the truth that presumably lies somewhere beneath the calm surface. In this moment, Raymond Burr has been transformed from a distant figure in a theatrical dumbshow into a Stanislavskian actor—a man who quietly thinks himself into the role and allows us to watch his ambiguous expression.

A good deal of *Rear Window*'s subtle commentary on the rhetoric of movie acting is made explicit early on, in a brief sequence involving a minor player. First we see Jefferies sipping a glass of wine and glancing out his window to the lower level of a building across the way, where "Miss Lonelyheart" (Judith Evelyn) stands before a candlelit table roughly comparable to the one in his own room. She is opening a bottle of wine when she seems to hear a sound from the hallway outside her door. Smiling, she crosses the room, opens the door, and greets an imaginary visitor, holding out her cheek for a kiss. Shyly touching her face and looking down as if to hide a blush, she indicates a chair at the dinner table. As she pours out two glasses of wine, she laughs extravagantly, responding to a witticism; then she takes a seat at the opposite end of the table and raises her glass in a toast to an empty chair. Cut to an extreme close-up of Jefferies, who smiles wryly and raises his own glass in response. (See next page.) Return to the previous view of Miss Lonelyheart, who suddenly breaks into tears, lowering her head to the table and resting it in her arms in a gesture of despair.

At the level of the diegesis, this sequence helps elaborate the theme of life-as-drama implicit in all the vignettes we observe in the apartment windows; at the same time, it establishes a contrast between Jeffries, an isolated man who is trying to keep free of relationships, and Miss Lonelyheart, an isolated woman who longs for a companion. At a purely formal level, however, the shot/reverse shot between James Stewart and Judith Evelyn is even more interesting, providing a vivid counterpoint between two types of rhetoric, one a "melodramatic" form of pantomime, framed at a distance and executed in a relatively long take and the other an intimate, naturalistic technique that involves little more than a brief glint in Stewart's eyes. Thus when Evelyn raises her glass for a toast, she lifts her arm in a grand, sweeping arc; but when Stewart responds, he merely tilts the glass, conveying the whole meaning with the shadow of a movement.

Because Stewart and Evelyn are momentarily linked by the raised wineglasses and by Stewart's glance, the sequence also calls attention to fundamental similarities in their work. For example, both players are required to perform within a specific, rigidly limited space established by the camera. Evelyn's exaggerated gestures are centered and played from a strong frontal position through a window, and the set has doubtless been marked to indicate exactly where she must cross or stand.[2] Meanwhile Stewart's more "natural"

2. A more obvious instance of how the activity in the apartment house is framed, centered, and choreographed would be the early views of Miss Torso (Georgine Darcy), who literally

Two actors share a toast.

movement is no less framed, confined to the small muscles of his face and angled outward toward the window of the movie screen itself. But an even more important similarity between the two is suggested by the bittersweet pantomime in Evelyn's room. The fact is, nearly every movie turns its principal actors into versions of Miss Lonelyheart, forcing them to respond and gesture to an imaginary "other." Thus when close-ups were taken of James Stewart in conversation with Grace Kelly during their romantic dinner, he, too, was speaking to nobody. And when he lifts his glass to toast a woman in another apartment, he, as much as she, is looking at nothing—or perhaps at a spot on the studio floor. The difference between Evelyn's situation and the normal scene in a film is simply that she performs in long shot rather than close-up, so that the camera neither masks the empty spot toward which she looks nor provides emphasis for the expression on her face. By calling attention to this situation, *Rear Window* playfully threatens to expose its own illusions, all the while inviting us to admire the ingenuity of its dramatic conception.

As I have indicated, *Rear Window* also involves a third type of actorly behavior, depicting the busy goings-on inside L. B. Jefferies's room. Here the situation is more conventionally theatrical, requiring the players to move about and exchange dialogue, often sharing the same frame. Hitchcock was probably as interested in the formal possibilities of these scenes as he was in the Kuleshovian montages. Ever since *Lifeboat* (1943), he had enjoyed working with films involving a single stagelike space—in the same year as *Rear Window,* for example, he adapted *Dial M for Murder,* a Broadway thriller set mainly in the front room of a London flat. Such films made his status as enunciator more evident, showing off his skillful blocking of players and camera, displaying his narrative and theatrical virtuosity in the midst of extreme physical limitations.

One of the obvious challenges of *Rear Window* is to give the activity inside Jefferies's room a theatrical vivacity, making the photographer's apartment attract our eye and stimulate our curiosity in much the same way as the silent dramas across the courtyard. To solve the problem, Hitchcock and his collaborators employ devices that are the stock-in-trade of the playwright and the stage performer: snappy dialogue, clever entrances and exits, and lots of business. And because Stewart's behavior is drastically limited, the major responsibility for keeping everything amusing and in provocative motion falls to three supporting players—Grace Kelly, Thelma Ritter, and Wendell Corey.

---

dances around her room while preparing breakfast. She is first seen through a small kitchenette window, standing with her back to us as she puts on a bra; then she reaches down to touch her toes, so that her derriere is positioned at the exact center of the composition.

Familiar as images from other movies, these three bring a wealth of connotation to the film, playing complex, explicitly *theatricalized* characters; repeatedly, they execute little performances-within-performance, subtly calling attention to themselves as actors. The work of each deserves a separate comment.

Of the three, Kelly is the most obvious object of display, providing the small room with a sense of erotic spectacle and giving the audience a pleasure in looking that is only dimly gratified by activities glimpsed in far-off windows. Kelly plays the most intimate scenes in a grand manner, ostentatiously displaying Edith Head's costumes and parts of her own flesh; at the same time, the film visibly molds her star image, making her at once an aristocratic *Vogue* fantasy and a perky tease—the most successful incarnation of the "Hitchcock woman."

Before this, Kelly had seemed ethereal and almost annoyingly upper class, having been cast as the spoiled eastern wife of Gary Cooper in *High Noon* (1952) and as the sexy but unsympathetic society woman in *Mogambo* (1953). Hollywood clearly regarded her as a princess (the role she was later to act in real life), too refined and aloof to become a major attraction. Thus near the beginning of *Rear Window* James Stewart seems to be voicing a public complaint: "She belongs to that rarified atmosphere of Park Avenue," he says. She is "too perfect. . . . If only she were ordinary."[3] But for Hitchcock, who was both a snob and a fetishist, such a woman offered distinct possibilities. Here was a blond with breeding and elocution-school diction; but here, too, as *Mogambo* had proved, was a steamy kisser. Her long embraces of Stewart in this film, modeled after the extended love scene in *Notorious,* established her as the most erotically adept of Hitchcock's leading ladies—less radiant than Ingrid Bergman, less gorgeously voluptuous than Kim Novak, but far more aggressive at displaying her amatory skills. Throughout, the Stewart character remains inactive, preferring to watch rather than perform; distracted by the activity outside his window, he is little more than an irritably nervous face that Kelly nibbles and taunts. "How's your leg?" she whispers, brushing her lips along his cheek. "And your stomach?" she asks, moving closer to his lips. "And your lovelife?" Finally she gives him a soft kiss on the mouth, melting against him.

In the era of Monroe and Mansfield, it was no simple matter for Kelly to become an emblem of screen sex; nevertheless, her gentility seems to have fired Hitchcock's imagination. In true fifties style, her wispy, otherwise uninteresting voice is kept at the level of a breathy invitation. The lines she speaks and the objects she touches are nearly always suggestive, and she is lit, costumed, and composed with loving care; hence if she is not exactly

3. In order to establish the "rarified atmosphere" to which Lisa Fremont belongs, the film has her remark to Jeff that she has just been visiting with Leland Hayward. In real life, Hayward was James Stewart's agent.

"ordinary," she at least becomes alluring in a conventional movie-star way. To enhance her appeal further, the filmmakers have adopted strategies from the old Katharine Hepburn vehicles. Kelly's character is given a latent "boy-ishness"—a desire for adventure and a willingness to sling her high-heeled leg over a fire escape with the same delight she exhibits when she models a dress. She is even cast alongside James Stewart, Hepburn's companion in *The Philadelphia Story,* so that her partial submission to a plain, no-nonsense fellow will give her a "down to earth" quality. (Significantly, Kelly later played the Hepburn role in a remake of *The Philadelphia Story,* entitled *High Society* [1956].) Perhaps equally important, Kelly in *Rear Window* is placed alongside Thelma Ritter, who is both a foil and an advocate, constantly prais-ing her virtues and proposing her as a mate for Stewart. Since there never was a screen character less likely to put up with fools or snobs than Ritter, the audience is predisposed to like the actress who plays Lisa Fremont.

But the project of making Kelly a star is secondary to the immediate needs of the film as spectacle. For this reason as much as any other, Kelly's move-ments have been specifically marked or coded as a type of theatricality, so that her work takes on a self-reflexive wit. Lisa Fremont literally *performs* for L. B. Jefferies, who acts the role of audience. And because she is a woman who has a career in the world of haute couture, her stylized, extravagant behavior is easily motivated. Consider her dramatic entrance. After leaning down to the audience in a gigantic close-up, she awakens Jeffries with a kiss and steps back to introduce herself like a character on a stage. The camera pans as she crosses the room and turns on three lamps which function like spotlights: "Reading from top to bottom," she says, "Lisa. . . ." Turning on the first lamp in medium close-up, she holds her pose and lets the light fall romantically along the side of her face. Then she steps farther back into the room. "Carol. . . ." She turns the switch of a second lamp and pauses, framed from the waist up, showing off the dark bodice of a dress and a pair of slender arms. Next she crosses to a deep corner, where she switches on the third lamp, suddenly illuminating the expanse of her long white skirt. "Fre-mont," she says, sweeping her hand along the skirt and assuming a fashion model's stance. "It's right off the Paris plane," she tells Stewart, and begins moving like a mannequin on a runway, turning gracefully to give us a back view, then posing with a small black bag slung over her shoulder. "Think it'll sell?" she asks.

As Kelly and Stewart exchange lines, she continues to stand in long shot, slowly peeling off a pair of long white gloves. Suddenly remembering some-thing, she dashes "upstage" and mounts three steps to a doorway, where the lamplight strikes her from below, casting a dramatic shadow along the wall. Her petticoated skirt billows and swirls as she makes a quick turn to face the room. "21!" she announces—opening the door, standing aside like a con-jurer, and revealing a red-jacketed waiter who has brought a meal along. This

Grace Kelly introduces herself.

prompts another round of busy, showy activity; Kelly and the waiter scurry about the room, leaving Stewart to struggle with a corkscrew and then sit idly by with his hands in his lap.

Like the setting for any well-made theater piece, Jefferies's apartment has been designed to give the players an opportunity to become the focus of attention as they come in or out of the doorway, and the script supplies them with witty entrance or exit lines. For example, when Stewart and Kelly have an argument after dinner, her feelings are hurt and she hurriedly starts to leave, promising not to come back "for a long time." She crosses to the door, opens it and pauses, her hand on the knob: "At least," she says hesitantly, "not until tomorrow night." Exit, closing the door to punctuate the sentence. When she returns the next evening, she replays nearly the same spectacular entrance as before, crossing the room to turn on three lights that reveal a new outfit—a straight, pale green skirt and jacket with white accessories. Once again she slowly removes a pair of gloves as Stewart talks; this time, however, her striptease is more elaborate and is prefaced by a suggestive piece of business. Clearing a space by removing a tray and a glass of milk from Stewart's side, she takes off her pillbox hat, unpinning it from her hair as she delivers a speech about the cleverness of women. After climbing onto Stewart's lap for a short kissing scene, she shows him a glistening black overnight bag that she balances on her knees, its clasps facing toward her. "I bet yours isn't this small," she says, and flicks the clasps so that the lid springs open, a silky pink negligee spilling over the edges.[4]

Smiling as if she appreciated her own wit, Kelly puts the bag aside and crosses to a cot in the foreground, where she reclines briefly and listens to music from the courtyard. For a moment her body is spread out before us for the full length of the screen; then she gets up and takes off her jacket, showing off a tiny white vest and bare shoulders. All this is prelude to another "act," when she models the negligee. Feeling guilty because Stewart has drawn her into the game of looking into other people's rooms, she gives him a mild lecture about "rear-window ethics." Crossing to lower the matchstick blinds, she remarks, "Show's over," and picks up the black bag, its contents still spilling out. "Preview of coming attractions," she announces, sweeping across the room toward a bedroom door. The image dissolves and she reenters, wearing the gown, standing with one arm lifted, her hand on the doorframe. "What do you think?" she asks Stewart and then parades across the room in long shot. Here as elsewhere, Kelly's elaborate show-within-the-show has both a conventionally theatrical purpose and an underlying irony, putting the male spectators of the film in the same place as Stewart. (The parallel between the imaginary audience and the central character is most clearly emphasized in two "subjective" close-ups—first in Kelly's opening appearance, when she bends down as if to kiss the camera lens, and then in the climactic scenes, when Raymond Burr lunges toward the camera as if to strangle it.)

But Kelly is not the only theatrical personage in the apartment. Thelma Ritter, her opposite in every other way, brings another kind of showy flamboyance to the film, providing a realist analogue to the more domesticated pantomimes Stewart has observed across the courtyard. Perpetually cast as a housemaid or a servant, Ritter is a classic instance of what Hollywood once meant by a "character actor"—a minor player, usually over the age of forty, with a face and voice so vividly eccentric that it saves writers and directors a good deal of trouble. Performers of her sort usually specialized in humorous or sinister overplaying; in the era of studio moviemaking, they gave the screen a more brilliant stylization than anyone since the Sennett clowns. A late manifestation of the type, Ritter was a small woman who could be alternately flinty and sweet. She had a round, rather tired, face offset by gleaming

4. The fluffy mound of pink surging out of a black box in Kelly's lap is one of the more explicit pieces of sexual symbolism in Hitchcock's films—more sensual but just as obvious as the train thundering into a tunnel at the end of *North by Northwest*. It has a precedent in *Suspicion*, where Joan Fontaine's purse is repeatedly used as a vaginal symbol, but I want to stress that it is also a pragmatic device of theater, a prime instance of how *Rear Window*, like most other films, tries to invent activity to complement the dialogue.

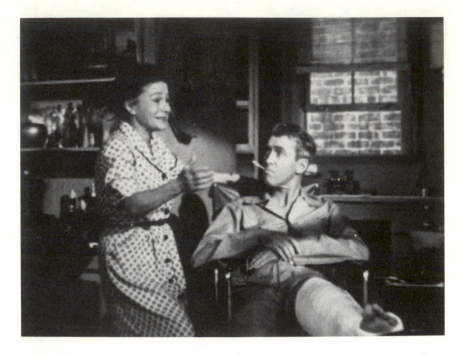

Thelma Ritter "acts" for James Stewart.

button eyes and a jack-o'-lantern smile; her voice was good onstage and on the radio, but it was equally effective in movies, where her exaggerated Bronx accent instantly established her as a hard-boiled, working-class character—a cynic with a heart of gold. In fact, she enters *Rear Window* voice first, warning James Stewart about the "New York state sentence for a peeping Tom." Throughout her first long sequence she never stops talking or moving, executing everything with a gusto and strength somewhat different from her other Hollywood roles. First she shakes out a thermometer, pokes it into Stewart's mouth, and challenges him to "break one hundred." Then she goes about preparing a place to give him a rubdown, doing everything with swift mechanical dexterity and with a slightly sour look that is offset by her wisecracks.

Kuleshov once remarked that anyone performing labor on the screen is interesting to watch; but Ritter is especially fascinating because in classic theatrical style, she does two things at once, not only making a bed but delivering long comic speeches that provide important exposition. (Throughout all this, Stewart plays the straight man, looking bored or pained. The thermometer also becomes a useful expressive object; he can get laughs of his own by trying to drawl a few words around the edge of the instrument, and at one point he yanks it out of his mouth to deliver a speech, waving it around like an academic making a lecture point.) Ritter even lapses into little vaudeville routines, putting on shows-within-the-show that function theatrically much like Kelly's modeling act. After preparing the bed and laying out bottles for the rubdown, she crosses to Stewart, props a foot up on his chair, and begins chiding him about his habit of peering into other people's windows. Then she plays a little scene in which she pretends to be *him,* appearing before a judge: "You're pleading," she says. "You're saying, 'Judge, it was only a little bit of innocent fun!'" She makes a self-deprecating little laugh and then becomes solemn and stiff, taking on the role of the judge. Sentencing Stewart to ten years in Dannemora, she ends the performance by yanking the thermometer out of his mouth.[5]

The third important figure in Stewart's room is a male, and in contrast to Kelly and Ritter, he tends to underplay, perhaps because he is cast as a stolid detective. Never quite so handsome as the typical leading man, Wendell Corey was nonetheless tall and conventionally good-looking, cultivating a quiet, recessive style suitable for playing professional types or staunchly reliable friends of the hero. What made Corey particularly effective in movies were his pale, icy eyes and equally colorless brows, which sometimes gave him a vaguely sinister or even maniacal look.[6] Even in *Rear Window* Corey's eyes give an ambiguous effect to his character, a slightly unsettling feeling that keeps the role from becoming too bland. As Thomas J. Doyle, the New York detective who is Stewart's old war buddy, he is unusually dapper—a trait that is never alluded to in the dialogue. In his first scene he leans out of a window, looking skeptically toward the opposite building, and his posture calls attention to the lines of his well-pressed tan summer suit; later we discover that he has a matching straw hat with a fancy band. In the climactic scenes of the film, when he and a group of cops rush in to capture Thorwald, he is wearing a dinner jacket. These costumes lend a dash of male color and luxury to the *mise-en-scène,* offsetting Stewart's drab pyjamas; at the same time, they make the Doyle character seem "rounded" and individualized.

Corey is neither so deliberately ostentatious a fashion model as Grace Kelly nor so lively and eccentric as Thelma Ritter. Even so, his character is occasionally given the opportunity to behave like an actor. For example, he does a performance-within-the-performance similar to Thelma Ritter's courtroom parody: sitting on an arm of a chair, he imagines himself pleading before a judge for a search warrant to enter Thorwald's apartment. "Your honor,"

5. Ritter's behavior is of course modeled on a habit of everyday performance and is a common device of realist theater, where characters often lapse into what Goffman describes as a "say for," or an attitude of mimicry (*Frame Analysis,* "The Frame Analysis of Talk," 496ff.).

6. Hitchcock exploited this quality a few years after *Rear Window,* assigning Corey a role in "Poison," another one-room suspense story that appeared on the "Alfred Hitchcock Presents" television series.

Acting with brandy glasses.

he says, wrinkling his brow in an appeal for sympathy, "I have this friend who's an amateur sleuth. . . ." Later in the film, he is also given a dramatic exit. After a brief visit to Stewart and Kelly, he leaves, pausing to deliver a clever comment. "I love funny exit lines," Kelly remarks sarcastically, and Corey doffs his hat. "Don't stay up too late," he says, smiling and going out the door.

The film therefore contrives to make Corey, Ritter, and Kelly into spectacular, witty, highly "acted" figures and fills any encounter with dramatic movement. Borrowing from conventions of the realist stage, it requires the performers—often handling an object of some kind—to stand, sit, or cross the field of the camera in ways that emphasize points in a dialogue. One of the most obvious and effective instances of the technique is a scene that occurs midway through the film, when Doyle, Jefferies, and Lisa Fremont drink brandy as they discuss the Thorwald case. (My own persistent childhood memory of *Rear Window,* dating from the film's original release, is of three characters exchanging dialogue while they constantly twirl liquor around in snifters; long after I had forgotten any detail of what the actors said, I could remember the swirl of amber in sparkling glasses, and the comic effect of people talking about murder as they kept moving their hands in tiny circles.)

The brandy glasses have a hypnotic effect, serving as fetish points for the viewer's eye; but they also function as expressive objects, signaling the emotional ebb and flow of the scene, sometimes motivating the way players change their position or attitude at significant moments. The glasses are introduced in a sexually suggestive way when Kelly enters from the kitchen, holding two globed snifters at the level of her breasts. "I was just warming some brandy," she says to Corey in her sultry voice, and then offers him a drink. As the three players discuss Thorwald, they twirl the brandy meditatively, never sipping it; then, at the dramatic turning point of the scene, Corey crosses to a table in the distance, plunks his glass down, and walks back into a close-up, looking out the window and announcing, "Lars Thorwald is no more a murderer than I am." Stewart and Kelly immediately stop moving their snifters as a pregnant pause fills the room. Corey walks back, picks up his brandy, and turns to sit in an easy chair; casually crossing his legs, he begins twirling the liquor around as if nothing had happened. Stewart and Kelly continue to ignore the drinks in their hands, making urgent arguments against Thorwald. Corey has an answer for all their suspicions, and the constant motion of his glass shows his easy confidence. He proposes that they all forget about Thorwald and have a drink, but when he looks at their faces he realizes he has outworn his welcome. "I'd better be getting home," he says, and tries to take a quick gulp of the untasted brandy. It spills on his neat shirtfront and he awkwardly brushes it off. "I'm not much for snifters," he says, and the scene draws to a close as he puts the glass aside.

Having examined the spectacle in the apartment windows and the equally theatrical behavior in L. B. Jefferies's room, we are left with James Stewart— a body confined, a face looking off camera, a symbol not only of the film spectator but also of a certain kind of film acting. Certainly his performance is the type most often associated with the medium: concentrated on the face and upper body, it emphasizes flesh tones, expressions in the eyes, and the grain of a voice. It seems to rise out of the most intimate personal qualities of the actor—and it is enhanced by his celebrity, his very presence giving the impression of a fully "embodied" character.

I have saved Stewart for last because even though he seems to do little, his work merits special consideration. Before discussing his technical skills, however, it is important to note those aspects of his career and acting style that make him especially effective in the role. To begin with, he is the most successful actor of the "common man" in the history of movies. He emerged from the late thirties looking rather like a right-wing version of his friend Henry Fonda and seemed prepared to inherit the mantle of Will Rogers. All the familiar signs were there: a lanky, awkward diffidence suggestive of Lincolnesque virtue; a drawling wit accompanied by a wise glint in the eye; a clod-kicking shyness and innocence concealing "natural" intelligence and passionate idealism. Thus in *Destry Rides Again* (1939) one almost expects him to do rope tricks as he needles the big-shot politicians of a western town; and in *Mr. Smith Goes to Washington* (1939), he plays a character similar to one Rogers himself had acted in *A Texas Steer* (1927). In fact Stewart was such an admired icon of Hollywood populism that Jack Warner once said he was the ideal actor to play the president of the United States, "with Ronald Reagan as his best friend."[7]

Beneath the folksy charm, however, Stewart had another important quality that made him different from any other male star of his period. He was the most intensely emotional leading man to emerge from the studio system— perhaps the only one who could regularly cry on the screen without losing the sympathy of his audience. There was also a troubled, cranky, slightly repressed feeling in his behavior: in comic moments he would frown in pain or speak with a slightly nervous stammer, and whenever he found himself in an especially tense situation, his normally earnest behavior would become harsh, shrill, and manic. Nowhere is his emotional breakdown more moving or frightening than in *It's a Wonderful Life* (1947)—his finest single performance, and his favorite—where George Bailey explodes in rage against his small-town family and goes out to drown his sorrow in a bar. A close-up of Stewart in that film—hunched over a drink, weeping and whispering a prayer—has a power that transcends the sentimentalities and evasions of Frank Capra's plot, as if the raw ends of a desperate but fundamentally decent personality had been exposed. The shot also contains a characteristic gesture I have illustrated in the third chapter of this book: Stewart lifts a trembling hand to his mouth and bites it in pain. He uses this mannerism as early as *After the Thin Man* (1936), when he was still an MGM contract player with no clearly defined image. Cast in the role of a Park Avenue murderer, he is trapped by Nick Charles and nearly goes berserk, all his youthful sincerity falling away as his hand rises compulsively to his mouth. Much later, playing the charmingly absent-minded professor in *No Highway in the Sky* (1951), he bites savagely at the same hand when he discovers that an airplane he is traveling aboard is likely to crash—a corny theatrical ploy, perhaps, but he invests it with so much shattered conviction that it inevitably works.

"There is something vulnerable about everything I do," Stewart once told an interviewer. When he starred in four memorable westerns directed by Anthony Mann, he was impressive precisely because he brought fragility and neurotic obsessiveness to his portrait of a cowboy; he almost fainted outright when he was shot in the hand by Alex Nicol in *The Man from Laramie*

---

7. Unlike Rogers, Stewart never became an outspoken ideologue, although his reactionary sentiments became visible in the fifties, when he sponsored such projects as *Strategic Air Command* (1955), *The Spirit of St. Louis* (1957), and *The FBI Story* (1959).

(1955), and in all four pictures there was a large band of sweat showing through his favorite Stetson hat. As he grew older, he became increasingly spindly, and in potentially violent situations he could raise the level of anxiety in an audience simply because he seemed so breakable. In *The Man Who Shot Liberty Valance* (1962), he bends tentatively down to a dusty street, trying to retrieve a gun lost in a shoot-out, and the angle of his thin, aging body makes it seem that one blow would splinter his entire frame.

Hitchcock must have been pleased by those brittle bones, because he was fond of dropping Stewart from high places. And despite Hitchcock's claim that the meaning of a face is controlled by montage, he must also have known that Stewart would bring a remarkable intensity to a picture like *Rear Window*. Stewart was important to Hitchcock primarily because he could elicit a strong sense of identification from the audience, serving as a perfect locus for a film's point of view; once that initial attachment was formed, he could exhibit unusual degrees of neurotic suffering, moral anguish, and physical pain. Without his contribution, *Rear Window* and *Vertigo* might have seemed far less disturbing.

In some respects, of course, Stewart does not have to give much energy to *Rear Window*. A known commodity for whom the audience has a special affection, he can "behave" less than the other players. His imprisonment in the wheelchair is a witty *reductio* of the technique in many films, and he can sometimes relax, his face encouraging us to accept the subject position offered by the narrative, his glance giving us a sense of where things are and ascribing a simple significance to what we see. The reference points of his various looks are determined by the editor, and often his expressions are quite rudimentary: for example he smiles at the composer who comes in drunk, and when he looks toward Thorwald's apartment, his eyes grow serious. At some points in the film, however, Stewart acts in more complex ways, as if to establish himself as a performer. Early on, a brief comic scene shows Jeffries alone in his room, seized by an itch. Stewart frowns restlessly and gives an irritable little scratch to the plaster sheath on his leg (a gesture that makes no sense in life but serves to inform us of his problem). Then he tries scratching with both hands, his lips compressed. He stops, looks helplessly down at the leg, and begins wiggling and shifting in the chair, his body stiff and his chin pulled in toward his neck. When this proves useless, he breaks into a moment of fury, his mouth grimacing and his hand slapping at the itchy spot. Twisting to look desperately at a table over his shoulder, he seizes a long wooden backscratcher and pokes it down into the cast. At first he makes a contorted, nearly wild face, but as he digs more deeply, his expression freezes into a mask, his tongue sticking out slightly from the effort of concentration. Arriving at the spot, he smiles, his body unclenching and his eyes closing with relief as he scratches busily.

This minor scene not only demonstrates how mobile Stewart's face can become but also provides him with an expressive object. Later in the film, he manipulates the backscratcher cleverly during a conversation with Wendell Corey. As they debate Thorwald's guilt, Stewart slaps impatiently at his cast with the scratcher or waves it loosely about. At one point he asks if the police need "bloody footprints" leading up to Thorwald's door, and at the same moment he lifts the stick like a conductor's baton, beating out the rhythm of his phrase while drawing little half-moon steps in the air.

Stewart also makes effective use of his voice. Long before the Method came to Hollywood, he knew how to seem unusually spontaneous in a two-shot, where he tends to overlap the other players or make little interjections. The familiar stammering hesitation of his speech is a calculated device, used to make his responses naturalistic—as when he tries to object to something Grace Kelly is saying: "Aw, well, now *wait* a minute—wa . . . now *wait* a minute!" This fumbling nervousness with language also contributes to his stylized, "folksy" persona and seems in keeping with the brittle quality of his body. For instance, he rarely curls or closes his hands, leaving the long fingers extended stiffly and moving them like flippers. He is not so frantic an actor as Jack Lemmon, but he seems just as impatient, harried, or uncomfortable when he does simple tasks, and he gives a sensory "contagion" to many of his scenes by making us feel his open nerve endings. Early in the film, tiny Thelma Ritter helps him take off his shirt and climb onto a cot, where she massages his back: Stewart is clearly older than the character he plays, and his soft flesh seems to need assistance in carrying the angular, inflexible length of his arms and legs; we can see the massive cast weighing him down, and at the same time it seems an almost logical appendage, consistent with a certain stiffness in his bodily style. When Ritter applies cold lotion to his shoulders, he makes a very plausible flinch ("D'ya . . . D'ya ever *heat* that stuff?"), and as she gives him a vigorous rubdown he speaks many of his lines into his pillow, producing a half-muffled vibrating sound that seems to put his voice under strain.

Much later, in the climactic moments of the film, Stewart reacts with far more intense discomfort. Sitting in a darkened room and waiting for Thorwald, he tries to whisper a conversation into a telephone, putting extreme pressure on his vocal cords. "*Lissen* to me! *Lissen* to me!" he says to the detective, clamping the telephone receiver between the flat extended fingers of both hands while hastily trying to explain all the evidence in the case. Certain words ("metal suitcase," for example) have an especially raspy sound in his throat, and he has no chance to gather breath as he forces a jumble of sentences through his whisper. (He had probably learned the dramatic value of torturing his voice fairly early in his career, in the filibuster scenes of *Mr. Smith Goes to Washington,* when he drank a solution prepared by a doctor to induce a mild laryngitis.) The subsequent confrontation between him and Raymond Burr is especially frightening because he seems overcome with

The backscratcher as expressive object.

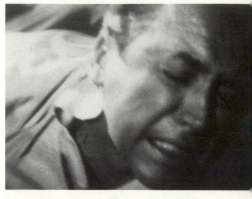

Stewart in the fight sequence.

nervous excitement. His quick, panicky manipulation of the wheelchair and his jittery handling of a flash unit suggest an aging invalid, and his wiry, scarecrow shape contrasts vividly with Burr's hulking figure standing in the doorway.

As befits this film, the most anguished, nerve-racking moments of Stewart's performance are delivered in close-ups, where his unusually beautiful and expressive eyes heighten the impact of the editing. As he watches the film's "primal scene"—Lisa's entry into Thorwald's apartment—he nearly cracks under the anxiety. "A man is assaulting a woman!" he whispers to the police on the telephone, and a large-scale close-up shows him looking out the window, his eyes tearing with pain. Throughout this rather extended shot there is no dramatic music to amplify his suffering—only Lisa's faraway screams echoing across the courtyard—and no objects to help him convey emotion. "No! No!" he whispers, holding his breath and wiping his full, slack lips with the back of a trembling hand. Typically, he almost bites the hand,

and then, nearly mad with frustration, he squirms in his seat, glancing down at his lap and straining his features as if he could not bear to watch. His breath becomes heavy, and he twists in the chair to look pathetically up at Thelma Ritter, whose body can be seen dimly behind him in the dark. "What do we do?" he says softly, raising both of his hands and clinching the back of his neck. He rubs at his shoulders and closes his hands into fists, looking down at his lap in humiliation and terror. Inhaling deeply, he lowers the fists out of sight and looks up with a grimace, his eyes welling with tears.

Stewart's role is constructed so that his slight frustration in the early scenes builds toward this horror; and whether he controlled the narrative structure of his performance or not, he is impressive at using close-ups to register the various stages in Jeffries's anxiety. At the same time, he conveys the darker side of the character, bearing the full weight of the film's commentary on sadistic voyeurism. Looking out the window early in the film, his bored list-lessness gives way to little flashes of casual pleasure, then to deep curiosity, and ultimately to fixation. At first he seems exhilarated by what he discovers, like a man who has overcome passivity with omniscience, sublimating all his frustrations to the scopic drive. (The plaster cast, covering him like a chastity belt from the waist down, makes the sublimation seem almost a necessity.) Hence there is an urgency in the way he grasps binoculars and camera lens in order to see better; at the crucial moment when Thorwald turns to look back at him, his excitement gives way to desperation.

In the closing moments of the film, Stewart makes an especially important contribution to the violent fight with Thorwald. During his interview with Truffaut, Hitchcock cited the battle between Stewart and Burr as another in-stance of the power of montage: "At first I had filmed the whole thing real-istically. It was a weak scene . . . so I did a closeup of a waving hand, a closeup of Stewart's face and another one of his legs; then I intercut all of this in proper rhythm and the final effect was just right" (201). It is true that cutting gives the battle its illusion of frantic activity, but the specific emo-tional tone comes from brief glimpses of Stewart's expression, which alter-nates between grotesquely distorted pain and a soft, almost erotic yielding. There are twenty-eight shots in the sequence, beginning at the point where Burr lunges toward the camera and ending where Stewart crashes onto the pavement outside his window. Of these, three close-ups are especially vivid: Stewart's head leaning backward over the edge of a bed, his eyes fluttering up in a swoon; Stewart gripped by his assailant's arm, eyes closed and mouth lax, as if he were about to faint; Stewart holding the windowsill as he is being shoved outside—eyes bulging, open mouth curled in strain, face growing red from an attempt to breathe.

The most expressive image of all, however, is the moment of his dizzying fall to the ground. The eerie quality of the shot has something to do with the

Stewart falls from the window.

composition and the evident artificiality of matte photography, but it also derives from Stewart, who looks straight upward toward us, his mouth open and his eyes popping in childlike fear. His body is fully extended, his arms wobbling, his hands and fingers held limply out to the lens, as if in helpless desire. The large white cast and the strange movement of limbs make him resemble a space-suited figure in free fall; but he is also an aging man, utterly vulnerable, struggling like a baby for its mother's breast.

Of all the performance techniques in *Rear Window*, this one might be described as the most specific to cinema. Stewart does not fall; he simply participates in an optical illusion that must have been almost comic to watch as it was being filmed. Even so, he gives the illusion much of its queasy, vertiginous power. He gazes back toward the "window" of the screen with a fear that mirrors our own look—a yearning for the camera's safe, solid position. In the process, he synthesizes two forms of acting upon which the film as a whole has depended: on the one hand, a simple pantomime involving his entire body, designed for a trick shot, and on the other, a naturalistic helplessness, conveyed by his inherently awkward arms and the unguarded emotional intensity of his face. His choice of expression is also important; instead of employing screams or squinty grimaces, he appears surprised and traumatized, falling away from us in openmouthed terror, as if he were unable to cry out. There is nothing innovative about his technique, but with another actor the scene might have been merely shocking or suspenseful. With Stewart, it has a surrealist quality appropriate to Hitchcock's best work. For a moment, the connotative power of the star's image, along with his willingness to forsake "charm" and expose his face in extreme anxiety, helps to make Hollywood's colored daydream a bit less cozy.

14

The King of Comedy (1983)

The previous chapter on *Rear Window* deliberately avoids mentioning a well-known minor player in the film whose work is more appropriately discussed at this point. Viewers will recall the moment when James Stewart glances into the window of a songwriter's studio, where Alfred Hitchcock makes a cameo appearance. Hitchcock's work is no different in kind from that of Ross Bagdasarian, who plays the songwriter; nevertheless, the gap between his professional identity and his minor part is so great that it breaks the fictional illusion. The effect he creates is ironic and witty—almost Brechtian, except that it has an aesthetic rather than a didactic purpose: it shifts our attention away from the diegesis and toward the apparatus, inviting us to think of the film as an art object crafted by an "author."

In a general sense, of course, we never forget that movies are fictional illusions; indeed a slight awareness of trickery seems necessary to the pleasure we take from dramatic rituals, enabling the artists to show off. Even so, there are different *kinds* of relation between players and fiction, and Hitchcock's famous personal appearances are good examples of how the casting of a particular actor can radically affect the audience's response. Moreover, the public's reception of the screen image can change over time, so that the casting in old movies sometimes creates unintended disjunctions between actors and roles. This phenomenon is especially noticeable since the advent of television, which regularly recycles old performances, turning every household into a *cinémathèque*. Thus, Raymond Burr was accepted by *Rear Window*'s original audience as a plausible villain, but his subsequent Perry Mason role on TV makes contemporary viewers see him as a humorous, unorthodox choice. (An even more glaring instance of the same effect is the dramatic scene near the end of *Psycho,* when a policeman hands a blanket to Norman Bates. Contemporary audiences usually laugh because the policeman is acted by Ted Knight, who later became famous as Ted Baxter on the "Mary Tyler Moore Show.")

I have argued that human figures in a film are received in three different ways: as actors playing fictional characters, as actors playing "themselves," and as facts in a documentary. As my examples indicate, however, we can make distinctions within these larger categories. Because movies are a specific form of cultural production with a relatively long and complex history, we typically notice whether an actor's presence in a film seems to correspond with his or her *professional* role. For similar reasons, we often notice differences between the actor's public "self" and the character, or changes in the kinds of roles played by a star. These perceptions can become part of a film's structure and meaning, even though they are subject to fluctuations over time. Stephen Heath has remarked that films "play between character and person with a variety of emphasis." The overriding irony of the situation is that "what is in question is so often the person as persona, the person as image, as— precisely—cinema; the living body of the human being exhausted in, converted to that" (181).

The shifting relation between public images created *by* media and persons acted *in* media has special importance to *The King of Comedy,* a film about performance and celebrity; indeed, some of the picture's most interesting formal effects arise from casting, or the art of playing off personae and roles. At the same time, *The King of Comedy* also involves an unusually self-conscious mix of acting *styles,* illustrating another important point about how we read performances. Critics often call attention to the ways intertextuality or a "horizon of expectations" can affect our response to a movie, but most discussion of the issue has focused on plots, genres, or the star system; *The King of Comedy* shows how intertextual cues function at the level of acting itself, in the form of allusions to familiar performance conventions or to the mannerisms of famous players. A modernist (and sometimes postmodernist) film, it continually makes use of parody or pastiche, foregrounding the work of performers and playfully undermining every form of behavioral sincerity.

Rupert Pupkin, the central character in the film, might be regarded as a perverse illustration of Brecht's thesis that all human education proceeds along theatrical lines. The difference between Pupkin and most of us is that he has rejected his shabby, imperfect family drama and has chosen show business as a more appealing entry into the Symbolic order. The father he both worships and wishes to dethrone is Jerry Langford, a television talk-show host whose career Pupkin describes as if it were the plot of *42nd Street:* "Remember the night you were with Jack Parr, when Jack Parr got sick?" he says to Langford. "That was your big break. . . . That was the night that convinced me I wanted to be a comedian." Pupkin's adoration of the star is undoubtedly strengthened each time he sees Langford on television—a transcendent presence, bathed in music, light, and applause, standing "in one" before an audience. "You are just as human as the rest of us," Pupkin tells him in a tape recorded message. "If not more so."

Although Pupkin is thirty-four years old, he spends much of his time in a sort of playroom in the New Jersey house where he lives with his (unseen) mother. He has arranged the room with life-sized cardboard cutouts of various stars; on a small stage in the corner, he acts out his obsessive fantasy of appearing on the Langford show. His material is bad, but he knows all the codes of behavior. "Hiya, Liza!" he says as he steps onto the makeshift stage, giving a kiss to Liza Minnelli's photo. "Jerry! Good seeing you! Don't get up!" Making himself comfortable in a favored spot, he crosses his legs and spreads his arms along the back of his chair. "Boy, I'll tell you," he remarks to Jerry's photo, "every time you come back from a tour, I dunno what it is, it must be something in the air or the tour, you look great!" Suddenly he glances around at his imaginary audience. "Isn't that so, everybody? Isn't that so? Heh, heh." At other moments, his extravagant fantasies of celebrity and power are depicted as actual television appearances, including one extended scenario in which the Langford show turns into a "This Is Your Life" surprise party for his benefit. His high school principal shows up as a mystery guest, publicly apologizing to him for having misjudged a great man and serving as a minister in a Tiny-Tim-style wedding between Pupkin and a neighborhood barmaid named Rita. Thanking Rupert for having given "meaning to our lives," the principal turns to the TV audience and promises to continue the ceremony right after a break for a commercial message.

When Pupkin is not imagining his life as a celebrity, he hovers outside the stage door of Langford's television studio, trying to be cool and disassociate himself from a pathetic flotsam of star worshippers. Unlike them, he is theatrically dressed, like a Vegas entertainer. "Hi Rupert, who'd you get?" one of the autograph seekers asks. "I'm not that interested," Pupkin says, inching his way through the crowd and leaning slightly forward in anticipation of Jerry's exit. "It's not my whole life—it's yours but not mine." Obviously, however, Pupkin's whole life is bound up in his desire for stardom, which motivates the plot of the film. In the opening scenes, he manages to force his way into Langford's presence, begging for a guest shot on TV. When he is unable to convince either the star or his staff that they have a chance to discover the new "King of Comedy," he makes increasingly aggressive and embarrassing attempts to see Langford personally, at one point invading his home. Ultimately, he decides on more drastic action, enlisting the aid of a wealthy young Manhattanite named Masha, who adores Langford in her own fashion.

As Beverle Huston has noted in her Lacanian reading of the film, Rupert wants to *be* the phallus, whereas Masha wants to *have* it. Together, they waylay Langford in the street, kidnapping him and demanding that Rupert be given an appearance on the show. Their insane plot somehow works: Masha stands guard over the prisoner, hoping to seduce him by behaving like Tina Turner, while Rupert does a five-minute monologue on late-night TV. Rupert's performance is not at all funny, but the audience gives him a warm reception. His crime makes him a celebrity, and after a short stay in prison he writes a best-selling book about his experience. He appears on the covers of *Newsweek, People, Life,* and *Rolling Stone;* when we last see him (in a slightly ambiguous, dreamy-looking sequence), he is hosting his own television show. The godlike voice of an announcer intones his name as he steps out to a spotlighted mark on a bare stage, wearing a fire-engine-red jacket and a matching bow tie. He smiles and bows with almost papal serenity, acknowledging a crowd that roars wildly at his every movement.[1]

Like *Network* (1976), *Being There* (1979), and a number of lesser Hollywood films of the eighties, *The King of Comedy* satirizes television as a medium that blurs the distinction between show business and reality, converting everything into theater and making heros out of boobs. In a more general sense, however, its theme is the connection between performance and identity in the age of mass media. Paul D. Zimmerman has said that in writing the script he wanted to explore "the need to exist publicly," and his original opening for the film was a question: "Are you someone?"[2] The question is symptomatic of an era when video technology and the ubiquity of human images have altered the very nature of social exchange, creating new determinants of self. (By contrast, a picture like *Rear Window* looks charmingly out of date, based on a world where we can still make clear divisions between public and private spheres of behavior.)

Rupert Pupkin is the child of a culture that makes celebrity an ever-proliferating commodity, displaying the theatrics of fame in every household. To some degree his mania seems the by-product of what sociologists Daniel Horton and R. Richard Wohl term "para-social interaction," or the tendency of television programming to coexist with personal relationships. In a pro-

1. Beverle Huston has discussed the "perhaps post-modernist implications" of this ending, citing the different views of Lewis and Scorsese about its meaning. Scorsese points out that many viewers have difficulty accepting Rupert's final appearance as "reality" (Huston, 91). In fact, the film hovers between techniques of social documentary and satiric fantasy, and critics who judge it in purely realist terms are likely to be disappointed. Consider Stanley Kauffmann's unfavorable review in *The New Republic,* which notes the implausible aspects of the script: had Rupert Pupkin been a real aspirant to show business, Kauffmann notes, he would surely have changed his name. And what are we to make of Masha's sudden disappearance from the narrative? Was she, too, put in prison? (Kauffmann, 79–81).

2. Information on the production of *The King of Comedy* comes from a lecture by Paul D. Zimmerman, and from my subsequent conversations with him in Bloomington, Indiana, in the spring of 1984.

phetic paper written in the fifties, Horton and Wohl point out that para-social interaction is a new phenomenon in human history: via television, the "most remote and illustrious men are met *as if* they were in the circle of one's peers." As a result, we in the audience begin to feel we "know" famous personalities in roughly the same way that we know actual acquaintances. Although the relation is mediated by a tube, in many ways it resembles a face-to-face encounter, and it has an especially important impact on what Horton and Wohl describe as the "socially isolated, the socially inept, the aged and invalid, the timid and rejected" (218). It makes stars out of "para-social performers" like talk-show hosts, who, as Joshua Meyrowitz notes, are less important for their "talent" than for their ability to establish "intimacy with millions," and who become "likeable and interesting in the same way that a close friend is likeable and interesting" (119).

Rupert Pupkin has been watching such performers all his life, but he is no simple misfit. A nerdy, laughable creature, played by Robert De Niro with a remarkable lack of sentimentality, he is also *our* representative—an expression of the audience's latent envy of celebrity and a reflection of Paul Zimmerman's own confessed desire to do a comic monologue on TV. It is difficult not to sympathize with him, even though he makes us cringe with discomfort when he becomes a nuisance in Langford's chrome-lined, Muzak-filled outer office or when he storms down the halls of corporate television demanding to see the star. Even though we know he is crazy and potentially dangerous, the film exploits our desire to see his act on the Langford show. And because television (not unlike movies) has always catered to dreams like his, there is a poetic justice to the ending of the picture—as if the hero had been given the "fifteen minutes" of celebrity Andy Warhol predicted for us all.

There is, in other words, a depressing logic to Rupert's mania, and his crime seems inadvertently ideological. He correctly perceives that television confers importance on "ordinary" lives and that the real key to American success is to be *on* the tube rather than watching it. A lowbrow version of the romantic idealist, he is convinced that his own grubby experience can be transformed through artistry; on television, he can rise above the insults of everyday life, becoming not only respected but fully human. Thus, he identifies with the biographies of the stars, and he discourses on Jerry Langford's childhood photographs as if they were memorabilia from his own family album. In fantasy, he concocts a scene in which Jerry Langford asks him for the secret of his comedy routines. "How do you do it?" Jerry wants to know, and Rupert replies, "I think it's that I look at my whole life, and I see the awful, terrible things and I turn it into something funny. It just happens!" Behind this cliché is the ironic truth that by simply crossing the boundary of the television screen and entering its system of representation, Rupert Pupkin can become a para-social performer; by learning the right gestures and playing out a grotesque parody of media personality, he can achieve importance, if not wholeness and intimacy. His corny act serves as a brilliant, if unintentional, exposure of talk-show conventions, a virtually Brechtian disruption of a certain type of comedy.

A character like Rupert offers especially attractive opportunities to a movie actor, and it is perhaps not surprising that Robert De Niro was the person most responsible for bringing *The King of Comedy* to the screen. Zimmerman's script had been circulating around Hollywood for a few years and was briefly in the hands of Buck Henry and Milos Foreman before De Niro saw it; he drew his old collaborator Martin Scorsese into the project, and between them they gave the film much of its New York accent and dark tone. *The King of Comedy* may also have appealed to them both because it explored materials that had been marginally present in *Raging Bull,* their previous picture. That film allowed De Niro to perform Jake LaMotta's seedy nightclub act, and it concluded with an astonishing piece of acting about acting: De Niro plays LaMotta playing Brando playing Terry Malloy—a *mise-en-abyme* in which the actor's personality becomes as insubstantial as the reflections in LaMotta's dressing room mirrors.

A thoroughgoing naturalist, De Niro is also a sophisticated theorist, a man who seems drawn to self-reflexive performances. (In one of his early pictures, *Jennifer on My Mind* [1971], we see him reading a copy of Bazin's *What is Cinema?*) But *The King of Comedy* is more than a showcase for his skill. The theme of the film overpowers the work of any single player, inevitably making us think about acting and celebrity (or lack of it) in the cast as a whole. There is, moreover, an inadvertent irony in the choice of the ensemble. The producers of *The King of Comedy* have clearly relied on the very phenomenon they wish to criticize, deriving many of their jokes from a "hip" audience's Pupkin-like knowledge of the players; in other words, the film could be regarded both as a satire and as a symptom of media culture, its casting dependent not only on realist *typage* and the manipulation of star images but also on subtle distinctions between degrees or kinds of celebrity. This point will become clearer if we examine the cast in detail, noting the various effects that arise from relations between personae and roles.

At one extreme, the film allows its audience to recognize a series of professionals who play fictional characters—including De Niro, Sandra Bernhard (Masha), Diahnne Abbott (Rita), and Shelly Hack (Miss Long). Within this category, however, the potential relation between player and role is variable. Abbott and De Niro were once married, and an audience's knowledge of their "true" relationship can give an ironic twist to the scenes they play together. By contrast, Sandra Bernhard was a less familiar name when the film was released, so that even though she exhibits impressive histrionic skill, the mass of viewers cannot know how much of her "self" has been absorbed into the character.

At the opposite extreme are a number of celebrities who do nothing more than play "themselves": Tony Randall, Ed Herlihy, Lew Brown, Victor Borge, and Dr. Joyce Brothers. They give a documentary-like authenticity to the "Jerry Langford Show," where they all make appearances, but they also embody the tawdriness of Pupkin's dreams.[3] By removing them from the actual frame of a TV variety hour, the film defamiliarizes their celebrity, making it seem vaguely silly; at the same time, however, it heightens their aura, presenting them to us "in person." Tony Randall, for example, is less of a star than De Niro, but when he appears on the screen he seems to stand out from the other players, creating a response similar to what we might feel if we saw him in real life. He is of course as much an image as anyone else in the film, and as much an actor in a movie. Nevertheless, because he is unmediated by a fictional characterization, he gives off an aura of "true" celebrity. Thus when De Niro appears in a scene with Dr. Joyce Brothers, the film presents a concrete demonstration of the difference between an actor and a talk-show guest: the actor, secure behind the mask of his characterization, stands at one remove from us, whereas the television personality seems like a famous person we are meeting in a fairly direct encounter.

Between these extremes are another set of figures whose roles partake equally of fictional characterization and public personae. The most notable among them is Jerry Lewis (born Joseph Levitch, the son of a burlesque comic), whose first name and last initial is echoed in the name of his character, Jerry Langford. Lewis has an opportunity to work against the grain of his usual image, and yet he is also "himself," for he appears in fact as an occasional talk-show host and is well-known to the film's audience as emcee for an annual Muscular Dystrophy Telethon. In other words, there is just enough distance between Lewis's professional identity and his character to ensure a fictional mask but not enough to keep him from seeming like a "guest star." Moreover, the distance between his persona and his character varies during the course of the film. Sometimes he is closer to Jerry Langford, as when he broods alone in his New York penthouse; sometimes he is closer to Jerry Lewis, as when he strolls down a Manhattan street while passersby yell "Hiya, Jerry," waving like old friends who have known him all their lives. The technique here is similar to what André Bazin once called "doubling"—

3. The choice of Joyce Brothers is of course significant. In fact, Brothers was able to obtain more than one movie job by playing "herself"—a person who signifies empty celebrity. She had originally become a media personality in the fifties, appearing on "The $64,000 Question" as a lady psychologist with an encyclopedic knowledge of boxing. She survived the scandals associated with rigged quiz shows, and reemerged as a guest on the Carson show, giving advice to the lovelorn. Ultimately, she was regarded as a sort of joke, making appearances not only in this film but in The Lonely Guy (1984), where she is shown in bed with Steve Martin. A symbol of the shameless desire to be "somebody," she seemed willing to be a good sport even when a movie wanted to make her look silly. And no wonder: the cinema was keeping her celebrity alive and paying her in the bargain.

the casting of a player in a fiction that parallels his or her public life. In this particular case, the film uses a real television star to authenticate the character's celebrity; at the same time, the occasional mismatches between Lewis and Langford keep the action safely fictional, enabling the star to play intimate scenes that do not reveal too much of his backstage life.

Because Lewis is a crucially important member of the cast who brings so much of "himself" to the project, he shapes the fiction in important ways. He insisted that he could not play Langford unless Zimmerman's original ending for the script was modified. That version had closed with Pupkin, now a full-fledged media personality, reappearing on the Langford show, where he and the host comically reenact the kidnapping for a television audience. Lewis rejected the idea, claiming that neither he nor any self-respecting talk-show star would do such a thing. (When the film was released, Lewis also criticized the revised ending, saying that it ought to be regarded as Rupert's fantasy. He told an interviewer at USC that "Rupert should have been Bickle . . . the picture suffers because no one was hurt" [quoted in Huston, 89].) But this slight change in the concluding scenes was as nothing compared to a series of adjustments that were necessary simply because the film needed to make use of Lewis's persona. The mere choice of him influences the slant of "The Jerry Langford Show," which in turn affects the characterization of Pupkin.

We can sense Lewis's importance if we imagine another celebrity in the role. The film obviously uses Johnny Carson as the structuring absence for the Langford character, but Zimmerman had also considered Dick Cavett as the actor who might play Pupkin's hero. Had Cavett actually made the film, Pupkin would need to seem more preppy or quasi-intellectual—a cinephile rather than an autograph collector. Lewis brings a different set of cultural stereotypes to the film, another sort of show-business career for Pupkin to emulate. However, it is important to stress that we are not watching the Jerry Lewis of the old days of live television—the anarchic, lunatic partner of Dean Martin, who ridiculed the very mechanics of TV and threatened chaos in each of his appearances on "The Ed Sullivan Show." We catch glimpses of that persona in *The King of Comedy*, but mainly the film draws on Lewis's more dubious contemporary reputation as a substitute talk-show host and glitzy personality who seldom says anything funny—an image that began to take shape after his breakup with Martin, when many of his nonfilm performances had the unfortunate effect of making him resemble a would-be Dino.

Soon after he and Martin were split, Lewis issued an LP of show tunes, and his manner onstage took on the style of Sinatra's "rat pack." He spoke with an especially low voice, establishing a distance from the adenoidal character he had played before, and he cultivated a laid-back, Vegas-style sophistication, often smoking a cigarette as he worked. As Langford in this film, he uses most of these techniques, wearing stylish glasses that suggest both a "cool" persona and a certain introspectiveness—the latter quality in keeping with his other, somewhat cultish, aura as an *auteur* at Paramount in the late fifties and early sixties. He is more vulgar and more theatrically impressive than Cavett would have been, and his New York background and vague "eth-nicity" make him a more plausible idol for De Niro. Lewis was, in fact, born in New Jersey—a place Carson and other stand-up comics regularly joke about on late-night television—and as a result Pupkin has been given the same origins. By such means, the film can hint at a latent similarity between its two principal characters even as it contrasts the work of the leading play-ers: Lewis, the comic, makes only minor adjustments of his typical on-screen behavior, appearing in an unexpected context but essentially playing a more realistic, serious version of "himself"; meanwhile De Niro, the dramatic ac-tor, constructs an unusual face, voice, and costume, always reminding us of the gap between his person and the character.[4]

Several other instances of "doubling" in the film function like allusions for the cognoscenti. For example, Mick Jones and the Clash, a rock group, have been cast as the "street scum" who stand on a corner and jeer at Sandra Bernhard. Here the fit between the actors and role constitutes a minor joke; in other places, the doubling is more literal, as when real-life New York autograph collectors—celebrities within their own narrow world—are re-cruited to play members of the crowd outside Langford's studio. Another instance of the same technique is the casting of Fred DeCordova, the producer for Johnny Carson, as Bert Thomas, the fictional producer of the Langford show. Because DeCordova is a behind-the-camera celebrity, he is probably received by some members of the audience as a professional actor; for others, he creates a complex effect, authenticating the backstage atmosphere, giving implicit endorsement from the Carson organization, and pointing us slightly toward the collective "authorship" or manufacture of the film.[5] Additionally, in an explicitly Hitchcock-like bit of casting, Martin Scorsese plays the role of Langford's director. He is shown in jeans and sneakers, standing behind the television cameras and talking with Tony Randall, who asks his opinion of a stale joke the writers have provided for an opening monologue. Scorsese says he thinks the joke is funny, but he gives a fake snigger as he looks at the script; his awkward behavior calls attention to the theme of acting and at the

4. In many respects, De Niro lacks the physical equipment of a movie star. He has narrow eyes, a rather harsh voice, and a smallish, bandy-legged body—a combination of traits that often gives the impression of a wiry country boy with a big city accent. Nevertheless, he converts his plainness into a powerful naturalistic instrument. He is the most austere of the actors with whom he is often compared—less boyish than Hoffman, and far less romantic than Al Pacino, who has a pretty face and a collection of narcissistic gestures borrowed from Brando. When De Niro plays the young Don Corleone in *The Godfather II*, he imitates a few of Brando's mannerisms, but he makes the character seem relatively ascetic.

5. Significantly, while *The King of Comedy* satirizes the Langford show and its fans, it de-picts the staff and celebrities as polite, hardworking professionals. Clearly it does not want to criticize the Carson organization or show business too deeply.

George Kapp.

same time flatters parts of the audience, making them feel privy to "secret" knowledge.

Most of the figures mentioned thus far possess a show-business identity that enables the audience to notice contrasts between personae and roles; they have what Jean-Louis Comolli, in another context, has termed "a body too much." But a number of less famous people also act in the film, some of whom can be identified retroactively from the credits at the end. For example, we learn that Cathy Scorsese, Charles Scorsese, and Catherine Scorsese play minor roles. (The last is another instance of "doubling," for she acts as the voice of Rupert's mother and is also the mother of the director.) The credits also tell us that George Kapp, the "mystery guest" on the fantasy version of the Langford show, is played by a fellow named George Kapp. Kapp is an interesting case of *typage*—a man with a quintessentially bland face, a flat, inexpressive voice, and the silly grin of a citizen from Peoria who has wandered into Television City. He is, however, difficult to classify in the schema I have been developing. He plays a fictional character, but the credits indicate that he is also "himself"; the film therefore turns his very lack of theatricality into a complex public persona, making him at once a "real person," a movie actor, and a para-social performer.

Most of the minor players are similarly difficult to label, if only because they have no "second self" beyond a proper name in the credits. Consider the FBI agent who accompanies Captain Burke during the investigation of the Langford kidnapping. He speaks one line of dialogue, offering to "put some color" into Pupkin's face, but most of the time he simply stands in a back corner of the screen at parade rest, muscles tightening in his tan suit. His blank face and stiffness of movement suggest an amateur—a quality he shares not only with Captain Burke (Richard Dioguardi) but also with Whitey Ryan, who plays the guard at the stage door of the Langford show, and with Kim Chan, who acts Langford's Oriental cook. It is possible that all these people are either professional actors or "doubles," but in one sense the distinction hardly matters. Lacking public identity, their chief function is to signify "ordinariness." They provide the film with a believable look and a charming awkwardness, throwing the work of the celebrities into relief and suggesting a world outside show business. Because of them, we can make a basic distinction between members of the cast, grouping not only the characters but also the players according to whether they are "somebodies." Hence the anonymous, amateurish actors make us aware of a social class or professional division within the film—a division very like the one Pupkin wishes to overcome.

The King of Comedy also contains a variety of performing styles, and their juxtaposition contributes just as much to its meaning. In itself there is nothing unusual about such an effect, since every film is composed of different kinds of easily-recognized theatrical behavior. All performance (and all art) is intertextual, and even the most classically "well-made" Hollywood movie is usually compounded of quite distinct acting traditions—*Casablanca* is one obvious example, but consider also *The Heiress,* whose three leading characters are played by an Ur-Method actor (Montgomery Clift), a star from the studio system (Olivia de Havilland), and an English Shakespearian (Ralph Richardson). Individual films can also elicit a wide range of rhetorical and expressive tasks, all of which are regulated by a narrative economy. Musicals provide an obvious example, since the actors are always breaking into song or dance; but even the ordinary realistic film could be described as a controlled heterogeneity of performing techniques. What makes *The King of Comedy* atypical is its comic self-consciousness about the process, its willingness to violate coherence openly by occasional shifts from one style to another, sometimes within individual roles.

Like much of Scorsese's work, the film shows the influence of early Godard and the *nouvelle vague,* especially in its tendency to mix generic conventions. Because it is also to some extent a comedy, it can more freely upset the normal balance between illusion and belief; as Steve Neale has written, "Comedy always and above all depends on an awareness that it is fictional. What comedy does, in its various forms and guises, is to set in motion a narrative process in which various languages, logics, discourses and codes are, at one point or another—at precisely the points of comedy itself—revealed to the audience as fictions" (40). And because *The King of Comedy* is above all a film about performance, it centers much of its comic disruption on the codes of behaving in front of a camera. The film presents itself as a multiverse of acting styles, shifting rapidly from one medium to another and continually alluding to kinds of performance we have seen before. Its form is not truly radical, because the different styles are arranged in a hierarchy that affords a typical narrative pleasure; nevertheless, *The King of Comedy* is more willing to forsake laws of classical unity than the usual film and could be used as a model to illustrate how we read conventions of movement and voice in the movies.

In what follows, I try to point out some conventions of behavior in the film, but I have been tentative about attaching stylistic labels. It would be useful if we could construct a typology of performing styles (as Richard Dyer tries to do in *Stars*), but acting is much older than cinema, and modern performance tends to draw on every available tradition. Vaudeville, radio, movies, and television have been profoundly eclectic institutions, developing specific techniques but at the same time allowing alternate traditions to combine and compete. Different genres have produced different styles of acting, but within the genre called comedy (or even within a manageable subgenre like "screwball comedy"), there are considerable variations of style from film to film. Therefore I have tried to be narrow and specific, confining myself to moments in *The King of Comedy* where the film seems to be "quoting" other actors and conventions or to moments when I can specify a given style in some detail.

Some of the performances in the film constitute an "amateur" form, marked by an expressive vacancy in the players' eyes and an unmotivated stiffness or awkwardness of movement. Significantly, the amateur effect is relegated to the minor roles, and while it calls attention to the film as an acted event, it never fundamentally upsets our ability to accept the dramatic illusion. In this regard, we may distinguish between three different uses of amateurs in movies: first, in neorealist cinema, which sometimes casts amateurs in important parts, seeking out "natural" performers who, at the technical level, seem indistinguishable from professionals; second, in "local color" films, which use amateurs in small ways for the purpose of authenticating the setting; third, in Brechtian or modernist experiments, where amateurs are cast throughout, their lack of expressive skill deliberately foregrounded. Of these three types, only the second is typical of Hollywood. See, for example, Bogdanovich's *The Last Picture Show* (1971), where minor roles have been assigned to the local Texas citizenry; the natives lend an aura of reality to the film, even though their wooden delivery is in stark contrast to the Method style of the leading players.

Hollywood increasingly relied on "local color" techniques after World War

II, and *The King of Comedy* is in this sense a typical film. It uses stars in lead roles, always maintaining expressive coherence between actors and characters, creating a strong sense of theatrical verisimilitude and psychological "depth." But *The King of Comedy* also allows its leading players to move back and forth between two media, signaled by direct cuts from 35mm film to video transfers. Whole sequences of the Langford show are shot with television cameras and played in the "hot" style of late-night variety, using a fair amount of direct address, a projected behavior aimed at a studio audience, and all the mannerisms we associate with stand-up comedy. By contrast, the sequences shot on film normally involve a more naturalistic, Stanislavskian form of playing. An instance of the latter technique is the early scene where Pupkin forces himself into the back of Langford's car, having "rescued" him from a swarm of admirers. As the automobile drives off from the theater, the two figures crowded together in the back seat resemble Brando and Steiger in *On the Waterfront,* and De Niro's speeches have all the redundancy and semi-coherence of Method dialogue: "That's why I'm asking you, if you'd just listen, I'm asking you if you'd just listen to my *act,* that's all, if you'll just listen to my *act* and tell me what you think about it. . . ."

The film oscillates between the extremes of video and film, sometimes appearing to put them in systematic formal opposition, as if to designate one as "performed" and the other as "real." Thus the blurry video image is contrasted with the full, clear resolution of film; flat lighting is contrasted with chiaroscuro; and presentational, public rhetoric is contrasted with representational acting. Within the two different worlds, however, the narrative motivates swift, complex changes of performance style. During the scene in the back of the car, for example, Pupkin is to some extent trying to audition for Langford. Sitting up and forward in the seat, he twists his body toward his audience and briefly adopts the timing of a club comic: "I just want to tell you, Jerry, my name is Rupert Pupkin, and, uh, I know the name doesn't mean much to you but it means an awful lot to me!" He talks rather softly, trying to calm Langford and get an urgent message across, but at the same time he makes flourishes with his hands and smiles slightly to signal attempts at wit. Langford, meanwhile, is like a figure out of a gangster movie or a *film noir,* slumped wearily in a dark corner, his tie loose, a sour, repressed anger in his glance. "Look, pal," he says in a deep voice. "I know this is a crazy business, but it's a business."

The TV monologues themselves are parodic. Langford's appearance at the beginning of the film reminds us of both Carson and Lewis, signifying an archetypal late-night entertainment. As the band strikes up a fanfare, Lewis strolls out to his mark, head held up, moving with a slightly Benny-ish sway. He pauses for the roar of applause, his hands clasped, and then makes a casual signal for everyone to keep on cheering. Smiling slyly at his own "humor," he glances confidently around the room, and as he chats with the

Lewis plays a monologue.

subservient announcer and the bandleader, he makes us aware of a great many flashy details—a glistening pinky ring; a rolled white collar and longish shirt-cuffs; a gleam of teeth and brilliantined hair.

By contrast, Rupert Pupkin's big opportunity as a stand-up comic is designed to indicate both Pupkin's awkwardness and De Niro's acting talent—hence the climactic moment of the film is equivalent to watching Olivier doing Archie Rice. Notice, however, that De Niro's monologue is especially subtle, never suggesting any breakdown or excessively awkward tone; perhaps for that reason, some critics have wondered whether it is intended to be funny. Beverle Huston has argued that we cannot tell because the film denies its audience the security of "controlled identification" with the point of view of an implied author (91). Certainly there are ambiguities in the scene: we hear the TV audience laughing uproariously, but we do not know whether they are laughing *at* or *with* Rupert, nor do we know whether the laughter is canned. Judged by traditional aesthetic criteria, it seems to me clear enough that the material is bad and that Rupert's performance is amateurish; nevertheless, in certain ways television has made these criteria irrelevant, repeatedly turning rank amateurs into cult figures and celebrities, players who seem witty by virtue of their very awkwardness. (The technique is especially noticeable on American TV commercials in the eighties, where an elderly woman named Clara Peller became an overnight star by asking "Where's the beef?" and where nonactors are regularly used as salespeople.)

De Niro plays the scene as if *he* (the dramatic actor) were being given a shot at comedy. He gives Rupert a reasonably good sense of timing, but he keeps his upper body stiff and his breathing a little anxious. He continually hunches his shoulders and gestures with both hands, like a man sending out semaphoric gestures from the prow of a ship: "Good evening, ladies and gentlemen!" His hands go up in a stop sign on either side of his body. "Let me introduce myself." Both hands point to his chest. "My name is Rupert Pupkin." His hands spread out to his sides, palms open. "I was born in Clifton, New Jersey. Is anyone here from Clifton?" He bends forward, one hand cupped over his ear to listen for a response. "Oh, good!" He crouches, arms extended, like an umpire signaling safe. "We can all relax now!" (When De Niro later played Al Capone in *The Untouchables* [1987] he used many of these same gestures, adding a bit of Pupkin to his portrait of the gangster.)

The routine has also been written so as to comment ironically on the character. Despite what Rupert has told Jerry about turning his own life into comedy, we know that most of what he says is fabrication—for example, when he claims that his mother has been dead for nine years. "But seriously," he reminisces, "you should have seen my mother. Blonde, beautiful, intelligent, alcoholic. . . ." After cheerfully listing a Kafkaesque series of family horrors, all of which open up the performance to a psychoanalytic subtext, he gets his biggest laughs by telling the truth, admitting he has kidnapped Jerry to get into show business: "I look at it this way: Better to be King for a night than schmuck for a lifetime!" The film's ultimate irony, of course, is that Rupert becomes a celebrity at the moment when he is most "natural," appearing before the audience as a madman who simply wants to be a star. By such means, *The King of Comedy* illustrates an oft-repeated, troubling fact about postindustrial culture: literally any act, no matter how outrageous, can be absorbed into mainstream media, becoming a source of amusement.

At various points both De Niro and Lewis "quote" other kinds of comic performance, sometimes deliberately violating the acted continuity of the film. Just before he leaps into Langford's limousine, Pupkin ties to restrain the zealous worshippers around the star: "Okay, stand back! Please let Mr. Langford get by!" he yells, turning his back to the crowd, spreading his arms and leaning like a figure in the Keystone Cops. Later, when the police chase him out of Langford's office, one of the shots is composed and played like something out of a Keaton film: the camera looks down a narrow corridor toward an open doorway, where we can see Rupert trotting past the frame of the door, first left to right, then right to left, with the law close behind.

As one might expect, the film is also filled with allusions to contemporary monologuists or celebrities—as when Rupert keeps pinching his tie and

Pupkin's monologue.

twisting his neck like Rodney Dangerfield. At one point, his fantasy appearance as a star on the Langford show becomes a derisive and fairly typical parody of Sammy Davis (probably influenced by "SCTV"'s "The Sammy Maudlin Show"). We see him talking to cardboard cutouts, rehearsing his reactions: "Yeh, you look wonderful, too, Jerry . . . What? . . . Yeah! Ha, ha, ha!" He tosses his arm in the air, slaps his thigh, and then leans forward in his chair, stomping his foot in uncontrollable laughter. "Oh, Jerry! I love this guy!" he says to the audience, getting up to kiss the cardboard picture on the cheek. "Always coming up with these great lines! I love him!" In a later sequence, where Pupkin imagines a meeting in Langford's office, Jerry Lewis breaks into a vaudeville shtick associated with Phil Silvers and Milton Berle: "Ya daffy bastard!" he says to De Niro, smiling and affectionately tapping him on the jaw with a fist. Suddenly he grabs De Niro around the neck with both hands and shakes his head back and forth, proclaiming "I-hate-you-but-I-love-you!" He then releases his grip, mashes De Niro's cheeks together like

Silly Putty, and shouts "I wouldn't lie to you, Rupe!" Perhaps the most obvious of these allusions, however, is the moment when Lewis quotes himself. Noticing that Marsha is following him through the streets of Manhattan, he breaks into the spastic run typical of the character he played in the fifties, as if he were tossing off the mask of Langford and suddenly becoming the clown in a Martin and Lewis farce.

These brief references to well-known comics function mainly as departures from what might be described as the film's dominant technique—a Method-inspired naturalism that, as we have seen, is typical of "social problem" or gangster movies. Sometimes this style, too, is subtly parodied or bracketed as simply one form of theatrical behavior among others. (In this regard, notice that the television programming depicted in the film consists not only of talk shows and news, but of old movies like *Pickup on South Street* and *Madigan*.) At one point, we see a suavely dressed Pupkin huddled over a restaurant table with Langford, who is begging him to work as a substitute host. "It's the show," Langford explains in a near whisper, nervously adjusting his glasses. "The pressure, the ratings. The same guests, the same questions." He leans his elbows on the table and cracks his knuckles, glancing down at his plate. "I really wish you would think about it again." Pausing for a moment before he replies, Pupkin touches his temples and then makes a little supplicating gesture, like a Broadway character out of *The Sweet Smell of Success*. "I'm thinking," he says, lightly tossing off the line. "I'm thinking. That's all I do." Suddenly a direct cut takes us to Rupert in his room, acting out the scene we have been watching. "How can I *not* think about it?" he shouts in a stagy voice. A big close-up shows his face twisted into a histrionic display of pain, his beseeching hands spread out like those of a tragedian who works in pantomime style. "You're asking me to do something that's im*pos*sible! It's im*poss*ible!" he yells, his voice growing increasingly nasal as his dramatic emotion rises. "Whadda you want?" he asks. "You want the tears to come outta my eyes?" Raising his fingers to his cheeks to indicate tears, he squints and makes a distorted, clownish expression of grief.

In this case as in others, *The King of Comedy* jokes about performance conventions even while it subordinates its more extravagant playing styles to the demands of realistic social satire. Ultimately, the acting is governed by the demands of verisimilitude—a quality that the film must have if Zimmerman's commentary on American culture is to do its work. The major characterizations are therefore strongly marked by three essential features of postwar naturalism: (1) Deliberate lapses in rhetorical clarity, signaled especially by overlapping speech and apparently contingent, spontaneous behavior. (2) Careful attention to the accents and manners of an indigenous, urban society. (3) Moments of expressive incoherence designed to indicate repression, or deep-seated psychological drives.

The last of these techniques is particularly important because most of the characters in the film are either neurotic or psychotic. Many of Jerry Lewis's scenes, for example, involve a quiet, relatively gestureless manner that is the very opposite of his comic persona, giving the impression of a sour, anxious man barely containing his anger. De Niro, on the other hand, makes Pupkin a highly animated figure, caught up in a frenzy of ambition and an eagerness to please (except during the moments—usually fantasized—when he feels himself in a position of power). According to Zimmerman, De Niro frequently asked questions about Pupkin's psychology as the film was being shot and even developed a posture for the role: a slightly bent-forward stance that looks obsequious in some contexts but elsewhere implies a nervous, pushy eagerness. Throughout, you can see Rupert nosing his way forward, adopting a mask of politeness to cover his desperate need. He wears a smile that pretends not to notice the jokes other people make at his expense, but then with Marsha or at home he regresses to adolescent derisiveness. (*"Mo-om! Puh-leeze!"* he shouts, rolling his eyes heavenward in response to his mother's voice.)

What is especially effective about De Niro's interpretation is that he makes us sense a basis for Pupkin's identification with Langford without ever falling into direct imitation of Lewis. Rupert emerges as a "weak" and slightly different version of his hero—onstage, he lacks Langford's vivid expressiveness and vocal power (partly because of De Niro's own squinty eyes and swift, nasal speech), but he has a roughly parallel set of mincing gestures, a similar accent, and the same neurotic intensity. In appearance, he is like a bargain-basement celebrity, wearing ducktailed hair, a trim mustache, and white shoes; nevertheless, he is close enough to Langford's sensibility to make us see the links between the two characters. De Niro also captures some of the weird balance between fantasy and reality in Pupkin's thinking—especially in the scene in Langford's house where he seems momentarily aware of his delusion yet determined to go on behaving as if he had been invited. Most of all, he is good at conveying Pupkin's sadly dull-witted, childlike rebellion against network television. Seated in Langford's outer office, he looks like Kafka's Joseph K. waiting in a cosmic airport lounge. Mixing prissy sarcasm with an air of mock innocence, he glances at the secretary and makes a lame joke: "Which reminds me of the guy who waited so long he forgot what he waited for!"

De Niro is able to invest his otherwise naturalistic portrayal of a psychopath with a good deal of comic expressiveness simply because Pupkin is a character who is "onstage" even in his intimate encounters; in fact, one of Rupert's problems is that he tries to adopt the style of the TV talk-show host to situations where he ought to behave more like a Method actor. He uses cue cards to instruct Langford on calling in a ransom demand, and when he takes Rita to a Chinese restaurant, he puts on as many pathetically ludicrous airs as Stella Dallas at a country club. "Ah, ha, ha. *Really?*" he responds to one of

Chuck Low "upstages" Pupkin / De Niro.

her cool insults, squinting his eyes and making a forced smile. After insisting that she name her favorite movie star, he puts down his chopsticks with a great to-do, swells his chest in satisfaction, and reaches under the table for a "Talent Register." As he points to Marilyn Monroe's autograph, he offers a learned commentary: "She wasn't a great actress, but she did have a gift for comedy. You know she died tragically and alone, like many of the world's most beautiful women." Turning to an illegible scrawl on another page, he cocks his head and beams, his voice becoming a sing-song: "The more scribbled the name, the bigger the fame!" Rita gives him a bored look, and he announces the mystery signature as if he were introducing the star of a talk show: "Ru-pert Pup-kin!" Then he leans over the table with a squirmy, grinning display of confidentiality. "I surprised you, didn't I?" he says, his tone suggesting that at some level he does not believe his own boast.

Here, as elsewhere, De Niro has the opportunity to show off skill by performing a man who is performing badly. Equally important, he makes us aware of a contrast between Pupkin, who yearns for glamour, and De Niro— who, since becoming a famous actor, has avoided tacky celebrity interviews and whose work usually lacks "charm" or sex appeal. The scene is also a good indication of how much care De Niro gives to the social and psycholog-

ical determinants of character; it embodies all of Rupert's smarmy graceless-
ness, all his madness, and all his underlying awareness that the world has
labeled him a "schmuck."

At the same time, however, the scene is typical of *The King of Comedy*'s
unusual self-consciousness, because it does not let De Niro's performance
stay at the level of pure illusion. At the very moment when he makes the
character seem vividly present to us, there is a barely visible element in the
staging that tends to alienate his behavior. Near the beginning of the sequence
a man (identified in the credits as Chuck L. Low) can be seen strolling past
the spot where Rupert and Rita are sitting; a moment later he sits in the
background, out of focus at a distant table. Each time the shot/reverse shot
pattern of the conversation takes us to a close-up of De Niro, we can see
Chuck Low in a corner, smiling in the direction of the camera. At first he
does nothing, but then he begins gesticulating broadly, watching De Niro's
hands and aiming the movements back at us. For a while he "apes" everything
De Niro does, and then he gets up and exits from the rear of the shot. In some
ways he seems to be a character in the scene—a man who watches Rupert's
flamboyant act and makes fun of it, perhaps trying to make a pass at Rita;
nevertheless, he is oddly positioned, looking not at the place Rita occupies,
but at *us*. He never acts like a man who is having dinner in the restaurant,
and he leaves the scene in a peculiar way, as if an extra, virtually ignored by
the camera, had suddenly decided to comment on the process of filming. In
effect, Low acts just like De Niro, who is acting like a man who is acting like
a show-business personality.

The naturalism of the film is also estranged by a feeling of improvisational
comedy—especially when Sandra Bernhard makes an appearance. I use the
term "improvisational" guardedly, because I do not want to suggest that the
actors are unrehearsed. What I have in mind is the contemporary comic style
made famous in the early work of Mike Nichols and Elaine May and associated with troupes like Second City. This style can be easily distinguished
from that of stand-up routines, and it differs markedly from the farcical skits
of vaudeville or burlesque, the high comedy of Grant and Hepburn, or the
typical situation comedy on television. It requires a special form of dramatic
writing, but its signs are chiefly evident at the level of the players, who frequently resemble Brechtian Method actors. In essence, it consists of Stanislavskian techniques applied to an absurdist mode and is clearly related to the
urban realism that suffuses so much of *The King of Comedy*.

The actors who work in this vein (the public usually recognizes them as
actors, rather than as "personalities" or pure comics) have a hip sensibility
and a satiric, often socially-critical attitude. They are experts at close observation of city life, but they also specialize in a kind of psychodrama, deriving
humor from signals of anxiety and neurosis. As a rule, they are not much
concerned with slapstick or even jokes; in place of acrobatic skill or witty

language, they rely on naturalistic clumsiness—a halting, nervous incoherence, together with little indications of tension and repression. Their style is less presentational, less clearly enunciated than any comedy in history, more given to free-associational monologues, quick, overlapping responses, and apparently extemporaneous outbursts of emotion.

Such a style affects nearly all the scenes in *The King of Comedy* that are not part of the "Jerry Langford Show." It conforms easily to De Niro's usual acting technique, but it contrasts sharply with what we normally expect of Jerry Lewis. In fact, the film seems to be using Lewis to suggest a difference between generations: on the one hand is a type of comedy derived from vaudeville, nowadays practiced in the Borscht belt, in Las Vegas, or on the "Tonight Show"; on the other is a comedy influenced by naturalist ensembles, seen on "Saturday Night Live." Inevitably, *The King of Comedy* favors the latter form. Thus Lewis seldom seems amusing, whereas Sandra Bernhard gives a performance that is frightening, sexy, and savagely funny.

Bernhard is in fact a club comic, and in many ways she relies on the conventional devices of clowns. She lacks the symmetrical face of "serious" actors like Fonda or Streep, so she pushes her features into grotesque extremes—poking out her lips or curling them up against her long nose, frowning or letting her jaw hang lax. When she moves, she is all angles, a gangling stick figure who looks like an anorexic bobbysoxer; when she speaks, her voice pitches up to the register of a New York teenager on the verge of hysteria. Nevertheless she inflects her exaggerated behavior in ways quite different from old-fashioned zanies like Fanny Brice or Martha Raye. Hers is a comedy of neurosis, a mingling of anxiety and laughter, and she behaves as if the whole weight of an Oedipal scenario were on her shoulders.

Bernhard's Masha is the neglected child of a rich Manhattan family, and her passion for Jerry is like a passion for Daddy; her sudden moments of expressive incoherence serve not merely as conventional gags but as deliberate indexes of repressed sexual emotion, scary breakdowns of rationality. When she gets Jerry alone, she is like a patient revealing her wildest fantasies to a therapist, and she becomes a parody of every seductress she has seen in the movies. Wearing a slinky black dress, she does a sultry walk down a candlelit hallway, high heels clicking against the marble floor with the remorseless tick of a time bomb. She stops in front of Jerry, who is bound and gagged, and plocks a champagne bottle and two glasses down on a romantically-prepared table. Then she takes two slow steps forward and peels the tape from his mouth like a stripper removing clothing.[6] Throughout the scene, Lewis is a mummified figure in a chair—a literal straight man—looking deadpan as she launches into a loopy, free-associative confession involving

---

6. As Beverle Huston has noted, Jerry has his tape removed at the very moment when Rupert is being "taped" for TV (86).

her parents, her desire to be black like Tina Turner, and her need to cast off restraint. A mad delight enters her eyes, and to demonstrate her impulsiveness she tosses her champagne glass over her shoulder without warning. Looking passionately across at Jerry, she slowly runs an arm along the top of the table, sweeping an entire dinner onto the floor with a crash. Then she suddenly breaks into a torchy rendition of "Come Rain or Come Shine" (a tune Lewis himself once recorded), rising and circling Jerry's chair like a panther. Sitting in his lap, she tells him she feels like "getting crazy," her voice bursting into a near scream and then subsiding just as quickly into a nervous calm. Finally she gets up and begins awkwardly taking off the dress. "I'm having a good time," she says, "That's right, havin' fun . . . all-American fun!"

Bernhard's scenes with De Niro have an equally dark, clinical humor and are played in an exceptionally loose, improvisational fashion, as if the two actors were sharing a rhythm, overlapping one another and playing from emotion. Their work together is the best instance of the kind of performance toward which most of the film aspires—a funky, big-city realism, counterpointed with signs of comic absurdity. Consider the protracted argument between Masha and Rupert that breaks out in the street in front of Jerry's offices: the scene belongs to De Niro because he has the biggest speech and the most intensely emotional outburst; but it also depends on Bernhard's ability to engage in a rapid exchange, a semicoherent overflow of powerful feeling between two characters who are exposing their private lives in public. It is played at a swift march—almost a run—with Rupert trying to avoid Masha, who is begging him for a favor. Finally, unable to escape her, he tries to out-embarrass her, stopping dead in his tracks and yelling at the top of his voice. De Niro gives his sudden outburst a heavily accented whine, running the sentences together and pausing toward the end for an aftersurge of grandiose self-pity:

> And what about the things I did for *you?* I did things for you that no money can buy, *no* money can buy! You came over there and I gave you my *spot!* You stood there and you wanted to get next to Jerry and you got next to him! And what about the time I gave you my last album of "The Best of Jerry," what about *that!* . . . I can't even pay my *rent!* Whatta you talking about, I live in a *hovel!* I can't believe this girl!

The sequence is assembled in documentary fashion, with the camera scurrying alongside De Niro and Bernhard as they move down an actual street, the angles shifting rapidly and the sounds of New York mixed heavily into shouted, systematically overlapping dialogue. Even so, we recognize the acting as a parody based on the dominant tradition of postwar American theater. What makes its status as a self-conscious artifact all the more evident is that

De Niro and Bernhard on the street.

even as the exchange between De Niro and Bernhard catches us up in its spontaneity and urgency, Scorsese once again violates a principle of naturalistic staging. In the background, behind the two players, we can see a few people on the sidewalk who are not behaving like extras. They signal their presence because they look at the camera instead of the action, reminding us of the presence of a great deal of machinery.

I would like to emphasize these anonymous faces here at the end. Probably some of them were unpaid volunteers who were simply asked to sign releases for appearing in the film. They mix with more actorly types and have the look of bystanders not yet elevated to the status of amateur players. A gaggle of curious "civilians" enlisted to play a crowd, they are only briefly registered on the screen, and are usually so much out of focus that it is difficult to tell how much Scorsese wanted them to be noticed. Nevertheless, they emphasize an important theme in *The King of Comedy,* functioning less as characters than as observers of celebrity. Their slightly awkward presence gives the sequence an aleatory, *cinéma-vérité* quality reminiscent of Godard's *Breathless* and helps bring the study I have been conducting full circle. For although the bystanders are barely there, they are not unlike the people behind Chaplin in *Kid's Auto Race,* participating in a movie in the most completely amateurish way, uncertain how they ought to behave. Neither public personae nor agents of the narrative, they are the least dramatized figures of all—styleless, not yet possessed of a cinematic "self." The apparatus has merely gathered them up into a performance, like props or raw material, letting their unrealized presence comment on the way acting makes persons of us all.

Selected Bibliography

Affron, Charles. *Star Acting: Gish, Garbo, and Davis*. New York: Dutton, 1977.

Affron, Mirella Jona. "Bresson and Pascal: Rhetorical Affinities." *Quarterly Review of Film Studies* 10, no. 2 (Spring 1985).

Aristotle. *Poetics*. Trans. Thomas Twining. London: Everyman's Library, 1941.

Aubert, Charles. *The Art of Pantomime*. Trans. Edith Sears. New York: Henry Holt and Co., 1927.

Bakhtin, Mikhail. *Rabelais and His World*. Trans. Helene Iswolsky. Bloomington: Indiana University Press, 1984.

Barkworth, Peter. *About Acting*. London: Seker and Warburg, 1984.

Barthes, Roland. *S / Z: An Essay*. Trans. Richard Miller. New York: Hill and Wang, 1974.

———. *Image / Music / Text*. Trans. Stephen Heath. New York: Hill and Wang, 1977.

———. *The Grain of the Voice*. Trans. Linda Coverdale. New York: Hill and Wang, 1985.

Battcock, Gregory, and Robert Nickas. *The Art of Performance*. New York: Dutton, 1984.

Baudry, Jean-Louis. "Ideological Effects of the Basic Cinematographic Apparatus." *Film Quarterly* (Winter 1973–74).

Bauml, Betty and Franz. *A Dictionary of Gestures*. Metuchen, N.J.: Scarecrow Press, 1975.

Baxter, John. *The Cinema of Josef von Sternberg*. London: A. Zwemmer, 1971.

Baxter, Peter. "On the Naked Thighs of Miss Dietrich." *Wide Angle* 2, no. 2 (1978).

Bazin, André. *What Is Cinema?* 2 vols. Berkeley and Los Angeles: University of California Press, 1967.

Bell-Metereau, Rebecca. *Hollywood Androgeny*. New York: Columbia University Press, 1985.

Belsey, Catherine. *Critical Practice*. London: Methuen, 1980.

Benjamin, Walter. *Illuminations*. Trans. Harry Zohn. Ed. Hannah Arendt. New York: Harcourt, Brace, and World, 1968.

———. *Reflections*. Trans. Edmund Jephcott. New York: Harcourt, Brace, Jovanovitch, 1978.

Bergman, Andrew. *James Cagney*. New York: Pyramid, 1974.

Berko, Lili. "Discursive Imperialism." *USC Spectator* 6, no. 2 (Spring 1986).

Birdwhistle, Ray L. *Kinesics and Context*. London: Allen Lane, 1971.

Biskind, Peter. *Seeing Is Believing*. New York: Pantheon, 1986.

Blum, Richard. *American Film Acting: The Stanislavsky Heritage*. Ann Arbor: UMI, 1984.

Bordwell, David, Janet Staiger, and Kristin Thompson. *The Classical Hollywood Cinema: Film Style and Mode of Production to 1960*. New York: Columbia University Press, 1985.

Braudy, Leo. *The World in a Frame*. Garden City: Doubleday, 1976.

Brecht, Bertolt. *Brecht on Theater*. Trans. John Willet. New York: Hill and Wang, 1964.

Britton, Andrew. *Cary Grant: Comedy and Male Desire*. Newcastle upon Tyne, England: Tyneside Cinema, 1983.

———. *Katharine Hepburn: The Thirties and After*. Newcastle upon Tyne, England: Tyneside Cinema, 1984.

Brooks, Louise. *Lulu in Hollywood*. New York: Knopf, 1983.

Bruder, Melissa, Lee Michael Cohn, Madeleine Olnek, Nathaniel Pollack, Robert Privito, and Scott Zigler. *A Practical Handbook for the Actor*. New York: Vintage, 1986.

Buñuel, Louis, and Jean-Claude Carrière. *My Last Sigh*. Trans. Abigail Israel. New York: Vintage, 1984.

Burke, Kenneth. *The Philosophy of Literary Form*. New York: Vintage, 1957.

Burns, Elizabeth. *Theatricality*. London: Longman, 1972.

Cagney, James. *Cagney on Cagney*. Garden City, N.Y.: Doubleday, 1976.

Callenbach, Ernest. "Classics Revisited: *The Gold Rush*." *Film Quarterly* 8, no. 1 (1959).

Campbell, Russell, ed. *The Velvet Light Trap* 7 (1972–73). Special issue on film acting.

Chapkis, Wendy. *Beauty Secrets: Women and the Politics of Appearance*. Boston: South End Press, 1986.

Chaplin, Charles. *My Autobiography*. New York: Simon and Schuster, 1964.

Ciment, Michel. *Kazan on Kazan*. London: Secker and Warburg, 1973.

Cole, Toby, and Helen Krich Chinoy, eds. *Actors on Acting*. New York: Crown, 1970.

Comolli, Jean-Louis. "Historical Fiction: A Body Too Much." Trans. Ben Brewster. *Screen* 19, no. 2 (1978).

Darwin, Charles. *The Expression of Emotions in Man and Animals*. Chicago: University of Chicago Press, 1965.

Delman, John, Jr. *The Art of Acting*. New York: Harper, 1949.

De Cordova, Richard. "The Emergence of the Star System in America." *Wide Angle* 6, no. 4 (1985).

———. "Genre and Performance: An Overview." In *Film Genre Reader,* edited by Barry Keith Grant. Austin: University of Texas Press, 1986.

Demaris, Ovid. "I Didn't Want to Be Who I Was." Interview with Michael Caine. *Parade,* 27 July 1986.

Dickens, Homer. *The Films of James Cagney.* Secaucus, N.J.: Citadel Press, 1974.

Downing, David. *Marlon Brando.* New York: Stein and Day, 1984.

Durgnat, Raymond. *The Crazy Mirror.* New York: Delta, 1970.

———. "Six Films of Josef von Sternberg." In *Movie Reader,* edited by Ian Cameron. London: November Books, 1972.

Dyer, Richard. *Stars.* London: BFI, 1979.

———. *Heavenly Bodies: Film Stars and Society.* New York: St. Martin's, 1986.

Eagleton, Terry. "Brecht on Rhetoric." *New Literary History* 16, no. 3 (Spring 1985).

———. *The Rape of Clarissa.* Minneapolis: University of Minnesota Press, 1982.

Eckert, Charles. "The Carole Lombard in Macy's Window." *Quarterly Review of Film Studies* 3, no. 1 (Winter 1978).

Ekman, Paul, ed. *Darwin and Facial Expression.* New York: Academic Press, 1973.

———. *Emotion in the Human Face.* Cambridge: Cambridge University Press, 1982.

Elam, Keir. *The Semiotics of Theater and Drama.* London: Methuen, 1980.

Eliot, T. S. *Selected Prose.* Harmondsworth: Penguin, 1953.

Ellis, John. *Visible Fictions: Cinema, Television, Video.* London: Routledge and Kegan Paul, 1982.

Elsaesser, Thomas. "Tales of Sound and Fury: Observations on the Family Melodrama." *Monogram* 4 (1973).

Erb, Cynthia. "Claude Rains as Character Actor: The Invisible Man in *Casablanca.*" SCS–FSAC Conference, Montreal, Canada, 24 May 1987. Typescript.

Farell, Tom. "Nick Ray's German Friend, Wim Wenders." *Wide Angle* 5, no. 4 (1983).

Fell, John L. *Film and the Narrative Tradition.* Norman: University of Oklahoma Press, 1974.

Freud, Sigmund. *The Complete Psychological Works of Sigmund Freud.* 24 vols. Trans. James Strachey. London: Hogarth Press, 1961.

Gaines, Jane M. and Charlotte C. Herzog, eds. *Fabrications: Costume and the Female Body* (forthcoming).

Geduld, Harry M. *Chapliniana.* Bloomington: Indiana University Press, 1987.

Gish, Lillian. *The Movies, Mr. Griffith, and Me.* Englewood Cliffs, N.J.: Prentice-Hall, 1969.

Godard, Jean-Luc. *Godard on Godard.* Trans. Tom Milne. New York: Viking, 1972.

———, and Jean-Pierre Gorin. "Excerpts from the Transcript of Godard-Gorin's *Letter to Jane.*" *Women and Film* 1, nos. 3 / 4 (1973).

Goffman, Erving. *The Presentation of Self in Everyday Life.* Garden City, N.Y.: Doubleday, 1959.

———. *Frame Analysis.* New York: Harper, 1974.

Gombrich, E. H. *Art and Illusion.* Princeton: Princeton University Press, 1961.

Greimas, A. J. *On Meaning.* Trans. Paul J. Perron and Frank H. Collins. Minneapolis: University of Minnesota Press, 1987.

Hall, Edward T. *The Silent Language.* Garden City, N.Y.: Doubleday, 1973.

Harre, Rom, ed. *The Social Construction of Emotion*. London: Basil Blackwell, 1986.

Haskell, Molly. *From Reverence to Rape*. New York: Holt, Rinehart and Winston, 1974.

Heath, Stephen. *Questions of Cinema*. Bloomington: Indiana University Press, 1981.

Henderson, Brian. *A Critique of Film Theory*. New York: E. P. Dutton, 1980.

Higham, Charles. *Kate: The Life of Katharine Hepburn*. New York: Norton, 1975.

Higson, Andrew. "Acting Taped: An Interview with Mark Nash and James Swinson." *Screen* 26, no. 5 (September–October 1985).

Hirsch, Foster. *A Method to Their Madness*. New York: Norton, 1984.

Holland, Norman N. "Psychoanalysis and Film: The Kuleshov Experiment." *IPSA Research Paper No. 1*. Gainesville: Institute for Psychological Study of the Arts, University of Florida, 1986.

Hollander, Anne. *Seeing Through Clothes*. New York: Avon Books, 1978.

Hornby, Richard. "Understanding Acting." *Journal of Aesthetic Education* 17, no. 3 (1983).

Horton, Donald, and R. Richard Wohl. "Mass Communication and Para-Social Interaction: Observations on Intimacy at a Distance." *Psychiatry* 19 (1956).

Houseman, John. *Final Dress*. New York: Simon and Schuster, 1983.

Huston, Beverle. "*King of Comedy:* A Crisis of Substitution." *Framework* 24 (Spring 1984).

Jacobowitz, Florence. "Feminist Film Theory and Social Reality." *Cineaction* 3–4 (Winter 1986).

Jameson, Fredric. "*Dog Day Afternoon* as a Political Film." *Screen Education* 30 (Spring 1979).

Kahan, Stanley. *Introduction to Acting*. Boston: Allyn and Bacon, 1985.

Kalter, Joanmarie, ed. *Actors on Acting: Performance in Theatre and Film Today*. New York: Sterling, 1979.

Kaplan, E. Ann. *Women and Film: Both Sides of the Camera*. New York: Methuen, 1983.

Kauffmann, Stanley. *Personal Views*. New York: PAJ Publications, 1986.

King, Barry. "Articulating Stardom." *Screen* 26, no. 5 (September–October 1985).

———. "Stardom as an Occupation." In *The Hollywood Film Industry*, edited by Paul Kerr. London: Routledge Kegan Paul, 1986.

Kirby, E. T. "The Delsarte Method: Three Frontiers of Actor Training." *Drama Review* 16, no. 1 (March 1972).

Kobal, John. *The Art of the Great Hollywood Portrait Photographers*. London: Allen Lane, 1980.

Kristeva, Julia. "Gesture: Practice or Communication?" Trans. Johnathan Benthael. In *The Body Reader*, edited by Ted Polhemus. New York: Pantheon, 1977.

Kuleshov, Lev. *Kuleshov on Film*. Trans. and ed. Ronald Levaco. Berkeley and Los Angeles: University of California Press, 1974.

LaValley, Albert J., ed. *Focus on Hitchcock*. Englewood Cliffs, N.J.: Prentice-Hall, 1972.

Leyda, Jay. *Film Makers Speak*. New York: Da Capo, 1977.

MacCabe, Colin. "Realism and the Cinema: Notes on Some Brechtian Theses." *Screen* 15, no. 2 (1974).

Marsh, Mae. *Screen Acting*. Los Angeles: Photo-Star Publishing, n.d.

Marx, Karl, and Friedrich Engels. *On Literature and Art*. Ed. Lee Baxandall and Stefan Morawski. New York: International General, 1973.

Mayne, Judith. "Marlene Dietrich, *The Blue Angel*, and the Ambiguities of Female Performance." SCS–FSAC Conference. Montreal, Canada, 23 May 1987. Typescript.

Merritt, Russell. "Rescued from a Perilous Nest: D. W. Griffith's Escape from Theater into Film." *Cinema Journal* 21, no. 1 (Fall 1981).

McArthur, Benjamin. *Actors and American Culture, 1880–1920*. Philadelphia: Temple University Press, 1984.

McClellan, Elizabeth. *History of American Costume*. New York: Tudor, 1969.

McGilligan, Patrick. *Cagney: The Actor as Auteur*. South Brunswick: A. S. Barnes, 1975.

Merleau-Ponty, Maurice. *Sense and Non-Sense*. Trans. Herbert L. and Patricia Allen Dreyfus. Evanston, Ill.: Northwestern University Press, 1964.

Meyrowitz, Joshua. *No Sense of Place: The Impact of Electronic Media on Social Behavior*. New York: Oxford University Press, 1985.

Morin, Edgar. *The Stars*. Trans. Richard Howard. New York: Grove Press, 1960.

Mulvey, Laura. "Visual Pleasure and Narrative Cinema." *Screen* 16, no. 3 (1975).

———. "Afterthoughts on 'Visual Pleasure and Narrative Cinema' Inspired by *Duel in the Sun*." *Framework* 15 / 16 / 17 (Summer 1981).

———. "Melodrama in and out of the Home." In *High Theory / Low Culture*, edited by Colin McCabe. New York: St. Martin's, 1986.

Neale, Stephen. *Genre*. London: BFI, 1980.

Nichols, Bill. *Movies and Methods*, 2 vols. Berkeley and Los Angeles: University of California Press, 1976, 1986.

———. *Ideology and the Image*. Bloomington: Indiana University Press, 1981.

Oumano, Ellen. *Film Forum: Thirty-Five Top Filmmakers Discuss Their Craft*. New York: St. Martin's, 1985.

Pearson, Roberta E. "'The Modesty of Nature': Performance Style in the Griffith Biographs." Ph.D. dissertation, New York University, 1987.

Pudovkin, Vsevold. *Film Technique and Film Acting: The Cinema Writings of V. I. Pudovkin*. Trans. Ivor Montagu. New York: Bonanza Books, 1949.

Rodowick, D. N. "The Difficulty of Difference." *Wide Angle* 5, no. 1 (1982).

Rosenbaum, Ron. "Acting: The Creative Mind of Jack Nicholson." *New York Times Magazine*, 13 July 1986.

Salt, Barry. *Film Style and Technology: History and Analysis*. London: Starword, 1983.

Sarris, Andrew. *The Films of Josef von Sternberg*. New York: The Museum of Modern Art, 1966.

———. "The Actor as Auteur." *American Film* (May 1977).

———. "Cary Grant's Antic Elegance." *The Village Voice*, 16 December 1986.

Selznick, David O. *Memo*. Ed. Rudy Behmer. New York: Knopf, 1984.

Schechner, Richard, and Cynthia Mintz. "Kinesics and Performance." *Drama Review* 17, no. 3 (September 1973).

Schnitzer, Luda and Jean, and Marcel Martin. *Cinema in Revolution*. Trans. with additional material by David Robinson. New York: Hill and Wang, 1973.

Shaffer, Lawrence. "Some Notes on Film Acting." *Sight and Sound* 42, no. 2 (Spring 1973).

———. "Reflections on the Face in Film." *Film Quarterly* 31, no. 2 (Winter 1977–78).

Shaftesbury, Edmund. *Lessons in The Art of Acting: A Thorough Course*. Washington, D.C.: The Martyn College Press, 1889.

Shipman, David. *The Great Movie Stars*. London: Hamlyn, 1970.

Smith, Ella. *Starring Miss Barbara Stanwyck*. New York: Crown, 1974.

Sontag, Susan. *Against Interpretation*. New York: Delta, 1966.

Stanislavsky, Konstantin. *An Actor Prepares*. Trans. Elizabeth Reynolds Hapgood. London: Geoffrey Bles, 1936.

———. *My Life in Art*. Trans. J. J. Robbins. New York: Theater Arts, 1948.

Stebbins, Genevieve. *The Delsarte System of Expression*. New York: Edgar S. Werner, 1902.

Steiger, Janet. "The Eyes Are Really the Focus: Photoplay Acting and Film Form and Style." *Wide Angle* 6, no. 4 (1985).

Stein, Charles W. *American Vaudeville as Seen by Its Contemporaries*. New York: Knopf, 1984.

Steinberg, Cobbett. *Reel Facts*. New York: Vintage, 1982.

Strickland, F. Cowles. *The Technique of Acting*. New York: McGraw-Hill, 1956.

Studlar, Gaylyn. "Masochism and the Perverse Pleasures of the Cinema." *Quarterly Review of Film Studies* 9, no. 4 (Fall 1984).

Suleiman, Susan, ed. *The Female Body in Western Culture*. Cambridge, Mass.: Harvard University Press, 1986.

Taylor, John Russell. *Hitch: The Life and Times of Alfred Hitchcock*. New York: Berkley, 1980.

Thompson, F. Grahame. "Approaches to 'Performance.'" *Screen* 26, no. 5 (September–October 1985).

Thompson, John O. "Screen Acting and the Commutation Test." *Screen* 19, no. 2 (Summer 1978).

———. "Beyond Commutation—A Reconsideration of Screen Acting." *Screen* 26, no. 5 (September–October 1985).

Thomson, David. *A Biographical Dictionary of Film*. 2nd ed. New York: William Morrow, 1981.

———. "Charms and the Man." *Film Comment* (February 1984).

Thumim, Janet. "'Miss Hepburn Is Humanized': The Star Persona of Katharine Hepburn." *Feminist Review* 24 (October 1986).

Todd, Janet. *Sensibility: An Introduction*. New York: Methuen, 1986.

Truffaut, François. *Hitchcock / Truffaut*. New York: Simon and Schuster, 1968.

Turner, Victor J. *The Anthropology of Performance*. New York: Performing Arts, 1986.

Vardac, A. Nicholas. *From Stage to Screen: Theatrical Method from Garrick to Griffith*. Cambridge, Mass.: Harvard University Press, 1949.

Veltruský, Jiři. "Man and the Object in the Theater." *A Prague School Reader.* Trans. and ed. Paul L. Gregory. Washington, D.C.: Georgetown University Press, 1964.

von Sternberg, Josef. *Fun in a Chinese Laundry.* London: Secker and Warburg, 1965.

Wagenknecht, Edward. *The Movies in the Age of Innocence.* Norman: University of Oklahoma Press, 1962.

Walker, Alexander. *Stardom: The Hollywood Phenomenon.* London: Penguin, 1974.

Warshow, Robert. *The Immediate Experience.* Garden City, N.Y.: Doubleday, 1976.

Watney, Simon. "Katharine Hepburn and the Cinema of Chastisement." *Screen* 26, no. 5 (September–October 1985).

Weis, Elizabeth, ed. *The Movie Star.* Harmondsworth: Penguin, 1981.

Welles, Orson. "The New Actor." Typescript notes for a lecture, 1940. Orson Welles Collection (box 4, folder 26), Lilly Library, Bloomington, Indiana.

Wexman, Virginia Wright. "Kinesics and Film Acting: Humphrey Bogart in *The Maltese Falcon* and *The Big Sleep.*" *The Journal of Popular Film and Television* 7, no. 1 (1979).

————. "The Method, the Moment, and *On the Waterfront.*" MLA Conference, New York, Dec. 28, 1986. Typescript.

————, ed. *Cinema Journal.* 20, no. 1 (1980). Special issue on film acting (1980).

Whitehall, Richard. "*The Blue Angel.*" *Films and Filming* (November 1962).

Wiles, Timothy J. *The Theater Event.* Chicago: University of Chicago Press, 1980.

Williams, Linda. "'Something Else Besides a Mother': *Stella Dallas* and the Maternal Melodrama." *Cinema Journal* 24, no. 1 (Fall 1984).

Williams, Raymond. *The Long Revolution.* Harmondsworth: Penguin, 1961.

————. *Culture.* Glasgow: Fontana, 1981.

Wood, Robin. "Venus de Marlene." *Film Comment* 14, no. 2 (1978).

Worthen, William B. *The Idea of the Actor.* Princeton: Princeton University Press, 1980.

Yacowar, Maurice. "An Aesthetic Defense of the Star System." *Quarterly Review of Film Studies* 4, no. 1 (1979).

Index